The American Record

Fifth Edition

The American Record

IMAGES OF THE NATION'S PAST

Volume I: To 1877

Edited by

William Graebner

State University of New York
College at Fredonia

Leonard Richards

University of Massachusetts, Amherst

Boston   Burr Ridge, IL   Dubuque, IA   Madison, WI   New York   San Francisco   St. Louis
Bangkok   Bogotá   Caracas   Kuala Lumpur   Lisbon   London   Madrid   Mexico City
Milan   Montreal   New Delhi   Santiago   Seoul   Singapore   Sydney   Taipei   Toronto

Higher Education

THE AMERICAN RECORD: IMAGES OF THE NATION'S PAST, VOLUME I: TO 1877

Published by McGraw-Hill, a business unit of The McGraw-Hill Companies, Inc., 1221 Avenue of the Americas, New York, NY 10020. Copyright © 2006, 2001, 1995, 1988, 1982 by The McGraw-Hill Companies, Inc. All rights reserved. No part of this publication may be reproduced or distributed in any form or by any means, or stored in a database or retrieval system, without the prior written consent of The McGraw-Hill Companies, Inc., including, but not limited to, in any network or other electronic storage or transmission, or broadcast for distance learning.

This book is printed on acid-free paper.

1 2 3 4 5 6 7 8 9 0 DOC/DOC 0 9 8 7 6 5

ISBN 0-07-294958-9

Editor in Chief: *Emily Barrosse*
Publisher: *Lyn Uhl*
Senior Sponsoring Editor: *Steven Drummond*
Marketing Manager: *Katherine Bates*
Developmental Editor: *Larry Goldberg*
Editorial Assistant: *Jessica Badiner*
Managing Editor: *Jean Dal Porto*
Project Manager: *Meghan Durko*
Manuscript Editor: *Gretlyn Cline*
Art Director: *Jeanne Schreiber*
Associate Designer: *Srdjan Savanovic*
Text Designer: *Ellen Pettengell*
Cover Designer: *Ellen Pettengell*
Associate Art Editor: *Ayelet Arbel*
Senior Photo Research Coordinator: *Nora Agbayani*
Photo Researcher: *Robin Sand*
Cover Credit: *Courtesy, Winterthur Museum. Photo by Jim Schneck.*
Production Supervisor: *Janean A. Utley*
Composition: *10.5/12 Jansen by ElectraGraphics, Inc.*
Printing: *45 # New Era Matte, R. R. Donnelly and Sons, Inc./Crawfordsville, IN.*

Library of Congress Cataloging-in-Publication Data

Graebner, William
    The American record : images of the nation's past / edited by William Graebner, Leonard
    Richards.— 5th ed.
        p. cm.
    Includes bibliographical references.
    Contents: v. 1. To 1877
    ISBN 0-07-294958-9 (pbk. : acid-free paper)
    1. United States—History. 2. United States—History—Sources. I. Graebner, William. II.
    Richards, Leonard L.

E178.6 .A4145+
973–dc22
                                                                              2004063180

The Internet addresses listed in the text were accurate at the time of publication. The inclusion of a website does not indicate an endorsement by the authors of McGraw-Hill, and McGraw-Hill does not guarantee the accuracy of the information presented at these sites.
www.mhhe.com

About the Editors

William Graebner is Professor of History at the State University of New York at Fredonia. He received the Frederick Jackson Turner Award from the Organization of American Historians for *Coal-Mining Safety in the Progressive Period: The Political Economy of Reform*. Another book, *A History of Retirement: The Meaning and Function of an American Institution, 1885–1978*, was published in 1980. He is also the author of *The Engineering of Consent: Democracy and Authority in Twentieth-Century America* (1987); *Coming of Age in Buffalo: Youth and Authority in the Postwar Era* (1990); *The Age of Doubt: American Thought and Culture in the 1940s* (1991), and the editor of *True Stories from the American Past* (1993, 1997). In 1993, he was Fulbright Professor of American Studies at the University of Rome. He currently serves as Associate Editor of *American Studies*.

Leonard Richards is Professor of History at the University of Massachusetts at Amherst. He was awarded the 1970 Beveridge Prize by the American Historical Association for his book *"Gentlemen of Property and Standing": Anti-Abolition Mobs in Jacksonian America*. Professor Richards is also the author of *The Advent of American Democracy*, *The Life and Times of Congressman John Quincy Adams*, which was a finalist for the Pulitzer Prize, *The Slave Power: The Free North and Southern Domination, 1780–1860*, which was the second-place winner of the 2000 Lincoln Prize, and *Shays's Rebellion: The American Revolution's Final Battle*. He is currently writing a book on the California Gold Rush and the coming of the Civil War.

Contents

Preface   xii

Chapter 1   The European Conquest of America 1

INTERPRETIVE ESSAY

The Indians' New World   James H. Merrell 3

SOURCES

The Indians as Seen by European Artists 21

ILLUSTRATIONS:
John White's Engraving of Indians Making a Canoe near Roanoke, 1588; A Settlement of Virginia Indians; Florida Battle Scene, 1564

Broken Spears: The Aztec Account of the Conquest of Mexico 21

@ **ON THE WEB: JOHN WHITE'S ENGRAVINGS OF VIRGINIA INDIANS 22**

@ **ON THE WEB: MORE ABOUT THE AZTECS 29**

Race War: The New England Experience 29

King Philip's War: A Contemporary Account 30

Defeat of King Philip: Increase Mather's Account 31

@ **ON THE WEB: CULTURAL, GENDER, AND HISTORICAL IMPLICATIONS OF KING PHILIP'S WAR 31**

THE BIG PICTURE 32

Chapter 2   Jamestown 33

INTERPRETIVE ESSAY

The Labor Problem at Jamestown, 1607–1618 Edmund S. Morgan 35

@ **ON THE WEB: JAMESTOWN AND THE EFFORTS TO "REDISCOVER" IT 46**

SOURCES

Jamestown: The Physical Setting 47

ILLUSTRATIONS OF JAMESTOWN

VOICES: LIFE AND DEATH IN VIRGINIA: RICHARD FRETHORNE'S ACCOUNT, 1623 47

THE BIG PICTURE 52

@ **ON THE WEB: A VIRTUAL TOUR OF JAMESTOWN 52**

Chapter 3   Puritan Order 53

INTERPRETIVE ESSAY

Anne Marbury Hutchinson: This Great and Sore Affliction   Willard Sterne Randall and Nancy Nahra 55

@ **ON THE WEB: A TRANSCRIPT OF ANNE HUTCHINSON'S TRIAL 65**

SOURCES

The New England Primer, 1690 66

ILLUSTRATIONS:
The New England Primer

Harvard, 1636–1642
From "New England's First Fruits," 1643 66

Three Early New England Portraits 71

ILLUSTRATIONS:
Henry Gibbs; Thomas Smith's Self-Portrait; Ann Pollard

The Spiritual Journey of Anne Bradstreet
Several Poems Compiled with Great Variety of Wit and Learning by Anne Bradstreet 73

THE BIG PICTURE 76

@ ON THE WEB: DISCUSSION OF THE LEGACY OF THE PURITANS 76

Chapter 4 The Have-Nots in Colonial Society 77

INTERPRETIVE ESSAY

The Origin and Consolidation of Unfree Labor Peter Kolchin 79

@ ON THE WEB: 17TH CENTURY LAWS ENACTED TO SECURE SHIFT FROM INDENTURED SERVITUDE TO SLAVERY 91

SOURCES

Portraits of Poverty 92

ILLUSTRATIONS:
Hogarth Engraving; Elizabethan Beggar

VOICES: THE EXPERIENCE OF BONDAGE: GOTTLIEB MITTELBERGER'S ACCOUNT, 1754 93

@ ON THE WEB: VIRGINIA COLONY LAWS ENACTED TO CONTROL INDENTURED SERVANTS 96

Wanted: Runaway Servants 96 Eighteenth-Century Newspaper Advertisements for Runaway Servants 96

Portraits of Slavery 99

ILLUSTRATIONS:
Slaves on the Bark Wildfire; Slaves on the West Coast of Africa; Engraving by Alexander Anderson; Shock of Enslavement; Diagram of the Slave Ship La Vigilante de Nantes; Standard Equipment for the Middle Passage; Advertisement in a Charleston, South Carolina, Newspaper, 1766

@ ON THE WEB: EXPERIENCE OF THE "MIDDLE PASSAGE" 103

Wanted: Runaway Slaves 104

Eighteenth- and Nineteenth-Century Newspaper Advertisements for Runaway Slaves 104

THE BIG PICTURE 107

Chapter 5 The American Revolution 108

INTERPRETIVE ESSAY

The Shoemaker and the Revolution Alfred F. Young 110

SOURCES

George III 121

ILLUSTRATIONS:
Woodcut of George III; Pulling Down the Statue of George III

Common Sense, 1776 Thomas Paine 122
Silencing the Tories 126

ILLUSTRATION:
A London Cartoon

VOICES: LETTER FROM ANN HULTON TO MRS. LIGHTBODY, 1774 128

THE BIG PICTURE 129

@ ON THE WEB: VIRTUAL MARCHING TOUR OF THE PHILADELPHIA CAMPAIGN (1777) 129

Chapter 6 Creating the Constitution 130

INTERPRETIVE ESSAY

The Framers and the People Alfred F. Young 132

@ ON THE WEB: THE CONSTITUTION AND THE FIRST TEN AMENDMENTS 139

SOURCES

Ratification 140

TABLE:
Order of Ratification; Map: Voting for Ratification

DEBATES: THE VIRGINIA DEBATES 142

The Debates in the Several State Conventions on the Adoption of the Federal Constitution, Edited by Jonathan Elliott 142

@ **ON THE WEB: DEBATES SURROUNDING THE ADOPTION OF THE CONSTITUTION 146**

The Meaning of the Slave Trade Provision 147
Arguments of Charles Coatesworth Pinckney and James Wilson

@ **ON THE WEB: THE UNITED STATES CONSTITUTION AND THE INTERNATIONAL SLAVE TRADE 148**

Designing the Nation's Capitol 149

ILLUSTRATIONS:
Capitol Building Designs Submitted by Samuel Dobie, Charles Wintersmith, Etienne Hallet, James Diamond, and William Thornton; Portrait of William Thornton

THE BIG PICTURE 152

Chapter 7   Federalists and Republicans 153

INTERPRETIVE ESSAY

The Hamiltonian Miracle   John Steele Gordon 155

ILLUSTRATION:
Alexander Hamilton Engraving

SOURCES

The Fight Begins 167

Truth Versus Treason 169

ILLUSTRATIONS:
Federalist Depiction of Washington Putting Down the Whiskey Rebellion; Republican Handbills, 1804 and 1807

Roughhouse Politics 171

ILLUSTRATION:
Cartoon Lampooning Lyon-Griswold Brawl

Affairs of Honor 172

ILLUSTRATIONS:
DeWitt Clinton and John Swartout Duel;

Dueling Pistols Used in Burr-Hamilton Duel

@ **ON THE WEB: MORE ABOUT THE FEDERALIST ERA 175**

THE BIG PICTURE 175

Chapter 8   The Transformation of Northern Society 176

INTERPRETIVE ESSAY

Civilizing the Machine   John F. Kasson 178

SOURCES

Lowell, as It Was and as It Is, 1845 Henry A. Miles 199

@ **ON THE WEB: MORE ABOUT THE "BIRTHPLACE" OF INDUSTRY 203**

Portraits of Industrialism 203

ILLUSTRATIONS:
View of Lowell, Massachusetts; Title Page of the Lowell Offering; Engraving by Winslow Homer Depicting Textile Workers of Lawrence, Massachusetts; Striking Women and Local Militia

@ **ON THE WEB: ADDITIONAL PORTRAITS OF INDUSTRIALISM AT THE LOWELL MILLS 206**

THE BIG PICTURE 206

Chapter 9   Jacksonian Democracy 207

INTERPRETIVE ESSAY

The Hunger for Indian Land in Andrew Jackson's America   Anthony F. C. Wallace 209

@ **ON THE WEB: REMOVAL OF THE CHEROKEE AND THE TRAIL OF TEARS 215**

SOURCES

The Election of Jackson 216

MAP:
Results of the 1828 Presidential Election

@ **ON THE WEB: THE LIFE AND PRESIDENCY OF ANDREW JACKSON** 216

Removal of Eastern Tribes 217

ILLUSTRATION:
Expulsion of Eastern Tribes

The Anti-Jacksonians 218

ILLUSTRATIONS:
Anti-Jackson Cartoon and Broadside

"King Andrew" 220

ILLUSTRATIONS:
Anti-Jackson Cartoons

The Art of Democratic Politics Davy Crockett 221

The Election of 1840 223

ILLUSTRATION:
Painting Depicting Harrison Campaign

@ **ON THE WEB: MAP OF THE RESULTS OF THE ELECTION OF 1840** 224

Rally for William Henry Harrison in St. Louis, Missouri, as Reported by the St. Louis New Era 225

The Artist's View of Politics   George Caleb Bingham 227

ILLUSTRATIONS:
Canvassing for a Vote; County Election; Verdict of the People; Stump Speaking

THE BIG PICTURE 231

Chapter 10   Antislavery 232

INTERPRETIVE ESSAY

The Commitment to Immediate Emancipation James Brewer Stewart 234

@ **ON THE WEB: ABOLITION AND THE MOVEMENT FOR COLONIZATION IN LIBERIA** 243

SOURCES

Commission to Theodore Dwight Weld, 1834 244

From Letters of Theodore Dwight Weld, Angelina Grimké Weld, and Sarah Grimké, 1822–1844, *Edited by Gilbert H. Barnes and Dwight L. Dumond* 244

The Anti-Slavery Record, 1835–1836 248

ILLUSTRATIONS:
Images from the Front Page of the Anti-Slavery Record

"Fathers and Rulers" Petition 251

From Letters of Theodore Dwight Weld, Angelina Gimké Weld, and Sarah Grimké, 1822–1844, *Edited by Gilbert H. Barnes and Dwight L. Dumond* 251

Slavery as It Is, 1839 Theodore Dwight Weld 252

@ **ON THE WEB: THE AMERICAN ANTI-SLAVERY SOCIETY AND ITS EFFORTS TO END SLAVERY** 253

@ **ON THE WEB:** *SLAVERY AS IT IS* **IN ITS ENTIRETY** 253

THE BIG PICTURE 254

Chapter 11   Westward Expansion 255

MAP:
Overland Routes to California 256

INTERPRETIVE ESSAY

The World Rushed In   J. S. Holliday 257

SOURCES

Two Views of the West 270

ILLUSTRATIONS:
Manifest Destiny, John Gast; 1849 Cartoon Spoofing the Wild Rush to Get to California; 1849 Cartoon of a Greenhorn Setting Off for the Gold Fields; Another Greenhorn Going West; The True Value of California Gold; California Justice

Poker Flat and Points West 274

MAP:
The California Gold Fields Showing Some of the More Important Mining Camps, c. 1850 274

◎ VOICES: THE OTHER SIDE OF THE
STORY

Life Among the Piutes: Their Wrongs
and Claims, *by Sarah Winnemucca
Hopkins 275*

   ILLUSTRATION:
   *Sarah Winnemucca, Nevada Historical
   Society.*

@ ON THE WEB: "EXPERIENCE" THE
GOLD RUSH FOR YOURSELF **278**

THE BIG PICTURE 279

Chapter 12   Sectional Conflict 280

INTERPRETIVE ESSAY

   The Quest for Room   William L. Barney *282*

   MAP:
   Westward Expansion 282

@ ON THE WEB: WHAT NOTABLE
HISTORIANS HAVE HAD TO SAY
ABOUT WESTWARD EXPANSION
AND SLAVERY **293**

SOURCES

   The Kansas-Nebraska Act, 1854 294

   MAP:
   The United States, 1854 294

@ ON THE WEB: CONGRESSIONAL
DEBATES ON THE COMPROMISE
OF **1850** AND OTHER ISSUES **294**

   Two Portraits of the West 295

   ILLUSTRATIONS:
   *Cartoon from Punch Magazine;
    Forcing Slavery Down the Throat
    of a Free-Soiler*

@ ON THE WEB: NEWSPAPER
EDITORIALS ADDRESSING THE
KANSAS-NEBRASKA ACT AND OTHER
ISSUES **297**

▥ DEBATES: THE LINCOLN-DOUGLAS DEBATES,
1858 297

From Political Debates between Abraham
Lincoln and Stephen A. Douglas in
the Celebrated Campaign of 1858
in Illinois *298*

   ILLUSTRATIONS:
   *Illinois Senator Stephen A. Douglas;
    Abraham Lincoln in 1858*

@ ON THE WEB: FULL TEXT OF THE
LINCOLN-DOUGLAS DEBATES **304**

THE BIG PICTURE 305

Chapter 13   The Civil War 306

   MAP:
   *The Union Disintegrates; Table: Deaths
    in the Civil War and Other Wars 307*

INTERPRETIVE ESSAY

   A Band of Brothers   James M. McPherson *309*

@ ON THE WEB: COLLECTIONS
OF AMERICAN CIVIL WAR SOLDIERS'
DIARIES AND LETTERS **319**

SOURCES

   The Photographers' War 320

   ILLUSTRATIONS:
   *Abraham Lincoln, 1860 and 1865; Civil War
    Dead; Private Edwin Francis Jennison;
    The 107th U.S. Colored Infantry; Powder
    Monkey, USS New Hampshire; Ruins of
    Charleston, South Carolina, 1865; Union
    Dead; Union Wounded; The Richmond
    and Petersburg Railroad Depot, 1865;
    Richmond, Virginia, at War's End;
    Freedmen in Richmond, Virginia; John
    Wilkes Booth's Accomplices*

@ ON THE WEB: ADDITIONAL
PHOTOGRAPHS FROM THE
CIVIL WAR **326**

   *Sherman's March Through Georgia
   David P. Conyngham 327*

@ ON THE WEB: THE CIVIL WAR'S
IMPACT ON THE SOUTHERN
HOMEFRONT **334**

THE BIG PICTURE 335

Chapter 14 Reconstruction 336

INTERPRETIVE ESSAY

   Promised Land Elizabeth Rauh Bethel 338

@ **ON THE WEB: THE EXPERIENCE OF RECONSTRUCTION AFTER THE CIVIL WAR 350**

SOURCES

VOICES: THE MEANING OF FREEDOM 351

   Letter from Jourdon Anderson to his former master, from The Freedmen's Book, Edited by Lydia Maria Child, 1865 351

   The Cartoonist's View of Reconstruction 353

ILLUSTRATIONS:
Ten Political Cartoons by Thomas Nast, 1865–1876

@ **ON THE WEB: THOMAS NAST AND HIS POLITICAL CARTOONS RELATIVE TO RECONSTRUCTION 362**

The South Redeemed 363

MAP:
The Barrow Plantation, 1860 and 1880 363

@ **ON THE WEB: FREDERICK DOUGLASS'S PERCEPTION OF RECONSTRUCTION 363**

THE BIG PICTURE 364

Preface

*D*uring the past three or four decades, the study of history in the United States has become in many ways more sophisticated and more interesting. Until the mid-1960s the dominant tradition among American historians was to regard the historian's domain as one centered on politics, economics, diplomacy, and war. Now, at the start of the twenty-first century, historians are eager to address new kinds of subjects and to include whole sections of the population that were neglected in the traditional preoccupation with presidential administrations, legislation, and treaties. Women and children, the poor and economically marginal, African Americans and native Americans, have moved nearer the center of the historians' stage. We have become almost as eager to know how our ancestors dressed, ate, reared their children, made love, and buried their dead as we are to know how they voted in a particular presidential election. In addition, ordinary Americans now appear on the stage of history as active players who possess the power to shape their lives, rather than as passive victims of forces beyond their control. The result is a collective version of our national past that is more inclusive, more complex, and less settled.

About the New Edition

The fifth edition of *The American Record* continues the effort begun in previous editions. We have attempted to bridge the gap between the old history and the new, to graft the excitement and variety of modern approaches to the past on an existing chronological and topical framework with which most of us feel comfortable. Most of the familiar topics are here; we have included essays on the early colonial settlements, the Revolutionary War, the Constitution, progressivism, the Great Depression, and the consensual society of the 1950s. But by joining these essays to primary sources, we have tried to make it possible for teachers and students to explore the links between the Puritan social order and the lessons children learn from their primers; between the Revolutionary War and the colonial class structure; between the Constitution and the physical layout of the nation's capital; between progressivism and the photographs of Lewis Hine; between the Great Depression and the murals that were painted on post-office walls across the nation in the mid-1930s; and between the so-called "consensus" of the 1950s and the integration of Little Rock, Arkansas's public schools. The fifth edition also takes up themes and materials that are not so universally familiar, but which are beginning to reshape our understanding of the American past—among them religion, the rise of a consumer society, the history of popular music, the impact of television, draft resistance and, most recently, the war in Iraq. Reflecting the book's subtitle, both volumes make liberal use of drawings, cartoons, photographs, advertisements, and other visual materials. *The American Record* teaches the skill of making sense of one's whole world.

Throughout, we have attempted to incorporate materials with *texture:* documents that are not only striking but can be given more than one interpretation; photographs that invite real examination and discussion; tables and maps that have something new and interesting to contribute; and essays, such as James H. Merrell's account of the "New World" as it appeared to the Catawba Indians, Ronald Takaki's treatment of the wartime relocation of Japanese-Americans, or Beth Bailey's analysis of post–World War II dating customs, that are at once superb examples of recent historical scholarship and accessible to undergraduates. To foreground the agency of ordinary people, we have included sections called **Voices,** which feature firsthand commentaries such as Sarah Winnemucca's account of the California migrations and the testimony of John Morrison, a New York machinist, before the U.S. Senate in 1883. Another section, labeled **Debates,** juxtaposes differing perspectives on selected issues, including the adoption of the Constitution, the expansion of slavery into the territories, imperialism, Vietnam (featuring a young John Kerry), and 21st century nation-building. The fifth edition introduces a new **On the Web** feature, designed to encourage students to pursue topics of interest using some of the splendid materials available on the Internet.

Learning Aids for Students

From the beginning, we realized that our approach to American history would require some adjustment for many students and teachers. It was one thing to call on students to place an address by Albert J. Beveridge in the context of turn-of-the-century imperialism, yet quite another to ask them to do the same with a young woman's account of the African exhibit at the 1901 Pan-American Exposition in Buffalo, New York. For this reason, we have offered a good deal of guidance. **Introductions** to primary and secondary materials are designed not just to provide basic background information, but to suggest productive avenues of interpretation. Interpretive essays and questions are intended to create a kind of mental chemistry that provides students with enough information to experience the excitement of putting things together, and yet not so much guidance that conclusions become obvious. Each chapter concludes with a brief section called **The Big Picture,** where some of the larger questions are posed. In the second volume, we have often taken the The Big Picture a step further, presenting mini-essays that we hope will offer students a sense of how the materials in a chapter can yield a broad understanding or interpretation.

Acknowledgments

We remain indebted to R. Jackson Wilson, who inspired the first edition of this book. We also wish to thank our past editors at Alfred A. Knopf and McGraw-Hill—first David Follmer and Chris Rogers, later Niels Aaboe and Peter Labella, and Kristen Mellitt and Lyn Uhl—for their patient supervision of the previous edition. For the fifth edition, we have been fortunate to work with Steve Drummond and Larry Goldberg; we thank them for their concern and assistance at every stage of the project. And we are grateful to the teachers and students who used the first, second, third, and fourth editions of *The American Record* and showed us how to make the book better. In particular, we would like to thank the following reviewers of the fourth edition for their many helpful suggestions: Lane Fenrich, Northwestern University; Harvey H. Jackson, Jacksonville State University; Rusty Monhollon, Hood College; Christopher Olsen, Indiana State University; William A. Pencak, The Pennsylvania State University; Peter Richards, St. John's Preparatory School; and Rebecca S. Shoemaker, Indiana State University.

William Graebner
*State University of New York
at Fredonia*

Leonard Richards
*University of Massachusetts
at Amherst*

Chapter 1

The European Conquest of America

Interpretive Essay by James H. Merrell 3
Sources 21
    The Indians as Seen by European Artists 21
    Broken Spears: The Aztec Account of the Conquest of Mexico 21
    Race War: The New England Experience 29
The Big Picture 32

The idea that Europeans discovered America in 1492 is of course absurd. And so are the maps of the Mediterranean area that describe it as the "known" world. The Western Hemisphere and other areas that Europeans thought of as "terra incognita" were discovered and known to those who lived in them many centuries before white Europeans set sail on their momentous voyages. The importance of 1492 is not that Columbus stumbled on the New World—new, that is, to Europeans—in that year. What made his voyage, and those of other European explorers, important is what it set in motion: the conquest of vast areas of the world by a newly energized Europe. The Europeans discovered not simply new continents, but new continents they could subject to their power. The expansion of Europe was an event in *world* history.

Innovations in navigational technology, combined with the economic and political development of Europe, created a vast new arena for domination. "Native" societies in Africa and Asia proved to be more resistant than Europeans hoped. But in the Americas, Indian cultures fell with relative ease before the European onslaught. Some of the native American societies were weak and disunited, and were technologically little advanced beyond the levels achieved in the Stone Age. But there were mighty and sophisticated empires in the Americas, too, particularly those of the Aztecs in Mexico and the Incas in Peru. One of the major mysteries of world history is the explanation for the speed and the completeness of their defeat, the rapid and total European conquest that has made North and South America modern extensions of European culture.

How have historians accounted for this astonishing fact? On the surface, differences in technology seem to provide an easy answer. The horse, gunpowder, and other devices certainly made a difference—even the most advanced American cultures do not seem to have grasped the principle of the wheel. But technology cannot fully explain how a tiny handful of European adventurers managed to defeat Indian populations with hundreds of thousands of skillful and resourceful warriors. Disunity among the Indians, all over both North and South America, has also been invoked as a part of the explanation. But the native civilizations were hardly more disunited and contentious than their European conquerors.

More recently, historians have begun to pay attention to a silent factor that few of the participants in the European conquest were fully aware of—and that few used intentionally. For countless generations, Europe had been ravaged by diseases like tuberculosis and smallpox. In the process, Europeans had developed natural immunities to the worst effects of their illnesses. The isolated Americans, on the other hand, had not been exposed to these diseases and had no immunities. They could be slain by the hundreds of thousands by sicknesses as harmless to Europeans as the measles. Such diseases literally wiped out entire tribes and their cultures and made it possible for Europeans to simply walk in and take over.

The conquest of the Americas was a complex process, and there are no clear-cut answers to our questions about it. What we know for certain is this: very few events in the history of the human race have had more far-reaching consequences, for the conquerors and their victims alike.

The Indians' New World

James H. Merrell

The following essay, by the noted historian of native Americans James H. Merrell, turns the familiar story of European conquest on its head. Traditionally, the story has been told from the perspective of the European invaders. Merrell tells it from the perspective of the Catawbas, a collection of small tribes that had to cope with the strange "new world" of the European invaders. As you read this essay, you may want to think carefully about the various "new" factors that Europeans introduced. What order of importance does Merrell give them? How do you think these factors should be ranked? Also, you will notice that Merrell says that the Catawbas were able to "play the hand dealt them well enough to survive." How did they do this? And what did it cost them?

In August 1608 John Smith and his band of explorers captured an Indian named Amoroleck during a skirmish along the Rappahannock River. Asked why his men—a hunting party from towns upstream—had attacked the English, Amoroleck replied that they had heard the strangers "were a people come from under the world, to take their world from them." Smith's prisoner grasped a simple yet important truth that students of colonial America have overlooked: after 1492 native Americans lived in a world every bit as new as that confronting transplanted Africans or Europeans.

The failure to explore the Indians' new world helps explain why, despite many excellent studies of the native American past, colonial history often remains "a history of those men and women—English, European, and African—who transformed America from a geographical expression into a new nation." One reason Indians generally are left out may be the apparent inability to fit them into the new world theme, a theme that exerts a powerful hold on our historical imagination and runs throughout our efforts to interpret American development. From Frederick Jackson Turner to David Grayson Allen, from Melville J. Herskovits to Daniel C. Littlefield, scholars have analyzed encounters between peoples from the old world and conditions in the new, studying the complex interplay between Europeans or African cultural patterns and the American environment. Indians crossed no ocean, peopled no faraway land. It might seem logical to exclude them.

The natives' segregation persists, in no small degree, because historians still tend to think only of the new world as the New World, a geographic entity bounded by the Atlantic Ocean on the one side and the Pacific on the

From James H. Merrell, "The Indians' New World: The Catawba Experience," *William and Mary Quarterly*, ser. 3, vol. 41, October 1984, pp. 537–565. Reprinted by permission of the author.

other. Recent research suggests that process was as important as place. Many settlers in New England recreated familiar forms with such success that they did not really face an alien environment until long after their arrival. Africans, on the other hand, were struck by the shock of the new at the moment of their enslavement, well before they stepped on board ship or set foot on American soil. If the Atlantic was not a barrier between one world and another, if what happened to people was more a matter of subtle cultural processes than mere physical displacements, perhaps we should set aside the maps and think instead of a "world" as the physical and cultural milieu within which people live and a "new world" as a dramatically different milieu demanding basic changes in ways of life. Considered in these terms, the experience of natives was more closely akin to that of immigrants and slaves, and the idea of an encounter between worlds can—indeed, must—include the aboriginal inhabitants of America.

For American Indians a new order arrived in three distinct yet overlapping stages. First, alien microbes killed vast numbers of natives, sometimes before the victims had seen a white or black face. Next came traders who exchanged European technology for Indian products and brought natives into the developing world market. In time traders gave way to settlers eager to develop the land according to their own lights. These three intrusions combined to transform native existence, disrupting established cultural habits and requiring creative responses to drastically altered conditions. Like their new neighbors, then, Indians were forced to blend old and new in ways that would permit them to survive in the present without forsaking their past. By the close of the colonial era, native Americans as well as whites and blacks had created new societies, each similar to, yet very different from, its parent culture.

The range of native societies produced by this mingling of ingredients probably exceeded the variety of social forms Europeans and Africans developed. Rather than survey the broad spectrum of Indian adaptations, this article considers in some depth the response of natives in one area, the southern piedmont (see map). Avoiding extinction and eschewing retreat, the Indians of the piedmont have been in continuous contact with the invaders from across the sea almost since the beginning of the colonial period, thus permitting a thorough analysis of cultural intercourse. Moreover, a regional approach embracing groups from South Carolina to Virginia can transcend narrow (and still poorly understood) ethnic or "tribal" boundaries without sacrificing the richness of detail a focused study provides.

Indeed, piedmont people had so much in common that a regional perspective is almost imperative. No formal political ties bound them at the onset of European contact, but a similar environment shaped their lives, and their adjustment to this environment fostered cultural uniformity. Perhaps even more important, these groups shared a single history once Europeans and Africans arrived on the scene. Drawn together by their cultural affinities and their common plight, after 1700 they migrated to the Catawba Nation, a cluster of villages along the border between the Carolinas that became the focus of native life in the region. Tracing the experience of these upland communities both before and after they joined the Catawbas can illustrate

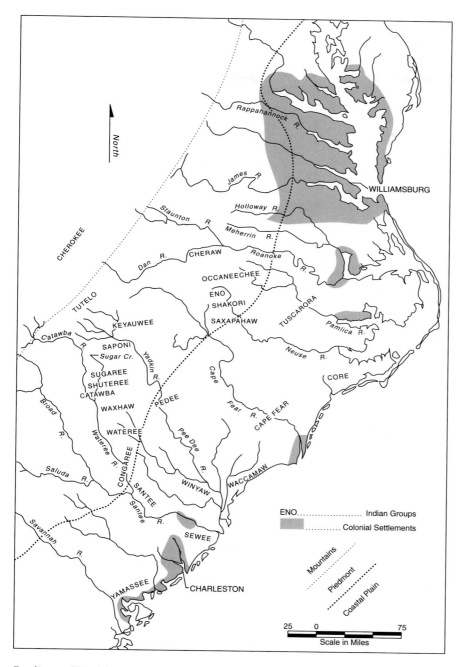

Carolinas and Virginia, 1700.

the consequences of contact and illuminate the process by which natives learned to survive in their own new world.

For centuries, ancestors of the Catawbas had lived astride important aboriginal trade routes and straddled the boundary between two cultural traditions, a position that involved them in a far-flung network of contacts and affected everything from potting techniques to burial practices. Nonetheless, Africans and Europeans were utterly unlike any earlier foreign visitors to the piedmont. Their arrival meant more than merely another encounter with outsiders; it marked an important turning point in Indian history. Once these newcomers disembarked and began to feel their way across the continent, they forever altered the course and pace of native development.

Bacteria brought the most profound disturbances to upcountry villages. When Hernando de Soto led the first Europeans into the area in 1540, he found large towns already "grown up in grass" because "there had been a pest in the land" two years before, a malady probably brought inland by natives who had visited distant Spanish posts. The sources are silent about other "pests" over the next century, but soon after the English began colonizing Carolina in 1670 the disease pattern became all too clear. Major epidemics struck the region at least once every generation—in 1698, 1718, 1738, and 1759—and a variety of less virulent illnesses almost never left native settlements.

Indians were not the only inhabitants of colonial America living—and dying—in a new disease environment. The swamps and lowlands of the Chesapeake were a deathtrap for Europeans, and sickness obliged colonists to discard or rearrange many of the social forms brought from England. Among native peoples long isolated from the rest of the world and therefore lacking immunity to pathogens introduced by the intruders, the devastation was even more severe. John Lawson, who visited the Carolina upcountry in 1701, when perhaps ten thousand Indians were still there, estimated that "there is not the sixth Savage living within two hundred Miles of all our Settlements, as there were fifty Years ago." The recent smallpox epidemic "destroy'd whole Towns," he remarked, "without leaving one *Indian* alive in the Village." Resistance to disease developed with painful slowness; colonists reported that the outbreak of smallpox in 1759 wiped out 60 percent of the natives, and, according to one source, "the woods were offensive with the dead bodies of the Indians; and dogs, wolves, and vultures were . . . busy for months in banqueting on them."

Survivors of these horrors were thrust into a situation no less alien than what European immigrants and African slaves found. The collected wisdom of generations could vanish in a matter of days if sickness struck older members of a community who kept sacred traditions and taught special skills. When many of the elders succumbed at once, the deep pools of collective memory grew shallow, and some dried up altogether. In 1710, Indians near Charleston told a settler that "they have forgot most of their traditions since the Establishment of this Colony, they keep their Festivals and can tell but little of the reasons: their Old Men are dead." Impoverishment of a rich cultural heritage followed the spread of disease. Nearly a century later, a South Carolinian exaggerated but captured the general trend when he noted that Catawbas "have forgotten their antient rites, ceremonies, and manufactures."

The same diseases that robbed a piedmont town of some of its most precious resources also stripped it of the population necessary to maintain an independent existence. In order to survive, groups were compelled to construct new societies from the splintered remnants of the old. The result was a kaleidoscopic array of migrations from ancient territories and mergers with nearby peoples. While such behavior was not unheard of in aboriginal times, population levels fell so precipitously after contact that survivors endured disruptions unlike anything previously known.

The dislocations of the Saponi Indians illustrate the common course of events. In 1670 they lived on the Staunton River in Virginia and were closely affiliated with a group called Nahyssans. A decade later Saponis moved toward the coast and built a town near the Occaneechees. When John Lawson came upon them along the Yadkin River in 1701, they were on the verge of banding together in a single village with Tutelos and Keyauwees. Soon thereafter Saponis applied to Virginia officials for permission to move to the Meherrin River, where Occaneechees, Tutelos, and others joined them. In 1714, at the urging of Virginia's Lt. Gov. Alexander Spotswood, these groups settled at Fort Christanna farther up the Meherrin. Their friendship with Virginia soured during the 1720s, and most of the "Christanna Indians" moved to the Catawba Nation. For some reason this arrangement did not satisfy them, and many returned to Virginia in 1732, remaining there for a decade before choosing to migrate north and accept the protection of the Iroquois.

Saponis were unusual only in their decision to leave the Catawbas. Enos, Occaneechees, Waterees, Keyauwees, Cheraws, and others have their own stories to tell, similar in outline if not in detail. With the exception of the towns near the confluence of Sugar Creek and the Catawba River that composed the heart of the Catawba Nation, piedmont communities decimated by disease lived through a common round of catastrophes, shifting from place to place and group to group in search of a safe haven. Most eventually ended up in the Nation, and during the opening decades of the eighteenth century the villages scattered across the southern upcountry were abandoned as people drifted into the Catawba orbit.

No mere catalog of migrations and mergers can begin to convey how profoundly unsettling this experience was for those swept up in it. While upcountry Indians did not sail away to some distant land, they, too, were among the uprooted, leaving their ancestral homes to try to make a new life elsewhere. The peripatetic existence of Saponis and others proved deeply disruptive. A village and its surrounding territory were important elements of personal and collective identity, physical links in a chain binding a group to its past and making a locality sacred. Colonists, convinced that Indians were by nature "a shifting, wandring People," were oblivious to this, but Lawson offered a glimpse of the reasons for native attachment to a particular locale. "In our way," he wrote on leaving an Eno-Shakori town in 1701, "there stood a great Stone about the Size of a large Oven, and hollow; this the *Indians* took great Notice of, putting some Tobacco into the Concavity, and spitting after it. I ask'd them the Reason for their so doing, but they made me no Answer." Natives throughout the interior honored similar places—graves of ancestors, monuments of stones commemorating important events—that could not be left behind without some cost.

The toll could be physical as well as spiritual, for even the most uneventful of moves interrupted the established cycle of subsistence. Belongings had to be packed and unpacked, dwellings constructed, palisades raised. Once migrants had completed the business of settling in, the still more arduous task of exploiting new terrain awaited them. Living in one place year after year endowed a people with intimate knowledge of the area. The richest soils, the best hunting grounds, the choicest sites for gathering nuts or berries—none could be learned without years of experience, tested by time and passed down from one generation to the next. Small wonder that Carolina Indians worried about being "driven to some unknown Country, to live, hunt, and get our Bread in."

Some displaced groups tried to leave "unknown Country" behind and make their way back home. In 1716 Enos asked Virginia's permission to settle at "Enoe Town" on the North Carolina frontier, their location in Lawson's day. Seventeen years later William Byrd II came upon an abandoned Cheraw village on a tributary of the upper Roanoke River and remarked how "it must have been a great misfortune to them to be obliged to abandon so beautiful a dwelling." The Indians apparently agreed: in 1717 the Virginia Council received "Divers applications" from the Cheraws (now living along the Pee Dee River) "for Liberty to Seat themselves on the head of Roanoke River." Few natives managed to return permanently to their homelands. But their efforts to retrace their steps hint at a profound sense of loss and testify to the powerful hold of ancient sites.

Compounding the trauma of leaving familiar territories was the necessity of abandoning customary relationships. Casting their lot with others traditionally considered foreign compelled Indians to rearrange basic ways of ordering their existence. Despite frequent contacts among peoples, native life had always centered in kin and town. The consequences of this deep-seated localism were evident even to a newcomer like John Lawson, who in 1701 found striking differences in language, dress, and physical appearance among Carolina Indians living only a few miles apart. Rules governing behavior also drew sharp distinctions between outsiders and one's own "Country-Folks." Indians were "very kind, and charitable to one another," Lawson reported, "but more especially to those of their own Nation." A visitor desiring a liaison with a local woman was required to approach her relatives and the village headman. On the other hand, "if it be an *Indian* of their own Town or Neighborhood, that wants a Mistress, he comes to none but the Girl." Lawson seemed unperturbed by this barrier until he discovered that a "Thief [is] held in Disgrace, that steals from any of his Country-Folks," "but to steal from the *English* [or any other foreigners] they reckon no Harm."

Communities unable to continue on their own had to revise these rules and reweave the social fabric into new designs. What language would be spoken? How would fields be laid out, hunting territories divided, houses built? How would decisions be reached, offenders punished, ceremonies performed? When Lawson remarked that "now adays" the Indians must seek mates "amongst Strangers," he unwittingly characterized life in native Carolina. Those who managed to withstand the ravages of disease had to redefine the meaning of the term *stranger* and transform outsiders into insiders.

The need to harmonize discordant peoples, an unpleasant fact of life for all native Americans, was no less common among black and white inhabitants of America during these years. Africans from a host of different groups were thrown into slavery together and forced to seek some common cultural ground, to blend or set aside clashing habits and beliefs. Europeans who came to America also met unexpected and unwelcome ethnic, religious, and linguistic diversity. The roots of the problem were quite different; the problem itself was much the same. In each case people from different backgrounds had to forge a common culture and a common future.

Indians in the southern uplands customarily combined with others like themselves in an attempt to solve the dilemma. Following the "principle of least effort," shattered communities cushioned the blows inflicted by disease and depopulation by joining a kindred society known through generations of trade and alliances. Thus Saponis coalesced with Occaneechees and Tutelos—nearby groups "speaking much the same language"—and Catawbas became a sanctuary for culturally related refugees from throughout the region. Even after moving in with friends and neighbors, however, natives tended to cling to ethnic boundaries in order to ease the transition. In 1715 Spotswood noticed that the Saponis and others gathered at Fort Christanna were "confederated together, tho' still preserving their different Rules." Indians entering the Catawba Nation were equally conservative. As late as 1743 a visitor could hear more than twenty different dialects spoken by peoples living there, and some bands continued to reside in separate towns under their own leaders.

Time inevitably sapped the strength of ethnic feeling, allowing a more unified Nation to emerge from the collection of Indian communities that occupied the valleys of the Catawba River and its tributaries. By the mid-eighteenth century, the authority of village headmen was waning and leaders from the host population had begun to take responsibility for the actions of constituent groups. The babel of different tongues fell silent as "*Kàtahba,*" the Nation's "standard, or court-dialect," slowly drowned out all others. Eventually, entire peoples followed their languages and their leaders into oblivion, leaving only personal names like Santee Jemmy, Cheraw George, Congaree Jamie, Saponey Johnny, and Eno Jemmy as reminders of the Nation's diverse heritage.

No European observer recorded the means by which nations became mere names and a congeries of groups forged itself into one people. No doubt the colonists' habit of ignoring ethnic distinctions and lumping confederated entities together under the Catawba rubric encouraged amalgamation. But Anglo-American efforts to create a society by proclamation were invariably unsuccessful; consolidation had to come from within. In the absence of evidence, it seems reasonable to conclude that years of contacts paved the way for a closer relationship. Once a group moved to the Nation, intermarriages blurred ancient kinship networks, joint war parties or hunting expeditions brought young men together, and elders met in a council that gave everyone some say by including "all the Indian Chiefs or Head Men of that [Catawba] Nation and the several Tribes amongst them together." The concentration of settlements within a day's walk of one another facilitated contact and communication. From their close proximity, common experience, and shared concerns, people developed ceremonies and myths that compensated for those lost to disease and gave the Nation a stronger collective consciousness. Associations evolved that balanced traditional narrow ethnic allegiance with a new, broader, "national" identity, a balance that tilted steadily toward the latter. Ethnic differences died hard, but the peoples of the Catawba Nation learned to speak with a single voice.

Muskets and kettles came to the piedmont more slowly than did smallpox and measles. Spanish explorers distributed a few gifts to local headmen, but inhabitants of the interior did not enjoy their first real taste of the fruits of European technology until Englishmen began venturing inland after 1650. Indians these traders met in upcountry towns were glad to barter for the more efficient tools, more lethal weapons, and more durable clothing that colonists offered. Spurred on by eager natives, men from Virginia and Carolina quickly flooded the region with the material trappings of European culture. In 1701 John Lawson considered the Wateree Chickanees "very poor in *English* Effects" because a few of them lacked muskets.

Slower to arrive, trade goods were also less obvious agents of change. The Indians' ability to absorb foreign artifacts into established modes of existence hid the revolutionary consequences of trade for some time. Natives leaped the technological gulf with ease in part because they were discriminating shoppers. If hoes were too small, beads too large, or cloth the wrong color, Indian traders refused them. Items they did select fit smoothly into existing ways. Waxhaws tied horse bells around their ankles at ceremonial dances, and some of the traditional stone pipes passed among the spectators at these dancers had been shaped by metal files. Those who could not afford a European weapon fashioned arrows from broken glass. Those who could went to great lengths to "set [a new musket] streight, sometimes shooting away above 100 Loads of Ammunition, before they bring the Gun to shoot according to their Mind."

Not every piece of merchandise hauled into the upcountry on a trader's packhorse could be "set streight" so easily. Liquor, for example, proved both impossible to resist and extraordinarily destructive. Indians "have no Power to refrain this Enemy," Lawson observed, "though sensible how many of them (are by it) hurry'd into the other World before their Time." And yet even here, natives aware of the risks sought to control alcohol by incorporating it into their ceremonial life as a device for achieving a different level of consciousness. Consumption was usually restricted to men, who "go as solemnly about it, as if it were part of their Religion," preferring to drink only at night and only in quantities sufficient to stupefy them. When ritual could not confine liquor to safe channels, Indians went still further and excused the excesses of overindulgence by refusing to hold an intoxicated person responsible for his actions. "They never call any Man to account for what he did, when he was drunk," wrote Lawson, "but say, it was the Drink that caused his Misbehaviour, therefore he ought to be forgiven."

Working to absorb even the most dangerous commodities acquired from their new neighbors, aboriginal inhabitants of the uplands, like African slaves in the lowlands, made themselves at home in a different technological environment. Indians became convinced that "Guns, and Ammunition, besides a great many other Necessaries, . . . are helpful to Man" and eagerly searched for the key that would unlock the secret of their production. At first many were confident that the *"Quera,"* or good Spirit, would teach them to make these commodities "when that good Spirit sees fit." Later they decided to help their deity along by approaching the colonists. In 1757, Catawbas asked Gov. Arthur Dobbs of North Carolina "to send us Smiths and other Tradesmen to teach our Children."

It was not the new products themselves but the Indians' failure to learn the mysteries of manufacture from either Dobbs or the *Quera* that marked the real revolution wrought by trade. During the seventeenth and eighteenth centuries, everyone in eastern North America—masters and slaves, farmers near the coast and Indians near the mountains—became producers of raw materials for foreign markets and found themselves caught up in an international economic network. Piedmont natives were part of this larger process, but their adjustment was more difficult because the contrast with previous ways was so pronounced. Before European contact, the localism characteristic of life in the uplands had been sustained by a remarkable degree of self-sufficiency. Trade among peoples, while common, was conducted primarily in commodities such as copper, mica, and shells, items that, exchanged with the appropriate ceremony, initiated or confirmed friendships among groups. Few, if any, villages relied on outsiders for goods essential to daily life.

Intercultural exchange eroded this traditional independence and entangled natives in a web of commercial relations few of them understood and none controlled. In 1670 the explorer John Lederer observed a striking disparity in the trading habits of Indians living near Virginia and those deep in the interior. The "remoter Indians," still operating within a precontact framework, were content with ornamental items such as mirrors, beads, "and all manner of gaudy toys and knacks for children." "Neighbour-Indians," on the other hand habitually traded with colonists for cloth, metal tools, and weapons. Before long, towns near and far were demanding the entire range of European wares and were growing accustomed—even addicted—to them. "They say we English are fools for . . . not always going with a gun," one Virginia colonist familiar with piedmont Indians wrote in the early 1690s, "for they think themselves undrest and not fit to walk abroad, unless they have their gun on their shoulder, and their shot-bag by their side." Such an enthusiastic conversion to the new technology eroded ancient craft skills and hastened complete dependence on substitutes only colonists could supply.

By forcing Indians to look beyond their own territories for certain indispensable products, Anglo-American traders inserted new variables into the aboriginal equation of exchange. Colonists sought two commodities from Indians—human beings and deerskins—and both undermined established relationships among native groups. While the demand for slaves encouraged piedmont peoples to expand their traditional warfare, the demand for peltry may have fostered conflicts over hunting territories. Those who did not fight each other for slaves or deerskins fought each other for the European products these could bring. As firearms, cloth, and other items became increasingly important to native existence, competition replaced comity at the foundation of trade encounters as villages scrambled for the cargoes of merchandise. Some were in a better position to profit than others. In the early 1670s Occaneechees living on an island in the Roanoke River enjoyed power out of all proportion to their numbers because they controlled an important ford on the trading path from Virginia to the interior, and they resorted to threats, and even to force, to retain their advantage. In Lawson's day Tuscaroras did the same, "hating that any of these Westward *Indians* should have any Commerce with the *English*, which would prove a Hinderance to their Gains."

Competition among native groups was only the beginning of the transformation brought about by new forms of exchange. Inhabitants of the piedmont might bypass the native middleman, but they could not break free from a perilous dependence on colonial sources of supply. The danger may not have been immediately apparent to Indians caught up in the excitement of acquiring new and wonderful things. For years they managed to dictate the terms of trade, compelling visitors from Carolina and Virginia to abide by aboriginal codes of conduct and playing one colony's traders against the other to ensure an abundance of goods at favorable rates. But the natives' influence over the protocol of exchange combined with their skill at incorporating alien products to mask a loss of control over their own destiny. The mask came off when, in 1715, the traders—and the trade goods—suddenly disappeared during the Yamassee War.

The conflict's origins lay in a growing colonial awareness of the Indians' need for regular supplies of European merchandise. In 1701 Lawson pronounced the Santees "very tractable" because of their close connections with South Carolina. Eight years later he was convinced that the colonial officials in Charleston "are absolute Masters over the *Indians . . .* within the Circle of their Trade." Carolina traders who shared this conviction quite naturally felt less and less constrained to obey native rules governing proper behavior. Abuses against Indians mounted until some men were literally getting away with murder. When repeated appeals to colonial officials failed, natives throughout Carolina began to consider war.

Persuaded by Yamassee ambassadors that the conspiracy was widespread and convinced by years of ruthless commercial competition between Virginia and Carolina that an attack on one colony would not affect relations with the other, in the spring of 1715 Catawbas and their neighbors joined the invasion of South Carolina.

The decision to fight was disastrous. Colonists everywhere shut off the flow of goods to the interior, and after some initial successes Carolina's native enemies soon plumbed the depths of their dependence. In a matter of months, refugees holed up in Charleston noticed that "the Indians want ammunition and are not able to mend their Arms." The peace negotiations that ensued revealed a desperate thirst for fresh supplies of European wares. Ambassadors from piedmont towns invariably spoke in a single breath of restoring "a Peace and a free Trade," and one delegation even admitted that its people "cannot live without the assistance of the English."

Natives unable to live without the English henceforth tried to live with them. No upcountry group mounted a direct challenge to Anglo-America after 1715. Trade quickly resumed, and the piedmont Indians, now concentrated almost exclusively in the Catawba valley, briefly enjoyed a regular supply of necessary products sold by men willing once again to deal according to the old rules. By mid-century, however, deer were scarce and fresh sources of slaves almost impossible to find. Anglo-American traders took their business elsewhere, leaving inhabitants of the Nation with another material crisis of different but equally dangerous dimensions.

Indians casting about for an alternative means of procuring the commodities they craved looked to imperial officials. During the 1740s and 1750s native dependence shifted from colonial traders to colonial authorities as Catawba leaders repeatedly visited provincial capitals to request goods. These delegations came not to beg but to bargain. Catawbas were still of enormous value to the English as allies and frontier guards, especially at a time when Anglo-America felt threatened by the French and their Indian auxiliaries. The Nation's position within reach of Virginia and both Carolinas enhanced its value by enabling headmen to approach all three colonies and offer their people's services to the highest bidder.

The strategy yielded Indians an arsenal of ammunition and a variety of other merchandise that helped offset the declining trade. Crown officials were especially generous when the Nation managed to play one colony off against another. In 1746 a rumor that the Catawbas were about to move to Virginia was enough to garner them a large shipment of powder and lead from officials in Charleston concerned about losing this "valuable people." A decade later, while the two Carolinas fought for the honor of constructing a fort in the Nation, the Indians encouraged (and received) gifts symbolizing good will from both colonies without reaching an agreement with either. Surveying the tangled thicket of promises and presents, the crown's superintendent of Indian affairs, Edmond Atkin, ruefully admitted that "the People of both Provinces . . . have I believe [sic] tampered too much on both sides with those Indians, who seem to understand well how to make their Advantage of it."

By the end of the colonial period delicate negotiations across cultural boundaries were as familiar to Catawbas as the strouds they wore and the muskets they carried. But no matter how shrewdly the headmen loosened provincial purse strings to extract vital merchandise, they could not escape the simple fact that they no longer held the purse containing everything needed for their daily existence. In the space of a century the Indians had become thoroughly embedded in an alien economy, denizens of a new material world. The ancient self-sufficiency was only a dim memory in the minds of the Nation's elders.

The Catawba peoples were veterans of countless campaigns against disease and masters of the arts of trade long before the third major element of their new world, white planters, became an integral part of their life. Settlement of the Carolina uplands did not begin until the 1730s, but once under way it spread with frightening speed. In November 1752, concerned Catawbas reminded South Carolina Governor James Glen how they had "complained already . . . that the white People were settled too near us." Two years later five hundred families lived within thirty miles of the Nation and surveyors were running their lines into the middle of native towns. "[T]hose Indians are now in a fair way to be surrounded by White People," one observer concluded.

Settlers' attitudes were as alarming as their numbers. Unlike traders who profited from them or colonial officials who deployed them as allies, ordinary colonists had little use for Indians. Natives made poor servants and worse slaves; they obstructed settlement; they attracted enemy warriors to the area. Even men who respected Indians and earned a living by trading with them admitted that they made unpleasant neighbors. "We may observe of them as of the fire," wrote the South Carolina trader James Adair after considering the Catawbas' situation on the eve of the American Revolution, "'it is safe and useful, cherished at proper distance; but if too near us, it becomes dangerous, and will scorch if not consume us.'"

A common fondness for alcohol increased the likelihood of intercultural hostilities. Catawba leaders acknowledged that the Indians "get very Drunk with [liquor] this is the Very Cause that they oftentimes Commit those Crimes that is offencive to You and us." Colonists were equally prone to bouts of drunkenness. In the 1760s the itinerant Anglican minister, Charles Woodmason, was shocked to find the citizens of one South Carolina upcountry community "continually drunk." More appalling still, after attending church services "one half of them got drunk before they went home." Indians sometimes suffered at the hands of intoxicated farmers. In 1760 a Catawba woman was murdered when she happened by a tavern shortly after four of its patrons "swore they would kill the first Indian they should meet with."

Even when sober, natives and newcomers found many reasons to quarrel. Catawbas were outraged if colonists built farms on the Indians' doorstep or tramped across ancient burial grounds. Planters, ignorant of (or indifferent to) native rules of hospitality, considered Indians who requested food nothing more than beggars and angrily drove them away. Other disputes arose when the Nation's young men went looking for trouble. As hunting, warfare, and other traditional avenues for achieving status narrowed, Catawba youths transferred older patterns of behavior into a new arena by raiding nearby farms and hunting cattle or horses.

Contrasting images of the piedmont landscape quite unintentionally generated still more friction. Colonists determined to tame what they considered a wilderness were in fact erasing a native signature on the land and scrawling their own. Bridges, buildings, fences, roads, crops, and other "improvements" made the area comfortable and familiar to colonists but uncomfortable and unfamiliar to Indians. "The Country side wear[s] a New face," proclaimed Woodmason proudly; to the original inhabitants, it was a grim face indeed. "His Land was spoiled," one Catawba headman told British officials in 1763. "They have spoiled him 100 Miles every way." Under these circumstances, even a settler with no wish to fight Indians met opposition to his fences, his outbuildings, his very presence. Similarly, a Catawba on a routine foray into traditional hunting territories had his weapon destroyed, his goods confiscated, his life threatened by men with different notions of the proper use of the land.

To make matters worse, the importance both cultures attached to personal independence hampered efforts by authorities on either side to resolve conflicts. Piedmont settlers along the border between the Carolinas were "people of desperate fortune," a frightened North Carolina official reported after visiting the area. "[N]o officer of Justice from either Province dare meddle with them." Woodmason, who spent even more time in the region, came to the same conclusion. "We are without any Law, or Order," he complained; the inhabitants' "Impudence is so very high, as to be past bearing." Catawba leaders could have sympathized. Headmen informed colonists that the Nation's people "are oftentimes Cautioned from . . . ill Doings altho' to no purpose for we Cannot be present at all times to Look after them." "What they have done I could not prevent," one chief explained.

Unruly, angry, intoxicated—Catawbas and Carolinians were constantly at odds during the middle decades of the eighteenth century. Planters who considered Indians "proud and deveilish" were themselves accused by natives of being "very bad and quarrelsome." Warriors made a habit of "going into the Settlements, robbing and stealing where ever they get an Oppertunity." Complaints generally brought no satisfaction—"they laugh and makes their Game of it, and says it is what they will"—leading some settlers to "whip [Indians] about the head, beat and abuse them." "The white People . . . and the Cuttahbaws, are Continually at varience," a visitor to the Nation fretted in June 1759, "and Dayly New Animositys Doth a rise Between them which In my Humble oppion will be of Bad Consequence In a Short time, Both Partys Being obstinate."

The litany of intercultural crimes committed by each side disguised a fundamental shift in the balance of physical and cultural power. In the early years of colonization of the interior the least disturbance by Indians sent scattered planters into a panic. Soon, however, Catawbas were few, colonists many, and it was the natives who now lived in fear. "[T]he white men [who] Lives Near the Neation is Contenuely asembleing and goes In the [Indian] towns In Bodys . . . ," worried another observer during the tense summer of 1759. "[T]he[y] tretton the[y] will Kill all the Cattabues."

The Indians would have to find some way to get along with these unpleasant neighbors if the Nation was to survive. As Catawba population fell below five hundred after the smallpox epidemic of 1759 and the number of colonists continued to climb, natives gradually came to recognize the futility of violent resistance. During the last decades of the eighteenth century they drew on years of experience in dealing with Europeans at a distance and sought to overturn the common conviction that Indian neighbors were frightening and useless.

This process was not the result of some clever plan; Catawbas had no strategy for survival. A headman could warn them that "the White people were now seated all round them and by that means had them entirely in their power." He could not command them to submit peacefully to the invasion of their homeland. The Nation's continued existence required countless individual decisions, made in a host of diverse circumstances, to complain rather than retaliate, to accept a subordinate place in a land that once was theirs. Few of the choices made survive in the record. But it is clear that, like the response to disease and to technology, the adaptation to white settlement was both painful and prolonged.

Catawbas took one of the first steps along the road to accommodation in the early 1760s, when they used their influence with colonial officials to acquire a reservation encompassing the heart of their ancient territories. This grant gave the Indians a land base, grounded in Anglo-American law, that prevented farmers from shouldering them aside. Equally important, Catawbas now had a commodity to exchange with nearby settlers. These men wanted land, the natives had plenty, and shortly before the Revolution the Nation was renting tracts to planters for cash, livestock, and manufactured goods.

Important as it was, land was not the only item Catawbas began trading to their neighbors. Some Indians put their skills as hunters and woodsmen to a different use, picking up stray horses and escaped slaves for a reward. Others bartered their pottery, baskets, and table mats. Still others traveled through the upcountry, demonstrating their prowess with the bow and arrow before appreciative audiences. The exchange of these goods and services for European merchandise marked an important adjustment to the settlers' arrival. In the past, natives had acquired essential items by trading peltry and slaves or requesting gifts from representatives of the crown. But piedmont planters frowned on hunting and warfare, while provincial authorities—finding Catawbas less useful as the Nation's population declined and the French threat disappeared—discouraged formal visits and handed out fewer presents. Hence the Indians had to develop new avenues of exchange that would enable them to obtain goods in ways less objectionable to their neighbors. Pots, baskets, and acres proved harmless substitutes for earlier methods of earning an income.

Quite apart from its economic benefits, trade had a profound impact on the character of Catawba-settler relations. Through countless repetitions of the same simple procedure at homesteads scattered across the Carolinas, a new form of intercourse arose, based not on suspicion and an expectation of conflict but on trust and a measure of friendship. When a farmer looked out his window and saw Indians approaching, his reaction more commonly became to pick up money or a jug of whiskey rather than a musket or an axe. The natives now appeared, the settler knew, not to plunder or kill but to peddle their wares or collect their rents.

The development of new trade forms could not bury all the differences between Catawba and colonist overnight. But in the latter half of the eighteenth century the beleaguered Indians learned to rely on peaceful means of resolving intercultural conflicts that did arise. Drawing a sharp distinction between "the good men that have rented Lands from us" and "the bad People [who] has frequently imposed upon us," Catawbas called on the former to protect the Nation from the latter. In 1771 they met with a prominent Camden storekeeper, Joseph Kershaw, to request that he "represent us when [we are] a grieved." After the revolution the position became more formal. Catawbas informed the South Carolina government that, being "destitute of a man to take care of, and assist us in our affairs," they had chosen one Robert Patten "to take charge of our affairs, and to act and do for us."

Neither Patten nor any other intermediary could have protected the Nation had it not joined the patriot side during the Revolutionary War. Though one scholar has termed the Indians' contribution to the cause "rather negligible," they fought in battles throughout the southeast and supplied rebel forces with food from time to time. These actions made the Catawbas heroes and laid a foundation for their popular renown as staunch patriots. In 1781 their old friend Kershaw told Catawba leaders how he welcomed the end of "this Long and Bloody War, in which You have taken so Noble a part and have fought and Bled with your white Brothers of America." Grateful Carolinians would not soon forget the Nation's service. Shortly after the Civil War an elderly settler whose father had served with the Indians in the revolution echoed Kershaw's sentiments, recalling that "his father never communicated much to him [about the Catawbas], except that all the tribe . . . served the entire war . . . and fought most heroically."

Catawbas rose even higher in their neighbors' esteem when they began calling their chiefs "general" instead of "king" and stressed that these men were elected by the people. The change reflected little if any real shift in the Nation's political forms, but it delighted the victorious revolutionaries. In 1794 the Charleston *City Gazette* reported that during the war "King" Frow had abdicated and the Indians chose "General" New River in his stead. "What a pity," the paper concluded, "certain people on a certain island have not as good optics as the Catawbas!" In the same year the citizens of Camden celebrated the anniversary of the fall of the Bastille by raising their glasses to toast "King Prow [*sic*]—may all kings who will not follow his example follow that of Louis XVI." Like tales of Indian patriots, the story proved durable. Nearly a century after the revolution one nearby planter wrote that "the Catawbas, emulating the examples of their white brethren, threw off regal government."

The Indians' new image as republicans and patriots, added to their trade with whites and their willingness to resolve conflicts peacefully, brought settlers to view Catawbas in a different light. By 1800 the natives were no longer violent and dangerous strangers but what one visitor termed an "inoffensive" people and one group of planters called "harmless and friendly" neighbors. They had become traders of pottery but not deerskins, experts with a bow and arrow but not hunters, ferocious warriors against runaway slaves or Tories but not against settlers. In these ways Catawbas could be distinctively Indian yet reassuringly harmless at the same time.

The Nation's separate identity rested on such obvious aboriginal traits. But its survival ultimately depended on a more general conformity with the surrounding society. During the nineteenth century both settlers and Indians owned or rented land. Both spoke proudly of their revolutionary heritage and their republican forms of government. Both drank to excess. Even the fact that Catawbas were not Christians failed to differentiate them sharply from nearby white settlements, where, one visitor noted in 1822, "little attention is paid to the sabbath, or religeon."

In retrospect it is clear that these similarities were as superficial as they were essential. For all the changes generated by contacts with vital Euro-American and Afro-American cultures, the Nation was never torn loose from its cultural moorings. Well after the revolution, Indians maintained a distinctive way of life rich in tradition and meaningful to those it embraced. Ceremonies conducted by headmen and folk tales told by relatives continued to transmit traditional values and skills from one generation to the next. Catawba children grew up speaking the native language, making bows and arrows or pottery, and otherwise following patterns of belief and behavior derived from the past. The Indians' physical appearance and the meandering paths that set Catawba settlements off from neighboring communities served to reinforce this cultural isolation.

The natives' utter indifference to missionary efforts after 1800 testified to the enduring power of established ways. Several clergymen stopped at the reservation in the first years of the nineteenth century; some stayed a year or two; none enjoyed any success. As one white South Carolinian noted in 1826, Catawbas were "Indians still." Outward conformity made it easier for them to blend into the changed landscape. Beneath the surface lay a more complex story.

Those few outsiders who tried to piece together that story generally found it difficult to learn much from the Indians. A people shrewd enough to discard the title of "king" was shrewd enough to understand that some things were better left unsaid and unseen. Catawbas kept their Indian names, and sometimes their language, a secret from prying visitors. They echoed the racist attitudes of their white neighbors and even owned a few slaves, all the time trading with blacks and hiring them to work in the Nation, where the laborers "enjoyed considerable freedom" among the natives. Like Afro-Americans on the plantation who adopted a happy, childlike demeanor to placate suspicious whites, Indians on the reservation learned that a "harmless and friendly" posture revealing little of life in the Nation was best suited to conditions in postrevolutionary South Carolina.

Success in clinging to their cultural identity and at least a fraction of their ancient lands cannot obscure the cost Catawba peoples paid. From the time the first European arrived, the deck was stacked against them. They played the hand dealt them well enough to survive, but they could never win. An incident that took place at the end of the eighteenth century helps shed light on the consequences of compromise. When the Catawba headman General New River accidentally injured the horse he had borrowed from a nearby planter named Thomas Spratt, Spratt responded by "banging old New River with a pole all over the yard." This episode provided the settler with a colorful tale for his grandchildren; its effect on New River and his descendants can only be imagined. Catawbas did succeed in the sense that they adjusted to a hostile and different world, becoming trusted friends instead of feared enemies. Had they been any less successful they would not have survived the eighteenth century. But poverty and oppression have plagued the Nation from New River's day to our own. For a people who had once been proprietors of the piedmont, the pain of learning new rules was very great, the price of success very high.

On that August day in 1608 when Amoroleck feared the loss of his world, John Smith assured him that the English "came to them in peace, and to seeke their loves." Events soon proved Amoroleck right and his captor wrong. Over the course of the next three centuries not only Amoroleck and other piedmont Indians but natives throughout North America had their world stolen and another put in its place. Though this occurred at different times and in different ways, no Indians escaped the explosive mixture of deadly bacteria, material riches, and alien peoples that was the invasion of America. Those in the southern piedmont who survived the onslaught were ensconced in their new world by the end of the eighteenth century. Population levels stabilized as the Catawba peoples developed immunities to once-lethal diseases. Rents, sales of pottery, and other economic activities proved adequate to support the Nation at a stable (if low) level of material life. Finally, the Indians' image as "inoffensive" neighbors gave them a place in South Carolina society and continues to sustain them today.

Vast differences separated Catawbas and other natives from their colonial contemporaries. Europeans were the colonizers, Africans the enslaved, Indians the dispossessed: from these distinct positions came distinct histories. Yet once we acknowledge the differences, instructive similarities remain that help to integrate natives more thoroughly into the story of early America. By carving a niche for themselves in response to drastically different conditions, the peoples who composed the Catawba Nation shared in the most fundamental of American experiences. Like Afro-Americans, these Indians were compelled to accept a subordinate position in American life yet did not altogether lose their cultural integrity. Like settlers of the Chesapeake, aboriginal inhabitants of the uplands adjusted to appalling mortality rates and wrestled with the difficult task of "living with death." Like inhabitants of the Middle Colonies, piedmont groups learned to cope with unprecedented ethnic diversity by balancing the pull of traditional loyalties with the demands of a new social order. Like Puritans in New England, Catawbas found that a new world did not arrive all at once and that localism, self-sufficiency, and the power of old ways were only gradually eroded by conditions in colonial America. More hints of a comparable heritage could be added to this list, but by now it should be clear that Indians belong on the colonial stage as important actors in the unfolding American drama rather than bit players, props, or spectators. For they, too, lived in a new world.

The Indians as Seen by European Artists

Europeans formed a fantastic variety of mental pictures of the lives and behavior of the natives of the Americas. On one hand, they might portray the Indians as vicious cannibals, with almost no social organization. On the other hand, Europeans often pictured Indian society as being rather orderly, advanced, and "civilized." Here are three very famous sixteenth-century representations. Pictures, we like to believe, tell us more than words. Suppose you were to try to translate these pictures into a few words, however. What would they be? Can you imagine other ways of depicting the Indians that Europeans might have used?

Broken Spears: The Aztec Account of the Conquest of Mexico

What about the violent side of the story? The Europeans, as the 1564 depiction of a Florida battle scene suggests, made much of the brutality of the "savages." By the same token, native groups had plenty of horror stories to tell about European

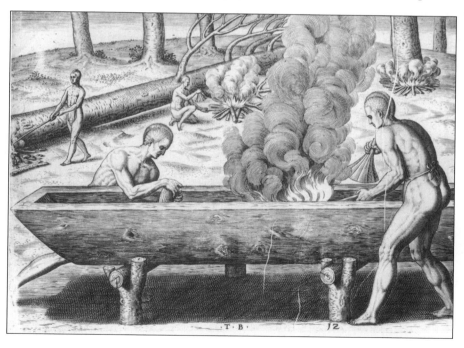

John White's engraving of Indians making a canoe near Roanoke, 1588. Rare Books and Manuscripts Division. The New York Public Library. Astor, Lenox and Tilden Foundations.

A settlement of Virginia Indians. From Part I, Plate XX, in Theodore DeBry's *America*. Rare Books and Manuscripts Division. The New York Public Library. Astor, Lenox and Tilden Foundations.

 ON THE WEB

For more information on John White's engravings of Virginia Indians, see the William W. Cole Collection on the Virginia Historical Society website at http://www.vahistorical.org/cole/overview.htm.

Florida battle scene, 1564. American Antiquarian Society.

atrocities. From various accounts, some written as early as 1528, the Mexican anthropologist Miguel Leon-Portilla has pieced together the Aztec memory of Cortés's invasion in 1521. At the time, almost a century before the Catawbas first encountered Europeans, the Aztecs ruled a mighty empire, thousands of times the size of the Catawba Nation, rich and spectacular by both New and Old World standards. As you read this story of the way Montezuma and his people experienced the shock of invasion and the bitterness of their defeat, keep these questions in mind: What do the Aztecs give as the cause of Spanish victory? Technology? Divine intervention? Disease? Was the Aztec experience the same as that of the Catawbas? In what respect was it different? Why?

❧ *Motecuhzoma Goes Out to Meet Cortes*

The Spaniards arrived in Xoloco, near the entrance to Tenochtitlan. That was the end of the march, for they had reached their goal.

Motecuhzoma now arrayed himself in his finery, preparing to go out to meet them. The other great princes also adorned their persons, as did the nobles and their chieftains and knights. They all went out together to meet the strangers.

They brought trays heaped with the finest flowers—the flower that resembles a shield; the flower shaped like a heart; in the center, the flower with the sweetest aroma; and the fragrant yellow flower, the most precious of all. They also brought garlands of flowers, and ornaments for the breast, and necklaces of gold, necklaces hung with rich stones, necklaces fashioned in the petatillo style.

Thus Motecuhzoma went out to meet them, there in Huitzillan. He presented many gifts to the Captain and his commanders, those who had come to make war. He showered gifts upon them and hung flowers around their necks; he gave them necklaces of flowers and bands of flowers to adorn their breasts; he set garlands of flowers upon their heads. Then he hung the gold necklaces around their necks and gave them presents of every sort as gifts of welcome. . . .

✎ *Motecuhzoma Awaits Word from the Messengers*

While the messengers were away, Motecuhzoma could neither sleep nor eat, and no one could speak with him. He thought that everything he did was in vain, and he sighed almost every moment. He was lost in despair, in the deepest gloom and sorrow. Nothing could comfort him, nothing could calm him, nothing could give him any pleasure.

He said: "What will happen to us? Who will outlive it? Ah, in other times I was contented, but now I have death in my heart! My heart burns and suffers, as if it were drowned in spices . . . ! But will our lord come here?"

Then he gave orders to the watchmen, to the men who guarded the palace: "Tell me, even if I am sleeping: 'The messengers have come back from the sea.'" But when they went to tell him, he immediately said: "They are not to report to me here. I will receive them in the House of the Serpent. Tell them to go there." And he gave this order: "Two captives are to be painted with chalk."

The messengers went to the House of the Serpent, and Motecuhzoma arrived. The two captives were then sacrificed before his eyes: their breasts were torn open, and the messengers were sprinkled with their blood. This was done because the messengers had completed a difficult mission: they had seen the gods, their eyes had looked on their faces. They had even conversed with the gods!

✎ *The Messengers' Report*

When the sacrifice was finished, the messengers reported to the king. They told him how they had made the journey, and what they had seen, and what food the strangers ate. Motecuhzoma was astonished and terrified by their report, and the description of the strangers' food astonished them above all else.

He was also terrified to learn how the cannon roared, how its noise resounded, how it caused one to faint and grow deaf. The messengers told him: "A thing like a ball of fire comes out its entrails: it comes out shooting sparks and raining fire. The smoke that comes out with it has a pestilent odor, like that of rotten mud. This odor penetrates even to the brain and causes the greatest discomfort. If the cannon is aimed against a mountain, the mountain splits and cracks open. If it is aimed against a tree, it shatters the tree into splinters. This is a most unnatural sight as if the tree had exploded from within."

The messengers also said: "Their trappings and arms are all made of iron. They dress in iron and wear iron casques on their heads. Their swords are iron; their bows are iron; their shields are iron; their spears are iron. Their deer carry them on their backs wherever they wish to go. These deer, our lord, are as tall as the roof of a house."

The strangers' bodies are completely covered, so that only their faces can be seen. Their skin is white, as if it were made of lime. They have yellow hair, though some of them have black. Their beards are long and yellow, and their mustaches are also yellow. Their hair is curly, with very fine strands.

"As for their food, it is like human food. It is large and white, and not heavy. It is something like straw, but with the taste of a cornstalk, of the pith of a cornstalk. It is a little sweet, as if it were flavored with honey; it tastes of honey; it is sweet-tasting food.

"Their dogs are enormous, with flat ears and long, dangling tongues. The color of their eyes is a burning yellow; their eyes flash fire and shoot off sparks. Their bellies are hollow, their flanks long and narrow. They are tireless and very powerful. They bound here and there, panting, with their tongues hanging out. And they are spotted like an ocelot."

When Motecuhzoma heard this report, he was filled with terror. It was as if his heart had fainted, as if it had shriveled. It was as if he were conquered by despair. . . .

The Spaniards Take Possession of the City

When the Spaniards entered the Royal House, they placed Motecuhzoma under guard and kept him under their vigilance. They also placed a guard over Itzcuauhtzin, but the other lords were permitted to depart.

Then the Spaniards fired one of their cannons, and this caused great confusion in the city. The people scattered in every direction; they fled without rhyme or reason; they ran off as if they were being pursued. It was as if they had eaten the mushrooms that confuse the mind, or had seen some dreadful apparition. They were all overcome by terror, as if their hearts had fainted. And when night fell, the panic spread through the city and their fears would not let them sleep.

In the morning the Spaniards told Motecuhzoma what they needed in the way of supplies: tortillas, fried chickens, hens' eggs, pure water, firewood and charcoal. Also: large, clean cooking pots, water jars, pitchers, dishes and other pottery. Motecuhzoma ordered that it be sent to them. The chiefs who received this order were angry with the king and no longer revered or respected him. But they furnished the Spaniards with all the provisions they needed—food, beverages, and water, and fodder for the horses.

✑ The Spaniards Reveal Their Greed

When the Spaniards were installed in the palace, they asked Motecuhzoma about the city's resources and reserves and about the warriors' ensigns and shields. They questioned him closely and then demanded gold.

Motecuhzoma guided them to it. They surrounded him and crowded close with their weapons. He walked in the center, while they formed a circle around him.

When they arrived at the treasure house called Teucalco, the riches of gold and feathers were brought out to them: ornaments made of quetzal feathers, richly worked shields, disks of gold, the necklaces of the idols, gold nose plugs, gold greaves and bracelets and crowns.

The Spaniards immediately stripped the feathers from the gold shields and ensigns. They gathered all the gold into a great mound and set fire to everything else, regardless of its value. Then they melted down the gold into ingots. As for the precious green stones, they took only the best of them; the rest were snatched up by the Tlaxcaltecas. The Spaniards searched through the whole treasure house, questioning and quarreling, and seized every object they thought was beautiful.

✑ The Seizure of Motecuhzoma's Treasures

Next they went to Motecuhzoma's storehouse, in the place called Totocalec [Place of the Palace of the Birds], where his personal treasures were kept. The Spaniards grinned like little beasts and patted each other with delight.

When they entered the hall of treasures, it was as if they had arrived in Paradise. They searched everywhere and coveted everything; they were slaves to their own greed. All of Motecuhzoma's possessions were brought out: fine bracelets, necklaces with large stones, ankle rings with little gold bells, the royal crowns, and all the royal finery—everything that belonged to the king and was reserved to him only. They seized these treasures as if they were their own, as if this plunder were merely a stroke of good luck. And when they had taken all the gold, they heaped up everything else in the middle of the patio.

La Malinche called the nobles together. She climbed up to the palace roof and cried, "Mexicanos, come forward! The Spaniards need your help! Bring them food and pure water. They are tired and hungry; they are almost fainting from exhaustion! Why do you not come forward? Are you angry with them?"

The Mexicans were too frightened to approach. They were crushed by terror and would not risk coming forward. They shied away as if the Spaniards were wild beasts, as if the hour were midnight on the blackest night of the year. Yet they did not abandon the Spaniards to hunger and thirst. They brought them whatever they needed, but shook with fear as they did so. They delivered the supplies to the Spaniards with trembling hands, then turned and hurried away. . . .

The Massacre in the Main Temple During the Fiesta of Toxcatl

At this moment in the fiesta, when the dance was loveliest and when song was linked to song, the Spaniards were seized with an urge to kill the celebrants. They all ran forward, armed as if for battle. They closed the entrances and passageways, all the gates of the patio: the Eagle Gate in the lesser palace, the Gate of the Canestalk and the Gate of the Serpent of Mirrors. They posted guards so that no one could escape, and then rushed into the Sacred Patio to slaughter the celebrants. They came on foot, carrying their swords and their wooden or metal shields.

They ran in among the dancers, forcing their way to the place where the drums were played. They attacked the man who was drumming and cut off his arms. Then they cut off his head, and it rolled across the floor.

They attacked all the celebrants, stabbing them, spearing them, striking them with their swords. They attacked some of them from behind, and these fell instantly to the ground with their entrails hanging out. Others they beheaded: they cut off their heads, or split their heads to pieces.

They struck others in the shoulders, and their arms were torn from their bodies. They wounded some in the thigh and some in the calf. They slashed others in the abdomen, and their entrails all spilled to the ground. Some attempted to run away, but their intestines dragged as they ran; they seemed to tangle their feet in their own entrails. No matter how they tried to save themselves, they could find no escape.

Some attempted to force their way out, but the Spaniards murdered them at the gates. Others climbed the walls, but they could not save themselves. Those who ran into the communal houses were safe there for a while; so were those who lay down among the victims and pretended to be dead. But if they stood up again, the Spaniards saw them and killed them.

The blood of the warriors flowed like water and gathered into pools. The pools widened, and the stench of blood and entrails filled the air. The Spaniards ran into the communal houses to kill those who were hiding. They ran everywhere and searched everywhere; they invaded every room, hunting and killing.

The Siege of Tenochtitlan

Now the Spaniards began to wage war against us. They attacked us by land for ten days, and then their ships appeared. Twenty days later, they gathered all their ships together near Nonohualco, off the place called Mazatzinta-malco. The allies from Tlaxcala and Huexotzinco set up camp on either side of the road.

Our warriors from Tlatelolco immediately leaped into their canoes and set out for Mazatzintamalco and the Nonohualco road. But no one set out from Tenochtitlan to assist us: only the Tlatelolcas were ready when the Spaniards arrived in their ships. On the following day, the ships sailed to Xoloco.

The fighting at Xoloco and Huitzillan lasted for two days. While the battle was under way, the warriors from Tenochtitlan began to mutiny. They said: "Where are our chiefs? They have fired scarcely a single arrow! Do they think they have fought like men?" Then they seized four of their own leaders and put them to death. The victims were two captains, Cuauhnochtli and Cuapan, and the priests of Amantlan and Tlalocan. This was the second time that the people of Tenochtitlan killed their own leaders. . . .

❧ *The Fighting Is Renewed*

The Spaniards made ready to attack us, and the war broke out again. They assembled their forces in Cuepopan and Cozcacuahco. A vast number of our warriors were killed by their metal darts. Their ships sailed to Texopan, and the battle there lasted three days. When they had forced us to retreat, they entered the Sacred Patio, where there was a four-day battle. Then they reached Yacacolco.

The Tlatelolcas set up three racks of heads in three different places. The first rack was in the Sacred Patio of Tlilancalco [Black House], where we strung up the heads of our lords the Spaniards. The second was in Acacolco, where we strung up Spanish heads and the heads of two of their horses. The third was in Zacatla, in front of the temple of the earth-goddess Cihuacoatl, where we strung up the heads of Tlaxcaltecas.

The women of Tlatelolco joined in the fighting. They struck at the enemy and shot arrows at them; they tucked up their skirts and dressed in the regalia of war.

The Spaniards forced us to retreat. Then they occupied the market place. The Tlatelolcas—the Jaguar Knights, the Eagle Knights, the great warriors—were defeated, and this was the end of the battle. It had lasted five days, and two thousand Tlatelolcas were killed in action. During the battle, the Spaniards set up a canopy for the Captain in the market place. They also mounted a catapult on the temple platform.

❧ *Epic Description of the Besieged City*

And all these misfortunes befell us. We saw them and wondered at them; we suffered this unhappy fate.

Broken spears lie in the roads;
we have torn our hair in our grief.
The houses are roofless now, and their walls
are red with blood.

Worms are swarming in the streets and plazas,
and the walls are splattered with gore.
The water has turned red, as if it were dyed,
and when we drink it,
it has the taste of brine.

We have pounded our hands in despair
against the adobe walls,
for our inheritance, our city, is lost and dead.
The shields of our warriors were its defense,
but they could not save it.

We have chewed dry twigs and salt grasses;
we have filled our mouths with dust and bits of adobe;
we have eaten lizards, rats and worms. . . .

When we had meat, we ate it almost raw. It was scarcely on the fire before we snatched it and gobbled it down.

They set a price on all of us: on the young men, the priests, the boys and girls. The price of a poor man was only two handfuls of corn, or ten cakes made from mosses or twenty cakes of salty couch-grass. Gold, jade, rich cloths, quetzal feathers—everything that once was precious was now considered worthless.

The captains delivered several prisoners of war to Cuauhtemoc to be sacrificed. He performed the sacrifices in person, cutting them open with a stone knife. . . .

Race War: The New England Experience

As the Aztecs' memory of their defeat indicates, the European conquest of America involved a good deal of brutality and terrorism. And brutality was not confined to Central or South America, either. Wherever Indians were able to mount a significant resistance, the European retaliation was likely to be swift and very harsh. The following selections attempt to justify the beheading and quartering— the cutting into four pieces—of an Indian leader, King Philip. He was the leader of Indian resistance in New England that culminated in what the English settlers called King Philip's War (1675–1676). The second selection was written by the most highly educated man in New England, Increase Mather, and thus represents the most "enlightened" view of the Indian in New England. Do you believe the two descriptions of the Indians' behavior? How does Mather explain the causes of the Indians' attacks on whites? How does he explain the white victory?

To learn more about the Aztecs and their world, explore http://www.indians.org/welker/ aztec.htm.

❧ *King Philip's War: A Contemporary Account*

A True but Brief Account of our Losses sustained since this Cruel and Mischievous War began, take as follows:

In *Narraganset* not one House left standing.
At *Warwick*, but one.
At *Providence*, not above three.
At *Potuxit*, none left.
Very few at *Seaconicke*.
At *Swansey*, two, at most.
Marlborough, wholy laid in Ashes, except two or three Houses.
Grantham and *Nashaway*, all ruined but one House or two.
Many Houses burnt at *Springfield, Scituate, Lancaster, Brookfield*, and
    Northampton.
The greatest Part of *Rehoboth* and *Taunton* destroyed.
Great Spoil made at *Hadley, Hatfield*, and *Chelmsford*.
Deerfield wholy, and *Westfield* much ruined
At *Sudbury*, many Houses burnt, and some at *Hingham, Weymouth*, and
    Braintree.

Besides particular Farms and Plantations, a great Number not be reckoned up, wholly laid waste, or very much damnified.

And as to Persons, it is generally thought, that of the English there hath been lost, in all, Men Women and Children, above Eight Hundred, since the War began. Of whom many have been destroyed with exquisite Torments, and most inhumane Barbarities; the Heathen rarely giving Quarter to those that they take, but if they were Women, they first forced them to satisfie their filthy Lusts and then murdered them; either cutting off the Head, ripping open the Belly, or skulping the Head of Skin and Hair, and hanging them up as Trophies; wearing Men's Fingers as Bracelets about their Necks, and Stripes of their Skins which they dress for Belts. They knockt one Youth of the Head, and laying him for dead, they flead (or skulp'd) his Head of Skin and Hair. After which the Boy wonderfully revived, and is now recovered, only he hath Nothing but the dry Skull, neither Skin nor Hair on his Head. Nor have our Cattle escaped the Cruelty of these worse than Brute and Savage Beasts: For what Cattle they took they seldom killed outright: or if they did, would eat but little of the Flesh, but rather cut their Bellies, and letting them go several Days, trailing their Guts after them, putting out their Eyes, or cutting off one Leg, &c.

From "A New and Farther Narrative of the State of New-England, July 22, 1676" by N. S., from *The Old Indian Chronicle*, Samuel G. Drake, ed., S. A. Drake, Boston, 1867, pp. 244–246.

❧ *Defeat of King Philip: Increase Mather's Account*

August 6. An *Indian* that deserted his Fellows, informed the inhabitants of *Taunton* that a party of *Indians* who might be easily surprised, were not very far off, and promised to conduct any that had a mind to apprehend those *Indians* in the right way towards them, whereupon about twenty Souldiers marched out of *Taunton*, and they took all those *Indians*, being in number thirty and six, only the *Squaw-Sachem of Pocasset*, who was next unto *Philip* in respect to the mischief that hath been done, and the blood that hath been shed in this Warr, escaped alone; but not long after some of *Taunton* finding an *Indian Squaw* in *Metapoiset* newly dead, cut off her head, and it happened to be *Weetamoo*, i.e. *Squaw-Sachem* her *head*. When it was set upon a pole in *Taunton*, the *Indians* who were prisoners there knew it presently, and made a most horrid and diabolical Lamentation, crying out that it was their Queens head. Now here it is to be observed, that God himself by his own hand brought his enemy to destruction. For in that place, where the last year, she furnished *Philip* with Canooes for his men, she her self could not meet with a Canoo, but venturing over the River upon a Raft, that brake under her, so that she was drowned, just before the *English* found her. Surely *Philips* turn will be next.

August 10. Whereas *Potock* a chief Counsellor to the old Squaw-Sachem of *Narraganset*, was by some of Road-Island brought into Boston, and found guilty of promoting the War against the *English*, he was this day shot to death in the Common at *Boston*. As he was going to his execution, some told him that now he must dy, he had as good speak the truth, and say how many *Indians* were killed at the Fort-Fight last winter. He replyed, that the *English* did that day kill above seven hundred fighting men, and that three hundred who were wounded, dyed quickly after, and that as to old men, women and Children, they had lost no body could tell how many; and that there were above three thousand *Indians* in the Fort, when our Forces assaulted them, and made that notable slaughter amongst them.

August 12. This is the memorable day wherein *Philip*, the perfidious and bloudy Author of the War and wofull miseryes that have thence ensued, was taken and slain. And God brought it to pass, chiefly by *Indians* themselves. For one of *Philips* men (being disgusted at him, for killing an *Indian* who had propounded an expedient for peace with the *English*) ran away from him, and coming to Road-Island, informed that *Philip* was now returned again to *Mount-Hope*, and undertook to bring them to the swamp where he hid himself. Divine Providence so disposed, as that Capt. *Church of Plymouth* was then in Road-Island, in order to recruiting his Souldiers, who had been

From Increase Mather, *A History of King Philip's War*, J. Munsell, Albany, 1862, pp. 191–195. *For more information about the cultural, gender, and historical implications of King Philip's War, see the Georgetown University site at* http://www.georgetown.edu/users/arsenauj/kpwtitle.html.

wearied with a tedious march that week. But immediately upon this Intelligence, he set forth again, with a small company of *English* and *Indians*. It seemeth that night *Philip* (like the man, in the Host of *Midian*) dreamed that he was fallen into the hands of the *English*, and just as he was saying to those that were with him, that they must fly for their lives that day, lest the *Indian* that was gone from him should recover where he was. Our Souldiers came upon him and surrounded the *Swamp* (where he with seven of his men absconded). Thereupon he betook himself to flight; but as he was coming out of the Swamp, an *English-man* and an *Indian* endeavoured to fire at him, the *English-man* missed of his aime, but the *Indian* shot him through the heart, so as that he fell down dead. The *Indian* who thus killed *Philip* did formerly belong to Squaw-Sachim of *Pocasset*, being known by the name of *Alderman*. In the beginning of the war, he came to the Governour of *Plymouth*, manifesting his desire to be at peace with the *English*, and immediately withdrew to an Island not having engaged against the *English* nor for them, before this time. Thus when *Philip* had made an end to deal treacherously, his own Subjects dealt treacherously with him. This Wo was brought upon him that spoyled when he was not spoyled. And in that very place where he first contrived and began his mischief, was he taken and destroyed, and there was he (like as Agag was hewed in pieces before the Lord) cut into four quarters, and is now hanged up as a monument of revenging Justice, his head being cut off and carried away to *Plymouth*, his Hands were brought to *Boston. So let all thine Enemies perish, O Lord!*

THE BIG PICTURE

Many reasons have been given to explain the ease with which Europeans conquered the New World. Which factors do you think were most important? What was the role of tribes like the Catawbas? Were they just hopeless victims? Or did they have an important role in shaping the "world" about them?

Chapter 2

Jamestown

Interpretive Essay by Edmund S. Morgan 35
Sources 47
    Jamestown: The Physical Setting 47
    Life and Death in Virginia: Richard Frethorne's Account, 1623 47
The Big Picture 52

We all know the story of Jamestown—or think we do. There was Captain John Smith, who put lazy gentlemen to work. There was Pocahontas, who made peace possible between whites and Indians. And there was John Rolfe, who figured out how to grow the "noxious weed," tobacco, successfully, and so ensured the struggling colony's eventual triumph.

But this familiar story had no meaning whatever to the original settlers of the colony of Virginia. For them, Virginia was not a setting for personal dramas. Life there was ugly, brutal, and very likely to be short. In fact, death was the most prominent feature of life. It came often and quickly—through illness, accident, and Indian resistance—but mainly through starvation.

The toll was awesome. The Virginia Company of London sent 144 colonists to Virginia late in 1606. Of these, thirty-nine died at sea. Forty-six more died within a few months of landing. Only thirty-eight were still alive when the next ship arrived in 1608. New settlers from England brought the population up to about five hundred. All but sixty of these died during the "starving time" of the winter of 1609–1610.

The figures for the longer run are almost as appalling. Between 1607 and 1624, four out of every five colonists who came over to Jamestown died.

Those who had been sent out to lose their lives in this deathtrap were the advance guard of a commercial concern, the Virginia Company. It had been chartered in 1606 by the English crown for the purpose of colonizing an area that was about half the size of the present United States. The investors in the company expected it to pay quick profits, perhaps from the discovery of gold or silver, or of an easy water passage through the continent (whose size no one yet knew) to the fabled markets of Asia.

The enterprise was, in short, a capital venture by a group of stockholders to whom the New World was an opportunity for investment. The investment failed. The stockholders eventually sank about 100,000 pounds (worth about 16 million of today's dollars) in their speculation. In return, they got nothing. The company paid no dividends, and its stock became worthless paper within a dozen years.

Why did the settlers and the investors alike fare so poorly? In the early years, the company did send over large numbers of "gentlemen," who wouldn't work. The original settlers also spent a lot of their time quarreling with each other and searching for gold. But surely such explanations do not account for the fact that Englishmen with the advantages of Iron Age technology had such difficulties, or why they starved to death in an area where Indians had lived successfully for years.

The Labor Problem at Jamestown, 1607–1618

Edmund S. Morgan

The following selection is by the most distinguished historian of the colonial period at work in the United States today. In it, he confronts the vexing problem of Jamestown. More precisely, he addresses a simple but puzzling question: why seventeenth-century English settlers had so much difficulty coping with the wilderness, why they starved to death rather than put in a hard day's work getting food. Morgan traces the problem back to English attitudes toward work and comes to the unhappy conclusion that the only way Virginians could solve their labor problem was to introduce black slavery. As you read, you should pay particular attention to the logic of the essay, which governs the introduction of its factual detail. Does that logic seem plausible? Or could other kinds of connections explain the facts that Morgan introduces?

The story of Jamestown, the first permanent English settlement in America, has a familiar place in the history of the United States. We all know of the tribulations that kept the colony on the point of expiring: the shortage of supplies, the hostility of the Indians, the quarrels among the leaders, the reckless search for gold, the pathetic search for a passage to the Pacific, and the neglect of the crucial business of growing food to stay alive. Through the scene moves the figure of Captain John Smith, a little larger than life, trading for corn among the Indians and driving the feckless crew to work. His departure in October 1609 results in near disaster. The settlers fritter away their time and energy, squander their provisions, and starve. Sir Thomas Gates, arriving after the settlement's third winter, finds only sixty men out of six hundred still alive and those sixty scarcely able to walk.

In the summer of 1610 Gates and Lord La Warr get things moving again with a new supply of men and provisions, a new absolute form of government, and a new set of laws designed to keep everybody at work. But when Gates and La Warr leave for a time, the settlers fall to their old ways. Sir Thomas Dale, upon his arrival in May 1611, finds them at "their daily and usuall workes, bowling in the streetes." But Dale brings order out of chaos. By enlarging and enforcing the colony's new law code (the famous *Lawes Divine, Morall and Martiall*) he starts the settlers working again and rescues them from starvation by making them plant corn. By 1618 the colony is getting on its feet and ready to carry on without the stern regimen of a Smith or a Dale. There are still evil days ahead, as the Virginia

From Edmund S. Morgan, "The Labor Problem at Jamestown, 1607–18," *American Historical Review*, vol. 76, 1971, pp. 595–610. Copyright by Edmund S. Morgan.

Company sends over men more rapidly than the infant colony can absorb them. But the settlers, having found in tobacco a valuable crop for export, have at least gone to work with a will, and Virginia's future is assured.

The story probably fits the facts insofar as they can be known. But it does not quite explain them. The colony's long period of starvation and failure may well be attributed to the idleness of the first settlers, but idleness is more an accusation than an explanation. Why did men spend their time bowling in the streets when their lives depended on work? Were they lunatics, preferring to play games rather than clear and plow and plant the crops that could have kept them alive?

The mystery only deepens if we look more closely at the efforts of Smith, Gates, La Warr, and Dale to set things right. In 1612 John Smith described his work program of 1608: "the company [being] divided into tennes, fifteenes, or as the businesse required, 4 hours each day was spent in worke, the rest in pastimes and merry exercise." Twelve years later Smith rewrote this passage and changed the figure of four hours to six hours. But even so, what are we to make of a six-hour day in a colony teetering on the verge of extinction?

The program of Gates and La Warr in the summer of 1610 was no more strenuous. William Strachey described it:

> it is to be understood that such as labor are not yet so taxed but that easily they perform the same and ever by ten of the clock have done their morning's work: at what time they have their allowances [of food] set out ready for them, and until it be three of the clock again they take their own pleasure, and afterward, with the sunset, their day's labor is finished.

The Virginia Company offered much the same account of this period. According to a tract issued late in 1610, "the setled times of working (to effect all themselves, or the Adventurers neede desire) [requires] no more pains than from six of clocke in the morning untill ten, and from two of the clocke in the afternoone till foure." The long lunch period described for 1610 was also a feature of the *Lawes Divine, Morall and Martiall* as enforced by Dale. The total working hours prescribed in the Lawes amounted to roughly five to eight hours a day in summer and three to six hours in winter.

It is difficult, then, to escape the conclusion that there was a great deal of unemployment or underemployment at Jamestown, whether it was the idleness of the undisciplined in the absence of strong government or the idleness of the disciplined in the presence of strong government. How are we to account for this fact? By our standards the situation at Jamestown demanded hard and continuous work. Why was the response so feeble?

One answer, given by the leaders of the colony, is that the settlers included too many ne'er-do-wells and too many gentlemen who "never did know what a dayes work was." Hard work had to wait until harder men were sent. Another answer may be that the Jamestown settlers were debilitated by hunger and disease. The victims of scurvy, malaria, typhoid, and diphtheria may have been left without the will or the energy to work. Still another answer, which was echoed through the pages of our history books, attributed the difficulty to the fact that the settlement was conducted on a communal basis: everybody worked for the Virginia Company and everybody was fed (while supplies lasted) by the company, regardless of how much he worked or failed to work. Once land was distributed to individuals and men were allowed to work for themselves, they gained the familiar incentives of private enterprise and bent their shoulders to the wheel. These explanations are surely all valid—they are all supported by the testimony of contemporaries—and they go far toward explaining the lazy pioneers of Jamestown. But they do not reach a dimension of the problem that contemporaries would have overlooked because they would have taken it for granted. They do not tell us what ideas and attitudes about work, carried from England, would have led the first English settlers to expect so little of themselves in a situation that demanded so much. The Jamestown settlers did not leave us the kind of private papers that would enable us to examine directly their ideas and attitudes, as we can those of the Puritans who settled New England a few years later. But in the absence of direct evidence we may discover among the ideas current in late sixteenth- and early seventeenth-century England some clues to the probable state of mind of the first Virginians, clues to the way they felt about work, whether in the old world or the new, clues to habits of thinking that may have conditioned their perceptions of what confronted them at Jamestown, clues even to the tangled web of motives that made later Virginians masters of slaves.

Englishmen's ideas about the new world at the opening of the seventeenth century were based on a century of European exploration and settlement. The Spanish, whose exploits surpassed all others, had not attempted to keep their success a secret, and by the middle of the sixteenth century Englishmen interested in America had begun translating Spanish histories and memoirs in an effort to rouse their countrymen to emulation. The land that emerged from these writings was, except in the Arctic regions, an Eden, teeming with gentle and generous people who, before the Spanish conquest, had lived without labor, or with very little, from the fruits of a bountiful nature. There were admittedly some unfriendly exceptions who made a habit of eating their more attractive neighbors; but they were a minority, confined to a few localities, and in spite of their ferocity were scarcely a match for Europeans armed with guns. Englishmen who visited the new world confirmed the reports of natural abundance. Arthur Barlowe, for example, reconnoitering the North Carolina coast for Walter Raleigh, observed that "the earth bringeth foorth all things in aboundance, as in the first creation, without toile or labour," while the people were "most gentle, loving and faithfull, void of all guile, and treason, and such as lived after the manner of the golden age."

English and European readers may have discounted the more extravagant reports of American abundance, for the same authors who praised the land often gave contradictory accounts of the hardships they had suffered in it. But anyone who doubted that riches were waiting to be plucked from Virginia's trees had reason to expect that a good deal might be plucked from the people of the land. Spanish experience had shown that Europeans could thrive in the new world without undue effort by exploiting the natives. With a mere handful of men the Spanish had conquered an enormous population of Indians in the Caribbean, Mexico, and Peru and had put them to work. In the chronicles of Peter Martyr Englishmen learned how it was done. Apart from the fact that the Indians were naturally gentle, their division into a multitude of kingdoms, frequently at odds with one another, made it easy to play off one against another. By aiding one group against its enemies the Spaniards had made themselves masters of both.

The story of English plans to imitate and improve on the Spanish strategy is a long one. It begins at least as early as Francis Drake's foray in Panama in 1572–73, when he allied with a band of runaway slaves to rob a Spanish mule train carrying treasure from Peru across the isthmus to Nombre de Dios on the Caribbean. The idea of joining with dissident natives or slaves either against their Spanish masters or against their wicked cannibalistic neighbors became an important ingredient in English plans for colonizing the new world. Martin Frobisher's experiences with the Eskimos in Baffin Land and Ralph Lane's with the Indians at Roanoke should perhaps have disabused the English of their expectations; but they found it difficult to believe that any group of natives, and especially the noble savages of North America, would fail to welcome what they called with honest pride (and some myopia) the "gentle government" of the English. If the savages first encountered by a colonizing expedition proved unfriendly, the thing to do was to make contact with their milder neighbors and rescue them from the tyranny of the unfriendly tribe, who must be their enemies and were probably cannibals to boot.

The settlers at Jamestown tried to follow the strategy, locating their settlement, as the plan called for, near the mouth of a navigable river so that they would have access to the interior tribes if the coastal ones were hostile. But as luck would have it, they picked an area with a more powerful, more extensive, and more effective Indian government than existed anywhere else on the Atlantic Coast. King Powhatan had his enemies, the Monacans of the interior, but he felt no great need of English assistance against them, and he rightly suspected that the English constituted a larger threat to his hegemony than the Monacans did. He submitted with ill grace and no evident comprehension to the coronation ceremony that the Virginia Company arranged for him, and he kept his distance from Jamestown. Those of his warriors who visited the settlement showed no disposition to work for the English. The Monacans, on the other hand, lived too far inland (beyond the falls) to serve as substitute allies, and the English were thus deprived of their anticipated native labor.

They did not, however, give up their expectations of getting it eventually. In 1615 Ralph Hamor still thought the Indians would come around "as they are easily taught and may be lenitie and faire usage . . . be brought, being naturally though ingenious, yet idlely given, to be no lesse industrious, nay to exceed our English." Even after the massacre of 1622 Virginians continued to dream of an Indian labor supply, though there was no longer to be any gentleness in obtaining it. Captain John Martin thought it better to exploit than exterminate the Indians, if only because they could be made to work in the heat of the day, when Englishmen would not. And William Claiborne in 1626 invented a device (whether mechanical or political is not clear) that he claimed would make it possible to keep Indians safely in the settlements and put them to work. The governor and council gave him what looks like the first American patent or copyright, namely a three-year monopoly, to "have holde and enjoy all the benefitt use and profitt of this his project or inventione," and they also assigned him a recently captured Indian, "for his better experience and tryall of his inventione."

English expectations of the new world and its inhabitants died hard. America was supposed to be a land of abundance, peopled by natives who would not only share that abundance with the English but increase it under English direction. Englishmen simply did not envisage a need to work for the mere purpose of staying alive. The problem of survival as they saw it was at best political and at worst military.

Although Englishmen long remained under the illusion that the Indians would eventually become useful English subjects, it became apparent fairly early that Indian labor was not going to sustain the founders of Jamestown. The company in England was convinced by 1609 that the settlers would have to grow at least part of their own food. Yet the settlers themselves had to be driven to that life-saving task. To understand their ineffectiveness in coping with a situation that their pioneering descendants would take in stride, it may be helpful next to inquire into some of the attitudes toward work that these first English pioneers took for granted. How much work and what kind of work did Englishmen at the opening of the seventeenth century consider normal?

The laboring population of England, by law at least, was required to work much harder than the regimen at Jamestown might lead us to expect. The famous Statute of Artificers of 1563 (re-enacting similar provisions from the Statute of Laborers of 1495) required all laborers to work from five in the morning to seven or eight at night from mid-March to mid-September, and during the remaining months of the year from day break to night. Time out for eating, drinking, and rest was not to exceed two and a half hours a day. But these were injunctions not descriptions. The Statute of Laborers of 1495 is preceded by the complaint that laborers "waste much part of the day . . . in late coming unto their work, early departing therefrom, long sitting at their breakfast, at their dinner and noon-meat, and long time of sleeping after noon." Whether this statute or that of 1563 (still in effect when Jamestown was founded) corrected the situation is doubtful. The records of local courts show varying efforts to enforce other provisions of the statute of 1563, but they are almost wholly silent about this provision, in spite of the often-expressed despair of masters over their lazy and negligent laborers.

It may be said that complaints of the laziness and irresponsibility of workmen can be met with in any century. Were such complaints in fact justified in sixteenth- and early seventeenth-century England? There is some reason to believe that they were, that life during those years was characterized by a large amount of idleness and underemployment. The outstanding economic fact of the sixteenth and early seventeenth century in England was a rapid and more or less steady rise in prices, followed at some distance by a much smaller rise in wages, both in industry and in agriculture. The price of provisions used by a laborer's family rose faster than wages during the whole period from 1500 to 1640. The government made an effort to narrow the gap by requiring the justices in each county to readjust maximum wages at regular intervals. But the wages established by the justices reflected their own nostalgic notions of what a day's work ought to be worth in money, rather than a realistic estimate of what a man could buy with his wages. In those counties, at least, where records survive, the level of wages set by the justices crept upward very slowly before 1630.

Wages became so inadequate that productivity was probably impaired by malnutrition. From a quarter to a half of the population lived below the level recognized at the time to constitute poverty. Few of the poor could count on regular meals at home, and in years when the wheat crop failed, they were close to starvation. It is not surprising that men living under these conditions showed no great energy for work and that much of the population was, by modern standards, idle much of the time. The health manuals of the day recognized that people normally slept after eating, and the laws even prescribed a siesta for laborers in the summer time. If they slept longer and more often than the laws allowed or the physicians recommended, if they loafed on the job and took unauthorized holidays, if they worked slowly and ineffectively when they did work, it may have been due at least in part to undernourishment and to the variety of chronic diseases that undernourishment brings in its train.

Thus low wages may have begot low productivity that in turn justified low wages. The reaction of employers was to blame the trouble on deficiencies, not of diet or wages, but of character. A prosperous yeoman like Robert Loder, who kept close track of his expenses and profits, was always bemoaning the indolence of his servants. Men who had large amounts of land that they could either rent or work with hired labor generally preferred to rent because labor was so inefficient and irresponsible.

Even the division of labor, which economists have customarily regarded as a means of increased productivity, could be a source of idleness. Plowing, for example, seems to have been a special skill—a plowman was paid at a higher rate than ordinary farm workers. But the ordinary laborer's work might have to be synchronized with the plowman's, and a whole crew of men might be kept idle by a plowman's failure to get his job done at the appropriate time. It is difficult to say whether this type of idleness, resulting from failure to synchronize the performance of related tasks, was rising or declining; but cheap, inefficient, irresponsible labor would be unlikely to generate pressures for the careful planning of time.

The government, while seeking to discourage idleness through laws requiring long hours of work, also passed laws that inadvertently discouraged industry. A policy that might be characterized as the conservation of employment frustrated those who wanted to do more work than others. English economic policy seems to have rested on the assumption that the total amount of work for which society could pay was strictly limited and must be rationed so that everyone could have a little, and those with family responsibilities could have a little more. It was against the law for a man to practice more than one trade or one craft. And although large numbers of farmers took up some handicraft on the side, this was to be discouraged, because "for one man to be both an husbandman and an Artificer is a gatheringe of divers mens livinges into one mans hand." So as not to take work away from his elders, a man could not independently practice most trades until he had become a master through seven years of apprenticeship. Even then, until he was thirty years old or married, he was supposed to serve some other master of the trade. A typical example is the case of John Pikeman of Barking, Essex, a tailor who was presented by the grand jury because he "being a singleman and not above 25 years of age, does take in work of tailoring and works by himself to the hindrance of other poor occupiers, contrary to the law."

These measures doubtless helped to maintain social stability in the face of a rapid population increase, from under three million in 1500 to a probable four and a half million in 1640 (an increase reflected in the gap between wages and prices). But in its efforts to spread employment so that every able-bodied person would have a means of support, the government in effect discouraged energetic labor and nurtured the workingman's low expectations of himself. By requiring masters to engage apprentices for seven-year terms and servants (in agriculture and in most trades) for the whole year rather than the day, it prevented employers from hiring labor only when there was work to be done and prevented the diligent and effective worker from replacing the ineffective. The intention to spread work is apparent in the observation of the Essex justices that labor by the day caused "the great depauperization of other labourers." But labor by the year meant that work could be strung out to occupy an unnecessary amount of time, because whether or not a master had enough work to occupy his servants they had to stay and he had to keep them. The records show many instances of masters attempting to turn away a servant or apprentice before the stipulated term was up, only to have him sent back by the courts with orders that the master "entertain" him for the full period. We even have the extraordinary spectacle of the runaway master, the man who illegally fled from his servants and thus evaded his responsibility to employ and support them.

In pursuit of its policy of full employment in the face of an expanding population, the government often had to create jobs in cases where society offered none. Sometimes men were obliged to take on a poor boy as a servant whether they needed him or not. The parish might lighten the burden by paying a fee, but it might also fine a man who refused to take a boy assigned to him. To provide for men and women who could not be foisted off on unwilling employers, the government established houses of correction in every county, where the inmates toiled at turning wool, flax, and hemp into thread or yarn, receiving nothing but their food and lodging for their efforts.

By all these means the government probably did succeed in spreading employment. But in the long run its policy, insofar as it was effective, tended to depress wages and to diminish the amount of work expected from any one man.

Above and beyond the idleness and underemployment that we may blame on the lethargy and irresponsibility of underpaid labor, on the failure to synchronize the performance of related tasks, and on the policy of spreading work as thinly as possible, the very nature of the jobs to be done prevented the systematic use of time that characterizes modern industrialized economies. Men could seldom work steadily, because they could work only at the tasks that could be done at the moment; and in sixteenth- and seventeenth-century England the tasks to be done often depended on forces beyond human control: on the weather and the seasons, on the winds, on the tides, on the maturing of crops. In the countryside work from dawn to dusk with scarcely an intermission might be normal at harvest time, but there were bound to be times when there was very little to do. When it rained or snowed, most farming operations had to be stopped altogether (and so did some of the stages of cloth manufacture). As late as 1705 John Law, imagining a typical economy established on a newly discovered island, assumed that the persons engaged in agriculture would necessarily be idle, for one reason or another, half the time.

To be sure, side by side with idleness and inefficiency, England exhibited the first signs of a rationalized economy. Professor J. U. Nef has described the many large-scale industrial enterprises that were inaugurated in England in the late sixteenth and early seventeenth centuries. And if the development of systematic agricultural production was advancing less rapidly than historians once supposed, the very existence of men like Robert Loder, the very complaints of the idleness and irresponsibility of laborers, the very laws prescribing hours of work all testify to the beginnings of a rationalized economy. But these were beginnings only and not widely felt. The laborer who seemed idle or irresponsible to a Robert Loder probably did not seem so to himself or to his peers. His England was not a machine for producing wool or corn. His England included activities and pleasures and relationships that systematic-minded employers would resent and that modern economists would classify as uneconomic. At the opening of the seventeenth century, England was giving him fewer economic benefits than she had given his grandfathers so that he was often ready to pull up stakes and look for a better life in another county or another country. But a life devoted to more and harder work than he had known at home might not have been his idea of a better life.

Perhaps we may now view Jamestown with somewhat less surprise at the idle and hungry people occupying the place: idleness and hunger were the rule in much of England of the time; they were facts of life to be taken for granted. And if we next ask what the settlers thought they had come to America to do, what they thought they were up to in Virginia, we can find several English enterprises comparable to their own that may have served as models and that would not have led them to think of hard, continuous disciplined work as a necessary ingredient in their undertaking.

If they thought of themselves as settling a wilderness, they could look for guidance to what was going on in the northern and western parts of England and in the high parts of the south and east. Here were the regions, mostly wooded, where wastelands still abounded, the goal of many in the large migrant population of England. Those who had settled down were scattered widely over the countryside in isolated hovels and hamlets and lived by pasture farming; that is, they cultivated only small plots of ground and ran a few sheep or cattle on the common land. Since the gardens required little attention and the cattle hardly any, they had most of their time to themselves. Some spent their spare hours on handicrafts. In fact, they supplied the labor for most of England's minor industries, which tended to locate in pasture-farming regions, where agriculture made fewer demands on the inhabitants, than in regions devoted to market crops. But the pasture farmers seem to have offered their labor sporadically and reluctantly. They had the reputation of being both idle and independent. They might travel to the richer arable farming regions to pick up a few shillings in field work at harvest time, but their own harvests were small. They did not even grow the wheat or rye for their own bread and made shift to live in hard times from the nuts and berries and herbs that they gathered in the woods.

Jamestown was mostly wooded, like the pasture-farming areas of England and Wales; and since Englishmen used the greater part of their own country for pasture farming, that was the obvious way to use the wasteland of the new world. If this was the Virginians' idea of what they were about, we should expect them to be idle much of the time and to get grain for bread by trading rather than planting (in this case not wheat or rye but maize from the Indians); we should even expect them to get a good deal of their food, as they did, by scouring the woods for nuts and berries.

As the colony developed, a pasture-farming population would have been quite in keeping with the company's expectation of profit from a variety of products. The Spaniards' phenomenal success with raising cattle in the West Indies was well known. And the proposed employment of the settlers of Virginia in a variety of industrial pursuits (iron works, silk works, glass works, shipbuilding) was entirely fitting for a pasture-farming community. The small gardens assigned for cultivation by Governor Dale in 1614 will also make sense: three acres would have been far too small a plot of land to occupy a farmer in the arable regions of England, where a single man could handle thirty acres without assistance. But it would be not at all inappropriate as the garden of a pasture farmer. In Virginia three acres would produce more than enough corn to sustain a man for a year and still leave him with time to make a profit for the company or himself at some other job—if he could be persuaded to work.

Apart from the movement of migrant workers into wastelands, the most obvious English analogy to the Jamestown settlement was that of a military expedition. The settlers may have had in mind not only the expeditions that subdued the Irish but also those dispatched to the European continent in England's wars. The Virginia Company itself seems at first to have envisaged the enterprise as partly military, and the *Lawes, Divine, Morall and*

Martiall were mostly martial. But the conception carried unfortunate implications for the company's expectations of profit. Military expeditions were staffed from top to bottom with men unlikely to work. The nucleus of sixteenth-century English armies was the nobility and the gangs of genteel ruffians they kept in their service, in wartime to accompany them into the field (or to go in their stead), in peacetime to follow them about as living insignia of their rank. Work was not for the nobility nor for those who wore their livery. According to the keenest student of the aristocracy in this period, "the rich and well-born were idle almost by definition." Moreover they kept "a huge labor force . . . absorbed in slothful and parasitic personal service." Aside from the gentlemen retainers of the nobility and their slothful servants the military expeditions that England sent abroad were filled out by misfits and thieves whom the local constables wished to be rid of. It was, in fact, government policy to keep the able-bodied and upright at home and to send the lame, the halt, the blind, and the criminal abroad.

The combination of gentlemen and ne'er-do-wells of which the leaders at Jamestown complained may well have been the result of the company's using a military model for guidance. The Virginia Company was loaded with noblemen (32 present or future earls, 4 countesses, 3 viscounts, and 19 barons). Is it possible that the large number of Jamestown settlers listed as gentlemen and captains came from among the retainers of these lordly stockholders and that the rest of the settlers included some of the gentlemen's personal servants as well as a group of hapless vagabonds or migratory farm laborers who had been either impressed or lured into the enterprise by tales of the new world's abundance? We are told, at least, that persons designated in the colony's roster as "laborers" were "for most part footmen, and such as they that were Adventurers brought to attend them, or such as they could perswade to goe with them, that never did know what a dayes work was."

If these men thought they were engaged in a military expedition, military precedent pointed to idleness, hunger, and death, not to the effective organization of labor. Soldiers on campaign were not expected to grow their own food. On the other hand they *were* expected to go hungry often and to die like flies even if they never saw an enemy. The casualty rates on European expeditions resembled those at Jamestown and probably from the same causes: disease and undernourishment.

But the highest conception of the enterprise, often expressed by the leaders, was that of a new commonwealth on the model of England itself. Yet this, too, while it touched the heart, was not likely to turn men toward hard, effective, and continuous work. The England that Englishmen were saddled with as a model for new commonwealths abroad was a highly complex society in which the governing consideration in accomplishing a particular piece of work was not how to do it efficiently but who had the right or the duty to do it, by custom, law, or privilege. We know that the labor shortage in the new world quickly diminished considerations of custom, privilege, and specialization in the organization of labor. But the English model the settlers carried with them made them think initially of a society like the one at home, in which each of them would perform his own special task and not encroach on the rights of other men to do other tasks. We may grasp some of the assumptions about labor that went into the most intelligent planning of a new commonwealth by considering Richard Hakluyt's recommendation that settlers include both carpenters and joiners, tallow chandlers and wax chandlers, bowyers and fletchers, men to rough-hew pike staffs and other men to finish them.

If Jamestown was not actually troubled by this great an excess of specialization, it was not the Virginia Company's fault. The company wanted to establish at once an economy more complex than England's, an economy that would include not only all the trades that catered to ordinary domestic needs of Englishmen but also industries that were unknown or uncommon in England: a list of artisans the company wanted for the colony in 1611 included such specialists as hemp planters and hemp dressers, gun makers and gunstock makers, spinners of pack thread and upholsterers of feathers. Whatever idleness arose from the specialization of labor in English society was multiplied in the new world by the presence of unneeded skills and the absence or shortage of essential skills. Jamestown had an oversupply of glass-makers and not enough carpenters or blacksmiths, an oversupply of gentle-men and not enough plowmen. These were Englishmen temporarily baffled by missing links in the economic structure of their primitive community. The later jack-of-all-trades American frontiersman was as yet unthought of. As late as 1618 Governor Argall complained that they lacked the men "to set their Ploughs to worke." Although they had the oxen to pull them, "they wanted men to bring them to labour, and Irons for the Ploughs, and har-nesse for the Cattell." And the next year John Rolfe noted that they still needed "Carpenters to build and make Carts and Ploughs, and skilfull men that know how to use them, and traine up our cattell to draw them; which though we indeavour to effect, yet our want of experience brings but little to perfection but planting Tobacco."

Tobacco, as we know, was what they kept on planting. The first shipload of it, sent to England in 1617, brought such high prices that the Virginians stopped bowling in the streets and planted tobacco in them. They did it without benefit of plows, and somehow at the same time they managed to grow corn, probably also without plows. Seventeenth-century Englishmen, it turned out, could adapt themselves to hard and varied work if there was sufficient incentive.

But we may well ask whether the habits and attitudes we have been examining had suddenly expired altogether. Did tobacco really solve the labor problem in Virginia? Did the economy that developed after 1618 represent a totally new set of social and economic attitudes? Did greater opportunities for profit completely erase the old attitudes and furnish the incentives to labor that were needed to make Virginia a success? The study of labor in modern underdeveloped countries should make us pause before we say yes. The mere opportunity to earn high wages has not always proved adequate to recruit labor in underdeveloped countries. Something more in the way of expanded needs or political authority or national consciousness or ethical imperatives has been required. Surely Virginia, in some sense, became a success. But how did it succeed? What kind of success did it have? Without attempting to answer, I should like very diffidently to offer a suggestion, a way of looking ahead at what happened in the years after the settlement of Jamestown.

The founders of Virginia, having discovered in tobacco a substitute for the sugar of the West Indies and the silver of Peru, still felt the lack of a native labor force with which to exploit the new crop. At first they turned to their own overpopulated country for labor, but English indentured servants brought with them the same haphazard habits of work as their masters. Also like their masters, they were apt to be unruly if pressed. And when their terms of servitude expired—if they themselves had not expired in the "seasoning" that carried away most immigrants to Virginia—they could be persuaded to continue working for their betters only at exorbitant rates. Instead they struck out for themselves and joined the ranks of those demanding rather than supplying labor. But there was a way out. The Spanish and Portuguese had already demonstrated what could be done in the new world when a local labor force became inadequate: they brought in the natives of Africa.

For more information about the Jamestown colony and the efforts to "rediscover" it today, see the website of the Association for the Preservation of Virginia Antiquities at http://www.apva.org/history.

Jamestown: The Physical Setting

The illustrations shown below and on the next page are representations of Jamestown as it looked in its early years. If these were the only sources of information you had about Jamestown, how would you describe the relationship between the town center and the outside world? Look back at the picture of the Indian village in Chapter 1 (p. 22). What similarities can you see between it and these representations of Jamestown? What details would signal to you that Jamestown was more technologically advanced?

Life and Death in Virginia: Richard Frethorne's Account, 1623

Today it is virtually impossible for us to fully understand those who lived and died in Virginia. Our world is much different, and most of us have never experienced the anxiety, suffering, and isolation that were so much a part of everyday life in early Virginia. Fortunately, a few personal documents have survived those miserable years, and they help us to understand the predicament of the first settlers. Most of these documents were written by leaders. But the one that follows

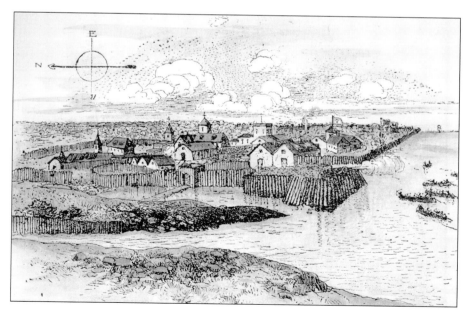

The Jamestown Settlement in 1622, wood engraving, 19th century. The Granger Collection, New York.

Re-creation/photo of daily life in Jamestown Settlement. Jamestown Settlement. Williamsburg, VA.
Photo Courtesy of Jamestown-Yorktown Foundation.

was written by an indentured servant, Richard Frethorne, in 1623, to his parents
in England. All we know of Frethorne is contained in this letter.

VOICES

Loving and kind father and mother:

My most humble duty remembered to you, hoping in God of your
good health, as I myself am at the making hereof. This is to let you understand that I your child am in a most heavy case by reason of the nature of the
country, [which] is such that it causeth much sickness, [such] as the scurvy
and the bloody flux and diverse other diseases, which maketh the body very
poor and weak. And when we are sick there is nothing to comfort us; for
since I came out of the ship I never ate anything but peas, and loblollie (that
is, water gruel). As for deer or venison I never saw any since I came into this
land. There is indeed some fowl, but we are not allowed to go and get it, but
must work hard both early and late for a mess of water gruel and a mouthful of bread and beef. A mouthful of bread for a penny loaf must serve for

Richard Frethorne, Letter to his father and mother, March 20, April 2 and 3, 1623, in Susan
M. Kingsbury, ed., *The Records of the Virginia Company of London*, IV, Government Printing
Office, Washington, D.C., 1935, pp. 58–62. Reprinted from Report of the Royal
Commission on Historical Manuscripts, *Report on the Mss. of His Grace the Duke of
Manchester*, London, 1881, VIII Report, Appendix II, pp. 40–41.

four men which is most pitiful. [You would be grieved] if you did know as much as I [do], when people cry out day and night—Oh! that they were in England without their limbs—and would not care to lose any limb to be in England again, yea, though they beg from door to door. For we live in fear of the enemy every hour, yet we have had a combat with them on the Sunday before Shrovetide, and we took two alive and made slaves of them. But it was by policy, for we are in great danger; for our plantation is very weak by reason of the death and sickness of our company. For we came but twenty for the merchants, and they are half dead just; and we look every hour when two more should go. Yet there came some four other men yet to live with us, of which there is but one alive; and our Lieutenant is dead, and [also] his father and his brother. And there was some five or six of the late year's twenty, of which there is but three left, so that we are fain to get other men to plant with us; and yet we are but 32 to fight against 3000 if they should come. And the nighest help that we have is ten miles of us, and when the rogues overcame this place [the] last [time] they slew 80 persons. How then shall we do, for we lie even in their teeth? They may easily take us, but [for the fact] that God is merciful and can save with few as well as with many, as he showed to Gilead. And like Gilead's soldiers, if they lapped water, we drink water which is but weak.

And I have nothing to comfort me, nor is there nothing to be gotten here but sickness and death, except [in the event] that one had money to lay out in some things for profit. But I have nothing at all—no, not a shirt to my back but two rags (2), nor no clothes but one poor suit, nor but one pair of shoes, but one pair of stockings, but one cap, [and] but two bands. My cloak is stolen by one of my own fellows, and to his dying hour [he] would not tell me what he did with it; but some of my fellows saw him have butter and beef out of a ship, which my cloak, I doubt [not], paid for. So that I have not a penny, nor a penny worth, to help me to either spice or sugar or strong waters, without the which one cannot live here. For as strong beer in England doth fatten and strengthen them, so water here doth wash and weaken these here [and] only keeps [their] life and soul together. But I am not half [of] a quarter so strong as I was in England, and all is for want of victuals; for I do protest unto you that I have eaten more in [one] day at home than I have allowed me here for a week. You have given more than my day's allowance to a beggar at the door; and if Mr. Jackson had not relieved me, I should be in a poor case. But he like a father and she like a loving mother doth still help me.

For when we go to Jamestown (that is 10 miles of us) there lie all the ships that come to land, and there they must deliver their goods. And when we went up to town [we would go], as it may be, on Monday at noon, and come there by night, [and] then load the next day by noon, and go home in the afternoon, and unload, and then away again in the night, and [we would] be up about midnight. Then if it rained or blowed never so hard, we must lie in the boat on the water and have nothing but a little bread. For when we go into the boat we [would] have a loaf allowed to two men, and it is all [we would get] if we stayed there two days, which is hard; and [we] must lie all that while in the boat. But that Goodman Jackson pitied me and made me a cabin to lie in always when I [would] come up, and he would give me some poor jacks [to take] home with me, which comforted me more than peas or water gruel. Oh, they be very godly folks, and love me very well, and will do anything for me. And he much marvelled that you would send me a servant to the Company; he saith I had been better knocked on the head. And indeed so I find it now, to my great grief and misery; and [I] saith that if you love me you will redeem me suddenly, for which I do entreat and beg. And if you cannot get the merchants to redeem me for some little money, then for God's sake get a gathering or entreat some good folks to lay out some little sum of money in meal and cheese and butter and beef. Any eating meat will yield great profit. Oil and vinegar is very good; but, father, there is great loss in leaking. But for God's sake send beef and cheese and butter, or the more of one sort and none of another. But if you send cheese, it must be very old cheese; and at the cheesemonger's you may buy very good cheese for twopence farthing or halfpenny, that will be liked very well. But if you send cheese, you must have a care how you pack it in barrels; and you must put cooper's chips between every cheese, or else the heat of the hold will rot them. And look whatsoever you send me—be it never so much—look, what[ever] I make of it, I will deal truly with you. I will send it over and beg the profit to redeem me; and if I die before it come, I have entreated Goodman Jackson to send you the worth of it, who hath promised he will. If you send, you must direct your letters to Goodman Jackson, at Jamestown, a gunsmith. (You must set down his freight, because there be more of his name there.) Good father, do not forget me, but have mercy and pity my miserable case. I know if you did but see me, you would weep to see me; for I have but one suit. (But [though] it is a strange one, it is very well guarded.) Wherefore, for God's sake, pity me. I pray you to remember my love to all my friends and kindred. I hope all my brothers and sisters are in good health, and as for my part I have set down my resolution that certainly will be; that is, that the answer of this letter will be life or death to me. Therefore, good father, send as soon as you can; and if you send me any thing let this be the mark.

ROT

Richard Frethorne,
Martin's Hundred

The names of them that be dead of the company [that] came over with us to serve under our Lieutenants:

John Flower	George Goulding
John Thomas	Jos. Johnson
Thos. Howes	our lieutenant, his father and brother
John Butcher	Thos. Giblin
John Sanderford	George Banum
Rich. Smith	a little Dutchman
John Olive	one woman
Thos. Peirsman	one maid
William Cerrell	one child

All these died out of my master's house, since I came; and we came in but at Christmas, and this is the 20th day of March. And the sailors say that there is two-thirds of the 150 dead already. And thus I end, praying to God to send me good success that I may be redeemed out of Egypt. *So vale in Christo.*

Loving father, I pray you to use this man very exceeding kindly, for he hath done much for me, both on my journey and since. I entreat you not to forget me, but by any means redeem me; for this day we hear that there is 26 of [the] Englishmen slain by the Indians. And they have taken a pinnace of Mr. Pountis, and have gotten pieces, armor, [and] swords, all things fit for war; so that they may now steal upon us and we cannot know them from [the] English till it is too late—[till the time] that they be upon us—and then there is no mercy. Therefore if you love or respect me as your child, release me from this bondage and save my life. Now you may save me, or let me be slain with infidels. Ask this man—he knoweth that all is true and just that I say here. If you do redeem me, the Company must send for me to my Mr. Harrod; for so is this Master's name. April, the second day.

Your loving son,
Richard Frethorne

Moreover, on the third day of April we heard that after these rogues had gotten the pinnace and had taken all furnitures [such] as pieces, swords, armor, coats of mail, powder, shot and all the things that they had to trade withal, they killed the Captain and cut off his head. And rowing with the tail of the boat foremost, they set up a pole and put the Captain's head upon it, and so rowed home. Then the Devil set them on again, so that they furnished about 200 canoes with above 1000 Indians, and came, and thought to have taken the ship; but she was too quick for them—which thing was very much talked of, for they always feared a ship. But now the rogues grow very bold and can use pieces, some of them, as well or better than an Englishman; for an Indian did shoot with Mr. Charles, my master's kinsman, at a mark of white paper, and he hit it at the first, but Mr. Charles could not hit it. But see the envy of these slaves, for when they could not take the ship, then our men saw them threaten Accomack, that is the next plantation. And now there is no way but starving; for the Governor told us and Sir George that except the *Seaflower* [should] come in or that we can fall foul of these rogues and get some corn from them, above half the land will surely be starved. For they had no crop last year by reason of these rogues, so that we have no corn but as ships do relieve us, nor we shall hardly have any crop this year; and we are as like to perish first as any plantation. For we have but two hogshead of meal left to serve us this two months, if the *Seaflower* do stay so long before she come in; and that meal is but three weeks bread for us, at a loaf for four [men] about the bigness of a penny loaf in England—that is but a halfpenny a day for a man. Is it not strange to me, think you? But what will it be when we shall go a month or two and never see a bit of bread, as my master doth say we must do? And he said he is not able to keep us all. Then we shall be turned up to the land and eat barks of trees or molds of the ground; therefore with weeping tears I beg of you to help me. Oh, that you did see my daily and hourly sighs, groans, and tears, and [the] thumps that I afford mine own breast, and [the way I] rue and curse the time of my birth, with holy Job. I thought no head had been able to hold so much water as hath and doth daily flow from mine eyes.

But this is certain: I never felt the want of father and mother till now; but now, dear friends, full well I know and rue it, although it were too late before I knew it.

I pray you talk with this honest man. He will tell you more than now in my haste I can set down.

Your loving son,
Richard Frethorne

Virginia, 3rd April, 1623

THE BIG PICTURE

What were the characteristics of English society on the eve of colonization? What role did they play in establishing Jamestown?

@ ON THE WEB

For a virtual tour of the Jamestown colony, see http://www.virtualjamestown.org/.

Chapter 3

Puritan Order

Interpretive Essay by Willard Sterne Randall and Nancy Nahra 55
Sources 66
    New England Primer, 1690 66
    Harvard, 1636–1642 66
    Three Early New England Portraits 71
    The Spiritual Journey of Anne Bradstreet 73
The Big Picture 76

The settling of Jamestown was proclaimed to be God's work, in which spreading the Gospel took precedence over everything else. But few Englishmen set off for Virginia to establish a holy community. The first to embark on such a venture were the Pilgrims, a small group of Puritan extremists who had separated from the Church of England on the grounds that the king's church was hopelessly corrupt. After a brief spell in Holland, they came to Plymouth in 1620 hoping to establish a Zion in the wilderness. Ten years later, a much larger and more affluent group of Puritans settled just north of the Pilgrims, in and around Boston. They too hoped to establish a holy commonwealth. In both the Pilgrim colony at Plymouth and the Puritan settlement in Massachusetts Bay order was a primary goal and value. The Puritans and Pilgrims both felt that they had escaped an England that was in decline. There, they believed, the poor, servants, children—the powerless in general—no longer felt bound to submit to authority. And those with power—the court and the nobility—had become hopelessly corrupt. New England was more than a new beginning, then. It was an attempt to recover something that had been lost in the Old World. And recovery meant discipline, the sacrifice of individual interests to the community's paramount interest in order. To the leaders, discipline also meant the rounding off of individual beliefs to fit an agreed-upon consensus. At both Plymouth and Massachusetts Bay, there was a heavy preoccupation with compacts and covenants—agreements signed by the adult males who were heads of house-holds, efforts to ward off dissent and disruption.

Despite their compacts and covenants, both groups had trouble with internal dissension. One of the ironies of Puritanism—with Protestantism generally—was its tendency to split into warring factions. Puritans never abandoned the ideal of establishing a single universal church. But the Bible—their sole source of authority—was subject to various interpretations. Truths that seemed self-evident to one Puritan did not seem so to others who were equally eager to find the true path to salvation. Ministers denounced one another for teaching false doctrine. Congregations split into bickering cliques. And community leaders constantly had to worry about firebrands such as Roger Williams and Anne Hutchinson who challenged established norms.

To overcome disunity, and to establish a godly community in an ungodly world, Puritans relied not only on deep religious faith but also on such basic social institutions as the family. Early Virginia was settled mainly by bachelors. New England Puritans would not even permit single persons to live as bachelors. Puritan New England was settled by families, and all single persons had to live within a family. Outside the family, so Puritans believed, ungodliness and anarchism were sure to gain the upper hand. In turn, all families had to live within a specified distance of the church, which was seen as the larger family to which all individual families were subordinate.

Anne Marbury Hutchinson: This Great and Sore Affliction

Willard Sterne Randall and Nancy Nahra

In the following selection, Willard Sterne Randall and Nancy Nahra examine one of the major religious controversies that developed in Puritan New England. Puritans thought they knew how one got to heaven. They accepted the doctrine taught by John Calvin that all humans deserved damnation, that all came short of the glory of God, but that God in His mercy had "chosen" some for salvation. But how did one tell whom God had chosen? Was it possible that the village drunk might be going to heaven, while the most pious woman in town might be bound for hell?

Anne Hutchinson thought she could tell, and she also thought most of New England's ministers were teaching false doctrine. She began to argue, publicly, that they were preaching too much about "works," or the behavioral obligations of Christians, and not enough about grace: God's free gift of salvation to the saved, a gift they could not earn through their own efforts. And she was effective; many women—and men—came to her home to hear what she had to say. Gradually, the leaders of the colony recognized a threat to their authority and the stability of their little society. They decided to try her. The colony's governor, John Winthrop, took the role of prosecutor. As you read, think about the way the various elements of Anne Hutchinson's society dealt with her. Think also about the way they dealt with questions of sex differentiation. Do you see any contradictions? Were they basically rigid or flexible?

The last European power to enter the race for New World territories and riches was England. While Portugal and Spain expanded their imperial possessions rapidly at the close of the fifteenth century, not until Elizabeth I came to the throne in 1558 did an English monarch think at all of competing with her mainland rivals—and then she was satisfied with commissioning marauders to poach the wealth of the New World from treasure ports and fleets. James I, who came to the throne in 1603, launched the first for-profit English settlement at Jamestown and also chartered the Plymouth Plantation (half the passengers on the *Mayflower* were merchants). By the time continued religious persecution in Europe sent a large English contingent toward Massachusetts Bay in 1629, prospective English colonists had their choice of colonial destinations—and the managers of colonies had to compete with each other for settlers.

From Wallace Sterne Randall and Nancy Nahra, *Forgotten Americans: Footnote Figures Who Changed American History*, Addison-Wesley, Reading, Mass., 1998, pp. 1–15. Reprinted by permission of DaCap, a member of Perseus Books, LLC.

For nearly a decade in the early years of New England's history, women enjoyed more rights and respect, less abuse, and the promise of a progressively better way of life than in Old England, their homeland. They emigrated willingly to Boston with their husbands, brothers, and fathers, as relieved as the men to escape the tightening noose of religious persecution, until by 1637 there were two women in Massachusetts Bay colony for every three men, the highest ratio in the American colonies. . . .

The Puritan fathers at first outdid themselves pampering, as they would have seen it, female colonists, probably not seeing where it could lead. In tracts such as William Wood's *New England's Prospect*, written to promote immigration to the edge of the wild American continent, women were told that members of their sex had already taken several upward steps in the New World. In England, wife beating was commonly used to keep women in their place; in New England, it was forbidden. Furthermore, men were forbidden to treat their wives as servants. Heavy fines punished infractions of either offense. In the early years after Boston's founding in 1630, New England authorities took pains to make women happy so that they would write glowing letters back to England to lure more of their sisters.

One of the more eager recipients of this good news from America was Anne Marbury Hutchinson, the cheerful, middle-aged wife of a prosperous silk manufacturer and, with all the hard work and risk it implied, already the mother of fourteen children. Married to a man who believed in equality of the sexes, Anne Hutchinson was also a devoted follower of a charismatic Puritan divine, a religious leader who also saw women and men as equals. As it became apparent that Puritans would have to flee intensifying persecution by the English government, Anne, her husband, and their seven younger children left behind the comfortable life of English gentry to become pioneers on the edge of the American wilderness.

Greater equality for women did not seem a distant prospect or a hypothetical philosophical concept when Anne Hutchinson was born in England in 1591. A woman was on the throne of England. Elizabeth I was not just a stand-in marking time between male rulers; she was the second queen in a row to rule England, and she spent much of her forty-five-year reign contending not only with less successful male European kings but with other powerful and ambitious women, including the cousin she would put to death, Mary Queen of Scots. It was, in fact, an age of queens in Europe, from Isabella of Spain to Margaret of Austria. The specter of enduring female power alarmed may Protestant rulers, including John Knox, Scottish founder of the Presbyterian Church and spiritual father of Puritanism, who denounced government by women in his treatise, *The First Trumpet Blast Against the Monstrous Regiment of Women* (1557). Elizabeth established herself as the unchallenged power of Europe by defeating the Spanish Armada three years before Anne Hutchinson's birth and remained, all through Anne's childhood, the figure of a brilliant woman towering over England.

Queen Elizabeth repeatedly jailed Anne's uncle, Sir Anthony Cope, for opposing her middle-of-the-road church policies. Cope once spent a month in the Tower of London on Elizabeth's instructions after he proposed a change known as Cope's Bill and Book; if passed, it would have allowed the Puritans to revise the official *Book of Common Prayer*, the defining religious document of the Church of England. When Elizabeth came to the throne, it was widely assumed that she would push ahead the radical Reformation agenda of the Puritans, who wanted to "purify" the Church of England of all remaining traces of the Church of Rome, including vestments, incense, and bishops. But her Act of Settlement suppressed zealous reformers: she preferred to downplay religious contention and made it clear from time to time by exemplary execution that on the subject of religion she would tolerate neither criticism nor open opposition, whether from Puritan reformers or Catholics.

The daughter of a Church of England preacher and a Puritan mother who was descended from a noble Lincolnshire family, Anne Marbury grew up in the small market town of Alford, 114 miles northeast of London, in a house full of books, daughters, and religious disputation. Her father, Francis Marbury, was master of Alford Grammar School and preacher at 250-year-old Saint Wilfrid's Church, hub of Alford's religious, social, and political life. Francis Marbury was frequently in trouble with the bishops for loudly denouncing the lazy, uneducated clergy of the Church of England. Twice he was tried by church courts and stripped of his living for his outspoken views. His pet targets were the "self-seeking soul-murdering" bishops and the low preaching standards of the country priests. In virtual house arrest throughout much of Anne's childhood, he had plenty of time to instruct his eager daughter, often his only appreciative audience, and treated her as a son.

A born bookworm with a retentive memory, Anne, a kinswoman of playwright John Dryden on her mother's side, spent more time reading than sewing. But she learned midwifery by helping at several of her mother's deliveries and also became a skilled nurse and herbalist. All these skills made her a respected figure among other women. Inspired no doubt by a queen who had not only mastered Latin but read Plato in the original Greek and could argue in French, Spanish, Portuguese, Italian, and Welsh, Anne grew up at a time when female literacy in England was higher than it had ever been or would be again until the late nineteenth century. One widely read London educator, Richard Mulcaster, argued "that young maidens can learn, nature doth give them, and that they have learned, our experience doth teach us. What can more assure the world of this truth," asked Mulcaster, headmaster of Saint Paul's School, "than our diamond [Queen Elizabeth] at home?"

At times, Francis Marbury was the sole voice advocating Puritan reforms to the Church of England. On trial, he argued bravely and uncompromisingly in the face of grillings by powerful bishops. Anne could not but mark the lesson. She also must have been aware that, after Elizabeth I died and the misogynist King James I ascended the throne, more Puritan women were beginning to lecture publicly across England—and that they, too, were persecuted. When Anne was thirteen, her father was knighted and made pastor of the vast parish of Saint Martin in the Vintry, London, in the shadow of Saint Paul's.

It was in London that Anne first imbibed the ideas of Familism, a radical sect that preached direct communication between each individual, male or female, and God. Its teachings rejected the Calvinist doctrines of predestination, which precluded individual free will, and original sin, which denounced Eve and blamed women for all sin. Young Anne began to listen closely to women's voices in the nonconformist sects sprouting in London—she was attracted at various times by Familism, Separatism, and Puritanism, to which her mother subscribed. London women took active roles in the Puritan movement. Some two hundred of them were hauled before the bishop of London in Star Chamber ecclesiastical courts. A majority of these women were tried. They suffered heavy fines and imprisonment for, among other offenses, keeping secret the locations of clandestine Puritan printing presses. London women not only supported the Puritan underground but held the equivalent of salons in their parlors to preach and lead religious discussions.

At James I's accession in 1603, he, too, was expected to unleash a Puritan reform movement, but at the Hampton Court conference of church leaders, he proclaimed that Puritanism "agrees as well with a monarchy as God and the Devil." He attacked not only Puritans but women, several times digressing from his prepared speech to disparage them. His bishops took his cue and imposed, among other strictures, a ban on infant baptism by midwives, even when no priest was available and the baby was dying. As James took every opportunity to reverse Elizabeth's policies toward women, he introduced a stiff new antiwitchcraft law and, in his best-selling book, *Demonology*, declared that of every twenty-one witches, twenty were women. James argued that all women were weak and lustful and easy prey to "the snares of the Devil as was ever well proved to be true by the Serpent's deceiving of Eve at the beginning." In his first speech to Parliament, James lashed out at women, paraphrasing Scripture: "The head of every man is Christ and the head of the woman is man." In a widely printed letter to his son, the king instructed his son, "Teach your wife that it is your office to command, hers to obey. Women must never be allowed to meddle in the government."

By the time Anne was seventeen, separatists who had given up on reforming the Church of England were trying to escape, first to Holland. Anne had her first glimpse of persecuted Englishwomen driven from their homeland as she witnessed the fleeing Pilgrims.

When Anne was twenty, her father, her soul mate and intellectual companion, died. He left his wife as the sole executrix of his will, an uncommonly liberal gesture for the time, and left each of his twelve children 200 marks, a tidy sum. One year later, Anne married William Hutchinson, aged twenty-six, a wealthy textile merchant. The first of their fifteen children was born soon after they moved back to their childhood home, Alford. Along the North Sea, in the shadow of Dutch windmills, new religious winds were blowing. Women were appearing in pulpits as preachers, a practice that had originated across the sea in Holland. Soon there were women ministers all over England, many of them preaching the reform doctrines of Familism. This sect held that the spirit was superior to the Bible, believed that women and men could return to the innocence that preceded the Fall, advocated the election of the clergy by the people, and put reason above ritual.

The rapid spread of this radical agenda by women preachers brought intensifying persecution by the established church. In January 1620, the bishop of London told all his clergy to preach vehemently against the insolence of women and to condemn their "wearing of broad-brimmed hats, pointed doublets, hair cut short or shorn" and their carrying of daggers and swords. One Londoner recorded, "Our pulpits ring continually of the insolence and impudence of women."

In rural Alford, Anne had little contact for many years with persecution until the mid-1620s, when Charles I succeeded James and stepped up persecution of dissenters even further. Anne flirted at first with separatism but then seems to have rejected the idea of leaving her father's church after she heard the preaching of a charismatic Puritan preacher, John Cotton, at Boston, on the east coast. Frequently, she and her husband journeyed to Boston, twenty-four miles away, to hear him preach his gentle version of Puritanism. Cotton had won a reputation all over England as a biblical scholar and, as the leading nonconforming minister in the Church of England, for his evangelical preaching of the "covenant of grace," which he described as a covenant between God and man whereby God drew the soul to salvation. He preached that there was nothing a man—or woman—could do to acquire this covenant. If Anne Hutchinson was predestined to salvation, God would endow her with faith and fulfill the covenant. This doctrine differed somewhat from the version that the founders of Massachusetts Bay Colony declared as orthodox when they sailed to Boston in 1630. The faithful were expected to "prepare" themselves for God's saving grace by good works, especially following the laws of the New England church state. Anne espoused John Cotton's evangelical preaching of divine omnipotence and human helplessness. She believed with him that to draw comfort from doing good works was presumptuous, that God acted alone, and that humans had no way of preparing for divine grace.

In the winter of 1629, as the persecution of Puritans worsened, John Winthrop, a Cambridge-educated London barrister, was elected governor of a company of a thousand Puritans preparing to establish a permanent settlement in New England. The company made strong overtures to women, clearly implying that the New World would have no use for Old World, women-trammeling traditions, one leader writing of "the kind usage of the English [in Massachusetts Bay] to their wives" and of households where "equals gather with equals." The 1620s had been years of severe restrictions and heavy taxes on English businessmen and of drought and famine in the English cities and towns. Reports from the New World, on the other hand, emphasized abundant game, seafood, fruit, berries, pumpkins for the taking. In the sermon John Cotton preached to the Puritans departing on the four ships commanded by Governor Winthrop, he emphasized the economic opportunities for merchants like Anne's husband:

> Nature teaches bees [that] when the hive is too full, they seek abroad for new dwellings . . . [so it is] when the hive of [England] is so full that the tradesmen cannot live one by another, but eat up one another. . . .

What may have pushed the Hutchinsons off the fence in favor of emigrating was the latest policy of King Charles I, who combined unparalleled taxation and religious persecution by exacting forced loans from Puritans. Anne's uncle, seventy-year-old Erasmus Dryden, owner of Canons Ashby, one of England's great houses, was jailed when he refused to lend the king money. William Hutchinson believed it was only a matter of time before his turn came. Anne's brother-in-law, the Puritan preacher John Wheelwright, was arrested even as she learned that John Cotton was on the run from Archbishop Laud's agents. In disguise and using an assumed name, he was living in hiding in a series of Puritan hideaways. In July 1633, the Reverend Cotton boarded the *Griffin* and escaped to New England. Two members of the Hutchinson family sailed with him to begin transferring the family business to Boston. Then, shortly after their twelfth child was born, Anne and William gave away their belongings, sold their home of twenty years, and prepared to emigrate.

Almost from the moment she stepped on board the *Griffin*, bound for Boston on Massachusetts Bay, Anne Hutchinson spoke her mind, perhaps feeling she was safely away from the inhibiting atmosphere of England's church spies. And almost immediately, she incurred the wrath of two Puritan ministers who, along with a hundred head of cattle, were crowded in among the voyagers to the New World. The Reverends Zechariah Symmes and William Bartholomew reported to Boston authorities that Anne had confided to Bartholomew "that she had never had any great thing done about her but it was revealed to her beforehand." To claim that she communicated directly with God through revelations was heretical enough for the two ministers: that a *woman* claimed direct contact with God smacked of witchcraft.

To make matters worse, Anne had quickly grown tired of the Reverend Symmes's five-hour, nonstop shipboard sermons, especially his constant belittling of women. After announcing that, as soon as she reached Boston, she would expose his claims as a tissue of errors, Hutchinson began holding women's meetings, as she had done for years unmolested in Alford, on board ship. She was surprised that some of the men aboard objected, confronting her with the verse, "And if they [women] will learn anything, let them ask their husbands at home" (1 Corinthians 14:35). Anne was next shocked on her arrival at the mean, uncouth look of Boston, a flat, swampy backwater town of crowded, unpaved streets with pigs rooting in the filth, its hundred-odd houses dominated by the square, barnlike Puritan meetinghouse. Inside, she received another shock: instead of automatic admission to membership, she was subjected to an all-day hearing conducted by Governor Thomas Dudley. Her other interrogators included her old pastor, the Reverend Cotton; the pastor of her new Boston church, the Reverend John Wilson; and the Reverend Symmes, one of the shipboard clergymen she had openly criticized. Finally "satisfied that she held nothing different from us," Governor Dudley urged her admission to the church. But if Anne Hutchinson had expected freedom of expression or the right to dissent in Massachusetts, she must have been sadly disappointed.

For the next two years, Anne and William Hutchinson were busy building and furnishing a spacious, thatch-roofed wattle-and-daub house in Boston's Cornhill section. They lived right across the street from John Winthrop, who had recently been displaced as governor because many country clergy thought he had been too lenient with dissenters and had closed an eye to sharp business practices. Demoted to the colony's council, he was waiting for the next election to prove his toughness: he had received a copy of Anne's hearing record and had already put her down as someone to watch. Oblivious and hard at work, Anne was busy building her practice as one of only four midwives in all Boston, while she cared for her large family. She still found a way to organize weekly meetings in her home to discuss with other women the finer points of Mr. Cotton's sermons, a joy for her to be able to hear every week.

In these meetings, soon so popular that sixty or seventy people packed in and stood for an hour or two as Anne elaborated Cotton's teachings, she began to take Cotton's principles of divine omnipotence and human helplessness in a new direction. Her first principle was "that the person of the Holy Ghost dwells in a justified person [predestined for salvation]." This view threatened the fundamental doctrine on which the Puritans had built their church state, namely, that God's will could be fathomed only in the pages of the Bible. She further claimed that a good life—"sanctification"—offered no guarantee of being saved—"justification." This dictum undermined the whole Puritan belief that good works were necessary to "prepare" for salvation. Anne's emphasis on personal revelation minimized the role of the clergy. She also maintained that "justified" people knew by revelation from the Holy Spirit that they were already "justified" and could tell on the basis of this mystical insight whether other people were "under a covenant of grace" (saved) or "under a covenant of works" (damned because they were depending on good works instead of divine grace). By October 1636, Governor Winthrop, now reelected, began to view these beliefs as damaging to the stable and clergy-dominated society of Boston.

At about that time Hutchinson hinted to her admirers that in all of Massachusetts only two churchmen, John Cotton and her brother-in-law John Wheelwright, were under a covenant of grace and therefore fit to preach. If she had given this opinion to only a handful of listeners, she might have only been censured by her pastor. But by late 1636 her house was being jammed three times a week by up to eighty eager auditors, many of them merchants disgruntled with clergy controls on trade and profits, and even more members of other congregations all over the colony who trekked great distances to see and hear this bold woman speaking out against the black-robed, all-male power structure. As historian Edmund Morgan has put it, "more was at stake here than the welfare of the Boston church."

When Hutchinson's mentor, John Cotton, applied to become teacher of the First Church of Boston, which had the largest congregation in the colony, Winthrop could not stop him. But when John Wheelwright, whose views were no different from Cotton's or his sister-in-law's, was proposed as a teacher at a church meeting on October 30, Winthrop saw his chance to block Anne's growing influence. Most recent among her followers was Sir Henry Vane, the new Puritan governor out from England. Winthrop opposed the appointment of Wheelwright, "whose spirit they knew not and [who] seemed to dissent in judgment," as the church's third minister. Despite the fact that Wheelwright had the support of most of the congregation, Winthrop was even more popular as the man who had led and shaped the Puritan colony over the years. And now he was putting all that influence at risk to rouse the entire colony to the threat posed by Anne Hutchinson.

By early 1637, the colony was divided into two hostile factions, the town of Boston versus the surrounding countryside. In January, the worried General Court, the colony's ruling body, declared a day of fasting and prayer, a compulsory holiday. John Cotton preached. When he finished, Wheelwright rose from his bench and criticized anyone adhering to the idea of a covenant of works: "The more holy they are, the greater enemies they are to Christ. . . . We must kill them with the word of the Lord." Speaking figuratively, Wheelwright no doubt thought that most of the clergy and magistrates were dead wood, but someone took down his words. At its next session, the General Court charged him with sedition, convicting him but deferring sentence until after the annual May election. When the General Court sat again, John Winthrop was back in power. He had moved the court and the elections out of Boston into the countryside, to remote Cambridge, where he had the support of orthodox country clergy. He therefore succeeded in ousting Governor Vane, who soon sailed back to England. To buttress his position further, Winthrop again put off sentencing Wheelwright and called a synod of ministers in late summer to examine the doctrines his informants told him were coming from Anne Hutchinson's parlor. In the meantime, to keep the dissenters' numbers from swelling further, Winthrop sponsored a General Court order forbidding anyone to entertain strangers for more than three weeks without permission of the magistrates. The order was pointed at new immigrants from England whose views accorded with Mrs. Hutchinson's. America had enacted its first immigrant-screening law, aimed at stifling religious dissent.

Indeed, the year 1637, the ninth year of the Massachusetts Bay colony, was the year in which Puritan New England lost its innocence. Massachusetts troops used the murder of a New England trader as an excuse to destroy the main stronghold of the Pequot Indians near Stonington, Connecticut; they then slaughtered the escaping remnants near New Haven.

On August 30, ministers converged from all over Massachusetts and Connecticut for twenty-four days to define orthodox Puritan doctrines and to spell out for each other the implications of some eighty-two "erroneous" doctrines that witnesses said were coming from Anne Hutchinson's parlor. Anne's old mentor, John Cotton, fell into line with the orthodox majority; only John Wheelwright dissented. When the General Court reconvened in November, Wheelwright refused to recant and was banished from the colony; he was expected to go off to Rhode Island to join Roger Williams, himself banished the year before and now starting a new colony among the

Indians. Then on November 12, the General Court, having already made up its collective mind that Anne Hutchinson must be silenced, tried the midwife and lay teacher, forty-six years old and five months pregnant, on charges of sedition and contempt.

The New Town (as Cambridge was then called) courthouse was unheated, stark, and crowded with some two hundred people when Hutchinson, dressed in black, was escorted in and told to stand facing the bench, a long table at which gowned and wigged General Court officials sat flanking Governor Winthrop. There was no jury, although this was a civil case. Only the judges had footwarmers with hot coals inside. Anne heard the charges read to her for the first time. She was accused of eighty-two "errors in conduct and belief," including "consorting with those that had been sowers of sedition." Did they mean her own brother-in-law Wheelwright? In England, all Puritans were nonconformists by definition; in New England, nonconformity had just become an indictable offense. She was also accused of breaking the fourth commandment. The Bible was the law book, and "Honor thy father and thy mother" now meant that the governors of the colony were the fathers and all women their dutiful children, who must honor and obey them. Her third offense was to claim revelation of God's word directly, and her fourth that she had misrepresented the conduct of the ministers.

Legally, the court was on slippery ground, handicapped by Anne Hutchinson's caution. She had written nothing down and had never spoken in public. Furthermore, Winthrop could accuse her only of "countenancing and encouraging" Wheelwright's seditious circulation of a petition to reform the clergy: she had not actually signed it. To hold home meetings had never been a crime in England or New England before: it was the bedrock of the persecuted underground Puritan tradition. Only the charge of traducing the authority of the ministers seemed serious.

Without a lawyer, Anne ably conducted her own defense. Standing and parrying the governor's questions for seven uninterrupted hours, with a devastating combination of nerve, logic, and expert knowledge of the Bible, she often reduced lawyer Winthrop to exasperated outbursts of pique: "We do not mean to discourse with those of your sex." Called on to justify teaching crowds in her home, she quoted the Bible to show that older women were required to teach younger women. When Winthrop would not accept two biblical sources as grounding for her meetings, she answered sarcastically, "Must I show my name written therein [in the Bible]?" One clergyman after another was brought in to testify that she had belittled and insulted the ministers. Winthrop seemed to prevail on this charge, but only after introducing notes from an off-the-record pretrial meeting with Anne.

The first day's grilling paused only when the pregnant Anne fainted after not being allowed to sit, eat, drink, or leave the courtroom for natural relief. That night, slipped notes by a supporter, she found discrepancies in the testimony of her principal accuser, her pastor, Reverend Wilson. The next day, she insisted that all witnesses be put under oath, including the clergy, nearly setting off a riot. One final witness was her old friend, John Cotton, who rebutted the testimony of Reverend Wilson that Anne had admitted accusing the clergy of being "under a covenant of works" (unsaved). The case against Anne Hutchinson collapsed.

In her moment of unexpected triumph, Anne blurted out that she had known from a revelation at the start of her trial that she would prevail. And then she went even further: "And see this scripture fulfilled this day in mine eyes. . . . Take heed what ye go about to do unto me. . . . God will ruin you and your posterity and this whole state." This public challenge was too much for Winthrop and his all-male panel of judges and clergy. Winthrop asked Anne how she knew "that it was God that did reveal these things" and Anne, condemning herself under the colony's biblical laws against claiming immediate revelation, replied, "By the voice of His own spirit to my soul."

Deliberating only briefly, the court agreed Hutchinson's words were enough grounds for banishment. And when Anne asked to "know wherefore I am banished," Winthrop gave her only a curt, high-handed answer: "Say no more, the court knows wherefore and is satisfied."

Ordered held under house arrest in the isolated manse of a clergyman safely away from Boston all winter, Anne still refused to recant. In March 1638, she was excommunicated and ordered to leave the colony. At her sentencing, the Reverend Hugh Peter summed up her principal offense: "you have stepped out of your place, you have rather been a husband than a wife." And Reverend Wilson, her nemesis, after noting, "you have so many ways troubled the church," added, "I do cast you out and deliver you up to Satan." Immediately after Anne's November 1637 hearing, the court had stripped Captain John Underhill, hero of the Pequot War, of his militia rank and had disfranchised him for supporting Wheelwright and Hutchinson. Twelve days after sentencing Anne Hutchinson, the court ordered fifty-eight Bostonians (William Hutchinson was third on the list) disfranchised and stripped of their guns, powder, and lead—seventeen others from other towns were punished similarly. Six more women were tried and expelled in 1638.

With eighteen inches of snow still in the woods, Anne, now nine months pregnant, and her children made the sixty-five-mile journey from Boston to Aquidneck by horse, canoe, and on foot over Indian paths. It took eight days. Her husband had gone ahead with twenty of her faithful adherents to build log cabins. By March 1639, Anne was preaching again, her following growing. But as excommunications continued in Boston and John Winthrop raged that Massachusetts would soon seize Rhode Island, Anne felt she could not stay there. After her husband died in 1642, she moved to New York province with several other families. Far from the reach of John Winthrop, she built a house on Pelham Bay on the outskirts of the Dutch settlements.

Anne Hutchinson did not believe in war or firearms. Her Boston adherents had refused to fight in the Pequot Wars; now, on the frontier, she steadfastly refused to defend herself as a new war against the native tribes broke out in 1643. When she opened her gate one day to a group of young braves who asked her for cold water from her well, they rushed in and killed her and all of her daughters except one, who was taken into captivity.

Unsympathetic even at the hour of the family's tragic death, the Reverend Thomas Weld, in whose house Hutchinson had been held under arrest, gleefully reported her death back to England: "Thus the Lord heard our groans to heaven, and freed us from this great and sore affliction."

To read a transcript of Anne Hutchinson's trial, see http://www.piney.com/ColAnnHutchTrial.html.

@ ON THE WEB

The New England Primer, 1690

Puritan New England may have been the most literate community in the world. The ability to read was essential to these Protestant reformers. Even more than other Protestants, they were committed to the idea of the "priesthood of all believers"—the notion that the individual church member had to understand God's truth as well as any priest. The ability to read the Bible was the most important key to this possibility. Therefore, the Puritans tried to make sure that their children learned to read by requiring each town to maintain a public school, long before any European country had such an educational system. One of the first books published in the English-speaking colonies was a reading book for children, The New England Primer *(1690). In format it was an alphabet book. But it was also a way of teaching morality and religion. How do the ideas presented in this alphabet book resemble those discussed in Randall and Nahra's essay? Can you detect any differences between these ideas and the attitudes of the Virginia settlers discussed by Morgan in Chapter 2?*

Harvard, 1636–1642

The New England colonists not only wanted to make certain that all the members of their society could read. They also wanted a supply of learned ministers. And they knew they could not count on the English universities to give them the

Pages from *The New England Primer*, 1690 (letters A–M). American Antiquarian Society.

Pages from *The New England Primer,* 1690 (letters N–Z). American Antiquarian Society.

preachers they needed. In 1636, very shortly after the first large migration to Massachusetts Bay, the colony founded a college, Harvard, to train its ministers. The following documents will give you considerable insight into the reasons why the college was created, its rules, and its program of study. How do the ideas that guided the college match up with the kinds of attitudes discussed in Randall and Nahra's essay? Or do they coincide at all? How would you compare this educational system to the one you have experienced? Many differences are obvious, but are there any continuities and similarities? What does the administration of the college tell you about the relationship of church and state in Massachusetts?

After God had carried us safe to New England, and we had builded our houses, provided necessaries for our livelihood, reared convenient places for God's worship, and settled the civil government, one of the next things we longed for, and looked after, was to advance learning and perpetuate it to posterity, dreading to leave an illiterate ministry to the churches when our present ministers shall lie in the dust. And as we were thinking and consulting how to effect this great work, it pleased God to stir up the heart of one Mr. Harvard (a godly gentleman and a lover of learning, there living amongst us) to give the one half of his estate (it being in all about 1700 £) towards the erecting of a College, and all his library. After him another gave 300 £, others after them cast in more, and the public hand of the state added the rest. The College was, by common consent, appointed to be

From "New England's First Fruits," London, 1643, in *Sabin's Reprints,* J. Sabin, New York, 1865, Quarto Series, no. vii.

at Cambridge (a place very pleasant and accommodate), and is called (according to the name of the first founder) Harvard College.

The edifice is very fair and comely within and without, having in it a spacious hall (where they daily meet at commons, lectures, [and] exercises), and a large library with some books to it, the gifts of divers of our friends, their chambers and studies also fitted for and possessed by the students, and all other rooms of office necessary and convenient, with all needful offices thereto belonging. And by the side of the College a fair grammar school, for the training up of young scholars, and fitting of them for academical learning, that still, as they are judged ripe, they may be received into the College of this school; Master Corlet is the master, who hath very well approved himself for his abilities, dexterity, and painfulness in teaching and education of the youth under him.

Over the College is Master Dunster placed, as President, a learned, conscionable, and industrious man, who hath so trained up his pupils in the tongues and arts, and so seasoned them with the principles of Divinity and Christianity, that we have to our great comfort, (and in truth) beyond our hopes, beheld their progress in learning and godliness also.* The former of these hath appeared in their public declamations in Latin and Greek, and disputations logical and philosophical which they have been wonted (besides their ordinary exercises in the college hall) in the audience of the magistrates, ministers, and other scholars, for the probation of their growth in learning, upon set days, constantly once every month to make and uphold. The latter hath been manifested in sundry of them by the savory breathings of their spirits in their godly conversation. Insomuch that we are confident, if these early blossoms may be cherished and warmed with the influence of the friends of learning and lovers of this pious work, they will by the help of God come to happy maturity in a short time.

Over the College are twelve Overseers chosen by the General Court. Six of them are of the magistrates, the other six of the ministers, who are to promote the best good of it and (having a power of influence into all persons in it) are to see that every one be diligent and proficient in his proper place.

Rules and Precepts That Are Observed in the College

1. When any scholar is able to understand Tully, or such like classical Latin author *extempore*, and make and speak true Latin in verse and prose . . . and decline perfectly the paradigms of nouns and verbs in the Greek tongue, let him then and not before be capable of admission into the College.

2. Let every student be plainly instructed and earnestly pressed to consider well [that] the main end of his life and studies is *to know God*

Henry Dunster (1609–1658/59), the first president of Harvard, was forced to resign in 1654 because of his heretical beliefs regarding the efficacy of infant baptism although he was a satisfactory president in all other respects.

and Jesus Christ which is eternal life, John 17:3, and therefore to lay Christ in the bottom, as the only foundation of all sound knowledge and learning. And seeing the Lord only giveth wisdom, let everyone seriously set himself by prayer in secret to seek it of him. . . .

3. Everyone shall so exercise himself in reading the Scriptures twice a day that he shall be ready to give such an account of his proficiency therein, both in theoretical observations of the language and logic, and in practical and spiritual truths, as his tutor shall require, according to his ability. . . .

4. That they, eschewing all profanation of God's name, attributes, word, ordinances, and times of worship, do study with good conscience carefully to retain God and the love of His truth in their minds, else let them know that (notwithstanding their learning) God may give them up to strong delusions, and in the end to a reprobate mind. . . .

5. That they studiously redeem the time: observe the general hours appointed for all the students, and the special hours for their own classes, and then diligently attend the lectures without any disturbance by word or gesture. And if in anything they doubt, they shall inquire, as of their fellows, so (in case of *non satisfaction*), modestly of their tutors.

6. None shall, under any pretence whatsoever, frequent the company and society of such men as lead an unfit and dissolute life. Nor shall any without his tutors leave, or (in his absence) the call or parents of guardians, go abroad to other towns.

7. Every scholar shall be present in his tutor's chamber at the seventh hour in the morning, immediately after the sound of the bell, at his opening the Scripture and prayer; so also at the fifth hour at night, and then give account of his own private reading, as aforesaid in particular the third, and constantly attend lectures in the hall at the hours appointed. But if any (without necessary impediment) shall absent himself from prayer or lectures, he shall be liable to admonition, if he offend above once a week.

8. If any scholar shall be found to transgress any of the laws of God, or the school, after twice admonition, he shall be liable, if not *adultus*, to correction; if *adultus*, his name shall be given up to the Overseers of the College, that he be admonished at the public monthly act.

The times and order of their studies, unless experience shall show cause to alter:

[1.] The second and third day of the week, read lectures as followeth: To the first year at eight of the clock in the morning Logic the first three quarters, Physics the last quarter.
To the second year, at the ninth hour, Ethics and Politics at convenient distances of time.

To the third year at the tenth [hour] Arithmetic and Geometry the three first quarters, Astronomy the last.

Afternoon   The first year disputes at the second hour.
The second year at the third hour.
The third year at the fourth, everyone in his Art.
[2.] The fourth day read Greek.
To the first year the Etymology and Syntax at the eighth hour.
To the second at the ninth hour, Prosodia and Dialects.

Afternoon   The first year at second hour practice the precepts of Grammar in such authors as have a variety of words.
The second year at third hour practice in Poesy, Nonnus, Duport, or the like.
The third year perfect their Theory before noon, and exercise Style, Composition, Imitation, Epitome, both in Prose and Verse, afternoon.
[3.] The fifth day read Hebrew and the Eastern Tongues.
Grammar to the first year hour the eighth.
To the second, Chaldee at the ninth hour.
To the third, Syriac at the tenth hour.

Afternoon   The first year practice in the *Bible* at the second hour.
The second in Ezra and Daniel at the third hour.
The third at the fourth hour in Trostius's New Testament.
[4.] The sixth day read Rhetoric to all at the eighth hour.
Declamations at the ninth. So ordered that every scholar may declaim once a month. The rest of the day [free from studies].
[5.] The seventh day read Divinity Catechetical at the eighth hour.
Commonplaces at the ninth hour.

Afternoon   The first hour reads history in the winter, the nature of plants in the summer.

The sum of every lecture shall be examined before the new lecture be read.

Every scholar, that on proof is found able to read the originals of the Old and New Testament into the Latin tongue, and to resolve them logically, withal being of godly life and conversation, and at any public act hath the approbation of the Overseers and Master of the College, is fit to be dignified with his first degree.

Every scholar that giveth up in writing a system, or synopsis, or sum of Logic, Natural and Moral Philosophy, Arithmetic, Geometry and Astronomy, and is ready to defend his theses or positions, withal skilled in the originals as abovesaid, and of godly life and conversation, and so approved by the Overseers and Master of the College, at any public act, is fit to be dignified with his second degree.

Three Early New England Portraits

Our knowledge of the literate Puritans comes mostly from their own writings. But they left to posterity other kinds of evidence, including a number of individual portraits. The first is of a young boy, Henry Gibbs. Do you think the artist's depiction of the boy presents an accurate picture of what he was really like? Or do you think the portrait was a Puritan dream of what little boys should be like? What do you make of his clothing? What does the background—the tessellated floor—tell you about his society? The second portrait is a self-portrait of Thomas Smith. Do you think it is more revealing than young Henry's portrait? Why? What does the background say about Smith's life, his concerns? The third portrait is of an ancient Puritan named Ann Pollard. Painted in 1721, she was one of the original settlers of Boston, coming over on one of the first ships as a "romping girl" of ten. She had outlived all her generation, and the portrait was done in honor of her 100th birthday. Does she share any traits with young Henry Gibbs or with Thomas Smith?

"Henry Gibbs," 1670, anonymous. Collection of Sunrise Museum, Charleston, West Virginia. Gift of Mrs. David M. Giltinan.

"Thomas Smith's Self-Portrait" ca. 1675. Worcester Art Museum.

"Ann Pollard," 1721, anonymous. Massachusetts Historical Society. Photo by M. Cushing.

The Spiritual Journey of Anne Bradstreet

At the heart of Puritanism was the belief in the intimate relationship between God and believer. For them God wasn't a distant figure; God was always present, and everything that happened in one's life—good or bad—was God's will. If a sick child got well, that was God's will. If the child died, that too was God's will. One must learn therefore to resign oneself to God's will. For some, however, that was easier said than done. Below is Anne Bradstreet's description of her lifelong struggle to resign herself to God's will. She wrote this piece for her eight children, thinking that giving birth to still another child might bring her own death. That didn't happen; she lived another twenty years. As you read this piece, try to put yourself in the shoes of her children. What did they get out of her spiritual journey?

To My Dear Children

> This book by any yet unread,
> I leave for you when I am dead,
> That being gone, here you may find
> What was your living mother's mind.
> Make use of what I leave in love
> And God shall bless you from above.
>
> *A.B.*

My dear children,—

I, knowing by experience that the exhortations of parents take most effect when the speakers leave to speak, and being ignorant whether on my death bed I shall have opportunity to speak to any of you much less to all, thought it the best whilst I was able to compose some short matters. . . .

The method I will observe shall be this—I will begin with God's dealing with me from my childhood to this day.

In my young years, about 6 or 7 as I take it, I began to make conscience of my ways, and what I knew was sinful as lying, disobedience to parents, etcetera, I avoided it. If at any time I was overtaken with the like evils, it was a great trouble. I could not be at rest 'till by prayer I had confessed it unto God.

I was also troubled at the neglect of private duties, though too often tardy that way. I also found much comfort in reading the Scriptures, especially those places I thought most concerned my condition, and as I grew to have more understanding, so the more solace I took in them.

In a long fit of sickness which I had on my bed, I often communed with my heart, and made my supplication to the most high who set me free from that affliction.

But as I grew up to be about 14 or 15 I found my heart more carnal, and sitting loose from God, vanity and the follies of youth take hold of me.

From Anne Bradstreet, *Several Poems Compiled with Great Variety of Wit and Learning*, John Foster, Boston, 1678.

About 16, the Lord laid his hand sore upon me and smote me with the small pox. When I was in my affliction, I besought the Lord, and confessed my pride and vanity and he was entreated of me, and again restored me. But I rendered not to him according to the benefit received.

After a short time I changed my condition and was married and came into this country, where I found a new world and new manners, at which my heart rose. But after I was convinced it was the way of God, I submitted to it and joined to the church at Boston.

After some time I fell into a lingering sickness like a consumption, together with a lameness, which correction I saw the Lord sent to humble and try me and do me good: and it was not altogether ineffectual.

It pleased God to keep me a long time without a child which was a great grief to me, and cost me many prayers and tears before I obtained one, and after him gave me many more, of whom I now take the care, that as I have brought you into the world, and with great pains, weakness, cares, and fears brought you to this, I now travail in birth again of you till Christ be formed in you.

Among all my experiences of God's gracious dealings with me I have constantly observed this, that he hath never suffered me long to sit loose from him, but by one affliction or other hath made me look home, and search what was amiss—so usually thus it hath been with me that I have no sooner felt my heart out of order, but I have expected correction for it, which most commonly hath been upon my own person, in sickness, weakness, pains, sometimes on my soul, in doubts and fears of God's displeasure, and my sincerity towards him. Sometimes he hath smote a child with sickness, sometimes chastened by losses in estate, and these times (through his great mercy) have been the times of my greatest getting and advantage, yea I have found them the times when the Lord hath manifested the most love to me. Then have I gone to searching, and have said with David, Lord search me and try me, see what ways of wickedness are in me, and lead me in the way everlasting: and seldom or never but I have found either some sin I lay under which God would have reformed, or some duty neglected which he would have performed. And by his help I have laid vows and bonds upon my soul to perform his righteous commands.

If at any time you are chastened of God, take it as thankfully and joyfully as in greatest mercies. For if ye be his, ye shall reap the greatest benefit by it. It hath been no small support to me in times of darkness, when the Almighty hath hid his face from me, that yet I have had abundance of sweetness and refreshment after affliction and more circumspection in my walking after I have been afflicted. I have been with God like an untoward child, that no longer than the rod has been on my back (or at least in sight) but I have been apt to forget him and my self too. Before I was afflicted I went astray, but now I keep thy statutes.

I have had great experience of God's hearing my prayers, and returning comfortable answers to me, either in granting the thing I prayed for, or else in satisfying my mind without it; and I have been confident it hath been from him, because I have found my heart through his goodness enlarged in thankfulness to him.

I have often been perplexed that I have not found that constant joy in my pilgrimage and refreshing which I supposed most of the servants of God have, although he hath not left me altogether without the witness of his Holy Spirit, who hath oft given me his word and set to his seal that it shall be well with me. I have sometimes tasted of that hidden manna that the world knows not, and have set up my Ebenezer, and have resolved with my self that against such a promise, such tastes of sweetness, the gates of Hell shall never prevail. Yet have I many sinkings and droopings, and not enjoyed that felicity that sometimes I have done. But when I have been in darkness and seen no light, yet have I desired to stay my self upon the Lord. And, when I have been in sickness and pain, I have thought if the Lord would but lift up the light of his countenance upon me, although he ground me to powder, it would be but light to me. Yea, often have I thought were it Hell itself and could there find the love of God toward me, it would be a Heaven. And, could I have been in Heaven without the love of God, it would have been a Hell to me. For, in Truth, it is the absence and presence of God that makes Heaven or Hell.

Many times hath Satan troubled me concerning the verity of the Scriptures, many times by atheism. How could I know whether there was a God if I never saw any miracles to confirm me, and those which I read of, how did I know, but they were feigned. That there is a God my reason would soon tell me by the wondrous works that I see, the vast frame of the Heaven and the earth, the order of all things, night and day, summer and winter, spring and autumn, the daily providing for this great household upon the earth, the preserving and directing of all to its proper end. The consideration of these things would with amazement certainly resolve me that there is an Eternal Being.

But how should I know he is such a God as I worship in Trinity, and such a Saviour as I rely upon? Though this hath thousands of times been suggested to me, yet God hath helped me over. I have argued thus with my self. That there is a God I see. If ever this God hath revealed himself, it must be in his word, and this must be it or none. Have I not found that operation by it that no humane invention can work upon the soul? Hath not judgements befallen diverse who have scorned and contend it? Hath it not been preserved through all ages maugre all the heathen tyrants and all of the enemies who have opposed it? Is there any story but that which shows the beginnings of times, and how the world came to be as we see? Do we not know the prophecies in it fulfilled which could not have been so long foretold by any but God himself?

When I have got over this block, then have I another put in my way. That admit this be the true God whom we worship, and that be his word, yet why may not the popish religion be the right? They have the same God, the same Christ, the same word. They only interpret it one way, we another.

This hath sometimes stuck with me, and more it would, but the vain fooleries that are in their religion, together with their lying miracles, and cruel persecutions of the saints, which admit were they as they term them, yet not so to be dealt withall.

The consideration of these things and many the like would soon turn me to my own religion again.

But some new troubles I have had since the world has been filled with blasphemy, and sectaries, and some who have been accounted sincere Christians have been carried away with them, that sometimes I have said, "Is there faith upon the earth?" And I have not known what to think; but then I have remembered the words of Christ that so it must be, and that, if it were possible, the very elect should be deceived. "Behold," saith our Saviour, "I have told you before," that hath stayed my heart, and I can now say, "Return, O my soul, to thy rest, upon this rock Christ Jesus will I build my faith, and if I perish, I perish." But I know all the powers of Hell shall never prevail against it. I know whom I have trusted, and whom I have believed, and that he is able to keep that I have committed to his charge.

Now to the King, immortal, eternal, and invisible, the only wise God, be honor and glory for ever and ever. Amen.

This was written in much sickness and weakness, and is very weakly and imperfectly done; but if you can pick any benefit out of it, it is the mark which I aimed at.

THE BIG PICTURE

The development of colonial New England has often been seen as strikingly different from that of Virginia. What accounts for the differences? The presence of women? Puritan ideology? Puritan discipline? The landscape?

@ ON THE WEB   *For a discussion of the legacy of the Puritans on American memory, see* http://xroads.virginia.edu/~CAP/PURITAN/purmain.html.

Chapter 4

The Have-Nots in Colonial Society

Interpretive Essay by Peter Kolchin 79

Sources 92

    Portraits of Poverty 92

    The Experience of Bondage: Gottlieb Mittelberger's Account, 1754 93

    Wanted: Runaway Servants 96

    Portraits of Slavery 99

    Wanted: Runaway Slaves 104

The Big Picture 107

Once the colonies were established, colonial leaders faced a long-term problem. If they were to become rich, they had to recruit a labor force. Acquiring land was easy for a man of means, since land in America was so plentiful. But acquiring *labor* was a constant problem. The small farmer could rely on his family, but a man with broad acres needed extra hands. Where were they to be found?

One possible source was obviously the Indian. And colonists repeatedly tried to enslave the Indian. As late as 1708, South Carolina held 1,400 native Americans in bondage as compared with 4,100 Africans. But colonists found to their chagrin that enslaving the Indian was more trouble than it was worth. In any case, the supply of Indian labor was minute compared with the need. Since enslaving the Indians proved unworkable, the earliest planters had to look to Europe—particularly to England—for their solutions. The most immediate solution to the labor problem seemed to lie in the English practice of "indentured" or contractual servitude. The arrangement was basically simple: in return for a promise of some kind—a promise to be fed and housed and trained in some work, for example—men or women could bind themselves to work for a master for a period of years. The most common term in England, and then in the colonies, was seven years. An agreement, called an indenture, would then be written and signed, and for the agreed-upon period of years, the servant would become the virtual property of the master.

As it happened, England in the seventeenth century contained thousands of young men and women who were desperate enough to bind themselves into servitude and risk the hazards of the Atlantic crossing—all in return for little more than the vague hope that they would somehow be better off at the end of their term. It is impossible to know just how many came, but probably as many as half the immigrants of the seventeenth and eighteenth centuries came in bondage of one kind or another. Most were indentured servants; others were "redemptioners," who had to work off only the costs of their passage. But, no matter what the form, their servitude had much in common with slavery. Their contracts could be bought and sold. They could not live where they pleased, or marry without their masters' permission, or work for themselves. They had no guarantee of fair treatment or of decent food, clothing, and shelter.

Africans were first purchased as servants in 1619, only a dozen years after Jamestown was settled. But it was not until after 1700 that black slavery displaced white servitude as the dominant form of forced labor. Gradually—at first in Virginia and then in other colonies, both north and south—the legal status of slave was defined. Especially in the southern colonies where large-scale commercial agriculture was the way of life, slaves became *the* work force on many plantations. By 1750, the largest single stream of immigration into British North America was composed of black slaves from Africa.

To understand this development, it is necessary to realize that North America was always on the fringes of the immense slave trade that developed between West Africa and tropical America. The Spanish colonies and Portuguese Brazil began importing slaves in the early 1500s, and by the time Jamestown was settled in 1607 some 250,000 African slaves had been brought to the New World. It was primarily the need for labor on the sugar plantations of Brazil and the Caribbean that stimulated the growth of the Atlantic slave trade after 1700. As that trade skyrocketed, the number of slave ships that wandered as far north as Virginia also increased. Yet, of the 6 million slaves who survived the Atlantic voyages between 1700 and 1810, less than 6 percent ended up in what is now the United States. So the growth of slavery in the thirteen colonies was only a small part of the growth of slavery in the New World.

It is also necessary to realize that very few people in colonial times had any qualms about slavery. Human bondage had been considered a part of the natural scheme of things since ancient times—and except for a few Quakers and kindred German sects, colonists everywhere accepted slavery as "normal." Even churches owned slaves. Indeed, the pious often bequeathed slaves to their ministers as tokens of affection. When the Reverend Cotton Mather, one of the leading New England ministers of his day, was honored with the gift of a slave, he recorded the event in his diary as "a smile from Heaven."

The Origin and Consolidation of Unfree Labor

Peter Kolchin

The following selection comes from the opening chapter of Peter Kolchin's imaginative book comparing American slavery and Russian serfdom. The two systems of human bondage developed at roughly the same time, became firmly entrenched by the 1750s, and played similar economic and social roles in the two countries. In this extract, Kolchin confronts the question of why the American elite embraced forced labor. As you read it, you should keep several questions in mind: Why did the wealthier colonists continue to rely on European indentured servants long after the arrival of the first African slaves? And why did white indentured servitude in some colonies eventually give way to black slavery? What was the importance of race in all this? And, finally, why did the elite fear the "giddy multitude" before 1700—and "servile insurrection" after 1700? How significant was this change?

A shortage of laborers . . . plagued English settlers in the American colonies, and . . . this situation led to the use of physical compulsion to secure workers. A vast abundance of virgin land together with a paucity of settlers defined the problem in all the mainland colonies; everywhere, land was plentiful and labor scarce. To attract laborers, the colonists consequently found it necessary to pay wages that in Europe would have been considered exorbitant. "Poor People (both men and women) of all kinds, can here get three times the wages for their Labour they can in *England* or *Wales*," reported an observer from Pennsylvania in 1698. In all the colonies complaints were rampant about the high cost of labor and about the resulting lack of submissiveness among the much-sought-after workers. The law of supply and demand rendered unsuccessful the early efforts of several colonial governments to legislate maximum wages, and both skilled and unskilled labor continued to command wages up to twice those prevalent in England.

The payment of high wages proved inadequate, however, to secure a sufficient number of workers, and in every colony highly paid free labor was supplemented by forced labor of one type or another. Like the Spaniards to the south, although with less success, the English forced Indians to work for them. Indian slavery was most prevalent in South Carolina, where in 1708 the governor estimated that there were 1400 Indian slaves in a population of 12,580, but Indians also served as house servants and occasional laborers in the other colonies: New Jersey wills reveal the continued presence of small numbers of Indian slaves in that colony as late as the middle of the eighteenth century.

For a variety of reasons, however, Indian slavery never became a major institution in the English colonies. The proximity of the wilderness and of friendly tribes made escape relatively easy for Indian slaves. The absence of a tradition of agricultural work among East Coast Indian males—women customarily performed the primary field labor—rendered them difficult to train as agricultural laborers. Because they were "of a malicious, surly and revengeful spirit; rude and insolent in their behavior, and very ungovernable," the Massachusetts legislature forbade the importation of Indian slaves in 1712. Finally, there were not enough Indians to fill the labor needs of the colonists. In New England, for example, most of the natives present when the Puritans arrived died from illness and war during the next half-century. The policy of eliminating the threat of Indian attack by eliminating the Indians themselves proved in the long run incompatible with the widespread use of Indians as slaves and necessitated the importation of foreign laborers.

For the greater part of the seventeenth century the colonists relied on the most obvious source for their labor: other Europeans. Although more prevalent in some colonies than in others, indentured servants were common everywhere in seventeenth-century America. Most served between four and seven years in exchange for free passage from Europe to America, although some were kidnapped and others transported as criminals. All found themselves highly prized commodities. In many colonies, such as Virginia, settlers received a headright—often fifty acres—for every person they imported. But even without such incentives, colonists eagerly snapped up newly arriving stocks of servants, who performed vital functions as agricultural laborers, domestics, and artisans. These immigrant servants, as well as colony-born Americans bound out for poverty, debt, or crime, were virtual slaves during their periods of indenture, bound to do as their masters ordered, subject to physical chastisement, forbidden to marry without permission, and liable to be bought and sold. Like slaves, some were forcibly separated from their relatives. Although a few servants became prosperous and influential in later life, for most the future was decidedly less rosy. In the mid-seventeenth century close to half the servants in Virginia and Maryland died before their terms of indenture were complete; once freed, many males continued to labor for others, living in their households and often—because of the excess of men over women—remaining unmarried.

Finally, the colonists turned to Africa for labor. As early as 1619 the forced labor of blacks supplemented that of whites in Virginia, and by the middle of the seventeenth century blacks were to be found in all the existing English colonies. Nevertheless, what is most striking about the early American labor force is the length of time it took for slavery to replace indentured servitude: throughout most of the seventeenth century white laborers, not black, prevailed in the English mainland colonies, and it was only between 1680 and 1730 that slaves became the backbone of the labor force in the south. This pattern raises two interrelated questions: why, despite the presence of some slaves, did the colonists continue for so long to rely primarily on indentured servants, and why, during the half-century beginning in the 1680s, did African slaves replace European servants in most of the colonies?

Despite the prevailing labor shortage, there were certain limitations on the colonists' demand for slaves. Very few could afford to buy them during the first three-quarters of the seventeenth century. Most early settlers were people of fairly modest means for whom the purchase of a servant—at one-third to one-half the price of an African slave—represented a substantial investment. Even if one could afford the initial outlay, the high mortality rate among the inhabitants of the early southern colonies made the purchase of slaves risky, and servants who were held for only a few years may have represented a better buy. Not only were servants cheaper than slaves, but their successful management required smaller investments of time and effort. They usually spoke the language—at least in the seventeenth century, when most of them came from the British Isles—and were at least partially familiar with the agricultural techniques practiced by the settlers. Given the circumstances, as long as European servants were readily available, their labor continued to make sense to most colonists.

Precisely such conditions prevailed during the first three-quarters of the seventeenth century, when the population of the colonies was small and the number of Englishmen anxious to come as servants was large. Readjustments in the English economy during the late sixteenth and early seventeenth centuries worked serious hardships on many British subjects, who suffered through periodic depressions and famines. Vagabondage, crime, and destitution all increased markedly, as did public awareness of these problems. Increased concern was expressed both by greater attention to charity and by savage repression of the criminal, the rowdy, and the idle. Impoverished Britons were only too anxious to start anew in America, where radically different conditions promised some hope of success and where they were actually wanted rather than regarded as a burden, but so too were many skilled and semiskilled workers who saw their opportunities decline at home. Recent studies of servant immigrants in the seventeenth century suggest that they were overwhelmingly young and male but represented a wide diversity of occupations with perhaps as many as one-half having some skill. The tide of immigration reached its peak in the third quarter of the seventeenth century when, spurred by a series of ten crop failures, political dislocations at home, and a strong colonial demand for labor, close to forty-seven thousand Englishmen came to Virginia alone.

If the supply of servants seemed abundant during most of the seventeenth century, that of slaves was limited at best. The English were latecomers to the African slave trade, which, throughout the first two-thirds of the century, was primarily in Portuguese and then Dutch hands. Only after the Anglo-Dutch war of 1664–1667 was English naval superiority established; shortly thereafter, in 1672, the Royal African Company, with a (theoretical) monopoly of the English slave trade, was formed. Even then, the supply of Africans remained limited. Despite the anguished cries of British planters in the West Indies (where the most lucrative colonies were located), the Royal African Company was unable to supply a sufficient quantity of slaves. West Indian planters mounted a vigorous attack on the company's monopoly, and even before 1698, when the monopoly was formally lifted, private traders illegally supplied a large portion of the islands' laborers. If there were not enough Africans for the West Indies, where the need was greatest, the number available for export to the mainland, which was of relatively small economic importance, was small indeed. Until the last third of the century, most of the slaves imported to the mainland colonies were probably bought from Dutch and other private merchants, so it is not surprising that New York, where the Dutch had early encouraged the importation of slaves, had a higher proportion of blacks in its population than any other English mainland colony except South Carolina as late as 1680.

During the half-century from 1680 to 1730 these conditions impeding the importation of slaves changed radically. The growing prosperity of many colonists meant that an increasing number of them were able to afford slaves. The growth in the number and wealth of large holdings was especially significant, because large planters, who could afford to make the initial investment and whose need for labor was greatest, were the principal purchasers of slaves. In Maryland, for example, the average net worth of the richest 10 percent of probated estates increased 241 percent between 1656–1683 and 1713–1719, far more than the increase among smaller estates; as a consequence the proportion of all wealth owned by the richest 10 percent increased from 43 to 64 percent.

Since servants were only temporarily bound and did not produce new servants, as the colonial population grew the number of servants imported would have had to increase sharply in order for them to form a constant proportion of the population. The 10,910 headrights issued in Virginia between 1650 and 1654 were the equivalent of more than 57 percent of the colony's estimated population in the former year; the 10,390 issued between 1665 and 1669 were only equal to about 29 percent of the population in 1670. Even if the number of immigrants had remained constant, they would have represented a continually decreasing percentage of the population and would soon have become inadequate to meet the colonies' labor needs.

In fact, the supply of English servants declined sharply at just the time that the demand for labor was increasing in many of the colonies. As the English social situation stabilized following the Restoration of 1660 and the British government adopted a strongly mercantilist policy, Englishmen no longer complained, as they had formerly, about an excess population; instead, with increasing economic productivity and well-being, a large population now seemed an asset in Britain's struggle for supremacy with other European powers. Although conditions for the poor remained hard, they no longer experienced the continual crises, famines, and unemployment of the early and middle seventeenth century. Conditions within the colonies also acted to discourage immigration. By the late seventeenth century land was no longer so easily acquired as it had been earlier; furthermore, generally declining tobacco prices may have led merchants to reduce intentionally their importation of servants to Maryland and Virginia.

The result was a rather abrupt decline in the number of British immigrants to the colonies. In no five-year period between 1650 and 1674 did the

number of headrights issued for whites in Virginia fall below 7,900; in none
between 1675 and 1699 did it rise above 6,000:

1650–1654:	10,910	1675–1679:	3,991
1655–1659:	7,926	1680–1684:	5,927
1660–1664:	7,979	1685–1689:	4,474
1665–1669:	10,390	1690–1694:	5,128
1670–1674:	9,876	1695–1699:	4,251

The number of English servants thus declined precisely when more were
needed. Although Britain continued to transport convict laborers to
Maryland and a growing number of German and Irish servants settled in
Pennsylvania, there simply were not enough Europeans willing to sell themselves into indentured servitude in America to continue filling the labor
needs of the colonies.

At the same time that the supply of servants was decreasing, that of enslaved Africans was increasing, and it was this changing relative supply (and
hence price) of labor in the face of high (indeed growing) demand that most
simply explains the shift in the nature of the colonial labor force. With the
founding of the Royal African Company in 1672, Britain became the foremost slave-trading country in the world. In 1713, by the Treaty of Utrecht,
the English won the *asiento* or monopoly awarded by the Spanish government to supply the Spanish colonies with slaves. The eighteenth century was
the golden era of the English slave trade, when British merchants provided
slave labor for most of the world's colonies.

Given the heightened demand for labor and the new availability of
Africans, planters who needed large, stable labor forces had good reason to
prefer slaves to indentured servants, even had the supply of the latter not begun to dwindle. For one thing, slaves were held permanently—as were their
children—while servants were freed after a definite term. As a consequence,
although slaves required a larger initial investment, a plantation using slaves
became a self-perpetuating concern, especially by the early eighteenth century, when slave fertility rates increased markedly, mortality rates declined,
and the black population began to grow through natural reproduction as
well as importation. A plantation using indentured servants, however, required the continual replenishment of the labor force.

Equally important, servants tended to disrupt the efficient working of
a farm or plantation by running away. Although slaves too attempted to escape, it was more difficult for them to succeed. Their color made them easily identifiable and naturally suspect. White servants, on the other hand, had
little trouble pretending to be free, and the shortage of labor rendered it easy
for fugitives to find employment. As a result, the flight of indentured servants was a common and widely lamented occurrence. The colonies adopted
stringent penalties for fugitives, usually involving their serving additional
time and, for subsequent offenses, branding or mutilation. Newspaper ad-

vertisements for fugitives give evidence of both the scope of the problem and the treatment of servants. A typical notice in the Pennsylvania *Gazette* of 18 June 1752 offered a five-pound reward for the return to his West Jersey master of "an Irish servant man, named Thomas Bunn, a thick well set fellow, of middle stature, full faced, a little pock mark'd, and his hair cut off; he speaks pretty good English, and pretends to be something of a shoemaker, he has a scar on his belly, and is mark'd on the upper side of his right thumb with TB."

A comparison of the number of slaves and servants from New Jersey listed in newspaper advertisements with the number of slaves and servants listed in New Jersey wills suggests how much more often indentured servants escaped than did slaves. Although more than four times as many slaves as servants were listed in the wills of 1751–1760, in 1753 and 1754 there were fifty-four notices of fugitive servants and only seventeen of slaves. In other words, servants were apparently escaping at a rate about thirteen times as high as that of slaves. For planters this kind of discrepancy must have been a powerful argument in favor of using slaves.

Discontent with white laborers was not confined to the problem of fugitives. The prevalent labor shortage together with the availability of land encouraged an independent mode of thought on the part of supposedly subordinate white workers—who knew they would have little trouble finding employment no matter what their behavior—that was extremely distasteful to employers. After complaining about the high price of blacks, New York planter-politician Cadwallader Colden noted that "our chief loss is from want of white hands. . . . The hopes of having land of their own & becoming independent of Landlords is what chiefly induces people into America, & they think they have never answer'd the design of their coming till they have purchased land which as soon as possible they do & begin to improve ev'n before they are able to mentain [*sic*] themselves." That slavery did not allow for the development of this kind of independence among the laboring class was one more consideration in its favor.

*   *   *

The key determinant of the kind of labor system that emerged in the American colonies was the degree to which agriculture was geared to market. Although the increased availability of Africans made *possible* the widespread adoption of slave labor after 1680, slavery became the backbone of the economy in some colonies while in others it made little or no advance. Where a basic subsistence agriculture was practiced (as in most of New England), farms were small, the labor of a farmer and his family—and perhaps one or two extra hands at harvest time—was quite sufficient, and there was little need for forced labor. Where crops were grown for export, planters sought to maximize their production and extend the acreage planted. In such areas, which included much but not all of the southern colonies, the demand for labor was great, and the indentured servitude that characterized agricultural operations prior to the 1680s gave way to slave labor. Where commercial agriculture was practiced on a smaller scale, as in the middle colonies, the labor system was less uniform: in some places, such as Pennsylvania, indentured servitude remained widespread; in others, families augmented their own labor with that of occasional hired hands; and in still others—most notably parts of New York—slavery was an institution of some importance.

*   *   *

A brief examination of the geographic distribution of slaves . . . illustrates the close connection between agricultural expansion and the spread of forced labor. In the British mainland colonies large-scale commercial agriculture developed first in the Chesapeake Bay region. As early as 1617 tobacco was grown "in the streets, and even in the market-place of Jamestown"; a Dutch traveler reported of Maryland and Virginia in 1679 that "tobacco is the only production in which the planters employ themselves, as if there were nothing else in the world to plant." Spurred by a seemingly insatiable European demand for the new weed and blessed with good soil, a mild climate, and an excellent system of water routes, Chesapeake Bay planters produced increasing quantities of tobacco throughout the seventeenth century; the 20,000 pounds exported in 1619 swelled to 175,590,000 in 1672 and 353,290,000 in 1697, after which, despite annual fluctuations varying with tobacco prices, average yields stabilized for the next generation.

With an abundance of land and a shortage of labor, the amount of tobacco a planter could raise depended primarily on the number of workers he could command. Relying throughout most of the seventeenth century on a continual supply of fresh indentured servants, beginning in the 1680s, when the number of white immigrants had begun to decline sharply and African slaves had become more readily available, planters turned to slave labor. Wesley Frank Craven's computation of slave imports into Virginia, based on the number of black headrights granted, shows a marked increase beginning in 1690:

1650–1654:	162	1675–1679:	115
1655–1659:	155	1680–1684:	388
1660–1664:	280	1685–1689:	231
1665–1669:	329	1690–1694:	804
1670–1674:	296	1695–1699:	1,043

He suggests, however, that "the greatly expanded number of black headrights in the 1690s . . . is substantially representative of postponed claims for Negroes reaching the colony somewhat earlier." Corroborative evidence comes from a calculation that in York County, Virginia, the ratio of servants to slaves plummeted from 1.90 in 1680–1684 to 0.27 in 1685–1689 to 0.07 in 1690–1694; within a decade servants had virtually stopped coming to the county. By 1700, when more than one-quarter of Virginia's population was black, the revolution in the composition of the colony's labor force had been largely completed. In Maryland, too, the number of slaves increased markedly, although because large parts of Maryland were unsuited for tobacco growing and because the colony continued to receive substantial shipments of convict servants, the change occurred slightly later than in Virginia and was less dramatic.

Even more heavily dependent on slave labor, although later in development, was South Carolina. First settled by Europeans in the 1660s, it grew slowly as colonists sought in vain to find a staple that would play for them the same role that tobacco did in Virginia. They raised cattle and hogs for sale to the West Indies and also exported deerskins and naval stores. Because of the large role played by West Indian planters in the settling of South Carolina, the colony from the beginning had a higher percentage of slaves than the other mainland colonies, although as elsewhere from Pennsylvania south most of the early immigrants were white indentured servants.

Then, in the 1690s, Carolinians discovered rice, a crop that within a few years became as much a staple for them as tobacco was to planters of the Chesapeake. American rice shipments to England—almost all of which came from South Carolina (and from the middle of the eighteenth century, Georgia)—increased from less than 1 percent of the total value of American shipments to England in 1697–1705 to 12 percent in 1721–1730 and 24 percent in 1766–1775. Even more than in Virginia, South Carolina's commercial orientation created a society in which most heavy labor was coerced. With a population of only a little more than a thousand in 1680, the colony by 1740 claimed forty thousand residents, of whom approximately two-thirds were slaves.

Slavery was much less central in the northern colonies and consequently proved relatively easy to abolish without serious social dislocations in the late eighteenth and early nineteenth centuries; . . . Nevertheless, it is worth noting that unfree labor was of some importance in parts of the north as late as the middle of the eighteenth century. In Pennsylvania, spurred in part by an active propaganda campaign waged by William Penn and his agents who sought to convince impoverished Europeans of the boundless opportunities that awaited them in the colony, tens of thousands of indentured servants, many of them German, continued to perform a significant share of the agricultural labor. By far the largest concentration of slaves outside the southern colonies, however, was located in New York: as late as 1760 about one of every seven New Yorkers was a black slave.

Although both the Dutch, who ruled the colony as the New Netherlands until 1667, and the British who came after them actively promoted the importation of Africans, this policy would have met with little success had conditions there not been conducive to their employment. Wherever water transportation was available, especially on Long Island, Staten Island, and along the banks of the Hudson River, large planters—beneficiaries of huge land grants from both the Dutch and the English—grew a variety of crops for sale. The most important of these was wheat. "Wheat is the staple of this Province . . ." explained New York's governor in 1734; "it's generally manufactured into flower [sic] and bread, and sent to supply the sugar collonys." Slaves appeared wherever large quantities of wheat or other crops were raised for export; on Long Island, for example, they increased from 14 percent of the population in 1698 to 21 percent in 1738. Of course, some New Yorkers, especially in the city, employed slaves as house servants, and others possessed slaves who performed various trades.

The typical owner, however, was a farmer with one to five slaves, who used them to supplement his family's labor and increase the amount of its product available for sale.

Slavery was least important in New England, where small farms and a largely self-sufficient agriculture required little labor that a farmer's family could not provide. In the seventeenth century the New England colonies contained relatively few indentured servants, and those few more often served as domestics and artisans than as agricultural laborers. In the early eighteenth century blacks constituted about 2 percent of the population in Connecticut, Massachusetts, and New Hampshire, and few of them were farm workers. They were a luxury for those who could afford them rather than an essential part of the economy.

The one area of New England where extensive use of slaves prevailed nicely illustrates the impact of commercially oriented agriculture on the labor system of colonial America. In the fertile flatlands of the Narragansett region of Rhode Island there arose a system of large-scale stock raising and dairy farming. There, on soil ideally suited for grazing, planters bred the famed Narragansett racehorses, raised herds of sheep and dairy cows, and developed an aristocratic lifestyle similar to that of Virginia and Carolina planters. Estates of hundreds and sometimes thousands of acres required a large, steady laboring population, and it is no accident that "slavery, both negro and Indian, reached a development in colonial Narragansett unusual in the colonies north of Mason and Dixon's line." In 1730 about 10 percent of Rhode Island's population was black, but this figure conceals widespread variations. In the Narragansett country townships of South Kingston and Jamestown from one-fifth to one-quarter of the inhabitants were black, and including Indians about one-third were slaves; in many other areas of Rhode Island blacks constituted no more than 3 or 4 percent of the population. As elsewhere in the colonies, slavery in Rhode Island was strong only where there was substantial market-oriented agriculture.

*   *   *

Over the course of the seventeenth and first part of the eighteenth centuries unfree labor gradually became entrenched and solidified in . . . the American south. If at first serfdom and slavery had emerged as institutions designed to help landholders cope with specific problems of labor shortage, by the middle of the eighteenth century they appeared part of the natural order, as God-given as government or agriculture itself. A central feature of this process of entrenchment was the hardening and clarification of class lines, so that . . . the welter of overlapping groups that still prevailed in much of the seventeenth century had coalesced by the eighteenth into well-delineated classes, the masters and their bondsmen. Of course, there remained intermediate groupings, people who did not fit into either of these major classes; these two, however, dominated society and gave shape to the social order.

It was not at first obvious that this would be so. In the English mainland colonies, class lines were still fluid during most of the seventeenth century, and a variety of laborers, ranging from slave through semifree to free, rubbed shoulders. Indentured servants continued to arrive and in some colonies—most notably Pennsylvania—continued to provide a large share of agricultural laborers well into the eighteenth century. There were still Indian slaves. Criminals and debtors were routinely bound out to work as servants, as were children learning a trade. Nor was the status of all blacks immediately clear: there were some who served as indentured servants, especially during the first two-thirds of the seventeenth century, and for several decades the notion persisted among some colonists that the conversion of African slaves to Christianity might necessitate their manumission. The very term *slave* lacked precision and was sometimes used for someone only temporarily deprived of freedom. In 1639, for example, a white man, "John Kempe, for filthy, uncleane attempts with 3 yong girles, was censured to bee whiped . . . very severely, and was committed for a slave." In this case and several others from the same period the slavery imposed was only temporary, but it is significant that the nature of slavery and freedom could remain so ill defined in the 1630s and 1640s. The early colonists were familiar with a continuum of unfree and semifree statuses and did not yet set the black slaves off from other laborers as an entirely separate class. Of course, the Africans were different and perceived as such, but so too were they differentiated from one another on the basis of national origins; among Carolina planters, for example, "Coromantes and Whydahs, because of their greater hardiness, were supposed to be especially desirable as field hands, whereas Ibos, Congos, and Angolas, allegedly weaker, were said to be more effective as house servants." The rigid dichotomy of later years between black and white, slave and free, did not yet exist.

A flexibility was evident in South Carolina slavery as late as the early years of the eighteenth century, when, although blacks were already a majority of the labor force, there was considerable leeway in what was expected of them. Until the 1720s "servants and masters shared the crude and egalitarian intimacies inevitable on a frontier." Because of the lack of white manpower in this frontier environment, slaves performed a multitude of jobs that would later be considered inappropriate and that sometimes involved considerable initiative, independence, and free association with whites. Thus, slaves served as hunters, trappers, guides, sailors, and fishermen; they were even used to fight Indians, as in the Yamassee war of 1715.

In Virginia, where until shortly before the turn of the century blacks were still a small proportion of the population and most unfree workers were white, racial lines seemed even less firmly drawn. Black and white agricultural laborers often worked together; in his 1705 description of Virginia Robert Beverley noted that "the male servants, and slaves of both sexes, are employed together in tilling and manuring the ground" although "some distinction indeed is made between them in their clothes, and food" and white women were no longer assigned field work. Black and white laborers also fraternized with one another, shared living accommodations, and sometimes ran away together. Indeed, black and white, slave, servant, and often exservant as well were all part of a general underclass, a "giddy multitude" that in the third quarter of the seventeenth century showed growing restiveness and caused considerable unease among the well-to-do.

Just how fluid class alliances still were was demonstrated by Bacon's Rebellion, a conflict that erupted in 1676 when Nathaniel Bacon led an uprising against the government of Governor William Berkeley, an uprising that achieved momentary success before its leader caught ill and died of the "bloody flux" and his forces disintegrated. One of a series of violent upheavals that shook the colonies in the 1670s and 1680s, Bacon's Rebellion seemed destined to bear out all the worst fears about the "giddy multitude." Although historians have disagreed sharply over the nature of the rebellion, what is significant here is not Bacon's goal so much as the composition of his forces, which cut across racial and class lines. Enlisted in Bacon's ranks was an incongruous medley of disaffected Virginians: slaves, indentured servants, debtors, ex-servants, frontiersmen chafing under Berkeley's restrained Indian policy, and political enemies of the governor. That such an alliance was possible and that the governor's supporters did not make an issue of the participation of blacks on the side of the rebels indicate how little slavery had yet shaped class attitudes.

Such a configuration of forces as was seen in Bacon's Rebellion would have been impossible in the southern colonies by the early eighteenth century. The rapid spread of slavery and the decline in the number of servant immigrants meant that blacks, instead of constituting one element of a complex, turbulent underclass, were now the backbone of the labor force. Class lines were coming more and more to approximate racial lines. The change was not just one of numbers: the social distance between blacks and whites increased too. As plantation labor came to be associated with slaves, there was a perceptible rise in the status, treatment, and economic well-being of most white colonists. Not only were fewer whites coming over as indentured servants, but those who did tended to be from a somewhat higher social rank, often possessing mechanical skills much in demand in the colonies. David W. Galenson, after examining the backgrounds of 2,955 servants leaving England for Jamaica, Maryland, Pennsylvania, and Virginia between 1718 and 1759, found that most were skilled, 65 percent of the men were literate, and only 6 percent listed their occupations as "laborers."

Equally important were the changed conditions they met in the colonies. As fewer servants arrived, the colonists felt stronger pressure to treat them tolerably, because only by convincing prospective immigrants that they faced a bright future in America could the colonists generate continued immigration. Of course, even at the height of the immigration in the 1650s and 1660s the need to attract laborers had militated against treatment so harsh as to discourage other would-be servants from indenturing themselves; here is one reason, as Edmund Morgan has suggested, that indentured servants were never actually reduced to slaves. But when the economic and political dislocations leading Englishmen to flee their country had largely disappeared, the need to offer positive incentives to potential immigrants was much greater. The relatively few immigrants who continued to perform agricultural labor were increasingly differentiated from slaves, as Beverley noted in stressing differences in food, clothing, and treatment of women. The economic well-being of white immigrants in the colonies also improved. Not only were they employed more often in skilled trades, but as the general economic level of the colonies improved they were more able to translate the heavy demand for their services into better material conditions.

There was no such improvement in the status of blacks, who came to America involuntarily and did not have to be lured by attractive conditions. In fact, as the ranks of indentured servants diminished and as their condition improved, the blacks seemed increasingly different and threatening, and there was a decrease in the fraternization and sense of common cause that had once existed between black and white in the laboring underclass. Contributing to this growing isolation of black slaves was the fact that whereas previously most had spent time in the West Indies, where they had already been "seasoned" before coming to the United States, from the 1680s the majority were imported directly from Africa, spoke no English on arrival, and consequently seemed more alien to white Americans. By the turn of the century the pervasive fear of the "giddy multitude" had disappeared. Southern colonists of the eighteenth century dreaded rebellion too, but their fear was of a "servile insurrection," an uprising by black slaves against whites. The growing tide of slave imports and the changed relations between whites and blacks led to a sharp rise in white racial consciousness and widespread expressions of fear that too large a slave population threatened the peace of the community. As Virginia planter William Byrd—himself a large slaveowner—wrote to the Earl of Egmont in 1736, congratulating him on the (temporary) prohibition of slavery in the new colony of Georgia, "They import so many Negros hither, that I fear this Colony will some time or other be confirmed by the Name of New Guinea. . . . The farther [*sic*] Importation of them in Our Colonys should be prohibited lest they prove as troublesome and dangerous everywhere, as they have been lately in Jamaica."

The result was a rash of colonial legislation designed to regulate slaves. Codification of slavery lagged well behind its actual establishment. In Virginia blacks "had an uncertain legal status" until 1661, and it was only in 1664 that a Maryland law spelled out that "all Negroes and other slaves . . . shall serve Durante Vita"; so long as there were relatively few blacks in the colonies there seemed little need to pass elaborate legislation defining their status and regulating their behavior. During the late seventeenth and early eighteenth centuries, however, the southern colonies passed a series of laws designed to set blacks off from whites, legitimize slavery, and protect society from potential servile insurrections. These laws ranged from reassurances that conversion to Christianity did not require manumission, as in Virginia's act of 1667 and Maryland's of 1671, to measures prohibiting free blacks from voting, testifying in court against whites, or marrying whites, to the establishment of slave patrols to guard against suspicious behavior and the passage of duties in part designed to stem the importation of Africans and thus safeguard public security.

By the middle of the eighteenth century slavery was solidly entrenched as the labor system of the southern colonies, from Maryland to Georgia. Whereas a century earlier freedom was a vague concept, and the lot of most laborers, white and black, was to one extent or another unfree, now the assumption was practically universal among whites that slavery was the natural state of blacks and freedom that of whites. Blacks were simply different: "Kindness to a Negroe by way of reward for having done well is the surest way to spoil him although according to the general observation of the world most men are spurred on to diligence by rewards," wrote Virginia planter Landon Carter in 1770. Eight years later he expressed the same sentiment more bluntly: blacks "are devils," he proclaimed, "and to make them otherwise than slaves will be to set devils free."

To explore the laws that were enacted during the seventeenth century to secure the shift from indentured servitude to slavery, see http://www.pbs.org/wgbh/aia/part1/1h315.html.

@ ON THE WEB

Portraits of Poverty

The following pictures are eloquent testimony about one of the social conditions in England that had fateful consequences for the American colonies: poverty. The first is an engraving by the great satirist William Hogarth. How would you describe the attitude toward the poor the illustration suggests was dominant in the upper classes? The beggar in the second illustration is an Elizabethan figure. Does he look pitiful? Or threatening?

Hogarth street scene. The Granger Collection, New York.

"A Caaveat or Weaening for Commen Cursetors," (detail), Dii verso. By permission of the Folger Shakespeare Library.

The Experience of Bondage: Gottlieb Mittelberger's Account, 1754

One of our richest sources of information about the life of the white bondsmen and women is the following autobiographical account. It was written by Gottlieb Mittelberger, a German who came to Pennsylvania in 1750 and spent four years in bondage. Mittelberger was a schoolmaster, and we can see his education and intelligence at work in this story. But the conditions he encountered were probably typical of those met by other indentured servants. What kind of impression do you think Mittelberger is trying to make on his German audience? Why do you think Mittelberger uses the term serf?

VOICES

Both in Rotterdam and in Amsterdam the people are packed densely, like herrings so to say, in the large sea vessels. One person receives a place of scarcely 2 feet width and 6 feet length in the bedstead, while many a ship carries four to six hundred souls; not to mention the innumerable implements, tools, provisions, water-barrels and other things which likewise occupy much space.

From Gottlieb Mittelberger, *Journey to Pennsylvania in the Year 1750 and Return to Germany in the Year 1754*, J. J. McVey, Philadelphia, 1898, pp. 19–20, 22, 24.

On account of contrary winds it takes the ships sometimes 2, 3, and 4 weeks to make the trip from Holland to Kaupp [Cowes] in England. But when the wind is good, they get there in 8 days or even sooner. Everything is examined there and the custom-duties paid, whence it comes that the ships ride there 8, 10 to 14 days and even longer at anchor, till they have taken in their full cargoes. During that time every one is compelled to spend his last remaining money and to consume his little stock of provisions which had been reserved for the sea; so that most passengers, finding themselves on the ocean where they would be in greater need of them, must greatly suffer from hunger and want. Many suffer want already on the water between Holland and Old England.

When the ships have for the last time weighed their anchors near the city of Kaupp [Cowes] in Old England, the real misery begins with the long voyage. For from there the ships, unless they have good wind, must often sail 8, 9, 10 to 12 weeks before they reach Philadelphia. But even with the best wind the voyage lasts 7 weeks.

But during the voyage there is on board these ships terrible misery, stench, fumes, horror, vomiting, many kinds of seasickness, fever, dysentery, headache, heat, constipation, boils, scurvy, cancer, mouth-rot, and the like, all of which come from old and sharply salted food and meat, also from very bad and foul water, so that many die miserably.

Add to this want of provisions, hunger, thirst, frost, heat, dampness, anxiety, want, afflictions and lamentations, together with other trouble, as c.v. the lice abound so frightfully, especially on sick people, that they can be scraped off the body. The misery reaches the climax when a gale rages for 2 or 3 nights and days, so that every one believes that the ship will go to the bottom with all human beings on board. In such a visitation the people cry and pray most piteously. . . .

Many sigh and cry, "Oh, that I were at home again, and if I had to lie in my pigsty!" Or they say: "O God, if I only had a piece of good bread, or a good fresh drop of water." Many people whimper, sigh and cry piteously for their homes; most of them get home-sick. Many hundred people necessarily die and perish in such misery and must be cast into the sea, which drives their relatives, or those who persuaded them to undertake the journey, to such despair that it is almost impossible to pacify and console them. In a word, the sighing and crying and lamenting on board the ship continues night and day so as to cause the hearts even of the most hardened to bleed when they hear it. . . .

At length, when, after a long and tedious voyage, the ships come in sight of land, so that the promontories can be seen, which the people were so eager and anxious to see, all creep from below on deck to see the land from afar, and they weep for joy, and pray and sing, thanking and praising God. The sight of the land makes the people on board the ship, especially the sick and the half-dead, alive again, so that their hearts leap within them; they shout and rejoice, and are content to bear their misery in patience, in the hope that they may soon reach the land in safety. But alas!

When the ships have landed at Philadelphia after their long voyage, no one is permitted to leave them except those who pay for their passage or can give good security; the others, who cannot pay, must remain on board the ships till they are purchased, and are released from the ships by their purchasers. The sick always fare the worst, for the healthy are naturally preferred and purchased first; and so the sick and wretched must often remain on board in front of the city for 2 or 3 weeks, and frequently die, whereas many a one, if he could pay his debt and were permitted to leave the ship immediately, might recover and remain alive. . . .

The sale of human beings in the market on board the ship is carried on thus: Every day Englishmen, Dutchmen and High-German people come from the city of Philadelphia and other places, in part from a great distance, say 20, 30, or 40 hours away, and go on board the newly arrived ship that has brought and offers for sale passengers from Europe, and select among the healthy persons such as they deem suitable for their business, and bargain with them how long they will serve for their passage money, which most of them are still in debt for. When they have come to an agreement, it happens that adult persons bind themselves in writing to serve 3, 4, 5, or 6 years for the amount due by them, according to their age and strength. But very young people, from 10 to 15 years, must serve till they are 21 years old.

Many parents must sell and trade away their children like so many head of cattle; for if their children take the debt upon themselves, the parents can leave the ship free and unrestrained; but as the parents often do not know where and to what people their children are going, it often happens that such parents and children, after leaving the ship, do not see each other again for many years, perhaps no more in all their lives. . . .

It often happens that whole families, husband, wife, and children, are separated by being sold to different purchasers, especially when they have not paid any part of their passage money.

When a husband or wife has died at sea, when the ship has made more than half of her trip, the survivor must pay or serve not only for himself or herself, but also for the deceased.

When both parents have died over halfway at sea, their children, especially when they are young and have nothing to pawn or to pay, must stand for their own and their parents' passage, and serve till they are 21 years old. When one has served his or her term, he or she is entitled to a new suit of clothes at parting; and if it has been so stipulated, a man gets in addition a horse, a woman, a cow.

When a serf has an opportunity to marry in this country, he or she must pay for each year which he or she would have yet to serve, 5 to 6 pounds. But many a one who has thus purchased and paid for his bride, has subsequently repented his bargain, so that he would gladly have returned his exorbitantly dear ware, and lost the money besides.

If some one in this country runs away from his master, who has treated him harshly, he cannot get far. Good provision has been made for such cases, so that a runaway is soon recovered. He who detains or returns a deserter receives a good reward.

If such a runaway has been away from his master one day, he must serve for it as a punishment a week, for a week a month, and for a month half a year. But if the master will not keep the runaway after he has got him back, he may sell him for as many years as he would have to serve him yet.

Wanted: Runaway Servants

We have learned a considerable amount about colonial servitude from documents like the following. They are advertisements for runaway servants, placed by their masters in eighteenth-century newspapers in Virginia, Georgia, and South Carolina. Why did the masters describe the clothes their servants were wearing when they ran away? Why would the servants not simply discard those clothes for others? In terms of purchasing power, the rewards offered were very large. What kinds of trades and skills did the runaways represent? These advertisements were published in an area where black slavery was well established. Does that fact make any sense? If there were thousands of slaves, why were there indentured servants?

Virginia *Gazette*, April 16, 1767. Advertisement.

Run away from King William court-house, on the 14th of March last, three apprentice boys, viz. James Axley, a carpenter, about 5 feet 8 inches high, and wears his own black hair cued behind; had on when he went away a gray cloth coat, without pockets or flaps, and a pair of leather breeches much daubed with turpentine. William Arter, a carpenter, rather taller and better set than the former, of a dark complexion, has black hair, but his clothes no way remarkable. William Kindrick, a bricklayer, which business he understands well, and is supposed to be gone with a view of carrying it on with the other boys; he is a fresh complexioned youth, wears a cap, and had on a bearskin coat with metal buttons, a dark brown waistcoat, and a pair of lead coloured serge breeches. It is supposed they are gone to Bedford, or into Carolina. Whoever brings the said apprentices to King William or Hanover court-houses shall have forty shillings reward for each, besides their expenses defrayed.

Francis Smith, Sen.-James Geddy

Virginia *Gazette*, Nov. 1767

Prince George, November 10, 1767

Supposed to be run away from the subscriber (having liberty about three weeks ago to go up to Osborne's and Warwick, on James river, to look

 **ON THE WEB**

To explore some of the laws put in place in the Virginia colony to control indentured servants and eventually separate them from slaves, see http://www.virtualjamestown.org/indlink.html.

From U. B. Phillips, ed., "Plantation and Frontier," Part I in John R. Commons et al., eds., *A Documentary History of American Industrial Society.* Copyright 1909, 1937 by John R. Commons; copyright 1958 by Russell & Russell. Russell & Russell, New York, 1958, pp. 352–354, 346–348.

for work, and not since heard of) an indented servant man named Alexander Cuthbert, by trade a bricklayer, born in Perth in Scotland, but came last from London in one Captain Grigg to Potowmack river. He is about 5 feet 6 or 7 inches high, about 22 years of age, wears his own hair of a dark brown colour, is a little pitted with the smallpox, and, as he was some time in England, has not much of the Scotch accent. Had with him when he went away a blue coarse cloth coat, blue and red striped silk and cotton jacket, blue breeches, several white and check linen shirts, and many other articles of apparel. He carried with him his bricklayer's and plaistering tools, a sliding rule, some books of architecture and mensuration, etc. From the little time I have had him, he appeared a harmless inoffensive lad, entirely sober and obliging, and if he has gone off must have been advised to such a measure by some more designing than himself. It is probable he may make to the northward and so to Philadelphia, having been heard to speak of some acquaintances gone that way. Whoever takes up the said servant (if run away) and delivers him to the subscriber, shall have five pounds if taken within the colony, and ten pounds if taken at any considerable distance out of it, paid by

William Black

N.B. All masters of vessels are desired to be cautious of not carrying such a person out of the country.

Virginia *Gazette*, March 26, 1767

Run away from the subscriber, in Northumberland county, two Irish convict servants named William and Hannah Daylies, tinkers by trade, of which the woman is extremely good; they had a note of leave to go out and work in Richmond county and Hobb's Hole, the money to be paid to Job Thomas, in said county; soon after I heard they were run away. The man wore a light coloured coarse cloth frock coat, a blue striped satin jacket, and plaid one, a pair of leather breeches, a pair of Russia drill white stockings, a little brown bog wig, and his hat cocked up very sharp. He is about 5 feet 8 inches high, of a sandy complexion, and freckled; is a well made fellow, somewhat bow legged. The woman had on an old stuff gown and a light coloured petticoat, and under petticoat of cotton with a blue selvedge at the bottom, a blue striped satin gown, the same with his jacket, two check aprons, and a pair of pale blue calimanco shoes. They both wore white shirts, with very short ruffles, and white thread stockings. They had a complete set of tinkers tools. They were seen to have two English guineas and a good deal of silver, and said in Essex county they lived in Agusta, and inquired the road that way. Whoever will apprehend both or either of said servants, and brings them to me, shall have five pounds reward for each, and reasonable travelling charges allowed by

William Taite

Virginia *Gazette*, Feb. 26, 1767. Advertisement.

Run away from the subscriber in Augusta, on the 17th of January last, a convict servant man named John Jones, an Englishman, about 35 years of age, about 5 feet 7 inches high, of a fair complexion, and fair short hair; had on when he went away a blue homemade drugget jacket lined with striped linen, a blue broad cloth do. under it, leather breeches, coarse spun shirt made out of hemp linen, sheep gray stockings, and country made shoes; he has been a sailor, and I suppose will endeavour to get on board some vessel. I have heard that he has altered his name at Fredericksburg, and stole from thence a ruffled shirt, a pair of everlasting breeches, an old whitish coloured jacket, and two razors. Whoever takes up the said servant, and brings him to me, or John Briggs at Falmouth, or secures him in any county gaol so that I may get him again, shall have five pounds reward, paid by me or John Briggs.

Andrew Burd

N.B. As he is a very good scholar, it is imagined he will forge a pass.

Virginia *Historical Register,* vol. vi, 96–97, advertisements reprinted from the Virginia *Gazette* (Williamsburg), 1736–1737.

Ran away lately from the Bristol Company's Iron Works, in King George County, a servant man named James Summers, a West Country [i.e., Cornish] Man, and speaks thick, he is a short thick fellow, with short black hair and a ruddy complexion. Whoever secures the said servant and brings him to the said Iron Works, or to the Hon. John Taylor, Esq., in Richmond County, or gives notice of him, so as he may be had again, shall be well rewarded besides what the law allows.

Nansemond, July 14, 1737

Ran away some time in June last, from William Pierce of Nansemond County, near Mr. Theophilus Pugh's Merchant: a convict servant woman named Winifred Thomas. She is Welsh woman, short black Hair'd and young; mark'd on the Inside of her Right Arm with Gunpowder W. T. and the Date of the Year underneath. She knits and spins, and is supposed to be gone into North Carolina by the way of Cureatuck and Roanoke Inlet. Whoever brings her to her master shall be paid a Pistole besides what the law allows, paid by

William Pierce

South Carolina *Gazette* (Charleston), June 16 to 23, 1739. Advertisement.

Savannah, May 7, 1739

Run away on the 5th Instant from Robert William's Plantation in Georgia, 3 Men Servants, one named James Powell, is a Bricklayer by Trade about Five Feet 9 inches high, a strong made man, born in Wiltshire, talks broad, and when he went away he wore his own short hair, with a White cap: Among his comrades he was call'd Alderman.

Another named Charles Gastril did formerly belong to the Pilot Boat at Pill near Bristol, is by Trade a Sawyer, about 5 feet 10 Inches high, of a thin spare make, raw boned, and has a Scar somewhere on his upper Lip, aged about 25.

The 3rd named Jenkin James, a lusty young fellow, about the same Height as Gastrill, has a good fresh complection, bred by trade a Taylor, but of late has been used to Sawing, talks very much Welshly, and had on when he went away a coarse red coat and waistcoat, the Buttons and Button holes of the Coat black.

Any person or Persons who apprehend them, or either of them, and bring them to Mr. Thomas Jenys in Charleston, or to the said Mr. Robert Williams in Savannah shall receive 10 1. Currency of South Carolina for each.

Robert Williams

Besides the above mentioned Reward, there is a considerable sum allow'd by the Trustees [of the colony of Georgia] for taking run away Servants.

N.B. About a Fortnight ago, three other of the said Robert William's Servants run away, who are already advertized.

Portraits of Slavery

Following is a collection of pictures representing the institution of black slavery, from its beginnings in Africa, through the horrors of the "middle passage," to life and suffering in the New World. What does the engraving of the slave being whipped suggest about the ways whites were able to keep discipline in the system? The slave ship shown is the infamous "négrier" (as it was called in French) La Vigilante de Nantes. Do you think that spending weeks in such a suffocating prison would break down the human cargo psychologically, or would they be able to maintain a hold on sanity and on their cultural identity? Does the advertisement for a slave sale in South Carolina suggest that the owners of the cargo would be ruthless or careless with their human commodity, or would they have reason to guard their investment against spoilage? Finally, remember that all these pictures were produced by white men. Can you imagine how pictures left by the slaves themselves would have looked?

Slaves on upper deck of the "bark" *Wildfire.* Culver Pictures, Inc.

F. A. Biard, "Slaves on the West Coast of Africa," c. 1833. Oil on canvas. Wilberforce Museum and Georgian Houses, Hull, Humberside, UK/Bridgeman Art Library, International.

Shock of enslavement. The Granger Collection, New York.

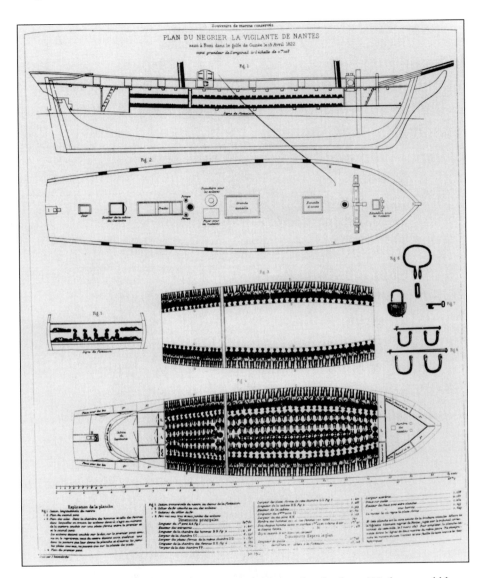

This is a diagram of the slave ship *La Vigilante de Nantes*, showing how 400 slaves could be crammed into a hold 36 feet in length and 3½ feet in height.

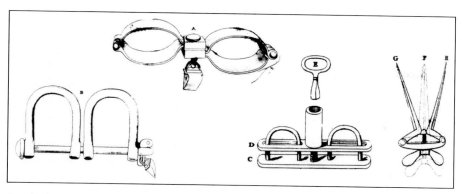

Standard equipment for the middle passage. (*A*) A pair of iron handcuffs by which one slave was padlocked to another. (*B*) A pair of leg irons, also for two slaves. (*C, D, E*) The thumbscrew, an instrument of torture. (*F, G, H*) A mouth opener for slaves who refused to eat.

TO BE SOLD, on board the Ship *Bance-Iſland*, on tueſday the 6th of *May* next, at *Aſhley-Ferry*; a choice cargo of about 250 fine healthy NEGROES, juſt arrived from the Windward & Rice Coaſt. —The utmoſt care has already been taken, and ſhall be continued, to keep them free from the leaſt danger of being infected with the SMALL-POX, no boat having been on board, and all other communication with people from *Charles-Town* prevented. *Auſtin, Laurens, & Appleby.*

N. B. Full one Half of the above Negroes have had the SMALL-POX in their own Country.

Advertisement in a Charleston, S.C., newspaper, 1766. Slaves from the Windward Coast were highly valued for their knowledge of growing rice. The Laurens of the commission merchants was Henry Laurens, later president of the Continental Congress. Library of Congress.

To better understand the experience of the "middle passage," see http://www.pbs.org/wgbh/aia/part1/1p277.html.

Wanted: Runaway Slaves

Angry masters advertised for runaway slaves just as they did for runaway indentured servants. The following notices, published in southern newspapers between 1767 and 1808, contain some of our most detailed descriptions and accounts of slaves. They also reveal much of the masters' attitudes toward their "property" and their general insensitivity toward pain and brutality. What do these advertisements mean, really? Do they suggest that slaves were, on the whole, so broken by their experience that they became submissive? Can you generalize about the kinds of backgrounds the runaways had? Is John Brown interested only in getting his property back, or does he want punishment, too? Notice that the last document in the set is signed with a famous name—Andrew Jackson, who was soon to become one of the nation's most popular presidents. Notice the reward offered and the additional payment Jackson offered to anyone who could whip this slave. Do these documents throw any additional light on the slave community? How do you think the owners could guess where the slaves might run to?

Advertisement from the Virginia *Gazette* (Williamsburg), March 26, 1767.

Run away about the 15th of December last, a small yellow Negro wench named Hannah, about 35 years of age; had on when she went away a green plains petticoat, and sundry other clothes, but what sort I do not know, as she stole many from the other Negroes. She has remarkable long hair, or wool, is much scarified under the throat from one ear to the other, and has many scars on her back, occasioned by whipping. She pretends much to the religion the Negroes of late have practised, and may probably endeavour to pass for a free woman, as I understand she intended when she went away, by the Negroes in the neighbourhood. She is supposed to have made for Carolina. Whoever takes up the said slave, and secures her so that I get her again, shall be rewarded according to their trouble, by

Stephen Dence

Advertisement from the Virginia *Gazette* (Williamsburg), April 23, 1767. Bounty on the head of an outlawed slave.

Run Away from the subscriber in Norfolk, about the 20th of October last, two young Negro fellows, viz. Will, about 5 feet 8 inches high, middling black, well made, is an outlandish fellow, and when he is surprised the white of his eye turns red; I bought him of Mr. Moss, about 8 miles below York, and imagine he is gone that way, or some where between York and Williamsburg. Peter, about 5 feet 9 inches high, a very black slim fellow, has a wife at Little Town, and a father at Mr. Philip Burt's quarter, near the half-way house between Williamsburg and York, he formerly belonged to Parson Fontaine, and

From U. B. Phillips, ed., "Plantation and Frontier," Part 2, in John R. Commons et al., eds., *Documentary History of American Industrial Society*, Russell & Russell, New York, 1958, pp. 92–93, 81–83, 86–89. Copyright 1909, 1937 by John R. Commons; copyright 1958 by Russell & Russell.

I bough[t] him of Doctor James Carter. They are both outlawed; and Ten Pounds a piece offered to any person that will kill the said Negroes, and bring me their heads, or Thirty Shillings for each if brought home alive.

John Brown

Advertisement from the Virginia *Gazette* (Williamsburg), Nov. 5, 1767.

Taken up on the 26th of July last, and now in Newbern gaol, North Carolina, Two New Negro Men, the one named Joe, about 45 years of age, about 5 feet 6 inches high, much wrinkled in the face, and speaks bad English. The other is a young fellow, about 5 feet 10 inches high, speaks English better than Joe, who he says is his father, has a large scar on the fleshy part of his left arm, and says they belong to Joseph Morse, but can give no account where he lives. They have nothing with them but an old Negro cloth jacket, and an old blue sailors jacket without sleeves. Also on the 21st of September was committed to the said gaol a Negro man named Jack, about 23 years of age, about 5 feet 4 inches high, of a thin visage, blear eyed, his teeth and mouth stand very much out, has six rings of his country marks round his neck, his ears full of holes, and cannot tell his master's name. And on the 27th of September two other Negro men, one named Sampson, about 5 feet 10 inches high, about 25 years of age, well made, very black, and is much marked on his body and arms with his country marks. The other named Will, about 5 feet 4 inches high, about 22 years of age, and marked on the chin with his country marks;* they speak bad English, and cannot tell their masters names. Whoever own the said Negroes are desired to come and pay the fees and take them away.

Richard Blackledge, Sheriff

Advertisement from the Virginia *Gazette* (Williamsburg), Jan. 13, 1774.

TWENTY POUNDS REWARD. Run away from Subscriber, a Mullatto Man named Abel, about forty Years old, near six Feet high, has lost several of his Teeth, large Eyebrows, a Scar or two on some Part of his Face, occasioned by a Brick thrown at him by a Negro, is very apt to stroke his Hand over his Chin, and plays on the Violin. He is well known as a Pilot for York River and the Bay. As I have whipped him twice for his bad Behaviour, I believe Scars may be seen upon his Body. He can write so as to be understood, and once wrote a Pass for a Negro belonging to the Honourable Colonel Corbin, wherein he said the Fellow had served his Time honestly and truly. He has been to England, but the Captain he went with took Care to bring him back, and since his Return from that Country is very fond of Liquor. He is gone off in a Boat with two Masts, Schooner rigged, once a Pilot Boat, but now the Property of the Magdalen Schooner of War, and was seen, I am told, fifty or sixty Leagues to the southward of Cape Henry, from which it is expected he intends for one of the Carolinas. He is a very great Rogue, and

---

*"*Country marks*" were the scars, tattooing, boring of ears, filing of teeth, etc., by which the Africans of certain tribes were accustomed to mark their persons.—Ed.*

is so instructed by several Persons not far from Wormeley's Creek, York River; one of whom, he told me, said I was not worthy to be his Master. He had some Cash of my Son's, and an Order drawn by Captain Punderson on Richard Corbin, Esq; payable to Ralph G. Meredith or myself. A White Lad went off with him, whom I cannot describe, never having seen him to my Knowledge. Whoever secures said Servant, so that I might get him again, shall have the above Reward.

Samuel Meredith, Senior

King and Queen, November 16, 1773

Advertisement from the Virginia *Gazette*, April 21, 1774.
A talented and wily mulatto.

Run away from the Neabsco Furnace, on the 16th of last Month, a light coloured Mulatto Man named Billy or Will, the Property of the Honourable John Taylor, Esquire. When I tell the Publick that he is the same Boy who, for many Years, used to wait on me in my Travels through this and the neighbouring Province, and, by his Pertness, or rather Impudence, was well known to almost all my Acquaintances, there is the less Occasion for a particular Description of him. However, as he is now grown to the Size of a Man, and has not attended me for some Time past, I think it not amiss to say that he is a very likely young Fellow, about twenty Years old, five Feet nine Inches high, stout and strong made, has a remarkable Swing in his Walk, but is much more so by a surprising Knack he has of gaining the good Graces of almost every Body who will listen to his be-witching and deceitful Tongue, which seldom or ever speaks the Truth; has a small Scar on the right Side of his Forehead, and the little Finger of his right Hand is quite straight by a Hurt he got when a Child. He had on when he went away a blue Fearnaught and an under Jacket of green Baize, Cotton Breeches, Osnabrug Shirt, a mixed Blue Pair of Stockings, a pair of Country made Shoes, and yellow Buckles. From his Ingenuity, he is capable of doing almost any Sort of Business, and for some Years past has been chiefly em-ployed as a Founder, a Stone Mason, and a Miller, as Occasion required; one of which Trades, I imagine, he will, in the Character of a Freeman, profess. I have some Reason to suspect his travelling towards James River, under the Pretence of being sent by me on Business. Whoever apprehends the said Mulatto Slave, and brings him to me, or his Master, the Honourable John Taylor of Mount Airy, or secures him so as to be had again, shall have dou-ble what the Law allows, and all reasonable Charges paid by

Thomas Lawson

Neabsco Furnace, April 1, 1774

Advertisement from the Georgia *Express* (Athens), Dec. 17, 1808.

Runaway from the subscriber living in Jackson county, on the Oconee river near Clarkesborough, on Sunday night the 13th of November last a mulatto man of the name of Joe. He is a very bright mulatto, almost white, about six feet high, tolerably well made, yellow gray eyes and yellow hair. He is branded on each cheek with the letter R, one of his upper fore teeth out, and, on examining under one of his arms there will be found a scar. He carried off with him clothes of different kinds, among them is a blue regimental coat turned up with red. He likewise took away with him a smooth bored gun. I suspect he will attempt to pass for a free man, and no doubt will aim northwardly or for the Indian Nation. Any person who will apprehend the above described negro, deliver him to me or confine him in jail shall be handsomely compensated.

Richard Thurmond

Advertisement from the Tennessee *Gazette & Mero District Advertiser* (Nashville), Nov. 7, 1804.

Andrew Jackson's way.

STOP THE RUNAWAY. FIFTY DOLLARS REWARD. Eloped from the subscriber, living near Nashville on the 25th of June last, a *Mulatto Man Slave*, about thirty years old, five feet and an inch high, stout made and active, talks sensible, stoops in his walk, and has a remarkably large foot, broad across the root of the toes—will pass for a free man, as I am informed he has obtained by some means, certificates as such—took with him a drab great-coat, dark mixed body coat, a ruffled shirt, cotton home spun shirts and overalls. He will make for Detroit, through the states of Kentucky and Ohio, or the upper part of Louisiana. The above reward will be given any person that will take him and deliver him to me or secure him in jail so that I can get him. If taken out of the state, the above reward, and all reasonable expenses paid—and ten dollars extra for every hundred lashes any person will give him to the amount of three hundred.

Andrew Jackson, near Nashville, State of Tennessee

THE BIG PICTURE

Indentured servitude was the most common form of forced labor in the seventeenth century, African slavery in the eighteenth century. Why the change? What role did race and racism play? The masters' desire for cheap labor? In what respects were the lives of indentured servants and slaves the same? How were they different? Of the differences, which was most important?

Chapter 5

The American Revolution

Interpretive Essay by Alfred F. Young 110

Sources 121
    George III 121
    Common Sense, 1776 122
    Voices: Silencing the Tories 126

The Big Picture 129

To Englishmen and colonists alike, the year 1763 was a great one. For almost a hundred years, the British had carried on an intense struggle with the French for the control of North America. For the colonists, this had meant involvement in one war after another, with Indians and their French allies sweeping down from Canada in raids on the New England and New York frontiers. Now, after the bloodiest of those wars, the French were finally beaten. Canada was British. In London and in all British North America, the loyal subjects of the now mighty British Empire looked forward to peace and prosperity. Small wonder that proud colonists toasted the British monarch, George III, and swore their undying allegiance to king and Parliament. Small wonder, too, that authorities in London now saw a chance to put their governmental house in order and to extend a more efficient administration to their growing colonies across the Atlantic.

Twelve years later, the same loyal colonists were at war with the same authorities in England. Twelve years later, the names of George III and even of Parliament were cursed all up and down the North American seaboard.

This astonishing turn of events had its seeds in the situation of 1763. The British government came out of its long series of wars with France with a large debt. And the wish to extend efficient government across the Atlantic was in part a wish to make the colonies profitable through taxes—primarily taxes on trade, on the goods the colonists shipped to Europe, and the manufactured items they imported. Parliament began to add to the list of taxes and duties the colonists were supposed to pay, and to send over officials to administer the duties and collect the taxes. The colonists, who had been virtually untaxed, responded vigorously and angrily. They began to boycott English goods, mob Crown officers, quarrel relentlessly with their royal governors, and destroy British property. The outcome of a succession of crises and protests was open rebellion, followed by a full-scale war for independence.

Who rebelled and why? And what effect did the American Revolution have on their lives? Historians have been grappling with these related questions ever since the revolution began in 1775. The only thing we know for certain is that there are no simple and easy answers. A number of general guesses have been proposed over the years. One takes the colonists more or less at their word and suggests that the cause of the rebellion was the attempt of the British to undercut some of the "liberties" the colonists had enjoyed as "free-born" Englishmen. Another kind of answer has been that the colonists were reacting basically to their economic interests, trying to protect a trading position that was vulnerable to British attempts to regulate commerce. Still others have argued that the issue was not the relationship between the home country and the colonies at all, but rather the tension *within* the colonies, and that the revolution was an *internal* revolution in which "radicals" in the colonies seized power from colonial elites who were dependent on their connection with authority in London. And within such general arguments, there are specific questions that still are unanswered. How much attention should be paid, for example, to the efforts of leading agitators like Sam Adams or Tom Paine? How important were the blundering shifts in policy in London, or the incompetence of British officials in the colonies?

Questions like these have made the interpretation of the American Revolution one of the most complicated and interesting of our historical problems. Underneath all the interpretations and disagreements lies a profoundly important question: Should the Revolution be seen as an anticipation of modern political and social history, or as an event rooted in local quarrels and the concerns of British and American politicians at the time? Was it a violent family squabble, or was it, as Ralph Waldo Emerson called it, the "shot heard round the world"? Or was it somehow and mysteriously *both?*

The Shoemaker and the Revolution

Alfred F. Young

Much has been written about the heroes of the American Revolution, men like Thomas Jefferson and John Hancock. In contrast, little is known about the ordinary men and women whose actions prompted Jefferson to write the Declaration of Independence and Hancock to sign it in large, bold letters. In the following selection, Alfred F. Young provides us with the opportunity to view the coming of the Revolution through the eyes of an ordinary citizen, a Boston shoemaker named George Robert Twelves Hewes, who once repaired a shoe for John Hancock. Hewes lived to be nearly a hundred, and in his old age was interviewed at length by two writers, James Hawkes and Benjamin Thatcher. Young, in turn, has relied heavily on the Hawkes and Thatcher interviews. As you read Young's essay, note the rigid class distinctions that existed in pre-Revolutionary Boston. Note also how Hewes's social outlook and political views changed. What caused him to become a Revolutionary? Why didn't he remain loyal to the king, as one of his brothers did? And, above all, what caused him to stop being a tongue-tied, deferential shoemaker and become a defiant citizen who "would not take off his hat to any man"?

Late in 1762 or early in 1763, George Robert Twelves Hewes, a Boston shoemaker in the last year or so of his apprenticeship, repaired a shoe for John Hancock and delivered it to him at his uncle Thomas Hancock's store in Dock Square. Hancock was pleased and invited the young man to "come and see him on New Year's day, and bid him a happy New-Year," according to the custom of the day, a ritual of noblesse oblige on the part of the gentry. We know of the episode through Benjamin Bussey Thatcher, who interviewed Hewes and wrote it up for his Memoir of Hewes in 1835. On New Year's Day, as Thatcher tells the story, after some urging by his master,

> George washed his face, and put his best jacket on, and proceeded straightaway to the Hancock House (as it is still called). His heart was in his mouth, but assuming a cheerful courage, he knocked at the front door, and took his hat off. The servant came:
> "Is 'Squire Hancock at home, Sir?" enquired Hewes, making a bow.
> He was introduced directly to the *kitchen*, and requested to seat himself, while report should be made above stairs. The man came down directly, with a new varnish of civility suddenly spread over his face. He ushered him into the 'Squire's sitting-room, and left him to make his obeisance. Hancock

From Alfred F. Young, "George Robert Twelves Hewes (1741–1840) a Boston Shoemaker and the Memory of the American Revolution," *William and Mary Quarterly*, ser. 3, vol. 38, October 1981, 561–562, 585–600.

remembered him, and addressed him kindly. George was anxious to get through, and he commenced a desperate speech—"as pretty a one," he says, "as he any way knew how,"—intended to announce the purpose of his visit, and to accomplish it, in the same breath.

"Very well, my lad," said the 'Squire—now take a chair, my lad."

He sat down, scared all the while (as he now confesses) "almost to death," while Hancock put his hand into his breeches-pocket and pulled out a crown-piece, which he placed softly in his hand, thanking him at the same time for his punctual attendance, and his compliments. He then invited his young friend to drink his health—called for wine—poured it out for him—and ticked glasses with him,—a feat in which Hewes, though he had never seen it performed before, having acquitted himself with a creditable dexterity, hastened to make his bow again, and secure his retreat, though not till the 'Squire had extorted a sort of half promise from him to come the next New-Year's—which, for a rarity, he never discharged.

The episode is a demonstration of what the eighteenth century called deference.

Another episode catches the point at which Hewes had arrived a decade and a half later. In 1778 or 1779, after one stint in the war on board a privateer and another in the militia, he was ready to ship out again, from Boston. As Thatcher tells the story: "Here he enlisted, or engaged to enlist, on board the Hancock, a twenty-gun ship, but not liking the manners of the Lieutenant very well, who ordered him one day in the streets to take his hat off to him—which he refused to do for any man,—he went aboard the 'Defence,' Captain Smedley, of Fairfield Connecticut." This, with a vengeance, is the casting off of deference.

What had happened in the intervening years? What had turned the young shoemaker tongue-tied in the face of his betters into the defiant person who would not take his hat off for any man? And why should stories like this have stayed in his memory sixty and seventy years later?

*   *   *

Between 1768 and 1775, the shoemaker became a citizen—an active participant in the events that led to the Revolution, an angry, assertive man who won recognition as a patriot. What explains the transformation? We have enough evidence to take stock of Hewes's role in three major events of the decade: the Massacre (1770), the Tea Party (1773), and the tarring and feathering of John Malcolm (1774). . . .

The presence of British troops in Boston beginning in the summer of 1768—four thousand soldiers in a town of fewer than sixteen thousand inhabitants—touched Hewes personally. Anecdotes about soldiers flowed from him. He had seen them march off the transports at the Long Wharf; he had seen them every day occupying civilian buildings on Griffin's Wharf near his shop. He knew how irritating it was to be challenged by British sentries after curfew (his solution was to offer a swig of rum from the bottle he carried).

More important, he was personally cheated by a soldier. Sergeant Mark Burk ordered shoes allegedly for Captain Thomas Preston, picked them up, but never paid for them. Hewes complained to Preston, who made good and suggested he bring a complaint. A military hearing ensued, at which Hewes testified. The soldier, to Hewes's horror, was sentenced to three hundred fifty lashes. He "remarked to the court that if he had thought the fellow was to be punished so severely for such an offense, bad as he was, he would have said nothing about it." And he saw others victimized by soldiers. He witnessed an incident in which a soldier sneaked up behind a woman, felled her with his fist, and "stripped her of her bonnet, cardinal muff and tippet." He followed the man to his barracks, identified him (Hewes remembered him as Private Kilroy, who would appear later at the Massacre), and got him to give up the stolen goods, but decided this time not to press charges. Hewes was also keenly aware of grievances felt by the laboring men and youths who formed the bulk of the crowd—and the principal victims—at the Massacre. From Hawkes and Thatcher three causes can be pieced together.

First in time, and vividly recalled by Hewes, was the murder of eleven-year-old Christopher Seider on February 23, ten days before the Massacre. Seider was one of a large crowd of schoolboys and apprentices picketing the shop of Theophilus Lilly, a merchant violating the anti-import resolutions. Ebenezer Richardson, a paid customs informer, shot into the throng and killed Seider. Richardson would have been tarred and feathered, or worse, had not whig leaders intervened to hustle him off to jail. At Seider's funeral, only a week before the Massacre, five hundred boys marched two by two behind the coffin, followed by two thousand or more adults, "the largest [funeral] perhaps ever known in America," Thomas Hutchinson thought.

Second, Hewes emphasized the bitter fight two days before the Massacre between soldiers and workers at Gray's ropewalk down the block from Hewes's shop. Off-duty soldiers were allowed to moonlight, taking work from civilians. On Friday, March 3, when one of them asked for work at Gray's, a battle ensued between a few score soldiers and ropewalk workers joined by others in the maritime trades. The soldiers were beaten and sought revenge. Consequently, in Thatcher's words, "quite a number of soldiers, in a word, were determined to have a row on the night of the 5th."

Third, the precipitating events on the night of the Massacre, by Hewes's account, were an attempt by a barber's apprentice to collect an overdue bill from a British officer, the sentry's abuse of the boy, and the subsequent harassment of the sentry by a small band of boys that led to the calling of the guard commanded by Captain Preston. Thatcher found this hard to swallow—"a dun from a greasy barber's boy is rather an extraordinary explanation of the origin, or one of the occasions, of the massacre of the 5th of March"—but at the trial the lawyers did not. They battled over defining "boys" and over the age, size, and degree of aggressiveness of the numerous apprentices on the scene.

Hewes viewed the civilians as essentially defensive. On the evening of the Massacre he appeared early on the scene at King Street, attracted by the clamor over the apprentice. "I was soon on the ground among them," he said, as if it were only natural that he should turn out in defense of fellow townsmen against what was assumed to be the danger of aggressive action by soldiers. He was not part of a conspiracy; neither was he there out of curiosity. He was unarmed, carrying neither club nor stave as some others did. He saw snow, ice, and "missiles" thrown at the soldiers. When the main guard rushed out in support of the sentry, Private Kilroy dealt Hewes a blow on his shoulder with his gun. Preston ordered the townspeople to disperse. Hewes believed they had a legal basis to refuse: "they were in the king's highway, and had as good a right to be there" as Preston.

The five men killed were all workingmen. Hewes claimed to know four: Samuel Gray, a ropewalk worker; Samuel Maverick, age seventeen, an apprentice to an ivory turner; Patrick Carr, an apprentice to a leather breeches worker; and James Caldwell, second mate on a ship—all but Christopher Attucks. Caldwell, "who was shot in the back was standing by the side of Hewes, and the latter caught him in his arms as he fell," helped carry him to Dr. Thomas Young in Prison Lane, then ran to Caldwell's ship captain on Cold Lane.

More than horror was burned into Hewes's memory. He remembered the political confrontation that followed the slaughter, when thousands of angry townspeople faced hundreds of British troops massed with ready rifles. "The people," Hewes recounted, "then immediately chose a committee to report to the governor the result of Captain Preston's conduct, and to demand of him satisfaction." Actually the "people" did not choose a committee "immediately." In the dark hours after the Massacre a self-appointed group of patriot leaders met with officials and forced Hutchinson to commit Preston and the soldiers to jail. Hewes was remembering the town meeting the next day, so huge that it had to adjourn from Fanueil Hall, the traditional meeting place that held only twelve hundred, to Old South Church, which had room for five to six thousand. This meeting approved a committee to wait on the officials and then adjourned, but met again the same day, received and voted down an offer to remove one regiment, then accepted another to remove two. This was one of the meetings at which property bars were let down.

What Hewes did not recount, but what he had promptly put down in a deposition the next day, was how militant he was after the Massacre. At 1:00 a.m., like many other enraged Bostonians, he went home to arm himself. On his way back to the Town House with a cane he had a defiant exchange with Sergeant Chambers of the 29th Regiment and eight or nine soldiers, "all with very large clubs or cutlasses." A soldier, Dobson, "ask'd him how he far'd; he told him very badly to see his townsmen shot in such a manner, and asked him if he did not think it was a dreadful thing." Dobson swore "it was a fine thing" and "you shall see more of it." Chambers "seized and forced" the cane from Hewes, "saying I had no right to carry it. I told him I had as good a right to carry a cane as they had to carry clubs."

The Massacre had stirred Hewes to political action. He was one of ninety-nine Bostonians who gave depositions for the prosecution that were published by the town in a pamphlet. Undoubtedly, he marched in the great funeral procession for the victims that brought the city to a standstill. He attended the tempestuous trial of Ebenezer Richardson, Seider's slayer, which was linked politically with the Massacre. ("He remembers to this moment, even the precise words of the Judge's sentence," wrote Thatcher.) He seems to have attended the trial of the soldiers or Preston or both. . . .

Four years later, at the Tea Party on the night of December 16, 1773, the citizen "volunteered" and became the kind of leader for whom most historians have never found a place. The Tea Party, unlike the Massacre, was organized by the radical whig leaders of Boston. They mapped the strategy, organized the public meetings, appointed the companies to guard the tea ships at Griffin's Wharf (among them Daniel Hewes, George's brother), and planned the official boarding parties. As in 1770, they converted the town meetings into meetings of "the whole body of the people," one of which Hutchinson found "consisted principally of the Lower ranks of the People & even Journeymen Tradesmen were brought in to increase the number & the Rabble were not excluded yet there were divers Gentlemen of Good Fortunes among them."

The boarding parties showed this same combination of "ranks." Hawkes wrote:

> On my inquiring of Hewes if he knew who first proposed the project of destroying the tea, to prevent its being landed, he replied that he did not; neither did he know who or what number were to volunteer their services for that purpose. But from the significant allusion of some persons in whom I had confidence, together with the knowledge I had of the spirit of those times, I had no doubt but that a sufficient number of associates would accompany me in that enterprise.

The recollection of Joshua Wyeth, a journeyman blacksmith, verified Hewes's story in explicit detail: "It was proposed that young men, not much known in town and not liable to be easily recognized should lead in the business." Wyeth believed that "most of the persons selected for the occasion were apprentices and journeymen, as was the case with myself, living with tory masters." Wyeth "had but a few hours warning of what was intended to be done." Those in the officially designated parties, about thirty men better known, appeared in well-prepared Indian disguises. As nobodies, the volunteers—anywhere from fifty to one hundred men—could get away with hastily improvised disguises. Hewes said he got himself up as an Indian and daubed his "face and hands with coal dust in the shop of blacksmith." In the streets "I fell in with many who were dressed, equipped and painted as I was, and who fell in with me and marched in order to the place of our destination."

At Griffin's Wharf the volunteers were orderly, self-disciplined, and ready to accept leadership.

> When we arrived at the wharf, there were three of our number who assumed an authority to direct our operations, to which we readily submitted. They divided us into three parties, for the purpose of boarding the three ships which contained the tea at the same time. The name of him who commanded the division to which I was assigned was Leonard Pitt [Lendell Pitts]. The names of the other commanders I never knew. We were immediately ordered by the respective commanders to board all the ships at the same time, which we promptly obeyed.

But for Hewes there was something new: he was singled out of the rank and file and made an officer in the field.

> The commander of the division to which I belonged, as soon as we were on board the ship, appointed me boatswain, and ordered me to go to the captain and demand of him the keys to the hatches and a dozen candles. I made the demand accordingly, and the captain promptly replied, and delivered the articles; but requested me at the same time to do no damage to the ship or rigging. We then were ordered by our commander to open the hatches, and take out all the chests of tea and throw them overboard, and we immediately proceeded to execute his orders; first cutting and splitting the chests with our tomahawks, so as thoroughly to expose them to the effects of the water. In about three hours from the time we went on board, we had thus broken and thrown overboard every tea chest to be found in the ship; while those in the other ships were disposing of the tea in the same way, at the same time. We were surrounded by British armed ships, but no attempt was made to resist us. We then quietly retired to our several places of residence, without having any conversation with each other, or taking any measures to discover who were our associates.

This was Hewes's story, via Hawkes. Thatcher, who knew a good deal more about the Tea Party from other sources, accepted it in its essentials as an accurate account. He also reported a new anecdote which he treated with skepticism, namely, that Hewes worked alongside John Hancock throwing tea overboard. And he added that Hewes, "whose whistling talent was a matter of public notoriety, acted as a boatswain," that is, as the officer whose duty it was to summon men with a whistle. That Hewes was a leader is confirmed by the reminiscence of Thompson Maxwell, a teamster from a neighboring town who was making a delivery to Hancock the day of the event. Hancock asked him to go to Griffin's Wharf. "I went accordingly, joined the band under one Captain Hewes; we mounted the ships and made tea in a trice; this done I took my team and went home as any honest man should." "Captain" Hewes—it was not impossible.

As the Tea Party ended, Hewes was stirred to further action on his own initiative, just as he had been in the hours after the Massacre. While the crews were throwing the tea overboard, a few other men tried to smuggle off some of the tea scattered on the decks. "One Captain O'Connor whom I well knew," said Hewes, "came on board for that purpose, and when he supposed he was not noticed, filled his pockets, and also the lining of his coat. But I had detected him, and gave information to the captain of what he was doing. We were ordered to take him into custody, and just as he was stepping from the vessel, I seized him by the skirt of his coat, and in attempting to pull him back, I tore it off." They scuffled. O'Connor recognized him and "threatened to 'complain to the Governor.'" "You had better make your will first,' quoth Hewes, doubling his fist expressively," and O'Connor escaped, running the gauntlet of the crowd on the wharf. "The next day we nailed the skirt of his coat, which I had pulled off, to the whipping post in Charlestown, the place of his residence, with a label upon it," to shame O'Connor by "popular indignation."

A month later, . . . Hewes won public recognition for an act of courage that almost cost his life and precipitated the most publicized tarring and feathering of the Revolution. The incident that set it off would have been trivial at any other time. On Tuesday, January 25, 1774, at about two in the afternoon, the shoemaker was making his way back to his shop after his dinner. According to the very full account in the *Massachusetts Gazette*,

> Mr. George-Robert-Twelves Hewes was coming along Fore-Street, near Captain Ridgway's, and found the redoubted John Malcolm, standing over a small boy, who was pushing a little sled before him, cursing, damning, threatening and shaking a very large cane with a very heavy ferril on it over his head. The boy at that time was perfectly quiet, notwithstanding which Malcolm continued his threats of striking him, which Mr. Hewes conceiving if he struck him with that weapon he must have killed him out-right, came up to him, and said to him, Mr. Malcolm I hope you are not going to strike this boy with that stick.

Malcolm had already acquired an odious reputation with patriots of the lower sort. A Bostonian, he had been a sea captain, an army officer, and recently an employee of the customs service. He was so strong a supporter of royal authority that he had traveled to North Carolina to fight the Regulators and boasted of having a horse shot out from under him. He had a fiery temper. As a customs informer he was known to have turned in a vessel to punish sailors for petty smuggling, a custom of the sea. In November 1773, near Portsmouth, New Hampshire, a crowd of thirty sailors had "genteely tarr'd and feather'd" him, as the *Boston Gazette* put it: they did the job over his clothes. Back in Boston he made "frequent complaints" to Hutchinson of "being hooted at in the streets" for this by "tradesmen"; and the lieutenant governor cautioned him, "being a passionate man," not to reply in kind.

The exchange between Malcolm and Hewes resonated with class as well as political differences:

> Malcolm returned, you are an impertinent rascal, it is none of your business. Mr. Hewes then asked him, what had the child done to him. Malcolm damned him and asked him if he was going to take his part? Mr. Hewes answered no further than this, that he thought it was a shame for him to strike the child with such a club as that, if he intended to strike him. Malcolm on that damned Mr. Hewes, called him a vagabond, and said he would let him know he should not speak to a gentleman in the street. Mr. Hewes returned to that, he was neither a rascal nor vagabond, and though a poor man was in as good credit in town as he was. Malcolm called him a liar, and said he was not, nor ever would be. Mr. Hewes retorted, be that as it will, I never was tarred nor feathered any how. On this Malcolm struck him, and wounded him deeply on the forehead, so that Mr. Hewes for some time lost his senses. Capt. Godfrey, then present, interposed, and after some altercation, Malcolm went home.

Hewes was rushed to Joseph Warren, the patriot doctor, his distant relative. Malcolm's cane had almost penetrated his skull. Thatcher found "the indentation as plainly perceptible as it was sixty years ago." So did Hawkes. Warren dressed the wound, and Hewes was able to make his way to a magistrate to swear out a warrant for Malcolm's arrest "which he carried to a constable named Justice Hale." Malcolm, meanwhile, had retreated to his house, where he responded in white heat to taunts about the half-way tarring and feathering in Portsmouth with "damn you let me see the man that dare do it better."

In the evening a crowd took Malcolm from his house and dragged him on a sled into King Street "amidst the huzzas of thousands." At this point "several gentlemen endeavoured to divert the populace from their intention." The ensuing dialogue laid bare the clash of conceptions of justice between the sailors and laboring people heading the action and Sons of Liberty leaders. The "gentlemen" argued that Malcolm was "open to the laws of the land which would undoubtedly award a reasonable satisfaction to the parties he had abused," that is, the child and Hewes. The answer was political. Malcolm "had been an old impudent and mischievious [*sic*] offender—he had joined in the murders at North Carolina—he had seized vessels on account of sailors having a bottle or two of gin on board—he had in other words behaved in the most capricious, insulting and daringly abusive manner." He could not be trusted to justice. "When they were told the law would have its course with him, they asked what course had the law taken with Preston or his soldiers, with Capt. Wilson or Richardson? And for their parts they had seen so much partiality to the soldiers and customhouse officers by the present Judges, that while things remained as they were, they would, on all such occasions, take satisfaction their own way, and let them take it off." The references were to Captain Preston who had been tried and found innocent of the Massacre, the soldiers who had been set off with token punishment, Captain John Wilson, who had been indicted for inciting slaves to murder their masters but never tried, and Ebenezer Richardson, who had been tried and found guilty of killing Seider, sentenced, and then pardoned by the crown.

The crowd won and proceeded to a ritualized tarring and feathering, the purpose of which was to punish Malcolm, force a recantation, and ostracize him.

> With these and such like arguments, together with a gentle crouding of persons not of their way of thinking out of the ring they proceeded to elevate Mr. Malcolm from his sled into a cart, and stripping him to buff and breeches, gave him a modern jacket [a coat of tar and feathers] and hied him away to liberty-tree, where they proposed to him to renounce his present commission, and swear that he would never hold another inconsistent with the liberties of his country; but this he obstinately refusing, they then carted him to the gallows, passed a rope around his neck, and threw the other end over the beam as if they intended to hang him: But this manoeuvre he set at defiance. They then basted him for some time with a rope's end, and threatened to cut his ears off, and on this he complied, and they then brought him home.

Hewes had precipitated an electrifying event. It was part of the upsurge of spontaneous action in the wake of the Tea Party that prompted the whig leaders to promote a "Committee for Tarring and Feathering" as an instrument of crowd control. The "Committee" made its appearance in broadsides signed by "Captain Joyce, Jun.," a sobriquet meant to invoke the bold cornet who had captured King Charles in 1647. The event was reported in the English newspapers, popularized in three or four satirical prints, and dramatized still further when Malcolm went to England, where he campaigned for a pension and ran for Parliament (without success) against John Wilkes, the leading champion of America. The event confirmed the British ministry in its punitive effort to bring rebellious Boston to heel.

What was lost to the public was that Hewes was at odds with the crowd. He wanted justice from the courts, not a mob; after all, he had sworn out a warrant against Malcolm. And he could not bear to see cruel punishment inflicted on a man, any more than on a boy. As he told the story to Thatcher, when he returned and saw Malcolm being carted away in tar and feathers, "his instant impulse was to push after the procession as fast as he could, with a blanket to put over his shoulders. He overtook them [the crowd] at his brother's [Shubael's] house and made an effort to relieve him; but the ruffians who now had the charge of him about the cart, pushed him aside, and warned him to keep off." This may have been the Good Samaritan of 1835, but the story rings true. While "the very excitement which the affront must have wrought upon him began to rekindle," Hewes conveyed no hatred for Malcolm.

The denouement of the affair was an incident several weeks later. "Malcolm recovered from his wounds and went about as usual. 'How do you do, Mr. Malcolm?' said Hewes, very civilly, the next time he met him. 'Your humble servant, Mr. George Robert Twelves Hewes,' quoth he,— touching his hat genteely as he passed by. 'Thank ye,' thought Hewes, 'and I am glad you have learned *better manners at last.*'" Hewes's mood was one of triumph. Malcolm had been taught a lesson. The issue was respect for Hewes, a patriot, a poor man, an honest citizen, a decent man standing up for a child against an unspeakably arrogant "gentleman" who was an enemy of his country.

Hewes's role in these three events fits few of the categories that historians have applied to the participation of ordinary men in the Revolution. He was not a member of any organized committee, caucus, or club. He did not attend the expensive public dinners of the Sons of Liberty. He was capable of acting on his own volition without being summoned by any leaders (as in the Massacre). He could volunteer and assume leadership (as in the Tea Party). He was at home on the streets in crowds but he could also reject a crowd (as in the tarring and feathering of Malcolm). He was at home in the other places where ordinary Bostonians turned out to express their convictions: at funeral processions, at meetings of the "whole body of the people," in courtrooms at public trials. He recoiled from violence to persons if not to property. The man who could remember the whippings of his own boyhood did not want to be the source of pain to others, whether Sergeant Burk, who tried to cheat him over a pair of shoes, or John Malcolm, who almost killed him. It is in keeping with his character that he should have come to the aid of a little boy facing a beating.

Nevertheless, Hewes was more of a militant than he conveyed or his biographers recognized in 1833 and 1835. He was capable of acting on his own initiative in the wake of collective action at both the Massacre and the Tea Party. He had "public notoriety," Thatcher tells us for his "whistling talent"; whistling was the customary way of assembling a crowd. According to Malcolm, Hewes was among the "tradesmen" who had "several times before affronted him" by "hooting" at him in the streets. And the patriots whose names stayed with him included Dr. Thomas Young and William Molineaux, the two Sons of Liberty who replaced Ebenezer McIntosh as "mob" leaders.

What moved Hewes to action? It was not the written word; indeed there is no sign he was much of a reader until old age, and then it was the Bible he read. "My whole education," he told Hawkes, "consisted of only a moderate knowledge of reading and writing." He seems to have read one of the most sensational pamphlets of 1773, which he prized enough to hold onto for more than fifty years, but he was certainly not like Harbottle Dorr, the Boston shopkeeper who pored over every issue of every Boston newspaper, annotating Britain's crimes for posterity.

Hewes was moved to act by personal experiences that he shared with large numbers of other plebeian Bostonians. He seems to have been politicized, not by the Stamp Act, but by the coming of the troops after 1768, and then by things that happened to him, that he saw, or that happened to people he knew. Once aroused, he took action with others of his own rank and condition—the laboring classes who formed the bulk of the actors at the Massacre, the Tea Party, and the Malcolm affair—and with other members of his family: his uncle Robert, "known for a staunch Liberty Boy," and his brother Daniel, a guard at the tea ship. Shubael, alone among his brothers, became a tory. These shared experiences were interpreted and focused more likely by the spoken than the written word and as much by his peers at taverns and crowd actions as by leaders in huge public meetings.

As he became active politically he may have had a growing awareness of his worth as a shoemaker. . . .

He may also have responded to the rising demand among artisans for support of American manufacturers, whether or not it brought him immediate benefit. He most certainly subscribed to the secularized Puritan ethic—self-denial, industry, frugality—that made artisans take to the nonimportation agreement with its crusade against foreign luxury and its vision of American manufactures. . . .

But what ideas did Hewes articulate? He spoke of what he did but very little of what he thought. In the brief statement he offered Hawkes about why he went off to war in 1776, he expressed a commitment to general principles as they had been brought home to him by his experiences. "I was continually reflecting upon the unwarrantable sufferings inflicted on the citizens of Boston by the usurpation and tyranny of Great Britain, and my mind was excited with an unextinguishable desire to aid in chastising them." When Hawkes expressed a doubt "as to the correctness of his conduct in absenting himself from his family," Hewes "emphatically reiterated" the same phrases, adding to a "desire to aid in chastising them" the phrase "and securing their independence." This was clearly not an afterthought; it probably reflected the way many others moved toward the goal of Independence, not as a matter of original intent, but as a step made necessary when all other resorts failed. Ideology thus did not set George Hewes apart from Samuel Adams or John Hancock. The difference lies in what the Revolution did to him as a person. His experiences transformed him, giving him a sense of citizenship and personal worth. Adams and Hancock began with both; Hewes had to arrive there, and in arriving he cast off the constraints of deference.

The two incidents with which we introduced Hewes's life measure the distance he had come: from the young man tongue-tied in the presence of John Hancock to the man who would not take his hat off to the officer of the ship named *Hancock*. Did he cast off his deference to Hancock? Hewes's affirmation of his worth as a human being was a form of class consciousness. Implicit in the idea, "I am as good as any man regardless of rank or wealth," was the idea that any poor man might be as good as any rich man. This did not mean that all rich men were bad. On the contrary, in Boston, more than any other major colonial seaport, a majority of the merchants were part of the patriot coalition; "divers Gentelmen of Good Fortunes," as Hutchinson put it, were with the "Rabble." This blunted class consciousness. Boston's mechanics, unlike New York's or Philadelphia's, did not develop mechanic committees or a mechanic consciousness before the Revolution. Yet in Boston the rich were forced to defer to the people in order to obtain or retain their support. Indeed, the entire public career of Hancock from 1765 on—distributing largesse, buying uniforms for Pope's Day marchers, building ships to employ artisans—can be understood as an exercise of this kind of deference, proving his civic virtue and patriotism. . . .

Hewes in effect had brought Hancock down to his own level. The poor shoemaker had not toppled the wealthy merchant; he was no "leveller." But the rich and powerful—the men in "ruffles"—had become, in his revealing word, his "associates." John Hancock and George Hewes breaking open the same chest at the Tea Party remained for Hewes a symbol of a moment of equality. To the shoemaker, one suspects, this above all was what the Revolutionary events of Boston meant, as did the war that followed.

George III

The American Revolution had many victims—the dead and wounded, the loyalists who went into exile, and a host of others. But perhaps the most dramatic victim (though the loss was bloodless) was the habitual reverence the king's loyal subjects felt for His Majesty. In fact, it was only at the moment of revolution that Americans could bring themselves to stop complaining about Parliament, or the Board of Trade, and to address their complaints directly to their revered monarch, George III. You can gather something about the completeness of the shift by comparing the following illustrations. The first is a woodcut depicting George III that appeared in a schoolbook published in America in 1770. The second shows a mob attacking a statue of the same king just five years later. Do the two pictures have implications about social class as well as politics? How would you characterize the dress and expression attributed to George III in the first picture? What generalization can you make about the dress and manner of the mob in the second picture? Do the pictures add anything to the essay on George Robert Twelves Hewes? Do they challenge his memory of urban unrest?

GEORGE III. by the Grace of GOD, of GREAT-BRITAIN, FRANCE and IRELAND, King, Defender of the Faith.

In ev'ry Stroke, in ev'ry Line,
Does some exalted Virtue shine;
And *Albion*'s Happiness we trace,
In every Feature of his Face.

Woodcut frontispiece to Watt's *Speller*, 1770. The Granger Collection, New York.

Pulling down the statue of George III. Print Collection, Miriam & Ira D. Wallach Division of Art, Prints & Photographs, The New York Public Library, Astor, Lenox and Tilden Foundations.

Common Sense, 1776

Thomas Paine

No one who wrote about the Revolution had an influence even remotely comparable to that of Thomas Paine, an English radical who had come to Philadelphia only in 1774. Paine's pamphlet Common Sense, *published in 1776, was quickly an astonishing success. Within months, it had sold 150,000 copies. Paine's success was a result, in part, of his rhetorical skills. He was simply a master propagandist. But* Common Sense *was significant for another reason, too: Paine realized before many of his countrymen that the time for reason had passed. And so had the time for emotional appeals to British sentiment. The colonies were at war, and* Common Sense *was a war document that intended to fasten words like brute and savage on the enemy. For whom do you think Paine thought he was writing? Englishmen or Americans? Men like John Hancock or ordinary folk like George Robert Twelves Hewes? Or was he addressing what he called "Mankind"?*

. . . Volumes have been written on the subject of the struggle between England and America . . . but all have been ineffectual, and the period of debate is closed. Arms, as the last resource, decide the contest; the appeal was the choice of the king, and the continent hath accepted the challenge. . . .

From Thomas Paine, *Common Sense* (1776) in Moncure Daniel Conway, ed., *The Writings of Thomas Paine*, Putnam, New York, 1894, vol. I, pp. 67–120.

I have heard it asserted by some, that as America hath flourished under her former connexion with Great-Britain, that the same connexion is necessary towards her future happiness. . . . Nothing can be more fallacious than this kind of argument. We may as well assert that because a child has thrived upon milk, that it is never to have meat, or that the first twenty years of our lives is to become a precedent for the next twenty. But even this is admitting more than is true, for I answer roundly, that America would have flourished as much, and probably much more, had no European power had any thing to do with her. The commerce, by which she hath enriched herself, are the necessaries of life, and will always have a market while eating is the custom of Europe.

But she has protected us, say some. . . .

Alas, we have been long led away by ancient prejudices, and made large sacrifices to superstition. We have boasted the protection of Great-Britain, without considering, that her motive was *interest* not *attachment*; that she did not protect us from *our enemies* on *our account*, but from *her enemies* on *her own account*, from those who had no quarrel with us on any *other account*, and who will always be our enemies on the *same account*. Let Britain wave her pretensions to the continent, or the continent throw off the dependance, and we should be at peace with France and Spain were they at war with Britain. . . .

But Britain is the parent country, say some. Then the more shame upon her conduct. Even brutes do not devour their young, nor savages make war upon their families; . . . but it happens not to be true, or only partly so. . . . Europe, and not England, is the parent country of America. This new world hath been the asylum for the persecuted lovers of civil and religious liberty from *every part* of Europe. Hither have they fled, not from the tender embraces of the mother, but from the cruelty of the monster; and it is so far true of England, that the same tyranny which drove the first emigrants from home, pursues their descendants still. . . .

But admitting, that we were all of English descent, what does it amount to? Nothing. Britain, being now an open enemy, extinguishes every other name and title: And to say that reconciliation is our duty is truly farcical. The first king of England, of the present line (William the Conqueror) was a Frenchman, and half the Peers of England are descendants from the same country; wherefore, by the same method of reasoning, England ought to be governed by France. . . .

I challenge the warmest advocate for reconciliation, to shew a single advantage that this continent can reap by being connected with Great-Britain. I repeat the challenge, not a single advantage is derived. Our corn will fetch its price in any market in Europe, and our imported goods must be paid for buy them where we will.

But . . . any submission to, or dependance on Great-Britain, tends directly to involve this continent in European wars and quarrels; and sets us at variance with nations, who would otherwise seek our friendship, and against whom we have neither anger nor complaint. As Europe is our market for trade, we ought to form no partial connection with any part of it. It is the true interest of America to steer clear of European contentions, which she never can do, while by her dependance on Britain, she is made the make-weight in the scale of British politics.

Europe is too thickly planted with kingdoms to be long at peace, and whenever a war breaks out between England and any foreign power, the trade of America goes to ruin, *because of her connection with Britain.* The next war may not turn out like the last, and should it not, the advocates for reconciliation now, will be wishing for separation then, because, neutrality in that case, would be a safer convoy than a man of war. Every thing that is right or natural pleads for separation. The blood of the slain, the weeping voice of nature cries, 'TIS TIME TO PART. Even the distance at which the Almighty hath placed England and America is a strong and natural proof that the authority of the one, over the other, was never the design of Heaven. The time likewise at which the continent was discovered adds weight to the argument, and the manner in which it was peopled encreases the force of it. The reformation was preceded by the discovery of America, as if the Almighty graciously meant to open a sanctuary to the persecuted in future years, when home should afford neither friendship nor safety.

The authority of Great-Britain over this continent, is a form of government, which sooner or later must have an end: And a serious mind can draw no true pleasure by looking forward, under the painful and positive conviction, that what he calls "the present constitution" is merely temporary. . . .

As to government matters, it is not in the power of Britain to do this continent justice: The business of it will soon be too weighty, and intricate, to be managed with any tolerable degree of convenience, by a power so distant from us, and so very ignorant of us; for if they cannot conquer us, they cannot govern us. To be always running three or four thousand miles with a tale or a petition, waiting four or five months for an answer, which when obtained requires five or six more to explain it in, will in a few years be looked upon as folly and childishness—There was a time when it was proper, and there is a proper time for it to cease.

Small islands not capable of protecting themselves are the proper objects for kingdoms to take under their care; but there is something very absurd in supposing a continent to be perpetually governed by an island. In no instance hath nature made the satellite larger than its primary planet, and as England and America, with respect to each other, reverses the common order of nature, it is evident they belong to different systems; England to Europe, America to itself. . . .

But admitting that matters were now made up, what would be the event? I answer, the ruin of the continent. And that for several reasons.

First. The powers of governing still remaining in the hands of the king, he will have a negative over the whole legislation of this continent. And as he hath shewn himself such an inveterate enemy to liberty, and discovered such a thirst for arbitrary power; is he, or is he not, a proper man to say to these colonies, *"You shall make no laws but what I please."* And is there any inhabitant in America so ignorant, as not to know, that according to what is called the *present constitution*, that this continent can make no laws but what the king gives leave to; and is there any man so unwise, as not to see, that (considering what has happened) he will suffer no law to be made here, but such as suit *his* purpose. We may be as effectually enslaved by the want of laws in America, as by submitting to laws made for us in England. After matters are made up (as it is called) can there be any doubt, but the whole power of the crown will be exerted, to keep this continent as low and humble as possible? Instead of going forward we shall go backward, or be perpetually quarrelling or ridiculously petitioning.—We are already greater than the king wishes us to be, and will he not hereafter endeavour to make us less? To bring the matter to one point. Is the power who is jealous of our prosperity, a proper power to govern us? Whoever says No to this question, is an *independant*, for independancy means no more, than, whether we shall make our own laws, or whether the king, the greatest enemy this continent hath, or can have, shall tell us *"there shall be no laws but such as I like."*

But the king you will say has a negative in England; the people there can make no laws without his consent. In point of right and good order, there is something very ridiculous, that a youth of twenty-one (which hath often happened) shall say to several millions of people, older and wiser than himself, I forbid this or that act of yours to be law. But in this place I decline this sort of reply, though I will never cease to expose the absurdity of it, and only answer, that England being the King's residence, and America not so, makes quite another case. The king's negative *here* is ten times more dangerous and fatal than it can be in England, for *there* he will scarcely refuse his consent to a bill for putting England into as strong a state of defence as possible, and in America he would never suffer such a bill to be passed. . . .

Secondly. That as even the best terms, which we can expect to obtain, can amount to no more than a temporary expedient, or a kind of government by guardianship, which can last no longer than till the colonies come of age, so the general face and state of things, in the interim, will be unsettled and unpromising. Emigrants of property will not choose to come to a country whose form of government hangs but by a thread, and who is every day tottering on the brink of commotion and disturbance; and numbers of the present inhabitants would lay hold of the interval, to dispose of their effects, and quit the continent.

But the most powerful of all arguments, is, that nothing but independance, i.e. a continental form of government, can keep the peace of the continent and preserve it inviolate from civil wars. I dread the event of a reconciliation with Britain now, as it is more than probable, that it will be followed by a revolt somewhere or other, the consequences of which may be far more fatal than all the malice of Britain.

Thousands are already ruined by British barbarity; (thousands more will probably suffer the same fate) Those men have other feelings than us who have nothing suffered. All they *now* possess is liberty, what they before enjoyed is sacrificed to its service, and having nothing more to lose, they disdain submission. . . .

But where, says some, is the King of America? I'll tell you. Friend, he reigns above, and doth not make havoc of mankind like the Royal Brute of Britain. Yet that we may not appear to be defective even in earthly honors, let a day be solemnly set apart for proclaiming the charter; let it be brought forth placed on the divine law, the word of God; let a crown be placed thereon, by which the world may know, that so far we approve of monarchy, that in America the law is king. For as in absolute governments the King is law, so in free countries the law ought to be King; and there ought to be no other. But lest any ill use should afterwards arise, let the crown at the conclusion of the ceremony, be demolished, and scattered among the people whose right it is.

A government of our own is our natural right: And when a man seriously reflects on the precariousness of human affairs, he will become convinced, that it is infinitely wiser and safer, to form a constitution of our own in a cool deliberate manner, while we have it in our power, than to trust such an interesting event to time and chance. . . .

Ye that tell us of harmony and reconciliation, can ye restore to us the time that is past? Can ye give to prostitution its former innocence? Neither can ye reconcile Britain and America. The last cord now is broken, the people of England are presenting addresses against us. There are injuries which nature cannot forgive; she would cease to be nature if she did. As well can the lover forgive the ravisher of his mistress, as the continent forgive the murders of Britain. The Almighty hath implanted in us these unextinguishable feelings for good and wise purposes. They are the guardians of his image in our hearts. They distinguish us from the herd of common animals. The social compact would dissolve, and justice be extirpated from the earth, or have only a casual existence were we callous to the touches of affection. The robber, and the murderer, would often escape unpunished, did not the injuries which our tempers sustain, provoke us into justice.

O ye that love mankind! Ye that dare oppose, not only the tyranny, but the tyrant, stand forth! Every spot of the old world is overrun with oppression. Freedom hath been hunted round the globe. Asia, and Africa, have long expelled her—Europe regards her like a stranger, and England hath given her warning to depart. O! receive the fugitive, and prepare in time an asylum for mankind. . . .

Silencing the Tories

The following documents tell us more about the patriot treatment of Tories, who probably constituted about 20 percent of the population—potentially a powerful and dangerous force opposing the American Revolution. The first is a cartoon drawn in London mocking the way the rebels treated John Malcolm, the haughty Boston Tory who played a central role in Hewes's life. What do the clothes tell you about the kinds of people the British thought were in rebellion? Look at the facial features. How does the cartoonist try to convince us that John Malcolm is made of finer stuff than the men who have tarred and feathered him?

The second document is part of a letter from a Tory woman, Ann Hulton, another Bostonian. How do the two documents differ? Which document do you find more convincing? More revealing? Do either help us understand the behavior of George Robert Twelves Hewes? Or why Hewes became an independent citizen who "would not take off his hat to any man"?

The BOSTONIAN'S Paying the EXCISE-MAN, or TARRING & FEATHERING

Library of Congress.

Ann Hulton to Mrs. Lightbody.

Boston, January 31, 1774

. . . But the most shocking cruelty was exercised a few nights ago, upon a poor old man, a tidesman, one Malcolm. He is reckoned creasy, a quarrel was picked with him, he was afterward taken and tarred and feathered. There's no law that knows a punishment for the greatest crimes beyond what this is of cruel torture. And this instance exceeds any other before it. He was stript stark naked, one of the severest cold nights this winter, his body covered all over with tar, then with feathers, his arm dislocated in tearing off his cloaths. He was dragged in a cart with thousands attending, some beating him with clubs and knocking him out of the cart, then in again. They gave him several severe whippings, at different parts of the town. This spectacle of horror and sportive cruelty was exhibited for about five hours.

The unhappy wretch they say behaved with the greatest intrepidity and fortitude all the while. Before he was taken, [he] defended himself a long time against numbers, and afterwards when under torture they demanded of him to curse his masters, the King, Governor, etc., which they could not make him do, but he still cried, "Curse all traitors!" They brought him to the gallows and put a rope about his neck, saying they would hang him. He said he wished they would, but that they could not, for God was above the Devil. The doctors say that it is impossible this poor creature can live. They say his flesh comes off his back in stakes.

It is the second time he has been tarred and feathered and this is looked upon more to intimidate the judges and others than a spite to the unhappy victim tho' they owe him a grudge for some things particularly. He was with Govr. Tryon in the battle with the Regulators and the Governor has declared that he was of great servise to him in that affair, by his undaunted spirit encountering the greatest dangers.

Govr. Tryon had sent him a gift of ten guineas just before this inhuman treatment. He has a wife and family and an aged father and mother who, they say, saw the spectacle which no indifferent person can mention without horror.

These few instances amongst many serve to shew the abject state of government and the licentiousness and barbarism of the times. There's no majestrate that dare or will act to suppress the outrages. No person is secure. There are many objects pointed at, at this time, and when once marked out for vengeance, their ruin is certain.

The judges have only a week's time allowed them to consider whether they will take the salaries from the Crown or no. Govr. Hutchinson is going to England as soon as the season will permit.

We are under no apprehension at present on our own account but we can't look upon our safety secure for long.

From Ann Hulton, *Letters of a Loyalist Lady . . . 1767–1776*, Cambridge, Mass., 1927, pp. 70–72.

THE BIG PICTURE

It often has been argued that the American Revolution took place first in the "hearts and minds" of the colonists, and that once the colonists decided to revolt the war that followed was secondary. What are the merits and weaknesses of this generalization?

Take a virtual marching tour of the Philadelphia Campaign (1777) of the American Revolution at http://www.ushistory.org/march/.   @ ON THE WEB

Chapter 6

Creating the Constitution

Interpretive Essay by Alfred F. Young 132

Sources 140

> Ratification 140
>
> The Virginia Debates 142
>
> The Meaning of the Slave Trade Provision 147
>
> Designing the Nation's Capitol 149

The Big Picture 152

The new nation brought into being by the Revolution stretched from the Atlantic to the Mississippi. It was a huge wilderness by European standards, six times the size of England and Wales combined, but thinly populated. Although most of the 3 to 4 million inhabitants lived near the Atlantic, the population had begun to move into the forests beyond the seaboard, farther and farther away from the centers of communication. So poor were communications and so rudimentary were transportation facilities that the country was little more than a collection of isolated communities. There were only six cities with over 8,000 inhabitants. The largest was Philadelphia, with some 40,000, followed by New York, Boston, Charleston, Baltimore, and Salem. Ninety-five percent of the population lived elsewhere, on isolated farms or in small villages, scattered from Maine to Georgia.

How could 3 to 4 million people, dispersed over a vast wilderness, be governed? That question was faced by every state in the Revolutionary period, and also by the new nation. But it was never really resolved. Laws were passed and orders were given, but there was simply no way that a handful of government officials could force a scattered—and somewhat unruly—population to obey the law. And few officials were foolish enough to try.

Instead, America's leaders were content to fashion a new system of government. And that, to them, was exciting. They saw themselves as daring innovators, creating a republic in a world of monarchies, establishing a new government not only for themselves but "for millions yet unborn." Wrote John Adams in 1776: "You and I, my dear friend, have been sent into life at a time when the greatest lawgivers of antiquity would have wished to live. How few of the human race have enjoyed an opportunity of making an election of government for themselves or their children."

It would be foolish to ignore this self-perception. But it would be equally foolish to forget that nine-tenths of those who had the chance to mold the new government were men of property, members of the colonial elite, old hands at government. Clearly, their vision of the new order was tempered by experience. But was it also tempered by self-interest? That question has been raised particularly in regard to the men who met in Philadelphia in 1787, destroyed the first system of federal government, and established the present system.

INTERPRETIVE ESSAY

The Framers and the People

Alfred F. Young

The modern debate over the nature of the Constitutional Convention has been dominated by two opinions. One is that the Founding Fathers were men of detached and lofty perceptions, men of principle who tried to embody those principles in a frame of government they hoped would endure for generations. The other is that the members of the convention were men of property whose actions were tied directly to their own economic stake in the outcome. In the following selection, Alfred F. Young takes a somewhat different stance. He agrees that the framers of the Constitution represented the interests of slaveholding planters, merchants, and "monied men." But they accommodated the "genius" of the people, not because they were saints but because they feared the wrath of ordinary citizens. As you read, try to determine what these accommodations were. And what, if anything, these accommodations cost the governing elite.

On June 18, 1787, about three weeks into the Constitutional Convention at Philadelphia, Alexander Hamilton delivered a six-hour address that was easily the longest and most conservative the Convention would hear. Gouverneur Morris, a delegate from Pennsylvania, thought it was "the most able and impressive he had ever heard."

Beginning with the premise that "all communities divide themselves into the few and the many," "the wealthy well born" and "the people," Hamilton added the corollary that the "people are turbulent and changing; they seldom judge or determine right." Moving through history, the delegate from New York developed his ideal for a national government that would protect the few from "the imprudence of democracy" and guarantee "stability and permanence": a president and senate indirectly elected for life ("to serve during good behavior") to balance a house directly elected by a popular vote every three years. This "elective monarch" would have an absolute veto over laws passed by Congress. And the national government would appoint the governors of the states, who in turn would have the power to veto any laws by the state legislatures.

If others quickly saw a resemblance in all of this to the king, House of Lords, and House of Commons of Great Britain, with the states reduced to colonies ruled by royal governors, they were not mistaken. The British constitution, in Hamilton's view, remained "the best model the world has ever produced."

Alfred F. Young, "The Framers of the Constitution and the 'Genius' of the People," *Radical History Review*, vol. 42, Fall 1988, pp. 8–18. Reprinted with permission from C MARHO: The Radical Historians' Organization. Originally published in *Radical History Review*, vol. 42, Fall 1988.

Three days later a delegate reported that Hamilton's proposals "had been praised by everybody," but "he has been supported by none." Acknowledging that his plan "went beyond the ideas of most members," Hamilton said he had brought it forward not "as a thing attainable by us, but as a model which we ought to approach as near as possible." When he signed the Constitution the framers finally agreed to on September 17, 1787, Hamilton could accurately say, "no plan was more remote from his own."

Why did the framers reject a plan so many admired? To ask this question is to go down a dark path into the heart of the Constitution few of its celebrants care to take. We have heard so much in our elementary and high school civics books about the "great compromises" within the Convention—between the large states and the small states, between the slaveholders and nonslaveholders, between north and south—that we have missed the much larger accommodation that was taking place between the delegates as a whole at the Convention and what they called "the people out of doors."

The Convention was unmistakably an elite body. The official exhibit for the bicentennial, "Miracle at Philadelphia," opens appropriately enough with a large oil portrait of Robert Morris, a delegate from Philadelphia, one of the richest merchants in America, and points out elsewhere that eleven out of fifty-five delegates were business associates of Morris's. The fifty-five were weighted with merchants, slaveholding planters and "monied men" who loaned money at interest. Among them were numerous lawyers and college graduates in a country where most men and only a few women had the rudiments of a formal education. They were far from a cross section of the 4 million or so Americans of that day, most of whom were farmers or artisans, fishermen or seamen, indentured servants or laborers, half of whom were women and about 600,000 of whom were African-American slaves.

❧ *I. The First Accommodation*

Why did this elite reject Hamilton's plan that many of them praised? James Madison, the Constitution's chief architect, had the nub of the matter. The Constitution was "intended for the ages." To last it had to conform to the "genius" of the American people. "Genius" was a word eighteenth-century political thinkers used to mean spirit: we might say character or underlying values.

James Wilson, second only to Madison in his influence at Philadelphia, elaborated on the idea. "The British government cannot be our model. We have no materials for a similar one. Our manners, our law, the abolition of entail and primogeniture," which made for a more equal distribution of property among sons, "the whole genius of the people, are opposed to it."

This was long-range political philosophy. There was a short-range political problem that moved other realistic delegates in the same direction. Called together to revise the old Articles of Confederation, the delegates instead decided to scrap [them] and frame an entirely new constitution. It would have to be submitted to the people for ratification, most likely to conventions elected especially for the purpose. Repeatedly, conservatives recoiled from extreme proposals for which they knew they could not win popular support.

In response to a proposal to extend the federal judiciary into the states, Pierce Butler, a South Carolina planter, argued, "the people will not bear such innovations. The states will revolt at such encroachments." His assumption was "we must follow the example of Solomon, who gave the Athenians not the best government he could devise but the best they would receive."

The suffrage debate epitomized this line of thinking. Gouverneur Morris, Hamilton's admirer, proposed that the national government limit voting for the House to men who owned a freehold, i.e., a substantial farm, or its equivalent. "Give the vote to people who have no property and they will sell them to the rich who will be able to buy them," he said with some prescience. George Mason, author of Virginia's Bill of Rights, was aghast. "Eight or nine states have extended the right of suffrage beyond the freeholders. What will people there say if they should be disfranchised?"

Benjamin Franklin, the patriarch, speaking for one of the few times in the convention, paid tribute to "the lower class of freemen" who should not be disfranchised. James Wilson explained, "it would be very hard and disagreeable for the same person" who could vote for representatives for the state legislatures "to be excluded from a vote for this in the national legislature." Nathaniel Gorham, a Boston merchant, returned to the guiding principle: "the people will never allow" existing rights to suffrage to be abridged. "We must consult their rooted prejudices if we expect their concurrence in our propositions."

The result? Morris's proposal was defeated and the convention decided that whoever each state allowed to vote for its own assembly could vote for the House. It was a compromise that left the door open and in a matter of decades allowed states to introduce universal white male suffrage.

❧ II. Ghosts of Years Past

Clearly there was a process of accommodation at work here. The popular movements of the revolutionary era were a presence at the Philadelphia Convention even if they were not present. The delegates, one might say, were haunted by ghosts, symbols of the broadly based movements elites had confronted in the making of the revolution from 1765 to 1775, in waging the war from 1775 to 1781, and in the years since 1781 within their own states.

The first was the ghost of Thomas Paine, the most influential radical democrat of the revolutionary era. In 1776 Paine's pamphlet *Common Sense* (which sold at least 150,000 copies), in arguing for independence, rejected not only King George III but the principle of monarchy and the so-called checks and balances of the unwritten English constitution. In its place he offered a vision of a democratic government in which a single legislature would be supreme, the executive minimal, and representatives would be elected from small districts by a broad electorate for short terms so they could "return and mix again with the voters." John Adams considered *Common Sense* too "democratical," without even an attempt at "mixed government" that would balance "democracy" with "aristocracy."

The second ghost was that of Abraham Yates, a member of the state senate of New York typical of the new men who had risen to power in the 1780s in the state legislatures. We have forgotten him; Hamilton, who was very conscious of him, called him "an old Booby." He had begun as a shoemaker and was a self-taught lawyer and warm foe of the landlord aristocracy of the Hudson Valley into which Hamilton had married. As James Madison identified the "vices of the political system of the United States" in a memorandum in 1787, the Abraham Yateses were the number-one problem. The state legislatures had "an itch for paper money" laws, laws that prevented foreclosure on farm mortgages, and tax laws that soaked the rich. As Madison saw it, this meant that "debtors defrauded their creditors" and "the landed interest has borne hard on the mercantile interest." This, too, is what Hamilton had in mind when he spoke of the "depredations which the democratic spirit is apt to make on property" and what others meant by the "excess of democracy" in the states.

The third ghost was a very fresh one—Daniel Shays. In 1786 Shays, a captain in the revolution, led a rebellion of debtor farmers in western Massachusetts that the state quelled with its own somewhat unreliable militia. There were "combustibles in every state," as George Washington put it, raising the specter of "Shaysism." This Madison enumerated among the "vices" of the system as "a want of guaranty to the states against internal violence." Worse still, Shaysites in many states were turning to the political system to elect their own kind. If they succeeded they would produce legal Shaysism, a danger for which the elites had no remedy.

The fourth ghost we can name the ghost of Thomas Peters, although he had a thousand other names. In 1775, Peters, a Virginia slave, responded to a plea by the British to fight in their army and win their freedom. He served in an "Ethiopian Regiment," some of whose members bore the emblem "Liberty to Slaves" on their uniforms. After the war the British transported Peters and several thousand escaped slaves to Nova Scotia from whence Peters eventually led a group to return to Africa and the colony of Sierra Leone, a long odyssey to freedom. Eighteenth-century slaveholders, with no illusions about happy or contented slaves, were haunted by the specter of slaves in arms.

III. Elite Divisions

During the revolutionary era elites divided in response to these varied threats from below. One group, out of fear of "the mob" and then "the rabble in arms," embraced the British and became active loyalists. After the war most of them went into exile. Another group who became patriots never lost their obsession with coercing popular movements.

"The mob begins to think and reason," Gouverneur Morris observed in 1774. "Poor reptiles, they bask in the sunshine and ere long they will bite." A snake had to be scotched. Others thought of the people as a horse that had to be whipped. This was coercion.

Far more important, however, were those patriot leaders who adopted a strategy of "swimming with a stream which it is impossible to stem." This was the metaphor of Robert R. Livingston, Jr., like Morris, a gentleman with a large tenanted estate in New York. Men of his class had to learn to "yield to the torrent if they hoped to direct its course."

Livingston and his group were able to shape New York's constitution, which some called a perfect blend of "aristocracy" and "democracy." John Hancock, the richest merchant in New England, had mastered his kind of politics and emerged as the most popular politician in Massachusetts. In Maryland Charles Carroll, a wealthy planter, instructed his anxious father about the need to "submit to partial losses" because "no great revolution can happen in a state without revolutions or mutations of private property. If we can save a third of our personal estate and all of our lands and Negroes, I shall think ourselves well off."

The major leaders at the Constitutional Convention in 1787 were heirs to both traditions: coercion and accommodation—Hamilton and Gouverneur Morris to the former, James Madison and James Wilson much more to the latter.

They all agreed on coercion to slay the ghosts of Daniel Shays and Thomas Peters. The Constitution gave the national government the power to "suppress insurrections" and protect the states from "domestic violence." There would be a national army under the command of the president and authority to nationalize the state militias and suspend the right of habeas corpus in "cases of rebellion or invasion." In 1794 Hamilton, as secretary of the treasury, would exercise such powers fully (and needlessly) to suppress the Whiskey Rebellion in western Pennsylvania.

Southern slaveholders correctly interpreted the same powers as available to shackle the ghost of Thomas Peters. As it turned out, Virginia would not need a federal army to deal with Gabriel Prosser's insurrection in 1800 or Nat Turner's rebellion in 1830, but a federal army would capture John Brown after his raid at Harpers Ferry in 1859.

But how to deal with the ghosts of Thomas Paine and Abraham Yates? Here Madison and Wilson blended coercion with accommodation. They had three solutions to the threat of democratic majorities in the states.

Their first was clearly coercive. Like Hamilton, Madison wanted some kind of national veto over the state legislatures. He got several very specific curbs on the states written into fundamental law: no state could "emit" paper money or pass "laws impairing the obligation of contracts." Wilson was so overjoyed with these two clauses that he argued that if they alone "were inserted in the Constitution I think they would be worth our adoption."

But Madison considered the overall mechanism adopted to curb the states "short of the mark." The Constitution, laws, and treaties were the "supreme law of the land" and ultimately a federal court could declare state laws unconstitutional. But this, Madison lamented, would only catch "mischiefs" after the fact. Thus they had clipped the wings of Abraham Yates but he could still fly.

The second solution to the problem of the states was decidedly democratic. They wanted to do an end-run around the state legislatures. The Articles of Confederation, said Madison, rested on "the pillars" of the state legislatures who elected delegates to Congress. The "great fabric to be raised would be more stable and durable if it should rest on the solid grounds of the people themselves"; hence, there would be popular elections to the House.

Wilson altered only the metaphor. He was for "raising the federal pyramid to a considerable altitude and for that reason wanted to give it as broad a base as possible." They would slay the ghost of Abraham Yates with the ghost of Thomas Paine.

This was risky business. They would reduce the risk by keeping the House of Representatives small. Under a ratio of one representative for every 30,000 people, the first house would have only 65 members; in 1776 Thomas Paine had suggested 390. But still, the House would be elected every two years, and with each state allowed to determine its own qualifications for voting, there was no telling who might end up in Congress.

There was also a risk in Madison's third solution to the problem of protecting propertied interests from democratic majorities: "extending the sphere" of government. Prevailing wisdom held that a republic could only succeed in a small geographic area; to rule an "extensive" country, some kind of despotism was considered inevitable.

Madison turned this idea on its head in his since famous *Federalist* essay No. 10. In a small republic, he argued, it was relatively easy for a majority to gang up on a particular "interest." "Extend the sphere," he wrote, and "you take in a greater variety of parties and interests." Then it would be more difficult for a majority "to discover their own strength and to act in unison with each other."

This was a prescription for a noncolonial empire that would expand across the continent, taking in new states as it dispossessed the Indians. The risk was there was no telling how far the "democratic" or "leveling" spirit might go in such likely would-be states as frontier Vermont, Kentucky, and Tennessee.

❧ IV. Democratic Divisions

In the spectrum of state constitutions adopted in the revolutionary era, the federal Constitution of 1787 was, like New York's, somewhere between "aristocracy" and "democracy." It therefore should not surprise us—although it has eluded many modern critics of the Constitution—that in the contest over ratification in 1787–1788, the democratic minded were divided.

Among agrarian democrats there was a gut feeling that the Constitution was the work of an old class enemy. "These lawyers and men of learning and monied men," argued Amos Singletary, a working farmer at the Massachusetts ratifying convention, "expect to be managers of this Constitution and get all the power and all the money into their own hands and then will swallow up all of us little folks . . . just as the whale swallowed up Jonah."

Democratic leaders like Melancton Smith of New York focused on the small size of the proposed House. Arguing from Paine's premise that the members of the legislature should "resemble those they represent," Smith feared that "a substantial yeoman of sense and discernment will hardly ever be chosen" and the government "will fall into the hands of the few and the great." Urban democrats, on the other hand, including a majority of the mechanics and tradesmen of the major cities who in the revolution had been a bulwark of Paineite radicalism, were generally enthusiastic about the Constitution. They were impelled by their urgent stake in a stronger national government that would advance ocean-going commerce and protect American manufacturers from competition. But they would not have been as ardent about the new frame of government without its saving graces. It clearly preserved their rights to suffrage. And the process of ratification, like the Constitution itself, guaranteed them a voice. As early as 1776 the New York Committee of Mechanics held it as "a right which God has given them in common with all men to judge whether it be consistent with their interest to accept or reject a constitution."

Mechanics turned out en masse in the parades celebrating ratification, marching trade by trade. The slogans and symbols they carried expressed their political ideals. In New York the upholsterers had a float with an elegant "Federal Chair of State" flanked by the symbols of Liberty and Justice that they identified with the Constitution. In Philadelphia the bricklayers put on their banner "Both buildings and rulers are the work of our hands."

Democrats who were skeptical found it easier to come over because of the Constitution's redeeming features. Thomas Paine, off in Paris, considered the Constitution "a copy, though not quite as base as the original, of the form of the British government." He had always opposed a single executive and he objected to the "long duration of the Senate." But he was so convinced of "the absolute necessity" of a stronger federal government that "I would have voted for it myself had I been in America or even for a worse, rather than have none." It was crucial to Paine that there was an amending process, the means of "remedying its defects by the same appeal to the people by which it was to be established."

❧ V. The Second Accommodation

In drafting the Constitution in 1787 the framers, self-styled Federalists, made their first accommodation with the "genius" of the people. In campaigning for its ratification in 1788 they made their second. At the outset, the conventions in the key states—Massachusetts, New York, and Virginia—either had an anti-Federalist majority or were closely divided. To swing over a small group of "antis" in each state, Federalists had to promise that they would consider amendments. This was enough to secure ratification by narrow margins in Massachusetts, 187 to 168; in New York, 30 to 27; and in Virginia, 89 to 79.

What the anti-Federalists wanted were dozens of changes in the structure of the government that would cut back national power over the states, curb the powers of the presidency as well as protect individual liberties. What they got was far less. But in the first Congress in 1789, James Madison, true to his pledge, considered all the amendments and shepherded twelve amendments through both houses. The first two of these failed in the states; one would have enlarged the House. The ten that were ratified by December 1791 were what we have since called the Bill of Rights, protecting freedom of expression and the rights of the accused before the law. Abraham Yates considered them "trivial and unimportant." But other democrats looked on them much more favorably. In time the limited meaning of freedom of speech in the First Amendment was broadened far beyond the framers' original intent. Later popular movements thought of the Bill of Rights as an essential part of the "constitutional" and "republican" rights that belonged to the people.

✎ VI. The "Losers" Role

There is a cautionary tale here that surely goes beyond the process of framing and adopting the Constitution and Bill of Rights from 1787 to 1791. The Constitution was as democratic as it was because of the influence of popular movements that were a presence, even if not present. The losers helped shape the results. We owe the Bill of Rights to the opponents of the Constitution, as we do many other features in the Constitution put in to anticipate opposition.

In American history popular movements often shaped elites, especially in times of crisis when elites were concerned with the "system." Elites have often divided in response to such threats and according to their perception of the "genius" of the people. Some have turned to coercion, others to accommodation. We run serious risk if we ignore this distinction. Would that we had fewer Gouverneur Morrises and Alexander Hamiltons and more James Madisons and James Wilsons to respond to the "genius" of the people.

To read the text of the Constitution and the first ten amendments, visit http://www.law.cornell. edu/constitution/constitution.overview.html.

@ ON THE WEB

Ratification

There was considerable agreement on at least the major point among the members of the Constitutional Convention: a stronger central government was needed to replace the Confederation of the States. But when the Constitution was sent out to the country, not even this initial assumption was widely shared. The result was that after sailing through four or five state ratifying conventions with ease, the Constitution ran into bitter opposition in such key states as Massachusetts, Virginia, and New York. In those states the supporters of the Constitution, as Young noted, were able to win majorities only by promising a host of amendments to the Constitution. The most exciting fight was in New York, where the Constitution squeaked through by a mere three votes. The map on page 141, and the table below giving the order of ratification, will give you some idea of how the Constitution fared from state to state. Do you see any patterns in the vote? Is it fair to say that the seaboard was for the Constitution and the back country was generally against it? What would have happened if New York, Virginia, or Massachusetts had gone the other way? It took only nine states to ratify the Constitution, but could the new government have survived without one of these key states?

Order of Ratification

State	Date	Vote in Convention	Rank in Population	1790 Population
1. Delaware	Dec. 7, 1787	Unanimous	13	59,096
2. Pennsylvania	Dec. 12, 1787	46 to 23	3	433,611
3. New Jersey	Dec. 18, 1787	Unanimous	9	184,139
4. Georgia	Jan. 2, 1788	Unanimous	11	82,548
5. Connecticut	Jan. 9, 1788	128 to 40	8	237,655
6. Massachusetts (incl. Maine)	Feb. 7, 1788	187 to 168	2	475,199
7. Maryland	Apr. 28, 1788	63 to 11	6	319,728
8. South Carolina	May 23, 1788	149 to 73	7	249,073
9. New Hampshire	June 21, 1788	57 to 46	10	141,899
10. Virginia	June 26, 1788	89 to 79	1	747,610
11. New York	July 26, 1788	30 to 27	5	340,241
12. North Carolina	Nov. 21, 1789	195 to 77	4	395,005
13. Rhode Island	May 29, 1790	34 to 32	12	69,112

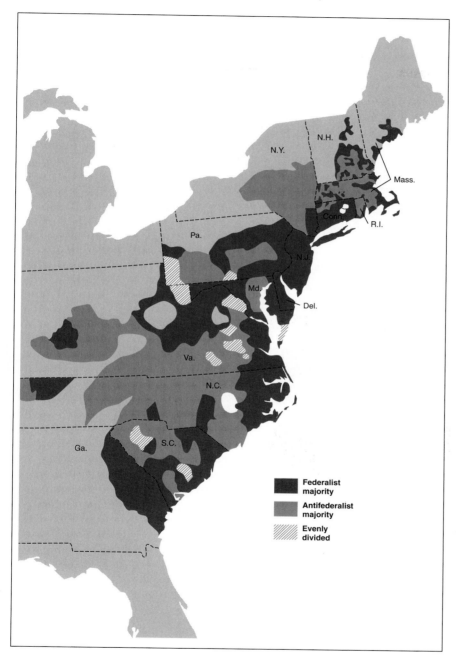

Voting for ratification.

The Virginia Debates

Proud Virginia, the biggest and most populous state, was sharply divided over the Constitution. Only by promising a Bill of Rights, and by making good use of the knowledge that Washington would undoubtedly be the first president, were the supporters of the Constitution able to win ratification by an 89 to 79 vote.

Here are some selections from one of the significant debates in Virginia. What opinions divided the proponents of the Constitution (who seized the name "Federalists" for themselves) from its opponents (who seem to have been left with the uninspired title of "Antifederalists")?

Some historians, notably Charles Beard early in the twentieth century, have argued that the Constitution was a political maneuver by the elite designed to protect their economic position and interests. Other historians have disagreed and have seen the Constitution as an able response to a political, not an economic or social, problem. What evidence can you find in the following debate to support either point of view?

Many years later, Abraham Lincoln argued that the nation had been conceived in liberty and dedicated to the proposition that all men are created equal. Which of these two values, liberty or equality, can you find expressed in the debate between Mason and Pendleton?

DEBATES

Mr. George Mason: Mr. Chairman, whether the Constitution be good or bad, the present clause clearly discovers that it is a national government, and no longer a Confederation. I mean that clause which gives the first hint of the general government laying direct taxes. The assumption of this power of laying direct taxes does, of itself, entirely change the confederation of the states into one consolidated government. This power, being at discretion, unconfined, and without any kind of control, must carry every thing before it. The very idea of converting what was formerly a confederation to a consolidated government, is totally subversive of every principle which has hitherto governed us. This power is calculated to annihilate totally the state governments. Will the people of this great community submit to be individually taxed by two different and distinct powers? Will they suffer themselves to be doubly harassed? These two concurrent powers cannot exist long together; the one will destroy the other: the general government being paramount to, and in every respect more powerful than the state governments, the latter must give way to the former. . . . Was there ever an instance of a general national government extending over so extensive a country, abounding in such a variety of climates, &c., where the people retained their liberty? I solemnly declare that no man is a greater friend to a firm union of the American states

From Jonathan Elliott, ed., *The Debates in the Several State Conventions on the Adoption of the Federal Constitution*, Jonathan Elliott, Washington, D.C., 1836, vol. 3, pp. 29–38, 80–84.

than I am; but, sir, if this great end can be obtained without hazarding the rights of the people, why should we recur to such dangerous principles? . . .

The mode of levying taxes is of the utmost consequence; and yet here it is to be determined by those who have neither knowledge of our situation nor a common interest with us, nor a fellow-feeling for us.

Why should we give up this dangerous power of individual taxation? Why leave the manner of laying taxes to those who, in the nature of things, cannot be acquainted with the situation of those on whom they are to impose them, when it can be done by those who are well acquainted with it? . . .

. . . There is one thing in it which I conceive to be extremely dangerous. Gentlemen may talk of public virtue and confidence; we shall be told that the House of Representatives will consist of the most virtuous men on the continent, and that in their hands we may trust our dearest rights. This, like all other assemblies, will be composed of some bad and some good men; and, considering the natural lust of power so inherent in man, I fear the thirst of power will prevail to oppress the people.

But my principal objection is, that the Confederation is converted to one general consolidated government, which, from my best judgment of it, (and which perhaps will be shown, in the course of this discussion, to be really well founded,) is one of the worst curses that can possibly befall a nation. Does any man suppose that one general national government can exist in so extensive a country as this? I hope that a government may be framed which may suit us, by drawing a line between the general and state governments, and prevent that dangerous clashing of interest and power, which must, as it now stands, terminate in the destruction of one or the other. When we come to the judiciary, we shall be more convinced that this government will terminate in the annihilation of the state governments: the question then will be, whether a consolidated government can preserve the freedom and secure the rights of the people.

MR. PENDLETON: Mr. Chairman, my worthy friend has expressed great uneasiness in his mind, and informed us that a great many of our citizens are also extremely uneasy, at the proposal of changing our government; but that, a year ago, before this fatal system was thought of, the public mind was at perfect repose. It is necessary to inquire whether the public mind was at ease on the subject, and if it be since disturbed, what was the cause. What was the situation of this country before the meeting of the federal Convention? Our general government was totally inadequate to the purpose of its institution; our commerce decayed; our finances deranged; public and private credit destroyed: these and many other national evils rendered necessary the meeting of that Convention. If the public mind was then at ease, it did not result from a conviction of being in a happy and easy situation: it must have been an inactive, unaccountable stupor. The federal Convention devised the paper on your table as a remedy to remove our political diseases. What has created the public uneasiness since? Not public reports, which are not to be depended upon; but mistaken apprehensions of danger, drawn from observations on government which do not apply to us. When we come to inquire into the origin of most governments of the world, we shall find that they are generally dictated by a conqueror, at the point of the sword, or are the offspring of confusion, when a great popular leader, taking advantage of circumstances, if not producing them, restores order at the expense of liberty, and becomes the tyrant over the people. It may well be supposed that, in forming a government of this sort, it will not be favorable to liberty: the conqueror will take care of his own emoluments, and have little concern for the interest of the people. In either case, the interest and ambition of a despot, and not the good of the people, have given the tone to the government. A government thus formed must necessarily create a continual war between the governors and governed.

Writers consider the two parties (the people and tyrants) as in a state of perpetual warfare, and sound the alarm to the people. But what is our case? We are perfectly free from sedition and war: we are not yet in confusion: we are left to consider our real happiness and security: we want to secure these objects: we know they cannot be attained without government. Is there a single man, in this committee, of a contrary opinion? What was it that brought us from a state of nature of society, but to secure happiness? And can society be formed without government? Personify government: apply to it as a friend to assist you, and it will grant your request. This is the only government founded in real compact. There is no quarrel between government and liberty; the former is the shield and protector of the latter. The war is between government and licentiousness, faction, turbulence, and other violations of the rules of society, to preserve liberty. Where is the cause of alarm? We, the people, possessing all power, form a government, such as we think will secure happiness: and suppose, in adopting this plan, we should be mistaken in the end; where is the cause of alarm on that quarter? . . .

But an objection is made to the form: the expression, We, the people, is thought improper. Permit me to ask the gentlemen who made this objection, who but the people can delegate powers? Who but the people have a right to form government? The expression is a common one, and a favorite one with me. The representatives of the people, by their authority, is a mode wholly inessential. If the objection be, that the Union ought to be not of the people, but of the state governments, then I think the choice of the former very happy and proper. What have the state governments to do with it? Were they to determine, the people would not, in that case, be the judges upon what terms it was adopted.

But the power of the Convention is doubted. What is the power? To propose, not to determine. This power of proposing was very broad; it extended to remove all defects in government: the members of that Convention, who were to consider all the defects in our general government, were not confined to any particular plan. Were they deceived? This is the proper question here. Then the question must be between this government and the Confederation. The latter is no government at all. It has been said that it has carried us, through a dangerous war, to a happy issue. Not that Confederation, but common danger, and the spirit of America, were bonds of our union: union and unanimity, and not that insignificant paper, carried us through that dangerous war. "United, we stand; divided, we fall!" echoed and reëchoed through America—from Congress to the drunken carpenter—was effectual, and procured the end of our wishes, though now forgotten by gentlemen, if such there be, who incline to let go this stronghold, to catch at feathers; for such all substituted projects may prove.

[*Mr. Madison* then arose. . . .]

Before I proceed to make some additions to the reasons which have been adduced by my honorable friend over the way, I must take the liberty to make some observations on what was said by another gentleman, (Mr. Patrick Henry.) He told us that this Constitution ought to be rejected because it endangered the public liberty, in his opinion, in many instances. Give me leave to make one answer to that observation: Let the dangers which this system is supposed to be replete with be clearly pointed out: if any dangerous and unnecessary powers be given to the general legislature, let them be plainly demonstrated; and let us not rest satisfied with general assertions of danger, without examination. If powers be necessary, apparent danger is not a sufficient reason against conceding them. He has suggested that licentiousness has seldom produced the loss of liberty; but that the tyranny of rulers has almost always effected it. Since the general civilization of mankind, I believe there are more instances of the abridgment of the freedom of the people by gradual and silent encroachments of those in power, than by violent and sudden usurpations; but, on a candid examination of history, we shall find that turbulence, violence, and abuse of power, by the majority trampling on the rights of the minority, have produced factions and commotions, which, in republics, have, more frequently than any other cause, produced despotism. If we go over the whole history of ancient and modern republics, we shall find their destruction to have generally resulted from those causes. If we consider the peculiar situation of the United States, and what are the sources of that diversity of sentiment which pervades its inhabitants, we shall find great danger to fear that the same causes may terminate here in the same fatal effects which they produced in those republics. This danger ought to be wisely guarded against. Perhaps, in the progress of this discussion it will appear that the only possible remedy for those evils, and means of preserving and protecting the principles of republicanism, will be found in that very system which is now exclaimed against as the parent of oppression.

I must confess I have not been able to find his usual consistency in the gentleman's argument on this occasion. He informs us that the people of the country are at perfect repose—that is, every man enjoys the fruits of his labor peaceably and securely, and that every thing is in perfect tranquility and safety. I wish sincerely, sir, this were true. If this be their happy situation, why has every state acknowledged the contrary? Why were deputies from all the states sent to the general Convention? Why have complaints of national and individual distresses been echoed and reëchoed throughout the continent? Why has our general government been so shamefully disgraced, and our Constitution violated? Wherefore have laws been made to authorize a change, and wherefore are we now assembled here? A federal government is formed for the protection of its individual members. Ours has attacked itself with impunity. Its authority has been disobeyed and despised. I think I perceive a glaring inconsistency in another of his arguments. He complains of this Constitution, because it requires the consent of at least three-fourths of the states to introduce amendments which shall be necessary for the happiness of the people. The assent of so many he urges as too great an obstacle to the admission of salutary amendments, which, he strongly insists, ought to be at the will of a bare majority. We hear this argument, at the very moment we are called upon to assign reasons for proposing a constitution which puts it in the power of nine states to abolish the present inadequate, unsafe, and pernicious Confederation! In the first case, he asserts that a majority ought to have the power of altering the government, when found to be inadequate to the security of public happiness. In the last case, he affirms that even three-fourths of the community have not a right to alter a government which experience has proved to be subversive of national felicity! nay, that the most necessary and urgent alterations cannot be made without the absolute unanimity of all the states! Does not the thirteenth article of the Confederation expressly require that no alteration shall be made without the unanimous consent of all the states? Could any thing in theory be more perniciously improvident and injudicious than this submission of the will of the majority to the most trifling minority? Have not experience and practice actually manifested this theoretical inconvenience to be extremely impolitic? Let me mention one fact, which I conceive must carry conviction to the mind of any one: the smallest state in the Union has obstructed every attempt to reform the government; that little member has repeatedly disobeyed and counteracted the general authority; nay, has even supplied the enemies of its country with provisions. Twelve states had agreed to certain improvements which were proposed, being thought absolutely necessary to preserve the existence of the general government; but as these improvements, though really indispensable, could not, by the Confederation, be introduced into it without the consent of every state, the refractory dissent of that little state prevented their adoption. The inconveniences resulting from this requisition, of unanimous concurrence in alterations in the Confederation, must be known to every member in this Convention; it is therefore needless to remind them of them. Is it not self-evident that a trifling minority ought not to bind the majority? Would not foreign influence be exerted with facility over a small minority? Would the honorable gentleman agree to continue the most radical defects in the old system, because the petty state of Rhode Island would not agree to remove them? . . .

To read more about the debates surrounding the adoption of the Constitution, see http://lcweb2.loc.gov/ammem/amlaw/lwed.html.

The Meaning of the Slave Trade Provision

Charles Cotesworth Pinckney and James Wilson

One of Young's arguments is that the Founding Fathers were canny politicians who knew the hopes and fears of their constituents. The following speeches were made by two members of the 1787 convention, in defense of the same clause of the Constitution—the provision that Congress could not prohibit the international slave trade until after 1808. In the first speech, Charles Cotesworth Pinckney defends the clause to a proslavery audience in his home state of South Carolina. In the second, Pennsylvanian James Wilson tells his audience why they should accept the provision. As you read the two speeches, note the extent to which each man defends the clause as the best compromise that could be achieved in the circumstances. Does this seem consistent with Young's way of characterizing the convention? If you thought the Constitution was a bundle of just such compromises, would you still regard it as a great document?

South Carolina

GEN. CHARLES COTESWORTH PINCKNEY: . . . then said he would make a few observations on the objections which the gentleman had thrown out on the restrictions that might be laid on the African trade after the year 1808. On this point your delegates had to contend with the religious and political prejudices of the Eastern and Middle States, and with the interested and inconsistent opinion of Virginia, who was warmly opposed to our importing more slaves. I am of the same opinion now as I was two years ago, when I used the expressions the gentleman has quoted—that, while there remained one acre of swamp-land uncleared of South Carolina, I would raise my voice against restricting the importation of negroes. I am as thoroughly convinced as that gentleman is, that the nature of our climate, and the flat, swampy situation of our country, obliges us to cultivate our lands with negroes, and that without them South Carolina would soon be a desert waste.

You have so frequently heard my sentiments on this subject, that I need not now repeat them. It was alleged, by some of the members who opposed an unlimited importation, that slaves increased the weakness of any state who admitted them; that they were a dangerous species of property, which an invading enemy could easily turn against ourselves and the neighboring states; and that, as we were allowed a representation for them in the House of Representatives, our influence in government would be increased in proportion as we were less able to defend ourselves. "Show some period," said the members from the Eastern States, "when it may be in our power to put a stop, if we please, to the importation of this weakness, and we will endeavor, for your convenience, to restrain the religious and political prejudices of our

From Jonathan Elliott, ed., *The Debates in the Several State Conventions on the Adoption of the Federal Constitution*, Jonathan Elliott, Washington, D.C., 1836, vol. 2, p. 452; vol. 4, pp. 285–286.

people on this subject." The Middle States and Virginia made us no such proposition; they were for an immediate and total prohibition. We endeavored to obviate the objections that were made in the best manner we could, and assigned reasons for our insisting on the importation, which there is no occasion to repeat, as they must occur to every gentleman in the house: a committee of the states was appointed in order to accommodate this matter, and, after a great deal of difficulty, it was settled on the footing recited in the Constitution.

By this settlement we have secured an unlimited importation of negroes for twenty years. Nor is it declared that the importation shall be then stopped; it may be continued. We have a security that the general government can never emancipate them, for no such authority is granted; and it is admitted, on all hands, that the general government has no powers but what are expressly granted by the Constitution, and that all rights not expressed were reserved by the several states. We have obtained a right to recover our slaves in whatever part of America they may take refuge, which is a right we had not before. In short, considering all circumstances, we have made the best terms for the security of this species of property it was in our power to make. We would have made better if we could; but, on the whole, I do not think them bad.

Pennsylvania

MR. JAMES WILSON: . . . With respect to the clause restricting Congress from prohibiting the *migration or importation of such persons* as any of the states now existing shall think proper to admit, prior to the year 1808, the honorable gentleman says that this clause is not only dark, but intended to grant to Congress, for that time, the power to admit the importation of *slaves*. No such thing was intended. But I will tell you what was done, and it gives me high pleasure that so much was done. Under the present Confederation, the states may admit the importation of slaves as long as they please; but by this article, after the year 1808, the Congress will have power to prohibit such importation, notwithstanding the disposition of any state to the contrary. I consider this as laying the foundation for banishing slavery out of this country; and though the period is more distant than I could wish, yet it will produce the same kind, gradual change, which was pursued in Pennsylvania. It is with much satisfaction I view this power in the general government, whereby they may lay an interdiction on this reproachful trade: but an immediate advantage is also obtained; for a tax or duty may be imposed on such importation, not exceeding ten dollars for each person; and this, sir, operates as a partial prohibition; it was all that could be obtained. I am sorry it was no more; but from this I think there is reason to hope, that yet a few years and it will be prohibited altogether; and in the mean time, the new states which are to be formed will be under the control of Congress in this particular, and slaves will never be introduced amongst them. . . .

To read more about the United States Constitution and the international slave trade, see http://www.archives.gov/research_room/alic/reference_desk/slavery_records.html.

Designing the Nation's Capitol

After the Constitution was ratified, the creative effort was not over with. It was followed by another bold plan, the creation of the city of rulers that the world today knows as Washington, D.C. Within four years of the ratification of the Constitution, the leaders of the new government, who met first at New York and then at Philadelphia, made plans to turn wetlands along the Potomac into the nation's capital. The plans were no less detailed than the Constitution, and they provide eloquent testimony about the kind of government that many of the Founding Fathers envisaged.

Consider, for example, the Capitol building, the home of the Senate and the House of Representatives, and until 1935 of the Supreme Court. In 1791 George Washington and other political leaders agreed with the French architect Pierre Charles L'Enfant that the Capitol should be located at the crest of Jenkins' Hill, the highest point in the envisioned city. And in 1792 the government offered a prize of $500 and a piece of property in the District of Columbia to whoever submitted the best design.

Following are some of the designs that were offered. You will notice that the designers, most of whom were rank amateurs, emphasized symmetry, domes, monumentality. Why do you think they did that? And why do you think the nation's leaders chose William Thornton's design as best suited for a community of republican rulers? Why did Etienne Hallet's plan rank as second best? What do the winning plans tell you about the kind of government that the Founding Fathers envisaged?

This design, submitted by Samuel Dobie, included three enormous statues on the building's roof. The Maryland Historical Society, Baltimore, Maryland.

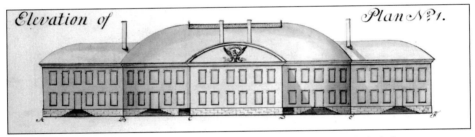

Contemporaries felt that the design submitted by Charles Wintersmith lacked elegance. The Maryland Historical Society, Baltimore, Maryland.

Etienne Hallet's plan placed second in the competition, but he was chosen to supervise the actual construction according to Thornton's design. Library of Congress.

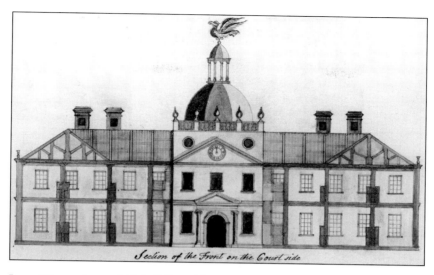

James Diamond capped his building with an enormous weathercock. The Maryland Historical Society, Baltimore, Maryland.

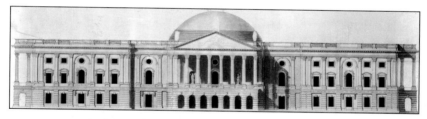

William Thornton's design was praised by President Washington for its "Grandeur, Simplicity and Convenience." It called for a central rotunda flanked by two identical wings, one for the Senate and the other for the House of Representatives. The above drawing is a slightly revised version of his first plan, which has been lost. Library of Congress.

William Thornton. Library of Congress.

THE BIG PICTURE

Both the Constitution of 1787 and the plans for building the nation's Capitol reflect the values of the Founding Fathers. What exactly were these values? What kind of society did the Founding Fathers have in mind? Which of their values to you find commendable? Contemptible?

Chapter 7

Federalists and Republicans

Interpretive Essay by John Steele Gordon 155
Sources 167
>   The Fight Begins 167
>   Truth Versus Treason 169
>   Roughhouse Politics 171
>   Affairs of Honor 172
The Big Picture 175

The Constitution created only the framework of the new government. The details still had to be worked out. At first the Federalists, under Presidents George Washington and John Adams, tried to build a consolidated and aristocratic nation. They were convinced that the fear of disunity and anarchy was so great that Americans would accept almost any sort of strong national government. They were dead wrong. Their goals ran against the grain of the Revolutionary impulse. Indeed, they were so out of touch with the realities of American life that they came close to provoking a second revolution. Only the electoral victory of the Republican opposition in 1800 ended this threat.

The very existence of a Republican opposition pointed to a serious problem on which the Constitution had been totally silent: the problem of political parties. To the men who wrote the Constitution, the idea of parties and factions was an evil one—as evil as the idea of democracy. Their conception of a successful government was one in which there were no factions. To a few sophisticated men, especially to James Madison, faction seemed to be an inevitable feature of human society. But, Madison believed, a well-framed government was one in which faction could *not* express itself in party.

The problem with political parties, of course, was that they led to disunity and disruption. They fed the ambitions of unscrupulous men. They gave demagogues a chance to excite the masses, and so led toward mob rule and an anarchic democracy. Madison, in a famous paper in the series known as *The Federalist*, had even argued that the republic should be large, so that no faction could easily seize control of it. In short, the leaders of the first period of American history were still committed to the idea of a society in which status and deference were more fundamental than ideology or faction.

In his famous farewell address, Washington spent much more time warning against the spirit of faction and party than he did trying to persuade his fellow citizens not to become involved in entangling alliances with European powers. And the warning was well taken. Washington, during his second administration especially, had watched while a faction developed into a party, a party of opposition to the very policies that he and his successor, John Adams, pursued.

The opposition leader was Thomas Jefferson, Washington's secretary of state, who lost the presidency to John Adams in 1796, but defeated him in 1800. He has been portrayed most vividly as an ideologist who feared both national and presidential power; who believed that states' rights should be predominant; that the small farmer was the foundation of the good society; that the threat to American life was the growth of big cities, industrialization, national banking, an urban proletariat, and a consolidated national government; that the best governments were those that governed least. He has also been portrayed as a revolutionary dreamer who made radical statements such as this about the need for revolutions every twenty years or so: "The tree of liberty must be refreshed from time to time with the blood of patriots and tyrants. It is its natural manure."

INTERPRETIVE ESSAY

The Hamiltonian Miracle

John Steele Gordon

What was the executive branch of the new government to be like? How was it to relate to Congress? The Constitution provided only a rough outline. The actual working arrangements had to be created by its first occupants, and in this respect the presidency of George Washington was critical.

Washington was the towering figure of his age, larger than life, treated like a god even before his presidency, a virtual monument long before his likeness was carved into stone. He self-consciously played the role of Father of his Country and did it very well. But no one expected him to handle the day-to-day business of the federal government. That was not his style. As expected, he created a cabinet to

Alexander Hamilton. Engraving by John F. E. Prud'homme after a miniature by Archibald Robertson. Courtesy American Antiquarian Society.

John Steele Gordon, *Hamilton's Blessing: The Extraordinary Life and Times of Our National Debt*, Walker and Company, New York, 1997, pp. 18–39.

formulate and implement executive policy. And, because the new nation had been born in debt and had terrible credit, the most important of the cabinet offices under Washington was certain to be the Treasury.

That he put in the hands of Alexander Hamilton, who had been his aide-de-camp during the Revolutionary War. Hamilton prided himself on being a doer, a man who weighed the options, made the tough decisions, and forged ahead. He quickly became a lightening rod in the nation's politics. For many he was a "miracle" worker—as the following account by John Steele Gordon makes clear. But "Hamilton's miracle" also generated violent opposition. Thousands sang his praises, but thousands more vilified him. Why was that the case? And why did "Hamiltonianism" become the springboard for one political battle after another, decade after decade, well into the nineteenth century?

. . . Hamilton was not like the other Founding Fathers. He was the only one of the major figures of the early Republic who was not born in what is now the United States. Instead he was born on the minor British West Indian island of Nevis and came to manhood on what was then the Danish island of St. Croix, now part of the U.S. Virgin Islands.

Further, he was the only Founding Father, other than the ancient and by then venerable Benjamin Franklin, who was not born into the higher levels of the local society of his native colony. Rather, in the brisk, if not altogether accurate, phrase of his political enemy John Adams, Hamilton was "the bastard brat of a Scotch pedlar."

Hamilton was certainly a bastard, but his father was not a peddler. He came, in fact, from an ancient Scottish family, being a younger son of the laird of Cambuskeith. But Hamilton's father was an utter failure as a businessman. He soon parted from his family, and Hamilton's mother was forced to open a small store to feed her two sons. Hamilton became a clerk in the trading concern of Nicholas Cruger and David Beekman at Christiansted, St. Croix, at the age of eleven or thirteen. (There is some doubt about Hamilton's birth date. Nearly contemporary documents imply it was 1755. Hamilton said it was 1757.) So bright and energetic was the young Hamilton—for his tainted birth had instilled a ferocious ambition to get ahead—that by the time he was in his midteens he was managing the concern.

Nicholas Cruger belonged to an old and powerful New York mercantile family, and he early recognized the talent of his young clerk. When he returned to New York in 1771 because of ill health, he left Hamilton in charge. Soon he helped his young employee come to New York to further his education including the study of law. Hamilton, still in his teens, left St. Croix in October 1772, never to see the West Indies again.

With the rapidly deteriorating relations between Great Britain and its American colonies, Hamilton threw in his lot with his new country. His immense talents and his capacity for work soon secured him an important role in the Revolution—as Washington's aide-de-camp—and its aftermath. When Washington became president under the new Constitution, on April 30th, 1789, he asked Robert Morris, known as "the financier of the Revolution" because of his success at finding money and supplies for the

Continental army, to become secretary of the treasury. But Morris, intent on making money, turned him down.

He recommended Hamilton instead. Morris and Hamilton had been in correspondence for several years about the country's fiscal crisis and how to solve it, and Hamilton, still in his early twenties, had greatly impressed the elder man. As early as 1781, as the Revolution still continued, Hamilton had written Morris regarding the establishment of a proper national debt on the British model. "A national debt, if it is not excessive, will be to us a national blessing," he wrote. "It will be a powerful cement to our union. It will also create a necessity for keeping up taxation to a degree which, without being oppressive, will be a spur to industry."

Washington was happy to appoint his old comrade in arms, and Hamilton, now in his early thirties, gladly gave up a lucrative law practice in New York to accept.

Hamilton's background would always set him apart and give him an outlook on life and politics the other Founding Fathers did not share. It also made him uniquely qualified to establish the financial basis of the new United States. Far more than Jefferson, Washington, Adams, and Madison, Hamilton was a nationalist. Perhaps because he had grown up viewing the colonies on the continent only from afar, his loyalty to the United States as a whole was unalloyed by any loyalty to a particular state, not even New York where he spent his adult life.

Also, Hamilton was by far the most urban and the most commercial-minded of the men who made the country. He had grown up, almost literally, in a counting house and lived most of his life in what had already long been the most cosmopolitan and commercial-minded city in the country. In 1784 he had founded a bank that continues to this day, the Bank of New York, and would found a newspaper that also lives, the *New York Post*. Washington, Jefferson, Madison, and even Adams were far more tied to the land than was Hamilton. Jefferson, especially, longed to see the United States as a country filled with self-sufficient yeoman farmers who shunned urban life. Hamilton, at home in the city and deeply learned in both the theory and practice of finance, saw far more clearly than Jefferson how the winds of economic change were blowing in the late eighteenth century.

Hamilton was always to be, to some extent, a social outsider. Today we tend to think of the American Revolution as having brought "democracy" to the thirteen colonies. In fact it brought no such thing. The eighteenth century was an age of aristocracy, and the American colonies were no exceptions. Each colony had its oligarchy of rich, established families who dominated the economic and, under the control of a royal governor, political affairs of that colony. To give just one instance of how pervasive was the sense of social hierarchy: Students enrolled at Harvard at this time were listed not according to the alphabetical order of their surnames but according to the social standing of their families in the community.

With the removal of royal control, these oligarchies inherited a near monopoly of political power in each colony. Although the population of the United States in 1787–88 was almost 4 million, only 160,000—4 percent of the whole—voted for delegates to the state conventions to ratify the new Constitution, the most important political event of their lives. Even when only adult white males are considered, fewer than 25 percent voted. It was not for lack of interest. Rather it was the right to vote was limited to those who owned substantial property, in other words, the oligarchs. That was precisely why the writers of the Constitution were so confident that Congress would be instinctively frugal.

The oligarchies, it need hardly be said, abused this monopoly of political power; monopolies, whether private or governmental, are always abused by those who hold them. The oligarchs often manipulated the legislatures to advance their own interests, such as suspending foreclosures for debt during the depressed economic conditions of the 1780s. And taxes tended to be laid more heavily on those without the vote such as small farmers and laborers. It was the latter that had led to Shays's Rebellion in Massachusetts.

Although Hamilton married the daughter of Philip Schuyler, one of the richest members of New York's "Knickerbocker Aristocracy," he never fully belonged to it himself. While he could be charming, especially with women, he was too driven, too ambitious for fame and glory, too unable to suffer fools gladly, to be completely accepted by the men. They recognized his brilliance, utilized his intellectual and financial skills, but they never forgot where Hamilton came from or the conditions of his birth.

Very nearly Congress's first act was to set about devising a federal tax system. On July 4, 1789, it passed the first Tariff Act, largely written by Hamilton, and henceforth import duties would usually provide the bulk of the federal government's revenues until the First World War. . . .

But, at first, tariffs were not enough. To gain more revenue, Congress passed excise taxes on carriages, distilled spirits, sugar, salt, and other items. Excise taxes are internal taxes on specific goods or on the privilege of doing business, and the tax on carriages was clearly a tax on the rich (only the rich, after all, could afford carriages) but a very modest one. Virginia quickly sued, claiming that the tax on carriages was a direct tax and thus had to be apportioned among the states according to population (in other words, according to the number of people, not carriages). Hamilton, at the request of the attorney general, argued the case for the federal government before the Supreme Court. The Court agreed with Hamilton that the carriage tax was an excise. This, as it happens, was the first time the Court addressed the constitutionality of an act of Congress.

The tax on liquor might seem to be the first of the "sin taxes," but the idea of alcohol as "demon rum" was, in fact, largely a nineteenth-century concept. Instead, liquor, sugar, and salt were taxed simply because they were three of the relatively few commodities then manufactured on an industrial scale and thus amenable to efficient tax collection.

The federal government quickly ran into a serious problem with the so-called whiskey tax. In most areas of the country, liquor distillers were too few in number to effectively protest the new tax, and, in any event, they could easily pass it along to their customers in higher prices. But the small farmers in western areas were blocked from eastern markets by the Appalachian Mountains. They had to convert their grain to whiskey before it was in a valuable enough form to bear the cost of transportation across the mountains. A 25 percent excise tax was a heavy economic burden for them, and they flared into rebellion in 1794, the first direct challenge to the authority of the new federal government. The rebellion was quickly and easily suppressed, and the two rebels who were convicted of treason were pardoned by President Washington. But the point was made that the new federal government could, and would, enforce its writ.

A revenue stream in place, Hamilton quickly turned to refunding the debt incurred in the Revolution and by the old national government. Indeed there was not much choice for the new Constitution commanded that the federal government assume the debts of the Confederation. The argument was over who should benefit from this refunding. Much of the debt, in the form of bonds, requisition IOUs, and continentals had fallen into the hands of wealthy merchants in the major cities, who had acquired it at far below par (its nominal face value), some for as little as 10 percent of that face value.

On January 14th, 1790, Hamilton submitted his first "Report on the Public Credit," which called for redeeming the old national debt on generous terms and issuing new bonds to pay for it, backed by the revenue from the tariff. The plan immediately became public knowledge in New York City—then the nation's temporary capital—but news of it spread only slowly, via horseback and sailing vessel, to the rest of the country. New York speculators moved at once to take advantage of the situation. They bought as many of the old bonds as they could, raising the price from 20–25 percent of par to about 40–45 percent.

There was an immediate outcry that these speculators should not be allowed to profit at the expense of those who had patriotically taken the old government's paper at par and then sold it for much less in despair or from necessity. James Jackson, a member of the House of Representatives from the sparsely settled frontier state of Georgia, was horrified by the avaricious city folk. "Since this report has been read in this house," he said in Congress, "a spirit of havoc, speculation, and ruin, has arisen, and been cherished by people who had access to the information the report contained, . . . Three vessels, sir, have sailed within a fortnight from this port [New York], freighted for speculation; they are intended to purchase up the State and other securities in the hands of the uninformed, though honest citizens of North Carolina, South Carolina, and Georgia. My soul rises indignant at the avaricious and immoral turpitude which so vile a conduct displays."

Elias Boudinot of New Jersey, wealthy and heavily involved in speculation himself, demurred. "I should be sorry," he said in reply, "if, on this occasion, the House should decide that speculations in the funds are violations of either the moral or political law. A government hardly exists in which such speculation is disallowed; . . . [I agree] that the spirit of speculation had now risen to an alarming height; but the only way to prevent its future effect, is to give the public funds a degree of stability as soon as possible." This, undoubtedly, was Hamilton's view as well.

James Madison, in the House of Representatives for Virginia, led the attempt to undercut the speculators. He proposed that the current holders of the old bonds be paid only the present market value and that the original bondholders be paid the difference between market value and face value. There were two weighty objections to this plan.

The first was one of simple practicality. Identifying the original holders of much of this paper would have been a bureaucratic nightmare, in many cases entirely impossible. Fraud would have been rampant. The second objection was one of justice. If an original bond holder had sold his bonds to another, "are we to disown the act of the party himself?" asked Elias Boudinot. "Are we to say, we will not be bound by your transfer, we will not treat with your representative, but insist on resettlement with you alone?"

Further, to have accepted Madison's scheme would have greatly impaired any future free market in U.S. government securities and thus greatly restricted the ability of the new government to borrow in the future. The reason was simple. If the government of the moment could decide, on its own, to whom it owed past debts, any government in the future would have a precedent to do the same. Politics would control the situation, and politics is always uncertain. There is nothing that markets hate more than uncertainty, and they weigh the value of stocks and bonds accordingly.

Hamilton, deeply versed in the ways of getting and spending, was well aware of this truth. Madison, a landowner and intellectual, was not. Hamilton, in his report, had been adamant. "It renders property in the funds less valuable, consequently induces lenders to demand a higher premium for what they lend, and produces every other inconvenience of a bad state of public credit."

Hamiton was anxious to establish the ability of the U.S. government to borrow when necessary. But he was also anxious to establish a well-funded and secure national debt for other reasons, for he was fully aware of the British experience with its national debt. Perhaps the greatest problem of the American economy at this time was a lack of liquid capital, which is to say, capital available for investment. Hamilton wanted to use the national debt to create a larger and more flexible money supply. Banks holding government bonds, he argued, could issue bank notes backed by them. He knew also that government bonds could serve as collateral for bank loans, multiplying the available capital, and that they would attract still more capital from Europe.

But there were still many people who failed to grasp the power of a national debt, properly funded and serviced, to bring prosperity to a national economy. John Adams, hardly stupid, was one. "Every dollar of a bank bill that is issued beyond the quantity of gold and silver in the vaults," he wrote, "represents nothing, and is therefore a cheat upon somebody."

Hamilton's reasoning eventually prevailed over Madison's, although not without a great deal of rhetoric. Hamilton's father-in-law, Philip Schuyler, by this time a senator from New York, owned more than $60,000 worth of government securities, a small fortune by the standards of the day. It was said that listening to the opposition speakers in the Senate made his hair stand "on end as if the Indians had fired at him." Rhetoric or no, the House passed Hamilton's funding proposals 36–13.

The second major part of Hamilton's program was for the new federal government to assume the debts that the individual states had incurred during the Revolutionary War. Hamilton thought these debts amounted to $25 million, although no one really knew for sure. It eventually turned out that only about $18 million in state bonds remained in circulation.

Again, opinion was sharply divided. Those states, such as Virginia, that had redeemed most of their bonds were adamantly opposed to assumption. Needless to say, those states, like the New England ones, that had not were all in favor of it. Financial speculators, hoping for a rise to par of bonds they had bought at deep discount, also favored the federal government assuming the state debts. But land speculators were opposed. Many states allowed public lands to be purchased with state bonds at face value, even when the bonds were selling in the open market for much less. Any rise in the price of bonds would increase the cost of land.

Madison and others argued that it was simply unfair for Virginians, who had nearly liquidated their state's bonded indebtedness, to pay all over again for the debts incurred by other states that had not. "Where, I again demand," thundered James Jackson of Georgia, "is the justice of compelling a State which has taxed her citizens for the sinking of her debt, to pay another proportion, not of her own, but the debts of other States, which have made no exertions whatever?"

Fisher Ames, a congressman from Massachusetts, argued that since the new Constitution gave all revenues from tariffs—the best and surest source of funds with which to pay the interest on the bonds—to the federal government, the federal government should now assume the debt. "Let the debts follow the funds," he demanded.

In the middle of April 1790, the House voted down Hamilton's proposal 31–29. Four more times it was voted down, each time by so narrow a margin that Hamilton had hopes of making a deal. He had to do something, for he had tied the funding of the old national debt and the assumption of the state debt into one bill. Many thought that the state debt issue was "a millstone about the neck of the whole system which must finally sink it."

Hamilton might have abandoned his effort to fund the state debts, but he had still one more reason for extinguishing as much state paper as possible and replacing it with federal bonds. The debts, of course, were largely held by the prosperous men of business, commerce, and agriculture—the oligarchs, in other words. These men's loyalties lay mainly with their respective states and the cozy local societies in which they had grown up. Although they had largely supported the creation of the new Union, Hamilton had every reason to suppose that their support would quickly fade away if their self-interest dictated it.

Hamilton, therefore, was anxious to make it in the self-interest of these men to continue their support of the Union. If they had a large share of their assets held in federal bonds, they would have powerful incentives for wishing the Union well. So he was willing to throw a very large bargaining chip onto the table to save his funding and assumption scheme. The new federal government had come into existence in New York City, and Hamilton, as well as nearly every other New Yorker, was hoping that the city would become the permanent capital. Certainly the city had gone to a lot of trouble to spruce itself up, spending £18,000 in the process. . . .*

Hamilton knew perfectly well that every state wanted the capital, and that Jefferson and Madison especially wanted the capital located in the rural South, away from what they regarded as the commerce and corruption of the cities. Hamilton intercepted Jefferson outside President Washington's Broadway mansion one day shortly after the bill's defeat and asked for help on getting his bill through Congress. Jefferson, who had opposed the adoption of the Constitution itself, and favored the states in nearly all federal-state disputes over the distribution of power, was opposed to the bill.

Nonetheless, he offered to meet Hamilton the following night for dinner, with Madison in attendance. There a deal was made. Enough votes would be switched to ensure passage of Hamilton's bill, in return for which Hamilton would throw his support to having the new capital located on the muddy and fever-ridden banks of the Potomac. To ensure Pennsylvania's cooperation, the temporary capital was to be moved to Philadelphia for ten years.

The deal was made, and the bill was passed and signed into law by President Washington. Hamilton was right that the bonds would find acceptance in the marketplace, and the entire issue sold out in only a few weeks. The new government, with a monopoly on customs duties and possessing the power to tax elsewhere, was simply a much better credit risk than the old government and the states had been. When it became clear that the U.S. government would be able to pay the interest due on these bonds, they quickly became sought after in Europe, just as Hamilton had hoped, especially after the outbreak of the war in which the other European powers tried to reverse the tide of the French Revolution.

The third major portion of Hamilton's program was the creation of a central bank, modeled after the Bank of England. Hamilton saw it as an instrument of fiscal efficiency, economic regulation, and money creation. Jefferson saw it as another giveaway to the rich and as a potential instrument of tyranny. Furthermore, Jefferson and Madison thought it was patently unconstitutional for the federal government to establish a bank, for the Constitution nowhere gives the federal government the explicit power to charter a bank or, for that matter, any other corporation.

There are three main purposes to a central bank. It acts as a depository for government funds and a means of transferring them from one part of the country to another (no small consideration in the primitive conditions of

---

*The dollar would largely replace the myriad other forms of currency in the 1790s, as the new federal government began to mint coins. Much old nomenclatural usage remained, however. An eighth of a dollar, twelve and a half cents, was known as a shilling until nearly the middle of the nineteenth century, despite the fact that the government never minted a coin of that denomination.

Hamilton's day). It is a source of loans to the government and to other banks, and it regulates the money supply.

The last was a great problem in the new Republic. Specie—gold and silver—was in critically short supply. Colonial coinage had been a hodge-podge of Spanish, Portuguese, and British coins, often cut into pieces in order to make small change.

The lack of specie forced merchants to be creative. In the southern colonies warehouse receipts for tobacco often circulated as money. Hamilton knew that foreign bonds could serve the same purpose. In his "Report on the Public Credit" he wrote: "It is a well-known fact that in countries in which the national debt is properly funded, and an object of established confidence, it answers most of the purposes of money. Transfers of stock, or public debt, are there equivalent to payments in specie; or, in other words, stock, in the principal transactions of business, passes current as specie. The same thing would, in all probability, happen here, under the like circumstances."

But the bonds, of course, were of very large denomination. There were a few state banks (three in 1790) to issue paper money, but these notes did not circulate on a national basis. Many business deals had to be accompanied by barter simply because there was no money to facilitate them.

Hamilton did not like the idea of the government itself issuing paper money because he felt that governments could not be trusted to exert self-discipline. Certainly the Continental Congress had shown none when it came to printing paper money, although at least it had the pretty good excuse of utter necessity. Hamilton thought that an independent central bank could supply not only a medium of exchange but the discipline needed to keep the money sound. If it issued notes that were redeemable in gold and silver on demand and accepted by the federal government in payment of taxes, those notes would circulate at par and relieve the desperate shortage of cash. Further, because the central bank could refuse the notes of state banks that got out of line—which would mean that no one else would take them either—it could supply discipline to those banks as well.

Hamilton proposed a capitalization of $10 million, a very large sum when it is considered that the three state banks in existence had a combined capital of only $2 million. The government was to subscribe 20 percent of this, but Hamilton intended the bank to be a private concern. "To attach full confidence to an institution of this nature," Hamilton wrote in his "Report on a National Bank" delivered to Congress on December 14th, 1790, "it appears to be an essential ingredient in its structure, that it shall be under a *private* not a *public* direction—under the guidance of *individual interest*, not of *public policy*; which would be supposed to be, and, in certain emergencies, under a feeble or too sanguine administration, would really be, liable to being too much influenced by *public necessity*." In other words, Hamilton did not believe that politicians could be trusted with the power to print money, whereas a privately held bank could, because its owners would go broke if they printed excessive amounts. The history of many countries, including, in his own time, France under the First Republic, would prove him right.

To make sure that the private owners of the bank did not pursue private interests at public expense, Hamilton wanted the bank's charter to require that its notes be redeemable in specie, that 20 percent of the seats on the board of directors be held by government appointees, and that the secretary of the treasury would have the right to inspect the books at any time.

There was little political discussion of the bank outside of Congress, which passed Hamilton's bill, the two houses splitting cleanly along sectional lines. Only one congressman from states north of Maryland voted against it, and only three from states south of Maryland voted for it.

Hamilton thought the bank was a fait accompli, but he had not reckoned on Thomas Jefferson and James Madison. Jefferson, the lover of rural virtues, had a deep, almost visceral hatred of banks, which he thought the epitome of all that was urban. "I have ever been the enemy of banks," he wrote years later to John Adams. "My zeal against those institutions was so warm and open at the establishment of the Bank of the U.S. that I was derided as a Maniac by the tribe of bank-mongers, who were seeking to filch from the public their swindling, and barren gains."

Jefferson and Madison, along with their fellow Virginian Edmund Randolph, the attorney general, wrote opinions for President Washington that the bank bill was unconstitutional. Their arguments revolved around the so-called necessary and proper clause, giving Congress the power to pass laws "necessary and proper for carrying into Execution the foregoing Powers."

The Constitution nowhere specifically authorizes the federal government to establish a central bank, they argued, and therefore one could be created only if it were indispensable for carrying out the government's enumerated duties. A central bank was not *absolutely* necessary and therefore was absolutely unconstitutional. This line of reasoning is known as *strict construction*—although the phrase itself was not actually coined until 1838—and has been a powerful force in the American political firmament ever since.

President Washington recognized the utility of a central bank, but Jefferson's and Randolph's argument had much force for him. Further, he may have worried that if the bank were established in Philadelphia, the capital might never make its way to his beloved Potomac. He told Hamilton that he could not sign the bill unless Hamilton was able to overcome Jefferson's constitutional argument.

To counter Jefferson's doctrine of strict construction, Hamilton devised a counter doctrine of *implied powers*. He said that if the federal government was to deal successfully with its enumerated duties, it must be supreme in deciding how best to perform those duties. "Little less than a prohibitory clause," he wrote to Washington, "can destroy the strong presumptions which result from the general aspect of the government. Nothing but demonstration should exclude the idea that the power exists." Moreover, he asserted that Congress had the right to decide what means were necessary and proper. "The national government like every other," he wrote, "must judge in the first instance of the proper exercise of its powers."

Hamilton's complete response to Jefferson and Randolph runs nearly 15,000 words and was written under an inflexible deadline, for the Constitution required President Washington to sign or veto the bill within ten days of its passage. Hamilton thought about his response for nearly a week but seems to have written it entirely in a single night. To read it today is to see plain the extraordinary powers of thought he possessed. Even John Marshall was awed by them. "To talents of the highest order," the great chief justice wrote, "he united a patient industry, not always the companion of genius, which fitted him in a peculiar manner for the difficulties to be encountered by the man who should be placed at the head of the American finances."

Washington, his doubts quieted, signed the bill in 1791, and the bank soon came into existence. Its stock subscription was a resounding success, for investors expected it to be very profitable, which it was. It also functioned as Hamilton intended and did much to further the early development of the American economy. State banks multiplied under its control—from 3 in 1790, to 29 by the turn of the century, to more than 100 a decade later.

Had Washington accepted Jefferson's argument and not Hamilton's, not only would the bank bill have been vetoed, but the development of the U.S. government would have been profoundly different. Indeed, it is hard to see how the Constitution could have long survived, at least without frequent amendment. Jefferson's doctrine of strict construction, rigorously applied, would have been a straitjacket, preventing the federal government from adapting to meet both the challenges and the opportunities that were to come in the future. Abraham Lincoln and Franklin Delano Roosevelt, for instance, would both push the Hamiltonian concept of implied powers very far in seeking to meet the immense national crises of the Civil War and the Great Depression.

Even Jefferson, once in the White House, would come to realize that strict constructionism was a doctrine that appeals mainly to those in opposition, not those who must actually exercise political power. Certainly he did not let the fact that the Constitution nowhere mentions the acquisition of territory from a foreign state stop him from snapping up the Louisiana Purchase from France when the opportunity arose.

Hamilton's financial program quickly, indeed utterly, transformed the country's financial circumstances. In the 1780s the United States had been a financial basket case. By 1794 it had the highest credit rating in Europe, and some of its bonds were selling at 10 percent over par. Talleyrand, who later became the French foreign minister, explained why. The United States bonds, he said, were "safe and free from reverses. They have been funded in such a sound manner and the prosperity of this country is growing so rapidly that there can be no doubt of their solvency." By 1801 Europeans held $33 million in U.S. securities, and European capital was helping mightily to build the American economy.

Less than two years after Hamilton's funding bill became law, trading in state and federal bonds had become so brisk in New York that brokers who specialized in them got together and formed an organization to facilitate trading. This organization would evolve into the New York Stock Exchange, and within a little more than 100 years it would be the largest such exchange in the world, eclipsing London's.

But Hamilton's program and its enactment had one great and entirely unanticipated consequence. It produced the first big political fight of the new federal union. It revealed deep and heretofore unsuspected cleavages in the American body politic. "When the smoke of the contest had cleared away," wrote Albert S. Bolles in his majestic *Financial History of the United States*, published a century ago, "two political parties might be seen, whose opposition, though varying much in conviction, power, and earnestness, has never ceased."

The Fight Begins

In protest to Hamilton's plan for the assumption of state debts, Patrick Henry drafted this remonstrance which was approved by both houses of the Virginia legislature. It caused Hamilton to remark: "This is the first symptom of a spirit which must either be killed, or will kill the Constitution of the United States." Strong words! But what triggered them? What were the two men fighting over? What was at stake? The debt and who would pay it? Political power and who would have it? Or the future of the nation?

In the House of Delegates,
    Thursday, the 16th of December, 1790.
    The General Assembly of the Commonwealth of Virginia to the United States in Congress assembled.
    Represent,
    That it is with great concern they find themselves compelled, from a sense of duty, to call the attention of Congress to an act of their last session, intitled "An act making provision for the debt of the United States," which the General Assembly conceive neither policy, justice nor the constitution warrants. Republican policy in the opinion of your memorialists could scarcely have suggested those clauses in the aforesaid act, which limit the right of the United States, in their redemption of the public debt. On the contrary they discern a striking resemblance between this system and that which was introduced into England, at the revolution; a system which has perpetuated upon that nation an enormous debt, and has moreover insinuated into the hands of the executive, an unbounded influence, which pervading every branch of the government, bears down all opposition, and daily threatens the destruction of everything that appertains to English liberty. The same causes produce the same effects! In an agricultural country like this, therefore to erect, and concentrate, and perpetuate a large monied interest, is a measure which your memorialists apprehend must in the course of human events produce one or other of two evils, the prostration of agriculture at the feet of commerce, or a change in the present form of federal government, fatal to the existence of American liberty.
    The General Assembly pass by various other parts of the said act which they apprehend will have a dangerous and impolitic tendency, and proceed to show the injustice of it as it applies to this Commonwealth. . . . Your memorialists turn away from the impolicy and injustice of the said act, and view it in another light, in which to them it appears still more odious and deformed.
    During the whole discussion of the federal constitution by the convention of Virginia, your memorialists were taught to believe "That every power not granted was retained;" under this impression and upon this

positive condition, declared in the instrument of ratification, the said government was adopted by the people of this Commonwealth; but your memorialists can find no clause in the constitution authorizing Congress to assume the debts of the states! As the guardians then of the rights and interests of their constituents, as sentinels placed by them over the ministers of the federal government, to shield it from their encroachments, or at least to sound the alarm when it is threatened with invasion, they can never reconcile it to their consciences, silently to acquiesce in a measure, which violates that hallowed maxim: a maxim on the truth and sacredness of which the federal government depended for its adoption in this Commonwealth. But this injudicious act not only deserves the censure of the General Assembly, because it is not warranted by the constitution of the United States, but because it is repugnant to an express provision of that constitution; this provision is "That all debts contracted and engagements entered into, before the adoption of this constitution, shall be as valid against the United States under this constitution as under the confederation," which amounts to a constitutional ratification of the contracts respecting the state debts in the situation in which they existed under the confederation, and resorting to that standard there can be no doubt that in the present question the rights of states as contracting with the United States must be considered as sacred.

The General Assembly of the Commonwealth of Virginia confide so fully in the justice and wisdom of Congress upon the present occasion, as to hope that they will revise and amend the aforesaid act generally, and repeal in particular, so much of it as relates to the assumption of the state debts.

December the 23d., 1790. Agreed to by the Senate.

Statutes at Large of Virginia, vol. XIII, pp. 237 ff.

Truth Versus Treason

American politics eventually was founded on the assumption that contests between major political parties are not struggles for control of the nation, but are contests between two groups, both legitimate and loyal, both with valid programs, both with patriotic voter support. In the early stages, however, this was not the assumption at all. The governing idea was simple: one party represented the real interests of the nation, the other was so misguided as to be downright treasonable. The following documents illustrate the point nicely.

The first is a Federalist depiction of Washington leading an army to put down the Whiskey Rebellion in western Pennsylvania. Notice how he is portrayed as saving the country. Notice also how Jefferson, the leader of the opposition party, is portrayed as giving traitorous aid and comfort to the enemy. His likeness speaks in pidgin French: "Stop de wheels of de gouvernement," thus supporting the Federalist notion that Jefferson was little better than an American agent of the French Revolution. The second set of documents are Republican handbills that appeared a decade later, in 1804 and 1807, after Jefferson won the presidency. Notice how they depict the Federalist followers of Washington and Hamilton as British agents, the servants of George III, and as men who would undo the hard-won triumphs of the American Revolution.

© Collection of The New-York Historical Society, [2737].

REPUBLICANS

Turn out, turn out and save your Country from ruin !

From an *Emperor*—from a *King*—from the iron grasp of a *British Tory Faction*—an unprincipled banditti of British speculators.   The hireling tools and emissaries of his majesty king George the 3d have thronged our city and diffused the poison of principles among us.

DOWN WITH THE TORIES, DOWN WITH THE BRITISH FACTION,

Before they have it in their power to enslave you, and reduce your families to distress by heavy taxation. Republicans want no Tribute-liars—they want no ship Ocean-liars—they want no Rufus King's for Lords —they want no Varick to lord it over them—they want no Jones for senator, who fought with the British against the Americans in time of the war.—But they want in their places such men as

Jefferson & Clinton,

who fought their Country's Battles in the year '76

The finiſhing
STROKE.
Every Shot's a Vote,
and every Vote
KILLS A TORY!

DO YOUR DUTY, REPUBLICANS,

Let your exertions this day

Put down the Kings

AND TYRANTS OF BRITAIN.

LAST DAY.

April, 1807.

Roughhouse Politics

On all sides, Americans were apparently convinced that party politics mobilized the worst passions of men. And it did seem to be true. In the early years of the republic, party politics was a roughhouse affair. Gentlemen fought in the streets, in taverns, and even in Congress itself. Here is a cartoon lampooning a famous brawl in the House of Representatives in February 1798. In the chair, wearing the silliest possible grin, is Speaker of the House Jonathan Dayton. The principals are, on the left, Republican Matthew Lyon, and, suitably on the right, Federalist representative Roger Griswold. What is the clerk at the lower left doing? Does any member have dignity, or are all shown as either involved or behaving almost as absurdly as Lyon and Griswold? The congressmen's clothing identifies them as members of the republic's elite. But what sets them apart from the impeccably upright George Washington? How have they failed? What connection can you draw between this cartoon and Jefferson's famous remark, after his victory in 1800, "We are all Republicans—we are all Federalists"?

He in a trice struck Lyon thrice
Upon his head, enraged sir.
© Collection of The New-York Historical Society, [33995].

Who seized the tongs to ease his wrongs
And Griswold thus engaged, sir.

Affairs of Honor

In addition to getting into brawls, politicians also challenged one another to duels. These so-called "affairs of honor" almost became commonplace. Hamilton was involved in eleven of them in the course of his life. The purpose was not to maim or kill, but to prove that a gentleman was willing to risk his life for his honor. Most thus followed a very precise ritual. There were, however, exceptions, and one of the more bizarre involved two Jeffersonian Republicans, DeWitt Clinton and John Swartout, who were locked in a fierce power struggle in 1802 for control of New York City and the New York Republican party. In most duels, the principals just stood face-to-face. In this duel, the seconds worked out a procedure where the principals had to spin and fire. Each time they missed, and each time Swartout insisted that he had not received "satisfaction" and they must fire again. Finally, after exchanging fire five times, Clinton declared the matter over. He was wrong. His enemies went after him, especially in this cartoon, portraying him as a coward, defecating into the wig of his second and saying "O my bowels! my bowels! they melt, they melt!"

A genuine View of the parties in an AFFAIR OF HONOR. after the fifth shot at Hobuken. 31st July 1802.

"*A Genuine View of the Parties in an Affair of Honor After the Fifth Shot, at Hobuken, 31st July, 1802.*" © Collection of the New-York Historical Society.

The most famous duel of the period involved Swartout's mentor, Vice President Aaron Burr, and Alexander Hamilton. Burr had risen rapidly in the New York Republican party in the 1790s, serving as the state's attorney general and as United States Senator. On several occasions Hamilton had campaigned against him, opposing his candidacy for vice president in 1792, his reelection to the United States Senate in 1796, and his candidacy for president in 1800. In fact, Jefferson's election to the presidency was largely the result of Hamilton's decision to support Jefferson over Burr. Four years later, when Burr sought the governorship of New York, the opposition circulated this broadside, which attacked Burr's morals and accused him of seducing countless young women.

Aaron Burr!

At length this Cataline stands confessed in all his villainy—His inveterate hatred of the Constitution of the United States has long been displayed in one steady, undeviating course of hostility to every measure which the solid interests of the Union demand—His political perfidiousness and intrigues are also now pretty generally known, and even his own party have avowed their jealousy and fear of a character, which, to great talents adds the deepest dissimulation and an entire devotion to self-interest, and self-aggrandizement—But there is a new trait in this man's character, to be unfolded to the view of an indignant public!—His abandoned profligacy, and the numerous unhappy wretches who have fallen victims to this accomplished and but too successful debauchee, have indeed been long known to those whom similar habits of vice, or the amiable offices of humanity have led to the wretched haunts of female prostitution—But it is time to draw aside the curtain in which he has thus far been permitted to conceal himself by the forbearance of his enemies, by the anxious interference of his friends, and much more by his own crafty contrivances and unbounded prodigality.

It is time to tear away the veil that hides this monster, and lay open a scene of misery, at which every heart must shudder. Fellow Citizens, read a tale of truth, which must harrow up your sensibility, and excite your keenest resentment. It is, indeed, a tale of truth! and, but for wounding, too deeply, the already lacerated feelings of a parental heart, as would be authenticated by all the formalities of an oath.

I do not mean to tell you of the late celebrated courtesan N———, nor U———, nor S———, nor of a half a dozen more whom first his intrigues have ruined, and his satiated brutality has afterwards thrown on the town, the prey of disease, of infancy, and wretchedness—It is to a more recent act, that I call your attention, and I hope it will create in every heart, the same abhorrence with which mine is filled.

When Mr. Burr last went to the city of Washington about 2 months ago, to take the oath of office, and his seat in the August senate of the U. States, he seduced the daughter of a respectable tradesman there, & had the cruelty to persuade her to forsake her native town, her friends and family, and to follow him to New-York. She did so—and she is now in keeping in Partition. Vice, however, sooner or later, meets its merited punishment. Justice, though sometimes slow, is sure. The villain has not long enjoyed this triumph over female weakness. The father of the girl has at length after a laborious and painful search, found out the author of his child's ruin, and his family's dishonor.—He is now in this city, and vengeance will soon light on the guilty head—Fellow-citizens, I leave you to make your own comments on this complicated scene of misery and vice.—I will conclude with a single observation.—Is that party at whose head is this monster, who directs all their motions and originates all their nefarious schemes worthy of your support?

Burr lost the 1804 New York gubernatorial election, and again many blamed it on Hamilton. A published account claimed that Hamilton at a dinner party had said that Burr was "a dangerous man, and one who ought not to be trusted with the reins of government." The account also said that Hamilton had expressed "a still more despicable opinion" of Burr, but provided no details and just left people guessing. (They have been guessing ever since.) On reading these words, Burr sent Hamilton a letter demanding an explanation. Hamilton responded at length, but Burr found the response to be unsatisfactory and challenged Hamilton to a duel. The "interview," as it was called, took place at Weehawken, New Jersey, on the morning of July 11, 1804. The two men used the same dueling pistols that Hamilton's brother-in-law had used in shooting a button off Burr's coat in 1799.

Dueling pistols used in the Burr-Hamilton duel. Chase Manhattan Archives.

Hamilton was killed. One week before, he wrote this letter to his wife. What do you make of it? Does it help you to understand his behavior? Burr's? DeWitt Clinton's? And that of other leaders of the early republic?

[New York, July 4, 1804]

This letter, my very dear Eliza, will not be delivered to you, unless I shall first have terminated my earthly career; to begin, as I humbly hope from redeeming grace and divine mercy, a happy immortality.

If it had been possible for me to have avoided the interview, my love for you and my precious children would have been alone a decisive motive. But it was not possible, without sacrifices which would have rendered me unworthy of your esteem. I need not tell you of the pangs I feel, from the idea of quitting you and exposing you to the anguish which I know you would feel. Nor could I dwell on the topic lest it should unman me.

The considerations of Religion, my beloved, can alone support you; and these you have a right to enjoy. Fly to the bosom of your God and be comforted. With my last idea, I shall cherish the sweet hope of meeting you in a better world.

Adieu best of wives and best of Women. Embrace all my darling children for me.

Ever yours,
A. H.

THE BIG PICTURE

The Founding Fathers regarded political parties as cancers on the body politic, and only a few accepted the legitimacy of political dissent. Yet most of them ended up joining political parties, and dissent was plentiful. How do you account for this? Why did parties develop? And why was there so much squabbling?

To read more about the Federalist Era including the conflict between the Hamiltonian and the Jeffersonian vision of America, see http://www.u-s-history.com/pages/h377.html.

@ ON THE WEB

Chapter 8

The Transformation of Northern Society

Interpretive Essay by John F. Kasson 178

Sources 199
> *Lowell, as It Was and as It Is,* 1845 199
> Portraits of Industrialism 203

The Big Picture 206

Thomas Jefferson wanted America to remain a nation of farmers. Identifying corruption and vice with the "dark satanic mills" of Europe, he hoped that America would never have an industrial revolution. There was a need, he acknowledged, for small rural mills to provide useful employment for "a few women, children and invalids, who could do little on the farm." But large industrial cities would destroy the moral fiber of the American people. Farming had to remain the basis of American life.

The South remained true to Jefferson's vision much longer than the North. Even though southerners moved west and turned to cotton as their cash crop, the basic structure of southern society changed very little after Jefferson's death in 1826. The South continued to be an agrarian society with few industries of its own and a small urban population. And, as always, the great planters ran things. In contrast, the North—and particularly the Northeast—underwent something of a metamorphosis. New York became a huge city. Factories sprang up throughout New England, New York, and Pennsylvania. Boatloads of Irish and German workers descended upon Boston, New York, Philadelphia, and other port cities. And between 1800 and 1850 the portion of the northern labor force in agriculture declined from 70 percent to 40 percent.

Our own society is so much a product of the industrial revolution that we sometimes find it difficult to appreciate just how deep the transformation went, just how disconcerting and exciting the process of "modernization" really was. Much of what a modern society is we take for granted and treat almost as "natural" or "human." But, though much lingered on from the past, the society that Americans were building in the first half of the nineteenth century was fundamentally new. And the newness reached into every detail of life. The ways Americans dressed and the ways they decorated their houses changed. So too did their ideas about child rearing and education, domestic architecture, and even diet. The nature and pace of work were altered in ways everyone knew about, but few understood.

Amid all the excitement about "progress" and "growth," there was a good deal of fear. Many Americans responded to change by trying to find ways to hold on to old values and habits. Religious revivalism, which swept across the nation in the period, was one way of trying to preserve inherited values. So was a rash of reform movements. But even the attempt to resist change employed the methods of modernity. Revivalists and reformers appealed to mass constituencies through the most modern means of communication. And they organized themselves in ways that paralleled the ways the new corporations were discovering to reach their markets.

All in all, the society that Lincoln would later look back on across his "fourscore and seven years" was a society in which little or nothing stood still. The South might still exhibit many eighteenth-century features, and might dress itself out as a kind of feudal scene of romance, but the reality was one of transformation.

Civilizing the Machine

John F. Kasson

Today, we normally think of cities when we think of factories; but in the early nineteenth century water power dictated the location of factories and hence factories were often located in rural areas. This was especially true of New England, where almost overnight cow pastures were turned into mill towns. Of these the most famous was Lowell, Massachusetts, which grew from nothing to a population of 28,000 in just two decades. Founded by rich Boston merchants, it was purposely laid out to take advantage of the peaceful rural setting as well as the water power of the Merrimack River. The town, in fact, became something of a tourist attraction, and everybody of importance—from Charles Dickens to the legendary Davy Crockett—came to see the "factory girls of Lowell."

Here is a modern account of the famous Lowell "system." It was written by John F. Kasson, a historian who is primarily interested in the question of whether it was possible to have industrial cities and still maintain the values of Jefferson's America.

The question of what social environment American manufacturers would create went to the heart of the republican venture. The introduction of new manufacturing centers portended dramatic changes in the structure of society. Their impact upon the character of American life was an issue of national concern. Could a system of manufactures be established that would nurture and protect the health, intelligence, independence, and virtue of their operatives, qualities essential to a republic? Or would factories breed disease, ignorance, dependence, and corruption? Would industrialization provide new prosperity and comfort for all levels of society? Or would industrialization prove an instrument of economic and political repression and social cleavage? In short, was the revolutionary ideal of a republican civilization compatible with rapid industrial development? On the answer to these questions much of the nation's future depended.

Americans in the early nineteenth century united in admiration of English machine technology; smuggling British industrial secrets and mechanics was the sincerest form of flattery. However, there was considerably less enthusiasm for the social consequences of the English factory system. Jefferson found cause to revise his earlier opposition to the promotion of domestic manufactures, but not his horror of the "mobs" of workmen in

European cities. In the late eighteenth and early nineteenth centuries, factory towns sprang up in England at unprecedented rates, stimulated by the colossal expansion in cotton manufactures in Lancashire. The capital of the cotton industry, Manchester, expanded from an ancient town of 17,000 people in 1770 to over 70,000 by 1801, 142,000 in 1831, and over 250,000 by mid-century, with more than an additional 150,000 in the sprawling towns that surrounded it. It stood as the "shock city" of the age, attracting numerous visitors from both England and abroad anxious to confront the symbol and embodiment of the new industrial order. Manchester's contrasts both fascinated and repelled: the advanced technology and immense productivity of its factories; the unbelievably primitive, cramped, and diseased hovels; the vitality of its magnates; the feebleness and despair of its workers. Wrestling with its conflicting characteristics during a visit in 1835, the astute social critic Alexis de Tocqueville concluded: "From this foul drain the greatest stream of human industry flows out to fertilise the whole world. From this filthy sewer pure gold flows. Here humanity attains its most complete development and its most brutish; here civilisation works its miracles, and civilised man is turned back almost into a savage." . . .

Such reports confirmed the popular American image of English factory towns in the first half of the nineteenth century as centers of advanced technology and productivity but also as cancers against both nature and society, producing an oppressed, ignorant, and debauched working class and threatening the civilization as a whole. Could the United States develop a system of manufactures that would avoid a similar fate? If American technology could indeed, as its proponents from Coxe to Everett claimed, integrate the country socially and politically and buttress its republican virtue, it would have to prove it first at the local level in the nation's new manufacturing towns. Here more than anywhere else would be the testing ground of the new republican industrial order.

No one was more aware of this challenge than American manufacturers themselves. The merchant-entrepreneurs who created the leading industrial towns of the nineteenth century shared their fathers' sense of republican mission and distrust of aristocratic Europe. Though some advocates of manufactures took heart in reports that pauperism pervaded England's agricultural counties to a much greater extent than her manufacturing ones, they were not generally inclined to dispute the sordid reputation of English factory towns. Many of them had observed firsthand what Nathan Appleton called the "misery and poverty" of English industrial workers, and they resolved that American manufactures must never be allowed to take a similar course. Manufacturing itself need not be debilitating, they reasoned. Many of the social and moral evils of the English system, they believed, stemmed from the establishment of factories in large cities, in which vice thrived and unchecked and a debased proletariat perpetuated itself. They shared the faith of some of the earliest American planners of industrial towns, including Tench Coxe and Alexander Hamilton, that by locating American manufactures in the countryside and instituting a strict system of moral supervision, the health and virtue of operatives would be protected. Thus situated, manufactures would harmoniously complement agricultural life, and the nation's agrarian character would remain undisturbed.

However, the leading American factory towns of the first half of the nineteenth century were shaped in response not only to the English factory system but to events in America as well. As we have seen, technology was absorbed into a conservative ideology of republicanism as early as the 1780s in part as an instrument of social order and control against both the insidious influences of European manufactures and symptoms of social discord and rebellion at home. As Americans advanced into the nineteenth century, pressures on a deferential society continued and the problems of republican order increased. The whole country surged with dramatic volatility and energy. The nation's population, which had more than doubled every twenty-five years in the eighteenth century, continued to grow at the same phenomenal rate through the first half of the nineteenth. People migrated restlessly not only along the vast new frontier but within the rapidly mushrooming urban centers as well. And the concept of republicanism, instead of controlling and containing this expansion, became in the hands of new egalitarian forces a weapon with which to challenge established authority in politics, religion, law, commerce—virtually every aspect of society. Social conservatives rubbed their eyes to see a reversion in American life from civilization to barbarism as the whole social order upon which the republican experiment was premised appeared to be collapsing around them. Some recent scholars, including Stanley Elkins and David Donald, have in effect supported their perception, arguing that ante-bellum America suffered from a general "institutional breakdown" and "an excess of democracy" that ultimately paved the way for Civil War. . . .

To the total institution, then, turned a group of merchants known as the Boston associates, who would become America's leading manufacturers before the Civil War, as they sought an alternative to the poverty and neglect of English industrial conditions and a safeguard against the fluidity and potential corruption of an expanding American society. Beginning in Waltham, Massachusetts, in 1815, they established a successful pattern of textile manufactures and extended it rapidly. By 1850 the Boston associates controlled mills in operation in Chicopee, Taunton, and Lawrence, Massachusetts; Manchester, Dover, Somersworth, and Nashua, New Hampshire; and Saco and Biddeford, Maine; and were making active preparations for new mills in Holyoke, Massachusetts. But the queen city of their system and the leading producer of cotton goods, the nation's largest industry before the Civil War, was Lowell, Massachusetts. Lowell's fame rested not only on its industrial capacity but even more on its reputed social achievement. One of the most important and influential of all total institutions of republican reform in the ante-bellum period, Lowell promised to resolve the social conflict between the desire for industrial progress and the fear of a debased and disorderly proletariat. Its founding sprang from the conviction that, given the proper institutional environment, a factory town need not be a byword for vice and poverty, but might stand as a model of enlightened republican community in a restless and dynamic nation. Lowell offers a dramatic example of the effort to put this conservative faith into practice. Its story is particularly interesting because within a few years of its founding, the basic assumptions of the Lowell factory system and its conception of republican community were challenged on both ideological and institutional grounds by the working class and their spokesmen. Branding Lowell's directors as a repressive new aristocracy, dissident workers increasingly rejected what they regarded as a manipulative social structure and an exploitative industrial capitalism. Against the conservative view of republicanism of Lowell's directors, protesting workers interpreted the American Revolution as the beginning of a continuing struggle toward a radical egalitarianism. The early history of Lowell thus provides an encapsulated version of the debate over the meaning of republicanism in an industrial society and the attempt to give that meaning institutional shape.

Lowell was conceived in the second decade of the nineteenth century by a trio of innovative and energetic young Boston merchants: Francis Cabot Lowell, Nathan Appleton, and Patrick Tracy Jackson. Touring Great Britain in 1810 and 1811 for his health, F. C. Lowell visited a large iron works in Edinburgh and grew excited over the enormous possibilities such large-scale manufacturing had for America. While in Edinburgh, he also met Nathan Appleton, his friend and fourth cousin, and the merchants discussed the idea of establishing cotton manufacture employing English technology in the United States. At the same time Lowell was corresponding on the subject with his business partner and brother-in-law, P. T. Jackson, and he determined, before his return to America, to study thoroughly the cotton mills at Manchester and Birmingham. He spent weeks in these factories, applying his keen mathematical and mechanical skill and questioning engineers eager to accommodate a wealthy potential customer. Thus Lowell circumvented stringent regulations against the exportation of English machinery or mechanical drawings and smuggled into America valuable mental baggage. His contemporaries would later acclaim him a hero and a genius, who had performed an act of patriotic espionage to rank with Samuel Slater's a generation earlier.

Shortly after Lowell's return from Europe, he and Jackson bought a waterpower site in Waltham, obtained a charter of incorporation from the Massachusetts legislature for their new Boston Manufacturing Company, and sought investors for the enterprise within their circle of friends and relatives among Boston's merchants. Some of Lowell's relations, including the Cabots whose pioneering 1787 cotton factory at Beverly had failed, attempted to dissuade him from what they considered "a visionary and dangerous scheme, and thought him mad." Nathan Appleton himself warily agreed to invest only five thousand dollars, half the amount Lowell and Jackson requested, "in order to see the experiment fairly tried." The two merchants also enlisted the financial support of Patrick Jackson's brothers; Israel Thorndike and his son; Uriah Cotting; James Lloyd; and two of Lowell's brothers-in-law, Benjamin Gorham and Warren Dutton.

Lowell hired a talented engineer, Paul Moody, and quickly set about a series of reinventions based upon his observations of English machinery and contemporary American developments. Of these the most important was the power loom, which promised to free American mills from dependence on neighborhood weavers and to permit the organization of all manufacturing processes from raw cotton to finished cloth within a single integrated mill complex. When Nathan Appleton first saw Lowell's loom in 1814, he was stupefied by its significance and, in a "state of admiration and satisfaction," sat with Lowell "by the hour, watching the beautiful movement of this new and wonderful machine, destined as it evidently was, to change the character of all textile industry." To exploit the capacity of large-scale mechanized production to its fullest extent while relying on unskilled labor, Lowell decided to concentrate production on standardized inexpensive cotton cloths, sheetings, and shirtings. Later, as new corporations arose at the town of Lowell and elsewhere, each manufactured a different type of cotton goods to avoid duplication and competition with fellow companies. Mills were designed to facilitate the flow of materials from one stage of processing to the next. Cotton was carded on the first floor, spun on the second, woven on the third and fourth, while machine shops resided in the basement. In the next fifteen years New England inventors would build upon this structure and introduce a series of labor-saving technological innovations which equaled or excelled British methods and machinery and mechanized all the basic processes of cloth manufacturing except spooling and warping. Even before some of these refinements, however, Lowell's system achieved dramatic gains in production. According to one technological historian, from its first years of operation the Waltham mill could with the same number of employees produce three and a half times as much as other American factories still operating according to pre-1812 methods. The achievement of Lowell and his colleagues, sometimes known as the "Massachusetts system," thus marked a significant stage in the development of modern mass production.

As a final stroke in his grand design, Lowell turned his attention to politics. Competition with British textiles had in the past been the bane of the American industry. Thus when Congress began deliberations over a new tariff measure in 1816, Lowell rushed to Washington to lobby for his cause. He adroitly steered through Congress a minimum valuation tariff that helped to establish the principle of protection to American industry and sheltered his own company's products from foreign competition, while leaving exposed rival manufacturers of more expensive cotton goods. Lowell made a powerful impression even on opponents of the protective tariffs, such as Daniel Webster, then a representative from New Hampshire. Only two years earlier, discussing another tariff measure Webster had declared he was "not in haste to see Sheffields and Birminghams in America." The grim image of English industrial towns dominated his thinking on the subject, and he gestured with foreboding toward the day "when the young men of the country shall be obliged to shut their eyes upon external nature, upon the heavens and the earth, and immerse themselves in close and unwholesome workshops; when they shall be obliged to shut their ears to the bleating of their own flocks, upon their own hills, and to the voice of the lark that cheers them at the plough, that they may open them in dust, and smoke, and steam, to the perpetual whirl of spools and spindles, and the grating of rasps and saws." Lowell helped Webster to change his opinion and to convert him gradually to the protectionist position. Webster's ambition was outgrowing New Hampshire, and he soon moved to Boston, where Lowell supplied him with letters of introduction. Such ministrations, including a later offer to obtain stock in the Boston associates' new enterprise at the town of Lowell, ultimately won Webster's services as a major apologist for American industrial interests.

In the eyes of his contemporaries, however, Lowell's greatest achievement lay in neither his technological success, nor his political skill, nor his business acumen. The special reverence with which his name was spoken in the period before the Civil War emerged from the sense that he had conceived a manufacturing system that concerned itself as much with the health, character, and well-being of its operatives as it did with profits. By allegedly protecting the integrity of America's workers, he had in important measure safeguarded the character of the republic itself. From the beginning, Lowell and his associates were mindful of the condition of European workers and particularly concerned to avoid a similar fate here. As Appleton recalled their earnest discussions, "The operatives in the manufacturing cities of Europe, were notoriously of the lowest character, for intelligence and morals. The question therefore arose, and was deeply considered, whether this degradation was the result of the peculiar occupation, or of other and distinct causes. We could not perceive why this peculiar description of labor should vary in its effects upon character from all other occupation."

Their solution was to organize the factory as a total institution, so that the company might exercise exclusive control over the environment. Unlike most English cotton factories of this time, which were powered by steam, American mills depended upon water power; and the necessity to locate the plant near an important rapids further insured that the community would be placed in the country, apart from urban contamination. But where Lowell's plan differed radically from both earlier English and American factory settlements was in his decision to establish a community with a rotating rather than a permanent population; this was central to the conception. Previous American factory settlements had retained the English system of hiring whole families, often including school-aged children. Lowell and his associates opposed the idea of a long-term residential force that might lead to an entrenched proletariat. They planned to hire as their main working force young, single women from the surrounding area for a few years apiece. For a rotating work force such women were an obvious choice. Able-bodied men could be attracted from farming only with difficulty, and their hiring would raise fears that the nation might lose her agrarian character and promote resistance to manufactures. Women, on the other hand, had traditionally served as spinners and weavers when textiles had been produced in the home, and they constituted an important part of the family economy. However, imports of European manufactured fabrics were eroding

American household industry. At the same time, southern New England farmers were gradually shifting from subsistence to commercial agriculture. By employing young farm women in American factories on a relatively short-term basis, the Lowell system in effect extended and preserved the family economy while at the same time avoiding incorporation into the factory of the family as a whole. Factory work, then, would not become a lifetime vocation or mark of caste, passed on from parent to child in the omnipresent shadow of the mill. Rather it might form an honorable stage in a young woman's maturation, allowing her to supplement her family's income or earn a dowry, before assuming what the founders regarded as "the higher and more appropriate responsibilities of her sex" in a domestic capacity. Her factory experience would be a moral as well as an economic boon, numerous spokesmen for American manufactures maintained, rescuing her from idleness, and vice, pauperism, possibly even confinement in an almshouse or penitentiary. Instead, in the cotton mill, under the watchful eyes of supervisors, she would receive a republican education, imbibing "habits of order, regularity and industry, which lay a broad and deep foundation of public and private future usefulness." During her term at Lowell, the worker would be protected *in loco parentis* by strict corporate supervision, lodged in company boardinghouses kept by upright matrons, and provided compulsory religious services. Such stringent standards of moral scrutiny and company control would serve a treble purpose: to attract young women and overcome the reluctance of their parents, most of them farmers; to provide optimal factory discipline and management control of the operatives; and to maintain an intelligent, honorable, and exemplary republican work force. Though Lowell's founders never regarded their efforts as utopian, they aimed to establish an ideal New England community, which would stand not as a blight but a beacon of republican prosperity and purity upon the American landscape.

Recently, however, some scholars have questioned the extent to which the Lowell system actually stemmed from any grand social vision or solicitude in behalf of the workers. How much choice, they ask, did Lowell's founders really have in developing their vaunted system? According to the economist Howard M. Gitelman, the complexity of the early power-driven machinery employed at Lowell and elsewhere made child labor unfeasible, and thus the economies of a family labor system were not a viable option for the founders. Moreover, he contends, the rural location of Waltham, Lowell, and similar mill towns was dictated mainly by considerations of available water power; company housing then had to be provided in order to staff the mills. Concerned parents and an aroused community, Gitelman speculates, would in any case have insisted upon supervised company housing and a strict system of rules and regulations for the operatives. Economic necessity, not employer magnanimity, so the argument runs, compelled the shape of Lowell.

But to conclude that because the Boston associates were not altruistic reformers, they were therefore simply capitalists following the line of least economic resistance clearly ignores a broad middle ground. A fuller, more satisfactory explanation of the founding of Lowell would recognize *both* commercial and social and ideological motives. For the Boston associates and many of their colleagues were in fact both capitalists and concerned citizens, hard-dealing merchants and public-spirited philanthropists, entrepreneurs and ideologues. Even as they helped to transform New England's economy, they sought to preserve a cohesive social order by adhering tenaciously to a rigorous code of ethics and responsibility. They took seriously their role as republican leaders, and the public turned to them for leadership. The Unitarian reformer Theodore Parker expressed the sense of gratitude of many when he praised the development of manufactures and improvements in transportation as helping to "civilize, educate, and refine men." "These are men," he concluded, "to whom the public owes a debt which no money could pay, for it is a debt of life." Whether it was sufficient payment or not, obviously these manufacturers received a great deal of money for their services. Nevertheless, they insisted both publicly and privately that wealth was not their goal. "My mind has always been devoted to many other things rather than moneymaking," Nathan Appleton declared toward the end of his life. "Accident, and not effort, has made me a rich man." Amos Lawrence, who with his brother Abbott joined forces with Lowell's investors in 1830, filled his diary and letters with reminders of the stewardship and public trust that wealth entailed. From 1829 through 1852 he personally and meticulously made charitable gifts of $639,000 in cash, as well as clothing, food, books, and other articles. He once wrote a factory agent, "We must make a good thing out of this establishment, unless you ruin us by working on Sundays. Nothing but works of necessity should be done in holy time." Boston's leading merchants generally scorned a narrowly acquisitive view of their role and participated in a wide variety of public affairs. They were active and influential in Federalist and later Whig politics and held important offices on both state and national levels. Their contributions to numerous charities and philanthropies, including hospitals, orphanages, and asylums, as well as libraries, historical societies, schools and colleges, helped to make Boston a center of social and cultural institutions in the nineteenth century. Such enterprises, they believed, were essential to the solidity and progress of society. As Francis Cabot Lowell's son John Lowell declared in establishing a series of public lectures, the Lowell Institute, in 1835, "The prosperity of my native land, New England, which is sterile and unproductive, must depend . . . 1st on the moral qualities and 2dly on the intelligence and information of its inhabitants."

Concern with the social consequences of Lowell, Massachusetts, as a tight-knit, carefully regulated republican community, then, was certainly consistent with the values and activities of the founders and their associates in a variety of other fields. Moreover, their philanthropic and industrial pursuits were related both historically and institutionally. Nineteenth-century textile mills were direct descendants of the manufacturing societies formed in various American colonies in the eighteenth century and more distant relatives of the work houses of the seventeenth century. Institutions such as the Boston Society for Encouraging Industry and Employing the Poor, established in 1751 and one of the colonies' most important prerevolutionary factories, had, as its name indicates, a dual purpose: not only to stimulate American manufactures but to provide work for the destitute; to encourage industry in both senses of the word, under official supervision. Undoubtedly, with increased mechanization in the textile industry, commercial motives were uppermost in the establishment of Lowell and other mill towns in the nineteenth century, but at the same time one should not lose sight of the social vision that accompanied them. Of course Lowell's founders and directors were not always as idealistic as they professed. But in instituting their factory system, they did not have to choose between their ethical and ideological convictions and their economic advantage as entrepreneurs—not in the beginning at least. The Lowell system united advanced technology, factory discipline, and conservative republicanism; and when it was eventually challenged, protest came on both economic and ideological grounds.

F. C. Lowell lived only until 1817, long enough to see the success of his Waltham experiment but before practical plans for the city that would bear his name had begun. Yet despite his premature death, he remained, in Nathan Appleton's words, "the informing soul, which gave direction and form to the whole proceeding." To carry on his work, Appleton and Jackson selected as agent Kirk Boott, a trained engineer with an autocratic personality who had perhaps acquired his rigorous standards of discipline and strong class-consciousness in his service in the British army under the Duke of Wellington. They purchased the Pawtucket canal on the Merrimack in what was then the town of Chelmsford, together with four hundred acres of farmland, in the fall of 1821. Boott quickly set about the planning and construction of the industrial town according to F. C. Lowell's general conception, opening the first factory complex, the Merrimack Manufacturing Company, for production in September 1823. The company's six factory buildings were grouped in a spacious quadrangle bordering the river and landscaped with flowers, trees, and shrubs. They were dominated by a central mill, crowned with a Georgian cupola. Made of brick, with flat, plain walls, and white granite lintels above each window space, the factories presented a neat, orderly, and efficient appearance, which symbolized the institution's goals and would be emulated by many of the penitentiaries, insane asylums, orphanages, and reformatories of the period. Beyond the counting house at the entrance to the mill yard stretched the company dormitories. Their arrangement reflected a Federalist image of proper social structure. The factory population of Lowell was rigidly defined into four groups, and their hierarchy immutably preserved in the town's architecture. As chief agent for the corporation, most of whose stockholders resided in Boston, Boott and the other company agents formed the unquestioned aristocracy of the community; a Georgian mansion with an imposing Ionic portico just below the original factory in Lowell powerfully symbolized Boott's authority. Beneath this class stood the overseers, who lived in simple yet substantial quarters at the ends of the rows of boardinghouses where the operatives resided, thus providing a secondary measure of surveillance. In the boardinghouses themselves lived the female workers, who outnumbered male employees roughly three to one. Originally these apartments were constructed in rows of double houses, at least thirty girls to a unit, with intervening strips of lawn. Later, in the 1830s, as companies expanded and proliferated, the houses were strung together, blocking both light and air. These quarters were intended to serve essentially as dormitories and offered few amenities beyond dining rooms and bedrooms, each of the latter shared by as many as six or eight girls, two to a bed. Boardinghouse keepers were responsible for both the efficient administration of the buildings and for enforcing company regulations as to the conduct of the workers. Similar tenements were provided for male mechanics and their families. At the bottom of this hierarchy were the Irish day laborers, who built the canals and mills and made possible the continuing expansion of Lowell. Significantly, no housing had been planned for this group, and they lived in hundreds of little shanties next to a small Catholic church in an area called "New Dublin" and the "Acre." This early corporate insensitivity to the needs of the immigrant presaged Lowell's response to the great mass of immigrants later on.

The adjustment of workers to factory life marked a critical juncture in America's transition to a mature industrial society. Many of Lowell's operatives had known long hours and hard tasks before in farms or shops; but the regularity and discipline of factory work were altogether new. They no longer labored at their own speeds in completing of a task, but to the clock at the pace of the machine. The employer aimed to standardize irregular labor rhythms and to make time the measurement of work. Thus the cupolas that crowned Lowell mills were not simply ornamental; their bells insistently reminded workers that time was money. Operatives worked a six-day week, approximately twelve hours a day, and bells tolled them awake and to their jobs (lateness was severely punished), to and from meals, curfew, and bed. Other factory owners also demanded long hours, even while they simultaneously claimed that the factory system had in large measure repealed the primeval curse "In the sweat of thy face shalt thou eat bread." In the hands of their operatives, they believed, leisure meant mischief; idleness at best; at worst vicious amusements, drink, gambling, and riot. Hence the resistance to shorter working hours throughout the nineteenth century and into the twentieth; work was a form of social control. Lowell's managers shared this perception and wove it into the entire social order. They established an elaborate structure of social deterrents and incentives, insisting at all times upon "respectability" and defining it to suit their needs. Here the heritage of the Puritan ethic served employers especially well. Many Lowell women had been raised in a strongly evangelical atmosphere, which placed heavy emphasis upon personal discipline and restraint. Injunctions to industry and the redemption of time pervaded their home communities, and their reading of popular didactic literature, from Isaac Watts's "How doth the little busy Bee," and Poor Richard's *Way to Wealth*, to the writings of Hannah More, reinforced these teachings. Company officials appropriated these values and adapted them to the imperatives of industrial capitalism. The Lawrence Company regulations, for example, stipulated that all employees "must devote themselves assiduously to their duty during working hours" and "on all occasion, both in their words and in their actions, show they are penetrated by a laudable love of temperance and virtue, and animated by a sense of their moral and social obligations."

A policy of strict social control, implicit in the residential architecture, enforced this code of factory discipline. The factory as a whole was governed by the superintendent, his office strategically placed between the boarding-houses and the mills at the entrance to the mill yard. From this point, as one spokesman enthusiastically reported, his "mind regulates all; his character inspires all; his plans, matured and decided by the directors of the company, who visit him every week, control all." Beneath his watchful eye in each room of the factory, an overseer stood responsible for the work, conduct, and proper management of the operatives therein. Should he choose to exercise it, an overseer possessed formidable power. The various mill towns of New England participated in a "black list" system. A worker who bridled at employers' demands was charged with an offense of character, such as "insubordination," "profanity," or "improper conduct." Issued a "dishonorable discharge," she would be unable to find similar work elsewhere. Supervision was thus constant. If the lines of social division occasionally relaxed on special occasions, it was only because the hierarchical authority of the community, which formed the basis of factory discipline, remained so indisputable.

In addition to these powerful institutional controls, corporate authorities relied upon the factory girls to act as moral police over one another. The ideal, as described by an unofficial spokesman of the corporation, represented a tyranny of the majority that would have made Tocqueville shudder. Declared the Rev. Henry A. Miles of Lowell, "Among the virtuous and high-minded young women, who feel that they have the keeping of their characters and that any stain upon their associates brings reproach upon themselves, the power of opinion becomes an ever-present, and ever-active restraint. A girl, *suspected* of immoralities, or serious improprieties of conduct, at once loses caste." As Miles approvingly described the ostracism, the girl's fellow-boarders would threaten to leave the house unless the house-keeper dismissed the offender. They would shun her on the street, refuse to work with her, and point her out to their companions. "From their power of opinion, there is no appeal." Eventually the outcast would submit to her punishment and leave the community. Even if, as one suspects, Miles overestimated the moral severity of Lowell women, his description nevertheless represented the official standard of behavior. On no account did employers wish to encourage independence of character, for it threatened the stability of the entire factory system.

During its first two decades of operation, Lowell's reputation as a model factory town, offering economic opportunity in a wholesome moral and intellectual atmosphere, proved notably successful in attracting labor. Eager and intelligent young women flocked to the city, mostly from farms in New Hampshire, Vermont, Massachusetts, and Maine. Though their pay was not great and declined relative to the general economy over the years, manufacturing initially offered the greatest income of any occupation open to women at the time; domestic service in particular suffered as a result. Women came for manifold reasons: for money to assist their families, to support a brother's education, or to earn a dowry, and in some cases to gain independence from family life. Often Lowell women offered more romantic explanations as well: a failed family fortune, infidel parents, a cruel mistress, a lover's absence. As Lowell operatives reported their experiences and the community's reputation spread, many came for an informal education and the stimulation of their peers in an urban setting. In addition, company recruiters traveled through New England painting glowing pictures of the life and wages to be enjoyed at Lowell and collecting a commission for each young woman they persuaded. With the construction of new factories and the rise of a middle class in the town to serve the needs of the enterprise, Lowell's population expanded rapidly: From roughly 200 in 1820, it climbed to 6477 in 1830, 21,000 in 1840, and over 33,000 in 1850. For many young women away from home and family for the first time, the factory town appeared overwhelming at first, though most soon adapted to the new industrial environment and institutional life. Some even found the community rather snug and reassuring. With memories tinged by the nostalgia of old age, Harriet Robinson described the early days of Lowell as a life of "almost Arcadian simplicity," and Lucy Larcom recalled "a frank friendliness and sincerity in the social atmosphere," a purposefulness and zest for life that contrasted warmly with her early days as a child on the Massachusetts seacoast. Despite Lowell's swelling population and the lack of public parks until the mid-1840s, the town retained at least suggestions of a rural life. House plants in windows often gave corners of the mills the effect of a bower, and some of the overseers cultivated flower gardens behind the factories as well. According to Miss Larcom, "Nature came very close to the mill gates . . . in those days. There was green grass all around them; violets and wild geraniums grew by the canals; and long stretches of open land between the corporation buildings and the street made the town seem countrylike."

Gradually, most of these young women adjusted to the demands of factory life. Probably the greatest challenge confronting them was the machinery itself. "The buzzing and hissing and whizzing of pulleys and rollers and spindles and flyers"—as one ex-worker described them—often proved bewildering and oppressive for people completely unaccustomed to such devices. As they mastered their machines' intricacies, they learned to defy the noise and tedium by distancing themselves from their work through private thoughts and daydreams. Furthermore, before operatives were given more looms to attend and the machines speeded up in the mid-1840s, they often had long periods of idleness between catching broken threads. Regulations prohibited books in the mill, but women frequently cut out pages or clippings from the newspaper and evaded the edict. Others worked on compositions in their spare moments or spent the time lost in contemplation. Thus they attempted to give meaning to the time that their work denied and to cultivate a mental separation from their activities and surroundings.

In the two or three hours they had remaining at the end of a long working day, and on Sundays, many Lowell women relentlessly pursued an education. They borrowed books from lending libraries, attended the lyceum at which Edward Everett, John Quincy Adams, and Ralph Waldo

Emerson spoke, met in church groups, and organized a number of "Improvement Circles," two of which produced their own periodicals, the *Operatives' Magazine* (1841–1842) and, most famous, the *Lowell Offering* (1840–1845), and its successor, the *New England Offering* (1848–1850). Writers in these journals were self-conscious of their position as "factory girls" and eager to vindicate their reputations. As they endeavored "to remove unjust prejudice—to prove that the female operatives of Lowell were, as a class, intelligent and virtuous"—they offered impressive support for the Lowell system as a model republican community. Factory life at Lowell, a number of writers maintained, did not injure their health or degrade their morals. On the contrary, they asserted, the conscientious worker's "intellect is strengthened, her moral sense quickened, her manners refined, her whole character elevated and improved, by the privileges and discipline of her factory life." To those who chafed against this regimen and thought of returning to the country, various authors replied that Lowell presented the most stimulating moral and intellectual climate, the most authentic republican community, in the land. Declared one woman in the *Lowell Offering*: "I believe there is no place where there are so many advantages within the reach of the laboring class of people, as exist here; where there is so much equality, so few aristocratic distinctions, and such good fellowship, as may be found in this community." A contributor to the *Operatives' Magazine* agreed: "We are, in fact, a truly republican community, or rather we have among us the only aristocracy which an intelligent people should sanction—an aristocracy of worth." While the stress of these remarks was more egalitarian than the conception of Lowell's founders, they effectively supported the existing system. The icon of the *Lowell Offering*'s title page depicted the symbolic landscape in which the operative stood: "the school girl, near her cottage home, with a bee-hive, as emblematical of industry and intelligence, and, in the background, the Yankee school-house, church and factory." With school and church, the factory thus formed a triad of republican instruction and uplift.

As Lowell's fame spread in the 1830s, 1840s, and 1850s, countless visitors made the pilgrimage to the town, were conducted through its factories by representatives of the corporations, and emerged awe-stricken by its technological splendor and moral sublimity. Their rhapsodic testimonies overwhelmingly endorsed the policies of F. C. Lowell, his associates, and successors. Not only did the town appear to sustain the nation's highest standards of health, intellect, prosperity, and character; its success was such that in many respects it presented a model for American communities. . . .

American enthusiasm over Lowell was eminently shared by European visitors. The town quickly emerged as the celestial countertype to infernal Manchester. By the 1830s it had become an obligatory stop on foreign itineraries, as distinctively a republican innovation as the American penitentiary, as established a landmark as Niagara Falls. Despite Lowell's international reputation, each traveler retained a European conception of factory towns that left him unprepared for what he saw. The dramatic natural setting along the banks of the Merrimack, nestled in the hills, with views reputedly as far

as the White Mountains, no less than the crisp, clean aspect of the town itself, gave Lowell an air of "rural freshness" that dazzled foreign guests. As
a result, each took his first glimpse of Lowell in amazement, even an air of
disbelief. Viewing the city from a hilltop one winter evening, the Swedish
novelist Fredrika Bremer compared it to "a magic castle on the snow-
covered earth." Upon closer inspection she exclaimed, "To think and to
know that these lights were not *ignes fatui*, not merely pomp and show, but
that they were actually symbols of a healthful and hopeful life." Alexander
Mackay found himself searching in vain for "the tall chimneys and the thick
volumes of black smoke" that characterized English manufacturing towns.
Lowell's appearance of newness overwhelmed Charles Dickens in the early
1840s, so that it seemed to him created only yesterday. And the perspicacious
French engineer Michel Chevalier, who had earlier experienced "the delu-
sive splendor" of the great Manchester mills, approached Lowell warily. His
sense of pleasure at the town, "new and fresh like an opera scene," warred
with his fear of its eventual decline, causing him to ponder, "Will this become like Lancashire?" Only gradually, watching Lowell operatives passing
neatly through the streets and learning of their wages, did he wholly credit
the enormous gulf between Lowell and Manchester. . . .

Lowell's planners and directors might thus have felt deservedly proud of
their accomplishment. For in Lowell and its sister cities—Chicopee,
Holyoke, Lawrence, Manchester, Saco, and the rest—they had apparently
built a productive, cohesive, and harmonious community based upon the
earlier ideological fusion of technology and republicanism. Lowell promised
not to compromise the nation's agrarian commitment, but rather to supplement it, to strengthen the country economically, socially, and morally. The
factory town ostensibly reconciled the myth of the American garden with a
new myth of the machine. Safely removed from Boston yet connected by the
railroad, Lowell represented in the public mind a region in the middle distance, between city and wilderness. In this setting among the hills and on the
banks of the Merrimack River, the town at once partook of the purifying influences of nature, yet—unwilling totally to submit to its siren song and reel
as debauchees of dew—retained the beneficial discipline of the factory. The
flowers in factory windows, so often noted by visitors, provided a fitting
token of the community's premise, that an oasis of harmony and joy was
attainable only through the maintenance of rigid moral standards and the
fulfillment of hard work. One may protest that this represented a vitiated
pastoralism, hardly worthy of the name; but this mythic fusion reconfirmed
America's self-image as a natural yet disciplined republic and a land of abundance and opportunity. Prosperity and republicanism, the directors might
have congratulated one another, had—despite John Adams's anguished
cry—indeed been reconciled in a temperate and industrious community.
This was the stunning achievement of Lowell. But was it?

Alongside the proud affirmations of company officials, the hosannas of industrial spokesmen and technological enthusiasts, and the admiring testimonies of

European visitors, the 1830s and 1840s saw an insurgent attack upon the basic assumptions of the Lowell factory system and its conception of republican community. This assault was launched by members of the working class and their spokesmen, who, with the emergence of the labor movement, protested their oppressive working conditions and the hierarchical conception of society that sustained them. Probably their sentiments were not shared by the preponderance of Lowell workers, many of whom shunned political opinions of any sort. But if these dissidents were a minority, they were nonetheless significant. Their very existence contradicted Lowell's image as a uniquely happy and harmonious community, and their arguments brought a radically different perspective to the institutionalization of the Lowell ideology and to the course of American technological development. Instead of remaining content in their station and allowing the social machinery to run smoothly, these workers rejected the notion that they shared a community of interests with mill-owners and called for the secret class war that was being waged against them to be fought in the open. The contrast between American and English factory systems did not appear to them so impressively distinct, and they were hardly inclined to join Whig politicians like Edward Everett in proclaiming Lowell as the fulfillment of the American Revolution and a model of republicanism. Quite the reverse; the more extreme among them charged that the manufacturing elite had betrayed everything the revolution stood for and were following in the footsteps of the luxury-loving and tyrannical British. Under the guise of humanitarian concern for the republic, they contended, Lowell's supporters were busily erecting a repressive new aristocracy. . . .

The attack against the Lowell factory system gained momentum . . . as Lowell women began to demonstrate on behalf of reform. In 1834 they participated in their first "turn-out," a demonstration and short-lived strike. Their numbers were estimated from "nearly eight hundred" (*Lowell Journal*) to two thousand (*The Man*), varying with the sympathies of newspaper reporters. The workers issued a proclamation asking the support of all "who imbibe the spirit of our patriotic ancestors," and ending with the verse:

> *Let oppression shrug her shoulders,*
> *And a haughty tyrant frown,*
> *And little upstart Ignorance*
> *In mockery look down.*
> *Yet I value not the feeble threats*
> *Of Tories in disguise,*
> *While the flag of Independence*
> *O'er our noble nation flies.*

The immediate occasion of the "turn-out" was the announcement of a 15 percent reduction in wages, but it represented as well a protest against Lowell's paternalism as unrepublican. As one of the demonstrators announced, "We do not estimate our liberty by dollars and cents; consequently it was not the reduction of wages alone which caused the excitement, but that haughty, overbearing disposition, that purse proud insolence, which was becoming more and more apparent." Two and a half years later, in October 1836, Lowell women struck against an increase in the price of board in company houses, amounting to a one-eighth cut in wages. Again they fortified their resolution by reminding one another of the revolutionary struggle against tyranny: "As our fathers resisted unto blood the lordly avarice of the British ministry," they declared, "so we, their daughters, never will wear the yoke which has been prepared for us."

Thus, despite the founders' best efforts and most stringent regulations, the radical, egalitarian strain of republicanism they had hoped to suppress broke out within the fortress of Lowell itself. Like other dissident workers throughout the nineteenth century, Lowell operatives returned repeatedly to the American Revolution and particularly to the Declaration of Independence to fortify and articulate their protest against what they regarded as a repressive social and industrial system. They insisted that since they were "created with certain unalienable rights," their labor could not simply be reduced to a commodity of which they were denied the fruits; human rights, "life, liberty, and the pursuit of happiness," took precedence over property rights. Lowell's leading investors were also acutely conscious of the revolution. Though Amos Lawrence, for example, was not born until 1786, so steeped was he in stories of that event that he felt himself "an actor in the scenes described," and a simple incident like the sound of a gunshot in 1843 instantly transported him back to the battles of Lexington and Concord in 1775. But the moral he and other manufacturers drew from the revolution was very different from the workers'. As his biographer Freeman Hunt wrote shortly after Lawrence's death, "In all [the revolution's] phases it was of a conservative character, aiming to maintain what was, and not seeking the development of fanciful theories. Our ancestors had no projects for the colonization of Utopia. The revolutionists were all on the other side." So the revolutionists must have seemed again in the 1830s and 1840s. Lowell's directors and other manufacturers were not about to surrender to these dangerous new visionaries. Prior to 1860 in Massachusetts not a single strike ended in victory for the workers or checked the reduction of wages.

The workers were handicapped not only in the lack of union organization; the very institutional character of the Lowell factory system placed immense obstacles in the way of labor resistance. As George Frederickson and Christopher Lasch have observed in considering the problem of resistance against another total institution, plantation slavery, "all total institutions are set up in such a way as to preclude any form of politics based on consent." In such a situation the conditions for organized and sustained resistance were meager. The authority of Lowell's staff was directed not just at the workers' productive performance but at their private activities and feelings as well; and traditional moral values were appropriated to reinforce the purposes and perspective of the institution. Political agitation not only smacked of "insubordination" but was also considered "unladylike" in the dominant culture. In this respect, extremely valuable allies to company management in quelling dissent were the much publicized journals that Lowell women produced themselves. The *Lowell Offering*, the *Operatives' Magazine*, and the *New England Offering*, though all nominally independent, served in effect as house organs, expressing solidarity between workers and management, and they were covertly encouraged by Lowell's directors. Wishing to elevate the reputation of the factory girl and to prove her virtue and intelligence, these periodicals rigidly excluded criticism of factory conditions or management policies and resolutely presented cheerful expressions to the public. Occasionally, an editor would sharply rebuke those who violated their decorous image. "Constant abuse of those from whom one is voluntarily receiving the means of subsistence," Harriet Farley lectured dissident workers, was "something more than bad taste." If an operative really wished to improve her condition, Miss Farley suggested, she should leave the mills altogether. A character in Lucy Larcom's poem *An Idyl of Work* supported this point of view when she asked:

> *Why should we,*
> *Battling oppression, tyrants be ourselves,*
> *Forcing mere brief concession to our wish?*
> *Are not employers human as employed?*
> *Are not our interests common? If they grind*
> *And cheat as brethren should not, let us go*
> *Back to the music of the spinning-wheel,*
> *And clothe ourselves at hand-looms of our own,*
> *As did our grandmothers.*

This theme that rather than protest, the dissatisfied worker should go elsewhere and seek a separate peace recurred in the pages of the *Offering*. If wages should finally drop too sharply, another young woman grandiloquently declared, "I fear not for the crust of black bread, the suppliant voice, and bended knee; for then the inducement to remain will be withdrawn. Our broad and beautiful country will long present her spreading prairies, verdant hills, and smiling vales, to all who would rather work than starve." In the last analysis, the supposedly "voluntary" character of Lowell and the fact that employment was temporary by design, encouraged cooperation between workers and management and mitigated against the formation of a class consciousness. High job turnover rates alone would have inhibited the development of a sense of solidarity among workers and of united opposition to their employers. In addition, as women who regarded their work in the mills as transient rather than a career, most Lowell workers were not disposed toward collective solutions to factory abuses.

Other obstacles also stood in the way of Lowell's protesting workers. The Panic of 1837 and subsequent depressions threw an estimated one-third of American laborers out of work and seriously damaged the union movement. With jobs scarce, workingmen's organizations came to regard the system of female labor as doubly pernicious; not only did it harm the women themselves, it brought women in competition with men, thereby either throwing the latter out of work or reducing their wages. In light of this situation, the National Trades' Union suggested in 1839 that the solution to the female labor problem might be to keep women at home where they belonged. Women operatives, clearly, could no longer depend upon male labor spokesmen always to uphold their position.

In spite of these impediments, however, resistance to the Lowell factory system gradually increased. By December 1844 Lowell's dissident workers, led by the redoubtable Sarah Bagley, had achieved sufficient strength to form an organization of their own, the Lowell Female Labor Reform Association. Its ranks swelled quickly: within three months it numbered three hundred members and by the end of 1845 it claimed six hundred workers in Lowell alone, plus branches in all major New England textile centers. Now workers were able to establish connections outside Lowell to the labor movement and hence to some degree to subvert institutional pressures. Immediately, they formed their own journal, *Factory Tracts*, and soon formed an alliance with the *Voice of Industry*, a new labor weekly newspaper, and brought it to Lowell. Denouncing the *Lowell Offering* as a "mouthpiece of the corporations," these dissident workers powerfully inveighed against the oppressive character of factory life. Like Luther and Douglas, they pointed with horror to the specter of a degenerate race, spawned in the mills to serve as slaves to a manufacturing aristocracy. And as in earlier appeals to labor, they attempted to rally and organize workers by applying the language and lessons of 1776 to their own times. "Is not," the *Voice of Industry* asked, "the same secret fawning, devouring monster, wilely [*sic*] drawing his fatal folds around us as a nation which has crushed the freedom, prosperity and existence of other republics whose sad fate, history long ago recorded. . . . ?" In such conspiracies, the paper charged, industrious and virtuous labor was inevitably targeted as the first victim. Every year its burdens grew more grievous, and the *Voice of Industry* demanded for all workingmen their God-given right to "'life, liberty, and the pursuit of happiness.'" The fact that conditions of European operatives might be even worse, the paper argued, was essentially irrelevant: "The American workingmen and women, will not long suffer this gradual system of *republican* encroachment, which is fast reducing them to dependence, vassalage and slavery; because the English, Irish or French operatives are greater slaves, their condition more deplorable or English capitalists and task masters have the power to be more tyrannical and oppressive." An article in *Factory Traits* similarly appealed to America's true nobility, its workers, to cast off the yoke of tyranny from about their necks before their country became "one great hospital, filled with worn out operatives and colored slaves!" It closed defiantly, "EQUAL RIGHTS, or death to the corporations."

Such rhetoric reasserted the radical egalitarianism of the republican message which conservatives had been struggling to contain ever since the revolution. References to the possibility of violent revolution formed a recurrent theme in the writings of Luther, Douglas, and other labor spokesmen of the period; now such phrases were being shouted outside the very mills of Lowell. How seriously is one to take them? Certainly no laborers were stockpiling arms and actively preparing for an insurrection. But neither should one dismiss such talk as a kind of verbal spice utterly without significance. In part, of course, it was intended to goad manufacturers toward reforms. Yet one cannot help but feel that it had an opposite effect: that such language only reconfirmed in Lowell's managers and stockholders their sense of the violence and chaos that would erupt should their institutional controls be removed. Of equal if not greater significance, this rhetorical violence also represented tacit admission of the immense gulf between labor reformers' vision of life in an ideal technological society, freed from the exigencies of industrial capitalism, and the formidable obstacles they encountered even to such minimal reforms as the ten-hour day. Indeed, the primacy of the ten-hour movement, as one historian has suggested, only reflects the extent to which workers accepted and fought within their employers' categories of time and work discipline. From this point of view, one might speculate that the apocalyptic rhetoric of dissident laborers and other antebellum reformers signaled, not the weakness of American institutions, but their strength and the difficulty of gaining any real leverage for resistance. While continuing to affirm their faith in the ballot box, they summoned forth the image of revolution not only because it made another link in the carefully elaborated analogy between nineteenth-century workers and the American revolutionists, but because it provided a vague yet powerful metaphor by which the bleak conditions of the present might suddenly be wrenched to their conception of the future.

Whatever efficacy the workers' protests had, then, was as symbolic rather than instrumental action; whatever gains they achieved were expressive rather than substantial. Efforts at specific reforms encountered powerful resistance. Workers from several mill towns had petitioned the Massachusetts legislature for establishment of a ten-hour day and other factory reforms as early as 1842, with no response. The petition of 1600 workers from Lowell and elsewhere the next year met a similar fate. In 1844 a third petition was tabled until the next session; so that at last in 1845 a legislative committee held hearings on labor conditions for the first time. In the absence of an existing labor committee, the task was assigned to William Schouler, publisher of the *Lowell Courier* and a staunch supporter of the corporations. Sarah Bagley and the Lowell Female Labor Reform Association feverishly circulated new petitions to support the ten-hour cause and gained over two thousand signatures, half of them from Lowell. Two conflicting groups of witnesses then paraded before the committee. Spokesmen for the employers defended the healthful environment of the mills, while Miss Bagley and a group of operatives personally testified that Lowell workers endured overlong work days for insufficient pay to the detriment of health, mind, and spirit. To examine conditions firsthand, a portion of the committee went to Lowell, and they returned substantially impressed. Of their visit to the Massachusetts and Boott Mills, they reported, "The rooms are large and well-lighted, the temperature, comfortable, and in most of the window sills were numerous shrubs and plants, such as geraniums, roses, and numerous varieties of the cactus. These were the pets of the factory girls, and they were to the Committee convincing evidence of the elevated moral tone and refined taste of the operatives." Thus Lowell's technological version of pastoral proved remarkably resilient; even in the midst of protest, legislators found confirmation of the essential rightness of the enterprise in a single whiff of a potted flower.

The committee as a whole affirmed the healthfulness of existing conditions and further shied away from a ten-hour law as jeopardizing Massachusetts' industry with respect to its neighbors. Paying left-handed tribute to Lowell's petitioners, the committee declared, "Labor is intelligent enough to make its own bargains, and look out for its own interests without any interference from us." While it acknowledged that hours should be lessened, mealtimes extended, ventilation improved, and other reforms instituted, the committee contended, "the remedy is not with us. We look for it in the progressive improvement in art and science, in a higher appreciation of man's destiny, in a less love for money, and a more ardent love for social happiness and intellectual superiority." The *Lowell Offering* could not have put it better. Protesting workers did gain official support in Dr. Josiah Curtis's report on public hygiene for 1849 and the minority report of the legislature's special committee on labor for 1850. Finally, the Lowell corporation voluntarily shortened the work day to eleven hours in 1853. But no ten-hour legislation was passed in Massachusetts until 1874. . . .

. . . The failure of the ten-hour movement added to discontent. When profits declined and new wage cuts were announced in 1848, the turnover of operatives rose sharply; at one of the most prosperous companies, the Merrimack, average workers' tenure dropped to nine months. In the past, the city's mystique had proved a powerful agent of employee recruitment. Now, as mechanization spread to other industries, such as boots and clothing, and other employment opportunities rivaled the textile mills, Lowell's companies appeared in danger of losing their command over their labor force.

Nevertheless, when the Lowell factory system was suddenly transformed in the late 1840s and 1850s, it was from quite another source than capitulation to workers' demands. At just the moment when company control of its traditional labor pool was growing shaky, Ireland's terrible potato famine that had begun in 1845 and the subsequent eviction of Irish peasants by their landlords triggered a massive immigration to America, over one and a half million people before the Civil War. As a major ship and railroad terminus, Boston received tens of thousands of these Irish immigrants. Upon arriving, however, they encountered a constricted social and economic life with little receptivity to foreigners. Nativist prejudice combined with the newcomers' lack of training and capital to shut them out of all but unskilled occupations. In such a position, Irish immigrants offered textile factories at Lowell and neighboring mill towns a ready and abundant supply of labor, and the incentive to accommodate demands of native workers diminished. Almost immediately, Irish began to take the places of departing New Englanders in the mills; once established, their presence further hastened the flow of native workers to other jobs and discouraged the entrance of other New England women into the industry. Only 7 percent of the operatives in Lowell mills were Irish in 1845, but by the early 1850s their proportion was estimated as one-half, and it grew still higher year by year. Later in the century, the labor force would be supplemented by French-Canadians and other immigrant groups. Instead of predominantly single women, the Irish came as families. As adult males were discriminated against, Irish women and, increasingly, children went to the mills, the last receiving lower wages than ever. High turnover rates thus persisted. But if the work force was not immobile, neither was the work force in Britain; it was certainly not the kind of circulatory labor force able to enter and leave the industrial economy at will with which the Lowell system had begun. Most lived not in company boardinghouses to be supervised by alien authority, but with family or friends in the town at large. With a different culture, training, aspirations, and status from earlier Lowell workers, the Irish obviously did not immerse themselves in improvement circles and literary magazines. And the Lowell mills, which had eagerly received credit for the talents and accomplishments of earlier operatives, now found themselves without their trophies. In less than a decade Lowell lost its prized population of well-educated and temporary New England women and with it the factory system's very rationale. Suddenly the basis that Lowell's founders and most ardent defenders had insisted constituted the principal difference between this city and English manufacturing towns and upon which its welfare would stand or fall—its lack of an established proletariat—was totally overthrown. . . .

The early history of Lowell, like that of other institutional innovations during this period, thus revealed complexities far beyond the shaping powers or expectations of its confident founders. The factory system they established, no matter how benign in intention, was still based upon a hierarchical and manipulative model in which workers were passive agents, tied to the demands of machine production and industrial capitalism as a whole. Ironically, Lowell's very success in attracting educated and independent New England women meant that at least an outspoken minority would refuse to accept the management's conception of "republicanism," inherent in its strict factory discipline, and insist upon a true egalitarian order. Reliance upon temporary workers, in any case, only postponed the question of what accommodations industry should make for a permanent labor force. But the arrival of the Irish triggered not a new concern upon the part of corporate officials and a re-examination of their conception of republican community, but, on the contrary, increased apathy. . . .

By the 1850s the possibility of an integrated and harmonious republican community seemed farther off than ever. Even while Lowell's praises echoed, its founders' optimistic vision lay tarnished, and its most ardent defenders were forced on the defensive. The problems of urban and industrial growth and social disorder that Lowell was established to correct had spread to the community itself.

SOURCES

Lowell, as It Was and as It Is, 1845

Henry A. Miles

When the owners of Lowell came under attack, they took pains to refute the charges made against them. Beginning in the 1840s they published articles, pamphlets, and books that defended Lowell's leading investors and company officials. Of these one of the most important was Lowell, As It Was and As It Is *by Henry A. Miles, a Unitarian minister at Lowell. Do you think he succeeded in convincing his fellow citizens that he was an impartial observer? That the influences going forth from Lowell were not "pernicious"?*

Lowell has been highly commended by some, as a model community, for its good order, industry, and general freedom from vice. It has been strongly condemned, by others, as a hotbed of corruption, tainting the whole land. We all, in New England, have an interest in knowing what are the exact facts of the case. We are destined to be a great manufacturing people. The influences that go forth from Lowell will go forth from many other manufacturing villages and cities. If these influences are pernicious, we have a great calamity impending over us. Rather than endure it, we should prefer to have every factory destroyed.

If, on the other hand, a system has been introduced, carefully provided with checks and safeguards, and strong moral and conservative influences, it is our duty to see that this system be faithfully carried out, so as to prevent the disastrous results which have developed themselves in the manufacturing towns of other countries. Hence the topics assume the importance of the highest moral questions. The author writes after a nine years' residence in this city, during which he has closely observed the working of the factory system, and has gathered a great amount of statistical facts which have a bearing upon this subject. He believes himself to be unaffected by any partisan views, as he stands wholly aside from the sphere of any interested motives.

A Lowell Boardinghouse

Each of the long blocks of boardinghouses is divided into six or eight tenements, and are generally three stories high. These tenements are finished off

From Henry A. Miles, *Lowell, As It Was and As It Is*, Powers and Bagley, Lowell, Mass., 1845, pp. 62–63, 66–67, 100–103, 128–135, 140–147.

in a style much above the common farmhouses of the country, and more nearly resemble the abodes of respectable mechanics in rural villages. These are constantly kept clean, the buildings well painted, and the premises thoroughly whitewashed every spring, at the corporation's expense.

As one important feature in the management of these houses, it deserves to be named that male operatives and female operatives do not board in the same tenement; and the following regulations, printed by one of the companies, and given to each keeper of their houses, are here subjoined, as a simple statement of the rules generally observed by all the corporations.

Regulations to be observed by persons occupying the boardinghouses belonging to the Merrimack Manufacturing Company.

They must not board any persons not employed by the company, unless by special permission.

No disorderly or improper conduct must be allowed in the houses.

The doors must be closed at ten o'clock in the evening.

Those who keep the houses, when required, must give an account of the number, names, and employment of their boarders; also with regard to their general conduct, and whether they are in the habit of attending public worship.

The buildings, both inside and out, and the yards about them, must be kept clean, and in good order.

The hours of taking meals in these houses are uniform throughout all the corporations in the city. The time allowed for each meal is thirty minutes for breakfast, when that meal is taken after beginning work; for dinner, thirty minutes.

The food that is furnished in these houses is of a substantial and wholesome kind, is neatly served, and in sufficient abundance. Operatives are under no compulsion to board in one tenement rather than another. And then, as to the character of these boardinghouse keepers themselves, on no point is the superintendent more particular than on this. Applications for these situations are very numerous. The rents of the company's houses are purposely low, averaging only from one-third to one-half of what similar houses rent for in the city. There is no intention on the part of the corporation to make any revenue from these houses. They are a great source of annual expense. But the advantages of supervision are more than an equivalent for this.

The influence which this system of boardinghouses has exerted upon the good order and good morals of the place, has been vast and beneficent. To a very great degree the future condition of Lowell is dependent upon a faithful adhesion to this system.

The following table shows the average hours per day of running the mills, throughout the year, on all the corporations in Lowell.

In addition to the above, it should be stated that lamps are never lighted on Saturday evening, and that four holidays are followed in the year, viz. Fast Day, Fourth of July, Thanksgiving Day, and Christmas Day.

Hours of Labor

	H.	M.		H.	M.
January	11	24	July	12	45
February	12	00	August	12	45
March	11	52	September	12	23
April	13	31	October	12	10
May	12	45	November	11	56
June	12	45	December	11	24

The average daily time of running the mills is twelve hours and ten minutes. Arguments are not needed to prove that toil, if it be continued for this length of time, each day, month after month, and year after year, is excessive, and too much for the tender frames of young women to bear. No one can more sincerely desire than the writer of this book, that they had more leisure time for mental improvement and social enjoyment. It must be remembered, however, that their work is comparatively light. All the hard processes, not conducted by men, are performed by machines, the movements of which female operatives are required merely to oversee and adjust.

❧ *Moral Police of the Corporations*

The productiveness of these works depends upon one primary and indispensable condition—the existence of an industrious, sober, orderly, and moral class of operatives. Without this, the mills in Lowell would be worthless. Profits would be absorbed by cases of irregularity, carelessness, and neglect; while the existence of any great moral exposure in Lowell would cut off the supply of help from the virtuous homesteads of the country. Public morals and private interests, identical in all places, are here seen to be linked together in an indissoluble connection. Accordingly, the sagacity of self-interest, as well as more disinterested considerations, has led to the adoption of a strict system of moral police.

The female operatives in Lowell do not work, on an average, more than four and a half years in the factories. They then return to their homes, and their places are taken by their sisters, or by other female friends from their neighborhood.

To obtain this constant importation of female hands from the country, it is necessary to secure *the moral protection of their characters while they are resident in Lowell.* This, therefore, is the chief object of that moral police.

No persons are employed on the corporations who are addicted to intemperance, or who are known to be guilty of any immoralities of conduct. As the parent of all other vices, intemperance is most carefully excluded.

In respect to discharged operatives, there is a system observed. Any person wishing to leave a mill is at liberty to do so, at any time, after giving a fortnight's notice. The operative so leaving, if of good character, and having worked a year, is entitled, as a matter of right, to an honorable discharge. That form is as follows:

Mr. or Miss _____, has been employed by the _____ Manufacturing Company, in a _____ room, _____ years _____ months, and is honorably discharged.

              _____, *Superintendent.*

LOWELL, _____ _____

This discharge is a letter of recommendation to any other mill in the city, and not without its influence in procuring employment in any other mill in New England. Those dishonorable have another treatment. The names of all persons dismissed for bad conduct, or who leave the mill irregularly, are also entered in a book, and these names are sent to all the counting rooms of the city. *Such persons obtain no more employment throughout the city.*

Any description of the moral care, studied by the corporations, would be defective if it omitted a reference to the overseers. Every room in every mill has its first and second overseer. At his small desk, near the door, where he can see all who go out or come in, the overseer may generally be found, and he is held responsible for the good order, and attention to business, of the operatives of that room. Hence, this is a post of much importance. It is for this reason that peculiar care is exercised in their appointment. The overseers are almost universally married men, with families; and as a body, numbering about one hundred and eighty in all, are among the most permanent residents, and most trustworthy and valuable citizens of the place. The guiding and salutary influence which they exert over the operatives is one of the most essential parts of the moral machinery of the mills.

It may not be out of place to present here the regulations, which are observed alike on all the corporations, which are given to the operatives when they are first employed, and are posted up conspicuously in all the mills. They are as follows:

Regulations to be observed by all persons employed by the Manufacturing Company, in the factories.

Every overseer is required to be punctual himself, and to see that those employed under him are so.

The overseers may, at their discretion, grant leave of absence to those employed under them, when there are sufficient spare hands in the room to supply their place; but when there are not sufficient spare hands, they are not allowed to grant leave of absence unless in cases of absolute necessity.

All persons are required to observe the regulations of the room in which they are employed. They are not allowed to be absent from their work without the consent of their overseer, except in case of sickness, and then they are required to send him word of the cause of their absence.

All persons are required to board in one of the boardinghouses belonging to the company, and conform to the regulations of the house in which they board.

All persons are required to be constant in attendance on public worship, at one of the regular places of worship in this place.

Persons who do not comply with the above regulations will not be employed by the company.

Persons entering the employment of the company are considered as engaging to work one year.

All persons intending to leave the employment of the company are required to give notice of the same to their overseer, at least two weeks previous to the time of leaving.

Anyone who shall take from the mills, or the yard, any yarn, cloth, or other article belonging to the company will be considered guilty of stealing—and prosecuted accordingly.

The above regulations are considered part of the contract with all persons entering the employment of the _____ Manufacturing Company. All persons who shall have complied with them, on leaving the employment of the company, shall be entitled to an honorable discharge, which will serve as a recommendation to any of the factories in Lowell. No one who shall not have complied with them will be entitled to such a discharge.

_____ _____, Agent.

Portraits of Industrialism

The following artwork illustrates some important features of the mental picture of industrialism that Americans began to form around the Lowell experience. The first is an engraving offering a view of Lowell. The second is the title page of the Lowell Offering of 1845, a collection of the writings of some of the young women who worked in the textile mill there. The third is an engraving by the famous painter Winslow Homer of workers in the nearby mill town of Lawrence. And the last is an artist's sketch of one of the most famous strikes of the century, the strike of 800 women shoemakers of Lynn, Massachusetts, in 1860. As you look at the pictures, think about the ways in which the artists have tried to resolve any potential contradiction between industry and nature, between industry and ordinary community life, between industry and femininity. Have the mills intruded on the greenery of the landscape, or do the artists create the impression that factories and trees can be integral parts of one harmonious landscape? What kind of relationship is suggested between the new factories and the traditional high points of a New England skyline, the church steeples? And what kind of relationship is suggested between the workers and the communities in which they lived? Notice the sign in the strike picture, comparing workers with slaves. Notice also that the Lynn City Guards, the local militia, preceded the striking women. What do you think middle-class women would have said upon seeing this picture?

To learn more about the "birthplace" of industry, go to the website of the Lowell National Historical Park History Pages at http://www.nps.gov/lowe/loweweb/Lowell%20History/prologue.htm.

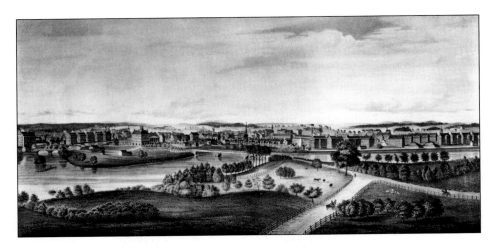

View of Lowell, Massachusetts.

Title page of the *Lowell Offering*.
Massachusetts Historical Society.

Engraving by Winslow Homer depicting textile workers of Lawrence, Massachusetts.
Culver Pictures, Inc.

Striking women and local militia. Culver Pictures, Inc.

THE BIG PICTURE

Industrialization, urbanization, and immigration brought dramatic changes to the lives of many men and women in the Northeast, while the lives of people in the South and the backcountry changed very little. Was there any truth to the proposition that the owners of the northern mills now had the same position in the North that the great slaveowners had in the South? Were northern factory workers no better off than southern slaves?

@ ON THE WEB   *To view more portraits of industrialism at Lowell Mills, visit* http://oldweb.uwp.edu/academic/ history/hist314/vmtedl/lowell.htm.

Chapter 9

Jacksonian Democracy

Interpretive Essay by Anthony F. C. Wallace 209

Sources 216

The Election of Jackson 216

Removal of Eastern Tribes 217

The Anti-Jacksonians 218

"King Andrew" 220

The Art of Democratic Politics 221

The Election of 1840 223

The Artist's View of Politics 227

The Big Picture 231

The dramatic changes that took place in the northern economy after the War of 1812 were accompanied by equally dramatic changes in national politics. Under President James Monroe (1817–1825) the party system that Jefferson helped to fashion fell apart. The Federalists dropped out of presidential politics after losing to Monroe in the election of 1816. The victorious Jeffersonian Republicans split into warring factions. Party leaders lost control of the political arena, and suddenly the most divisive issues of the day—slavery and southern power—came to dominate congressional debate when Missouri in 1819 asked to be admitted to the Union as a slave state. By 1824 Jefferson's party was in hopeless disarray. Instead of running one man for president, the party was unable to make a binding nomination, and four men—all calling themselves Jeffersonian Republicans—ran for the presidency. None of the four received the necessary majority of electoral votes, and hence the election went to the House of Representatives. There, after much wheeling and dealing, Andrew Jackson lost the presidency to John Quincy Adams. The outcome, said Jackson, was due to "bargain and corruption."

Along with the old party system went the old style of politics. James Monroe was the last president to dress like an aristocrat, powder his hair, and wear the knee-length pantaloons and white-topped boots of Washington's day. His successor, John Quincy Adams, wore long pants and was the least ostentatious of our early presidents. But he too was identified with the old style of politics in which ordinary citizens were expected to defer to their "betters." However, a new style was developing in which politicians sang the praises of "democracy," lauded the natural instincts of the ordinary white man, and even pretended to be just common folk. The new style came to be identified with General Andrew Jackson, the hero of the Battle of New Orleans, who defeated Adams in the election of 1828.

Historians have debated the meaning of Jacksonian democracy almost as vigorously as they have the American Revolution or the Civil War. The Jacksonian movement has seemed to some the expression of the rising spirit of democracy along the frontier, north and south. To others, the new democracy has appeared to be something even newer and more remarkable: the politics of a new urban working class in the North. Others, content enough with the label "Jacksonian," have doubted the element of democracy. To them, Jackson was a conservative who might manipulate the rhetoric of the "common man," but a conservative nonetheless, a slaveholder with all the political instincts of a member of the southern elite.

The Hunger for Indian Land in Andrew Jackson's America

Anthony F. C. Wallace

In debating the meaning of Jacksonian Democracy, there was one matter that many historians of a previous generation tended to overlook. That was Jackson's treatment of the various tribes that for centuries had dwelled on land east of the Mississippi River. In one book after another, the topic was scarcely mentioned—and sometimes neglected entirely—or treated as little more than a disgraceful footnote to the main course of American history.

That is no longer the case. Few historians today treat "Indian removal" as just a minor matter or a neglected episode in the story of Jacksonian America. It was central. It exposed many of the contradictions in American democratic values, and it also revealed much about Andrew Jackson and the society he dominated.

Of the many who have seen "Indian removal" as a key to understanding Jacksonian America, perhaps the most influential has been Anthony F. C. Wallace. Trained as both an anthropologist and a historian, Professor Wallace spent virtually his entire career, both as a student and as a teacher, at the University of Pennsylvania.

Andrew Jackson was a young lawyer of twenty-one when in 1788 he moved to Nashville, the principal town in the Cumberland Valley in what is now the state of Tennessee. The Cumberland Valley had been purchased from the Cherokee Indians only three years before. It was very much a frontier region, still subject to occasional raids from hostile natives. Fortunes were being made and lost in land speculations, trading in horses and slaves, betting on horse races, storekeeping, and cotton growing, and the young lawyer tried it all. He soon married Rachel Donelson Robards, the daughter of a powerful local clan, but unwittingly and unfortunately the ceremony was performed before Rachel's divorce from her first husband was final. The devoted couple had to be legally remarried later, and gossip about the "scandal" plagued them for years. Jackson's fortunes ebbed and flowed, but he eventually secured a prosperous cotton plantation on the outskirts of Nashville, The Hermitage, a one-square-mile estate which remained his residence for the rest of his life.

As a member of the Nashville gentry, he naturally took part in the political life of the area. In 1796, when Tennessee was about to be admitted into the Union, he became a member of the convention that wrote a constitution

Anthony F. C. Wallace, *The Long Bitter Trail: Andrew Jackson and the Indians*, Hill & Wang, New York, 1993, pp. 3–11. Reprinted by permission of Farrar, Straus, and Giroux, LLC.

for the new state, and in the same year was elected to serve as the first representative to Congress from the state of Tennessee. He entered the U.S. Senate in 1797, but resigned after one year, pleading financial difficulties. Soon, however, he was appointed a judge of the Superior Court of the state and stayed a member of that body until 1804.

In 1802, Jackson was elected major general of the Tennessee militia, and he retained that post through the War of 1812. At the end of that war, by defeating the Creek Indians in Alabama in 1814 and repulsing the British before New Orleans in 1815, he had achieved national prominence as the only American military hero of that inconclusive conflict. Appointed a commissioner to treat with the Southern Indians, in the six years immediately after the war he was able, personally, to force cessions of land upon both friendly and hostile tribes, and to begin the process of removal of the Southern Indians to the "Indian territory" west of the Mississippi. Jackson's success as treaty commissioner from 1815 to 1820 was phenomenal: in those years he and his fellow commissioners persuaded the tribes, by fair means or foul, to sell to the United States a major portion of their lands in the Southeast, including a fifth of Georgia, half of Mississippi, and most of the land area of Alabama.

Andrew Jackson had a personal financial interest in some of the lands whose purchase he arranged. His attention focused particularly on an area in northern Alabama, south of that part of the Tennessee River known as Muscle Shoals, acquired from the Cherokees in a treaty surrounded by allegations of fraud. The Senate, in fact, refused to ratify the treaty and it had to be renegotiated. The lands south of this stretch of river were in frontier times seen as a prospectively lucrative site for agricultural development, and efforts had been under way to acquire it from its Native American owners, the Cherokees, since the 1780s. More recently, the land south of the Shoals had been recognized as prime cotton acreage. Jackson and his troops had repeatedly marched through there during the war. Now that cotton prices were rising, and old cotton land to the east was reaching exhaustion, the demand for accessible agricultural land like that in northern Alabama had become intense. By the time the cession was completed, in 1816, 10,000 squatters had entered the territory now being described as the future "Garden of America."

Andrew Jackson and his nephew by marriage John Coffee, a former fellow officer in the war against the Creeks in 1813 and 1814, were at the center of the "Alabama fever." Jackson in late 1816 used his influence in Washington to have Coffee appointed head government surveyor of the Alabama land cessions. In this post, Coffee was in a position to know exactly where the most valuable lands were, and he made his fortune by it. At the suggestion of his Uncle Andrew, it is said, Coffee made an agreement with the Land Office clerks to receive half of any bribes they took for giving information about land or aiding in its acquisition. Coffee also took care of his relatives. Among other enterprises, he formed a land company whose shares were divided among Tennessee and Philadelphia speculators; Andrew Jackson was one of them. In 1818 Jackson bought land on his own near the

Shoals (with no one bidding against him), and in the same year Coffee bought eighty-three tracts totaling 16,000 acres. The officially recorded value of these lands was $76,000 (at $4.75 an acre), but comparable land in the same area was selling for $40 an acre and some for as much as $78 an acre. Jackson later also acquired a 2,700-acre plantation in Mississippi on erstwhile Indian land.

The hunger for Indian land was most intense in the Southern slave-owning states, and Jackson as a politician generally reflected Southern economic interests. He became the political prime mover of the Indian-removal process. In 1824 he ran unsuccessfully for President on the Democratic ticket. In 1828 he tried again, and won, and one of his first actions as President was to call, in his inaugural address in 1829, for the passage of a Removal Act that would effectively dislodge the Native Americans—and especially the Southern tribes—from their ancestral lands east of the Mississippi River and colonize them in an Indian territory west of the Mississippi. The Act was passed in 1830, and during the remainder of his presidency, and for several years thereafter, the government proceeded to persuade—with force when necessary—the tribes to "voluntarily"—surrender their territories and emigrate to allotted tracts, primarily in what is now the state of Oklahoma.

In all this mania for the land of the Native Americans, Jackson himself does not stand out as the greediest of speculators. He took care of himself, to be sure, and he was always ready to reward family, friends, and political constituents, but he was also concerned to develop the country by expanding its agriculture and commerce. By the time of his death in 1845 (after virtually all the Southern Indians had been removed), he had managed to amass an extensive estate, including the well-furnished mansion at The Hermitage, two plantations, 161 slaves, a valuable stable of fifty horses, and hundreds of head of livestock. He was in his financial dealings a typical man of his time, and by action, precept, and example he fed the land fever of others.

But although Jackson was the most visible, forceful, and effective exponent of the white man's desire to acquire Indian land, the source of his own and others' land hunger lay in larger processes of economic change. The appetite for Indian land in the American South in the 1820s and '30s was whetted by economic events outside the region, in Great Britain and the northern part of the United States. There an industrial revolution was under way. Steam engines had been developed to pump water out of coal mines, making access to the deeper veins for the first time practicable; steam engines now supplied power for factories, permitting a concentration of production in cities rather than in the old dispersed pattern along country streams that turned water-wheels; steam engines powered boats on the waters and steam locomotives drew trains of cars on land, opening up for economic development (along with a network of canals) new regions hitherto virtually inaccessible. And to supply the increasing need for iron and steel, English blast furnaces were now able to substitute for charcoal a seemingly inexhaustible supply of coke, cheaply made from soft coal; and American iron works (after the introduction of the hot blast in the late 1830s) were able to employ another seemingly inexhaustible supply of fuel, Pennsylvania anthracite.

In Great Britain, the centerpiece of the Industrial Revolution was cotton manufacturing. Large factories, powered by water or steam, crammed with long lines of automatic spinning and weaving machines, spewed out enormous quantities of yarn and cloth made from American raw cotton. British cotton goods were sold all over the world as the British Empire extended its global economic grip, and as a result the demand for American cotton was voracious.

America produced, in the mid-1830s, about 400 million pounds of cotton per year, most of it exported to Great Britain. According to one estimate, America sold abroad in 1836 about 384 million pounds of raw cotton, which amounted to two-thirds of all the cotton produced for export in the world. Upland Georgia cotton, a variety of middling quality, cost about ten cents a pound to produce; it sold on an average for sixteen cents a pound, but prices could go as high as forty-four cents a pound; a single acre would produce a crop of about two hundred pounds. A 500-acre cotton plantation thus could expect to make a profit on the order of $6,000 a year—a very large sum in those days.

The worldwide demand for manufactured cotton goods was enormous. In England, France, and the United States, about eight pounds of cotton cloth per capita was consumed each year, and although far less cotton was used in the nonindustrialized countries, it was estimated that worldwide consumption of manufactured cotton goods amounted to two pounds per capita per annum. With a world population of about 450 million at that time, the annual consumption of cotton goods was about 900 million pounds, nearly half of it made from raw cotton grown in the American South.

Americans of all sorts, in all kinds of places, were obsessed with Southern cotton. The hunger for new cotton lands affected all classes of Southern society. Not merely prospective growers of plantation cotton caught the "Alabama fever," but also land speculators, and settlers who expected to make their fortunes in subsidiary activities on which the plantations depended—millwrights, blacksmiths, and other artisans of all kinds, doctors and lawyers, teamsters and steamboat captains, storekeepers and small farmers and railway workers. The demand for raw cotton was also increasing in the Northern United States, particularly in New England and Pennsylvania, where American cotton mills were beginning to compete with the British in the expanding American market for cotton goods. The Northern factories were aided, to be sure, by a protective tariff, which drove up the cost of British goods in the North as well as the South, and was leading to a bitter interregional conflict over federal tariff policy.

The increasing resentment in the South against the protective tariff was only one factor in the rise of a separatist sentiment that was becoming increasingly virulent. Particularly in Georgia, there was real bitterness against the federal government (which alone had the constitutional authority to hold treaties with the Native Americans and to purchase their lands) for its failure to remove the Indians. It had promised to do so as long ago as

1802, when Georgia relinquished to the United States its claim to sovereignty over what became the states of Alabama and Mississippi. The promise to purchase all the Native American land in Georgia, turn it over to the state, and transport the Indians elsewhere still remained partially unfulfilled when the Removal Act was finally passed, after much debate, in 1830.

The urge to convert "unused" Indian land into commercially productive cotton fields affected not only the white folks but the Native Americans themselves. Among the Southern Indians particularly, there was a recognized social class called "half-breeds," distinguished from the "full-bloods" by some degree of white ancestry, usually on the father's side. Many of these half-breeds were sired by men of property who had taken refuge, or made their fortunes in, Indian country, had married Indian—or part-Indian—women, and had raised their children in homes where English was spoken. These children were sent to mission schools or even to white academies, where they received anything from a basic acquaintance with the three R's to an education in the classics and advanced training in one of the professions. Although they identified themselves as Indians in a native community where one's tribal and clan membership were inherited from the mother, they emulated their white cousins in economic behavior. For a considerable number of half-breeds, the form this emulation took—or perhaps competition would be a better word—was to establish a cotton plantation, complete with mansion house, livestock, and black slaves.

One of the most successful of the Native American plantation owners was the Cherokee chief John Ross (1790–1866). His father was a Loyalist of Scottish origin who fled the persecution of the rebels during the Revolution, married a Cherokee woman (herself actually of only one-quarter Indian descent), and remained with the tribe after independence. John Ross was educated at a white academy in Tennessee but returned to live in the Cherokee country. During the War of 1812, being literate in English as well as fluent in Cherokee, he volunteered to serve as adjutant officer to a regiment of Cherokee warriors recruited by Andrew Jackson to fight against the Creeks, who had joined the British. He took part with Jackson and Coffee in the bloody battle at Horseshoe Bend on the Tallapoosa River, where Ross's regiment played a major role in the slaughter of over five hundred Creek fighters and the sacking of their main fortified town.

In the years after the war, proud, aristocratic in manner, statesmanlike in policy, Ross became a man of great influence in the Cherokee nation. He established his own plantation in Georgia, at the head of the Coosa River near the Alabama line, where he served as federal postmaster and operated a lucrative ferry worth $1,000 per year in income. It was a substantial establishment on about three hundred acres, including a large two-story family residence, seventy feet long, boasting twenty glass windows and a covered porch running the length of it. There was an overseer's house, three cabins for his twenty or so slaves, a building where circuit preachers regularly held Methodist services, various barns and stables, a blacksmith shop, and fruit orchards. "Head of Coosa" was appraised, after he was driven out of it, at about $20,000. John Ross was not wealthy on the scale of an Andrew Jackson—but he was prosperous. Favoring the "civilization" of Native Americans in their ancestral territories, he supported the introduction of missionary academies and training schools for artisans. He was a prime mover in creating the Cherokee republican constitution, modeled after that of the United States, in 1827. He was, however, as one of the two principal chiefs established in the new government, the leader of the major faction that opposed Jackson and his removal policy. His opposition, of course, proved to be unsuccessful, and his former association with Andrew Jackson did him no good: an attempt was made on his life by a white man, his plantation was seized and sold in the Georgia lottery, he was briefly arrested and jailed, he was forced to organize the removal of most of the tribe, and his Indian wife, Quatie, died in Arkansas in 1839 during the emigration so aptly called "the trail of tears."

Yet John Ross did not give up the struggle to advance the fortunes of the Cherokees. He served as principal chief of the united Cherokee nation in Indian territory until his death in 1866. And he built a new cotton plantation, worked (until emancipation) by numerous slaves.

John Ross was, in a sense, the mirror image of Andrew Jackson, a gentleman of the Old South, stamped on the Indian side of the American coin. And what white Georgia feared most was the rise of men like John Ross. It was not the "savagery" of the Indians that land-hungry whites dreaded; it was their "civilization."

The consequences of the trans-Mississippi removal of the Southern Indians, and to a lesser extent of the Northern Indians as well, were momentous. The United States acquired millions of acres of fertile Southern land, which it sold at little or no profit to speculators and settlers, thereby in effect subsidizing the expansion of the cotton industry and the slave system along with it. The rapidly increasing population in the North also moved westward. For the Native Americans who were relocated in the Indian territory, the removal was of course an immediate disaster, costly in lives and wealth.

But it was a disaster that never really ended. The government thereafter pursued the same policy of buying Native American lands and relocating Native American tribes as the nation moved westward. The Indian territory (as did other reservations) became a vast, poverty-stricken concentration camp for dispossessed Native Americans, administered by a federal bureaucracy—the Bureau of Indian Affairs, created by Jackson's presidential directive—that largely controlled the local economy, the local police, and the local schools.

It is remarkable how little attention has been paid to the removal of the 1830s, and the events consequent upon it, by general historians of the United States. Despite the labors of a number of specialists in Indian history, the authors of textbooks and scholarly treatises that profess a national view have virtually ignored the Indian wars and removals of the post-colonial era. The Indians were big news in the seventeenth and eighteenth centuries; Francis Parkman memorialized their savage exploits during their wars against the French and the British. But the Native Americans appear only briefly as tiny blips on the screen of nineteenth-century history, unfriendly but fortunately feeble opponents of the manifest destiny that Jackson and his colleagues worked so ardently to fulfill, scarcely slowing the inevitable march of the redeemer nation to the Pacific. Attention has been lavished instead on the political and economic restructuring of America, on Jacksonian democracy, on the centrist vs. separatist issue as it affected the banking system, tariff policy, and the extension of slavery into states only recently liberated from thralldom to their aboriginal occupants.

To learn more about Indian removal, specifically the removal of the Cherokee and the Trail of Tears, visit http://www.ngeorgia.com/history/nghisttt.html.

@ ON THE WEB

 SOURCES

The Election of Jackson

Andrew Jackson was elected president twice—in 1828 and in 1832. Here is how the voters responded to Jackson in 1828. Overall he won 56 percent of the national vote, but he generally did better in the South than he did in the North. Why do you think that was the case? Do the results in any way surprise you?

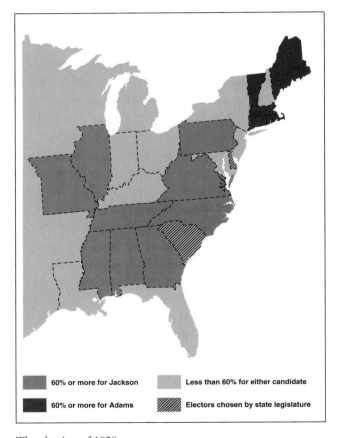

60% or more for Jackson	Less than 60% for either candidate
60% or more for Adams	Electors chosen by state legislature

The election of 1828.

 ON THE WEB
To learn more about the life and presidency of Andrew Jackson, visit the website of the North Carolina State Library at http://statelibrary.dcr.state.nc.us/nc/bio/public/jackson.htm.

Removal of Eastern Tribes

Andrew Jackson, elected president in 1828, pushed through the Indian Removal Act of 1830. The purpose of the bill was to get eastern tribes to sign away their current lands for reservations west of the Mississippi River. Jackson had an easy time getting the bill through the Senate, but had trouble in the House of Representatives, losing several test votes before finally prevailing by a vote of 102 to 97. Force, fraud, bribery, and murder were used to get the tribal chiefs to sign over tribal lands, and the United States Army was used to force tribe members to move west. The most famous removal, the Trail of Tears, involved John Ross's Cherokees. But others suffered just as much. All the major tribes of the Deep South lost their homelands and experienced the horrors of Indian removal. So too did some northern tribes.

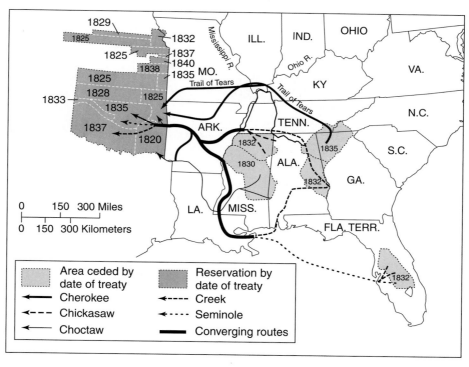

Expulsion of the eastern tribes.

The Anti-Jacksonians

The response to Andrew Jackson was intense. Most people either loved him or hated him, and only a handful were neutral about him. Those who hated him had to be organized and brought to the polls on election day. To get out this vote, his opponents attacked him with cartoons and broadsides as well as with speeches. While some attention was given to his mistreatment of the eastern tribes, much more was made of his violent nature, his street fights, and his many executions of army deserters and enemies. Why do you think this was the case? Do you think such propaganda had any effect on the voters? Undoubtedly it made little difference in states that Jackson either won or lost by big margins. But what about the close states? Who do you think would be influenced by such appeals? Why do you think the opposition decided not to emphasize his record as an "Indian killer"?

"*Jackson is to be President, and you will be HANGED.*"

Corbis images.

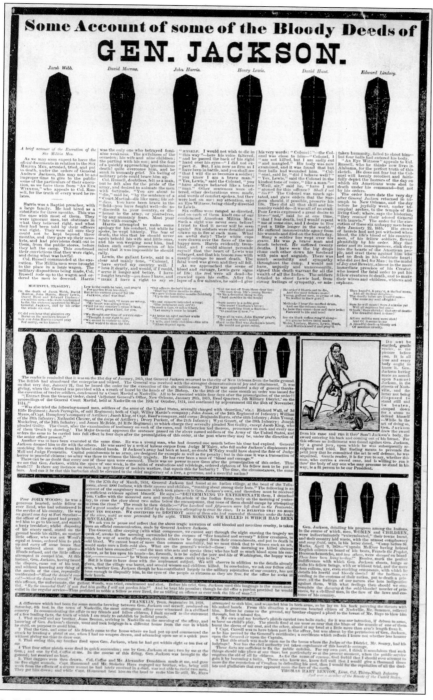

"King Andrew"

Later, when Jackson was president and vetoed more bills than all his predecessors combined and simply ignored the Supreme Court, the opposition tried to portray him as a tyrannical monarch. The first cartoon, which is quite famous, shows Jackson placing his will above that of the Constitution, the courts, and the good of the country. The second cartoon draws upon violent episodes from Jackson's military past and likens him to the English monarch Richard III, who was accused of murdering two young princes in the Tower of London. Which of the two cartoons do you think was more effective?

American Antiquarian Society.

The Art of Democratic Politics

Jackson was a rich Tennessee planter with over 100 slaves, but sometimes he was portrayed by his followers as a man of the people, an unlettered hero of the west, who spoke common sense and easily routed the learned eastern establishment. To counter this propaganda, anti-Jacksonians eventually found good copy in Davy Crockett, who had served in Congress since 1826 and had toasted Jackson for betraying the backwoodsmen of western Tennessee. Crockett played the role of a comic backwoods hero who claimed to be half-alligator, half-horse, with a touch of the snapping turtle. Here Crockett explains to a Little Rock audience the tricks of democratic politics.

From David Crockett, *The Life of Colonel David Crockett*, Porter and Coates, Philadelphia, 1865, pp. 275–278.

Having gone through with the regular toasts, the president of the day drank, "Our distinguished guest, Col. Crockett," which called forth a prodigious clattering all around the table, and I soon saw that nothing would do, but I must get up and make them a speech. I had no sooner elongated my outward Adam, than they at it again, with renewed vigor, which made me sort of feel that I was still somebody, though no longer a member of Congress.

In my speech I went over the whole history of the present administration; took a long shot at the flying deposites, and gave an outline, a sort of charcoal sketch, of the political life of "the Government's" heir-presumptive. I also let them know how I had been rascaled out of my election, because I refused to bow down to the idol; and as I saw a number of young politicians around the table, I told them, that I would lay down a few rules for their guidance, which, if properly attended to, could not fail to lead them on the highway to distinction and public honor. I told them, that I was an old hand at the business, and as I was about to retire for a time I would give them a little instruction gratis, for I was up to all the tricks of the trade, though I had practiced but few.

"Attend all public meetings," says I, "and get some friends to move that you take the chair; if you fail in this attempt, make a push to be appointed secretary; the proceedings of course will be published, and your name is introduced to the public. But should you fail in both undertakings, get two or three acquaintances, over a bottle of whisky, to pass some resolutions, no matter on what subject; publish them even if you pay the printer—it will answer the purpose of breaking the ice, which is the main point in these matters. Intrigue until you are elected an officer of the militia; this is the second step towards promotion, and can be accomplished with ease, as I know an instance of an election being advertised, and no one attending, the innkeeper at whose house it was to be held, having a military turn, elected himself colonel of his regiment." Says I, "You may not accomplish your ends with as little difficulty, but do not be discouraged—Rome wasn't built in a day.

"If your ambition or circumstances compel you to serve your country, and earn three dollars a day, by becoming a member of the legislature, you must first publicly avow that the constitution of the state is a shackle upon free and liberal legislation; and is, therefore, of as little use in the present enlightened age, as an old almanac of the year in which the instrument was framed. There is policy in this measure, for by making the constitution a mere dead letter, your headlong proceedings will be attributed to a bold and unshackled mind; whereas, it might otherwise be thought they arose from sheer mulish ignorance. 'The Government' has set the example in his attack upon the constitution of the United States, and who should fear to follow where 'the Government' leads?

"When the day of election approaches, visit your constituents far and wide. Treat liberally, and drink freely, in order to rise in their estimation, though you fall in your own. True, you may be called a drunken dog by some of the clean shirt and silk stocking gentry, but the real rough necks will style you a jovial fellow, their votes are certain, and frequently count double. Do all you can to appear to advantage in the eyes of the women. That's easily done you have but to kiss and slabber their children, wipe their noses, and pat them on the head; this cannot fail to please their mothers, and you may rely on your business being done in that quarter.

"Promise all that is asked," said I, "and more if you can think of anything. Offer to build a bridge or a church, to divide a county, create a batch of new offices, make a turnpike, or anything they like. Promises cost nothing, therefore deny nobody who has a vote or sufficient influence to obtain one.

"Get up on all occasions, and sometimes on no occasion at all, and make long-winded speeches, though composed of nothing else than wind— talk of your devotion to your country, your modesty and disinterestedness, or on any such fanciful subject. Rail against taxes of all kinds, office-holders, and bad harvest weather; and wind up with a flourish about the heroes who fought and bled for our liberties in the times that tried men's souls. To be sure you run the risk of being considered a bladder of wind, or an empty barrel, but never mind that, you will find enough of the same fraternity to keep you in countenance.

"If any charity be going forward, be at the top of it, provided it is to be advertised publicly; if not, it isn't worth your while. None but a fool would place his candle under a bushel on such an occasion.

"These few directions," said I, "if properly attended to, will do your business; and when once elected, why a fig for the dirty children, the promises, the bridges, the churches, the taxes, the offices, and the subscriptions, for it is absolutely necessary to forget all these before you become a thoroughgoing politician, and a patriot of the first water."

My speech was received with three times three, and all that; and we continued speechifying and drinking until nightfall, when it was put to vote, that we would have the puppet show over again, which was carried *nem.con.* The showman set his wires to work, just as "the Government" does the machinery in his big puppet show; and we spent a delightful and rational evening. We raised a subscription for the poor showman; and I went to bed, pleased and gratified with the hospitality and kindness of the citizens of Little Rock. There are some first-rate men there, of the real half horse, half alligator breed, with a sprinkling of the steamboat, and such as grow nowhere on the face of the universal earth, but just about the back bone of North America.

The Election of 1840

By 1840, political strategists of all stripes were willing to try what one newsman called the "Davy Crockett Line" and portray their candidates as simple backwoodsmen who had been raised on possum fat and hominy. The Harrison campaign for president in 1840 probably carried political hoopla to an extreme. As you look at the following picture and read the newspaper account of a St. Louis political rally, you will begin to understand not only why Harrison won but also why the election brought 78 percent of the electorate out to vote. In many ways the Harrison campaign was the first modern political campaign.

F.D.R. Library.

 ON THE WEB　　*To view of map of the results of the election of 1840, see* http://www.britannica.com/
elections/1840.html.

❧ Rally for William Henry Harrison in St. Louis, Missouri

We cannot believe that any friend of Harrison could, in his most sanguine moments, have anticipated so glorious a day, such a turn-out of the people, as was witnessed on Tuesday last in this city. Everything was auspicious. The heavens, the air, the earth all seemed to have combined to assist in doing honor to the services, the patriotism and the virtues of William Henry Harrison. Never have we seen so much enthusiasm, so much honest, impassioned and eloquent feeling displayed in the countenances and bursting from the lips of freemen. It was a day of jubilee. The people felt that the time had come when they could breathe freely—when they were about to cast from them the incubus of a polluted and abandoned party, and when they could look forward to better and happier days in store for them and for the country.

Preparations had been made for the reception and entertainment of the company, by the proper committees, at Mrs. Ashley's residence. The extensive park was so arranged as to accommodate the throng of persons who were expected. Seats were erected for the officers of the day, for the speakers and for the ladies. At the hour appointed by the marshal of the day, the people commenced to assemble at the court house, and several associations and crafts were formed in the procession as they advanced on the ground. While this was going on, the steamboats bringing delegations from St. Charles, Hannibal, Adams county, Ill., and Alton, arrived at the wharf, with banners unfurled to the breeze, and presenting a most cheering sight. The order of procession, so far as we have been able to obtain it, was as follows:

Music: Brass band.

1. Banner, borne by farmers from the northern part of St. Louis township. This banner represented the "Raising of the Siege of Fort Meigs" and bore as its motto, "It Has Pleased Providence, We Are Victorious." (Harrison's dispatch.)
2. Officers and members of the Tippecanoe club, preceded by the president, Col. John O'Fallon, with a splendid banner, representing a hemisphere surmounted by an American eagle, strangling with his beak a serpent, its fold grasped within its talons, and its head having the face of a fox in the throes of death.
3. Log cabin committee, six abreast.
4. Soldiers who served under Harrison in the late war—in a car, adorned with banners on each side—one, a view of a steamboat named Tippecanoe, with a sign board, "For Washington City."
6. Invited guests in carriages.

From "Rally for William Henry Harrison in St. Louis, Missouri," as reported by the St. Louis *New Era*, in A. B. Norton, ed., *The Election of 1840*, vol. I, 1888, pp. 141–146.

7. Citizens on foot, six abreast, bearing banners inscribed, "Harrison, the Friend of Pre-emption Rights," "One Term for the Presidency," "Harrison, the People's Candidate;" "Harrison, the People's Sober Second Thought;" "Harrison, He Never Lost a Battle;" "Harrison, the Protector of the Pioneers of the West;" "Harrison, Tyler and Reform;" "Harrison, the Poor Man's Friend;" "Harrison, the Friend of Equal Laws and Equal Rights."
8. Citizens on horseback, six abreast.
9. Delegation from Columbia Bottom.
10. Canoe, "North Bend."
11. Boys with banners, upon one of which was inscribed, "Our Country's Hope," and on another, "Just as the Twig is Bent, the Tree's Inclined."
12. Laborers, with their horses and carts, shovels, picks, etc., with a banner bearing the inscription, "Harrison, the Poor Man's Friend— We Want Work."
13. A printing press on a platform with banners, and the pressman striking off Tippecanoe songs, and distributing them to the throng of people as they passed along, followed in order by the members of the craft.
14. Drays, with barrels of hard cider.
15. A log cabin mounted on wheels, and drawn by six beautiful horses, followed by the craft of carpenters in great numbers. Over the door of the cabin, the words, "The String of the Latch Never Pulled In."
16. The blacksmiths, with forge, bellows, etc., mounted on cars, the men at work. Banner, "We Strike for Our Country's Good."
17. The joiners and cabinet-makers; a miniature shop mounted on wheels; men at work; the craft following it.
18. A large canoe, drawn by six horses, and filled with men.
19. Two canoes, mounted, and filled by sailors.
20. Fort Meigs, in miniature, 40 by 15 feet, drawn by nine yoke of oxen.

Arrived at the southern extremity of the park, the procession halted and formed in open order, the rear passing to the front.

The people were then successively addressed by Mr. John Hogan, of Illinois.

Colonial John O'Fallon was then called for, and mounted on Fort Meigs, he thus addressed the people:

> My Fellow Citizens:
> I feel deeply sensible of the honor you confer upon me by calling me to address this vast concourse of intelligent freemen.
> I had the honor of serving under General Harrison at the battle of Tippecanoe, during the siege of Fort Meigs, and at the battle of the Thames. I can say that, from the commencement to the termination of his military services in the last war, I was almost constantly by his side. I was familiar with his conduct as governor and superintendent of Indian affairs of the Territory of Indiana, and after the return of peace, as commissioner to treat

with all the hostile Indians of the last war in the Northwest, for the establishment of a permanent reconciliation and peace. I saw also much of General Harrison whilst he was in the Congress of the United States.

Opportunities have thus been afforded me of knowing him in all the relations of life, as an officer and as a man, and of being enabled to form a pretty correct estimate of his military and civil services, as well as his qualifications and fitness for office.

As a military man, his daring, chivalrous courage inspired his men with confidence and spread dismay and terror to his enemies. In all his plans he was successful. In all his engagements he was victorious. He has filled all the various civil and military offices committed to him by his country, with sound judgment and spotless fidelity. In every situation he was cautious and prudent, firm and energetic, and his decisions always judicious. His acquirements as a scholar are varied and extensive, his principles as a statesman sound, pure and republican.

If chosen President he will be the President of the people rather than of a party. The Government will then be administered for the general good and welfare.

His election will be drawn of a new era! The reform of the abuses of a most corrupt, profligate and oppressive Government. Then will end the ten years' war upon the currency and institutions of the country. The hard-money cry and hard times will disappear altogether. Then will cease further attempts to increase the wages of the office-holders and reduce the wages of the people to the standard of European labor.

Then shall we see restored the general prosperity of the people, by giving them a sound local currency, mixed with a currency of a uniform value throughout the land. The revival of commerce, of trade, enterprise and general confidence. Then the return of happier, more peaceful and more prosperous days, when cheerfulness and plenty will, once more, smile around the poor man's table.

The Artist's View of Politics

What were ordinary elections like? Fortunately, the painter George Caleb Bingham of Missouri provided some answers to this question. He broke into western politics in 1840 as an enthusiastic young orator for Harrison, and he eventually won a seat in the Missouri House of Representatives. He knew that every vote counted; he won one election by a mere three votes and another by twenty-five votes.

He painted these memorable political scenes out of his own experience. The first one, "Canvassing for a Vote," shows a campaigner with a saddlebag full of literature trying to win a vote outside a highway tavern. The second, "County Election," shows the voters lined up to cast their ballots verbally, with candidates on top of the steps tipping their hats politely, and the inevitable barrel of cider (or whiskey) on the left. The third, "Verdict of the People," shows a clerk reading election results aloud from the steps of the courthouse. The fourth, "Stump Speaking," is Bingham's masterpiece. It shows an experienced politician who has grown gray in the pursuit of office trying to influence a crowd. The man taking notes is his opponent, and the fat man at the far left is the former governor of

Missouri, Meredith Miles Marmaduke. He was so angry when he saw this painting that he challenged Bingham to a duel.

Compare these pictures with some earlier ones on pages 222 and 223. Do they help you understand why Jacksonian politics was regarded as being new and different? Was it really a complete break with the past? Or can you see some carryover from earlier days?

"Convassing for a Vote," George Bingham. George Caleb Bingham, "Canvassing for a Vote," 1852. Collection of Nelson—Atkins Museum of Art, Kansas City, MO. All Rights Reserved. W. R. Nelson Trust.

"County Election," George Bingham. George Caleb Bingham, "County Election," 1851/52. The Saint Louis Art Museum Purchase.

"Verdict of the People," George Bingham. George Caleb Bingham, "Verdict of the People." From the collection of Bank of America.

"Stump Speaking," George Bingham. George Caleb Bingham, "Stump Speaking." From the collection of Bank of America.

THE BIG PICTURE

The politics of Jacksonian America have often been seen as more vibrant and more violent than politics today. What was different about the politics of Jackson's day? Why was Jackson the towering figure of his age? How do you account for the fact that the two parties in the election of 1840 were able to get 78 percent of the electorate out to vote, while parties today are lucky to get 50 percent of the electorate to the polls?

Chapter *10*

Antislavery

Interpretive Essay by James Brewer Stewart 234

Sources 244

    Commission to Theodore Dwight Weld, 1834 244

    The *Anti-Slavery Record*, 1835–1836 248

    "Fathers and Rulers" Petition 251

    Slavery as It Is, 1839 252

The Big Picture 254

There was one issue that leaders of both parties, Whigs and Democrats alike, wanted to keep out of politics. And that issue was slavery. Politicians of all stripes knew that slavery could easily shatter their national parties—and perhaps the Union itself. They preferred to fight over "safe" political issues like banking, tariffs, roads, and canals. And they fought over such issues year in and year out. In working to keep slavery out of the limelight, of course, politicians were effectively supporting slavery, which was an old and well-established institution by Jackson's time.

Keeping slavery out of politics, however, became increasingly difficult. For one thing, the old institution of slavery, which had been "normal" throughout the Atlantic world since the 1500s, began to give way rapidly after the American Revolution. By 1804 all northern states had either freed their slaves or adopted programs of gradual emancipation. And by the time of Jackson's second administration (1833–1837) programs to abolish slavery had been adopted in Haiti, Argentina, Chile, Colombia, Central America, Mexico, Bolivia, and the British West Indies. The American South was beginning to stand out like a sore thumb.

For another thing, "reform" was in the air after the War of 1812, especially in the North, where all sorts of reformers suddenly emerged and tromped across the countryside. In contrast to the South, where one could go for weeks without hearing the cry of reform, there were parts of New

England, upstate New York, and the Ohio Valley that seemed to be overrun with revivalists, reformers, and enthusiasts espousing one cause or another.

Why? The answers have been almost as numerous as the reformers and abolitionists. One point of view is that the reformers, especially the men and women who came out against slavery, were simply working out the logic of modern egalitarianism. Did not the Declaration of Independence assert simply the equality of all men? How could such a faith coexist with slavery? Other historians have argued that reform, especially in its connection with revivalism, was a product of the experience of the frontier. Others have claimed that the reform leaders were members of an old elite that was afraid of being displaced by a new class of people whose wealth came from business, and so turned to reform to relieve their anxiety at losing control of the nation's social and political life.

Another point of view is that the prime recruits for reform movements were to be found among people whose ethnic and regional identities led them to undergo conversion to a militant Protestant revivalism. Immigrants from England and Wales, and migrants from New England to the west, so this argument goes, were the people most likely to answer the evangelical preachers' calls that they dedicate their lives to Christ. Out of this wave of revival, on both sides of the Atlantic, came an army of hundreds of thousands of converts. And it was from among them that a tiny minority was chosen, a minority who turned now to try to perfect society in the image of Christ, and in so doing to try to perfect themselves.

INTERPRETIVE ESSAY

The Commitment to Immediate Emancipation

James Brewer Stewart

The following essay, by the historian James Brewer Stewart, examines the relationship between nineteenth-century Protestantism and the commitment to the immediate end of slavery. There were a variety of antislavery positions, some favoring gradual abolition, others immediate; some advocating sending ex-slaves to Africa; others involving paying former slaveowners something like the market value of their freed slaves. The most radical position, which gained ground after 1830, was the uncompromising demand for the immediate, unconditional emancipation of slaves without compensation to their owners—and without regard for the consequences. Only a minority of Americans with antislavery opinions adopted this position, and this selection is a guide to understanding who they were and why they embarked on such a course.

American society in the late 1820s presented the pious, well-informed Yankee with tremendous challenges. For the better part of a decade, Protestant spokesmen had warned him against the nation's all-absorbing interest in material wealth, geographic expansion, and party politics. Infidelity, he was told, flourished on the western and southern frontiers; vice reigned supreme in the burgeoning eastern cities. In politics, he was exhorted to combat atheist demagogues called Jacksonians who insisted on popular rule and further demanded that the clerical establishment be divorced from government. Urban workingmen and frontier pioneers, morally numbed by alcoholism and illiteracy, were being duped in massive numbers by the blandishments of these greedy politicos. America, he was assured, faced moral bankruptcy and the total destruction of its Christian identity. Exaggerated as such claims may seem, they had some grounding in reality. Yankee Protestantism was indeed facing immense new challenges from a society in the throes of massive social change. As Protestants struggled to overcome these adversities, the abolitionists' crusade for immediate emancipation also took form.

By the end of the 1820s, America was in the midst of unparalleled economic growth. Powerful commercial networks were coming to link all sections of the country; canals, mass-circulation newspapers, and (soon) railroads reinforced this thrust toward regional interdependency. Northern business depended as never before on trade with the south. The "cotton revolution" that swept the Mississippi-Alabama-Georgia frontier in turn stimulated tex-

From James Brewer Stewart, *Holy Warriors: The Abolitionists and American Slavery*, Hill and Wang, New York, 1976, pp. 33–49. Copyright © 1976 by James Brewer Stewart. Reprinted with the permission of Hill and Wang, a division of Farrar, Straus & Giroux, Inc.

tile manufacturing and shipping in the northeast. In the northwest, yet another economic boom took shape as businessmen and farmers in Ohio, Indiana, and Illinois developed lucrative relationships with the eastern seaboard, and the population of northern cities grew apace. Politicians organized party machines that catered to these new interests and to the "common man's" mundane preferences.

The cosmopolitan forces of economic interdependence, urbanization, democratic politics, and mass communication posed major challenges to provincial New England culture. The Protestant response, in John L. Thomas's apt phrase, was "to fight democratic excess with democratic remedies." Throughout the 1820s New Englanders mounted an impressive counterattack against the forces of "immorality" by commandeering the tools of their secular opponents: the printing press, the rally, and the efficiently managed bureaucratic agency. With the hope of renovating American religious life, the American Tract Society spewed forth thousands of pamphlets that exhorted readers to repent. The Temperance Union carried a similar message to the nation's innumerable hard drinkers. Various missionary societies sent witnesses to backcountry settlements, the waterfront haunts of Boston's seamen, the bordellos of New York City. These societies envisioned a reassertion of traditional New England values on a national scale. At the same time, although unintentionally, these programs for Christian restoration were stimulating in pious young men and women stirrings of spiritual revolt.

All of these reform enterprises drew their vitality from revivalistic religion. Once again, social discontent and political alienation found widespread expression through the conversion experience; the Great Revivals announced the Protestant resurgence of the 1820s. Like their eighteenth-century predecessors, powerful evangelists such as Charles G. Finney and Lyman Beecher urged their audiences that man, though a sinner, should nonetheless strive for holiness and choose a new life of sanctification. Free will once again took precedence over original sin, which was again redefined as voluntary selfishness. As in the 1750s, God was pictured as insisting that the "saved" performed acts of benevolence, expand the boundaries of Christ's kingdom, and recognize a personal responsibility to improve society. Men and women again saw themselves playing dynamic roles in their own salvation and preparing society for the millennium. By the thousands they flocked to the Tract Society, the Sunday School Union, the temperance and peace organizations, and the Colonization Society. Seeking prevention, certainly not revolution, evangelicals thus dreamed of a glorious era of national reform: rid of liquor, prostitution, atheism, and popular politics, the redeemed masses of America would gladly submit to the leadership of Christian statesmen. So blessed, Americans would no longer fall prey to the blandishments of that hard-drinking gambler, duelist, and unchurched slaveowner, President Andrew Jackson.

From this defensive setting sprang New England's crusade against slavery. Indeed, radical reformers of all varieties, not just abolitionists, traced their activism to the revivals of the 1820s. . . .

While revivalism's ambiguities stimulated anxiety in the 1820s, its network of benevolent agencies opened opportunities for young Americans that their eighteenth-century counterparts could never have foreseen. The missionary agencies and even the revivals themselves were organized along complex bureaucratic lines. Volunteers were always needed to drum up donations or to organize meetings. New careers were also created. For the first time in American history, young people could regard social activism as a legitimate profession. Earnest ministerial candidates began accepting full-time positions as circuit riders, regional agents, newspaper editors, and schoolteachers, with salaries underwritten by the various benevolent agencies. One important abolitionist-to-be, Joshua Leavitt, spent his first years after seminary editing the *Seaman's Friend*, an evangelical periodical for sailors. Another, Elizur Wright, Jr., was employed by the American Tract Society.

Most important to abolitionism was the effect of revivalism on the ministry itself. Once open to only an elite, the ministry had by the 1820s become a common profession. Spurred by expanding geography, seminaries increased their enrollments as they attracted young New Englanders who burned to aid in America's regeneration. Included were some destined to number among abolitionism's dominant figures: Samuel J. May, Amos A. Phelps, Theodore D. Weld, Joshua Leavitt, and Stephen S. Foster, to name only a few. First as seminarians, then as volunteers, paid agents, clergymen, and teachers, many pious young Americans dedicated themselves to fighting sin and disbelief. Given the intensity of the evangelical temperament, the results of such experiences were to suggest, to some, far more radical courses of action, and there can be no question that these abolitionists-to-be took their responsibilities in deadly earnest.

There is some persuasive evidence that family background and upbringing predisposed young New Englanders toward a radical outlook. Over twenty years ago, David Donald gathered information that suggests the influence of parental guidance on abolitionism's most prominent spokesmen. Abolitionism, he reported, was a revolt of youth raised by old New England families of farmers, teachers, ministers, and businessmen. The parents of abolitionists were usually well-educated Presbyterians, Congregationalists, Quakers, and Unitarians who participated heavily in revivalism and its attendant benevolent projects. Many scholars have effectively criticized Donald's methods and have raised serious questions about the reliability of his evidence regarding the movement's rank-and-file. Donald also erred in concluding that commitments to abolitionism were reactions to a loss of social status to nouveau riche neighbors. Actually, abolitionism flourished among groups with rising social prospects during the 1830s. Nevertheless, Donald's findings remain extremely suggestive as to the influence of parental guidance of abolitionism's most prominent leaders.

In such families, as numerous biographers have since attested, a stern emphasis on moral uprightness and social responsibility generally prevailed. In the words of Bertram Wyatt-Brown, young men and women "learned that integrity came not from conformity to the ways of the world, but to the principles by which the family tried to live." Parents were usually eager to inculcate a high degree of religious and social conscience. In their reminiscences, abolitionists commonly paid homage to strong-minded mothers or fathers whose intense religious fervor dominated their households. In his early years, Wendell Phillips constantly turned to his mother for instruction, and after her death he confessed that "whatever good is in me, she is responsible for." Thomas Wentworth Higginson, Arthur and Lewis Tappan, and William Lloyd Garrison became, like Phillips, leading abolitionists and also internalized the religious dictates of dominating mothers. Sidney Howard Gay, James G. Birney, Elizur Wright, Jr., and Elijah P. Lovejoy are examples of abolitionists who modeled their early lives to fit the intentions of exacting fathers. Young women who were to enter the movement usually sought the advice of their fathers, as in the cases of Elizabeth Cady Stanton and Maria Weston Chapman. Yet whatever the child's focus, the expectations of parents seldom varied. Displays of conscience and upright behavior brought the rewards of parental love and approval.

Children also learned that sexual self-control was a vital part of righteous living. Parents stressed prayer and benevolent deeds as substitutes for "carnal thoughts" and intimacy; they associated sexual sublimation with family stability and personal redemption. During his years at boarding school and later at Harvard, Wendell Phillips strove to satisfy his mother on all these counts. Lewis Tappan, too, remembered how hard he had worked "to be one of the best scholars, often a favorite with the masters, and a leader among the boys in our plays." When he was twenty and living away from home, Tappan still received admonitions from his mother about the pitfalls of sex. Recalling a dream, she wrote, "Methought you had, by frequenting the theatre, been drawn into the society of lewd women, and had contracted a disease that was preying upon your constitution." For his part, Tappan had already sworn to "enjoy a sound mind and body, untainted by vice." A strong sense of their individuality, a deadly earnestness about moral issues, confidence in their ability to master themselves and to improve the world—these were the qualities that so often marked abolitionists in their early years. Above all, these future reformers believed in their own superiority and fully expected to become leaders.

Of course, not all children of morally assertive New England parents became radical abolitionists. William Lloyd Garrison's brother, for example, emerged from his mother's tutelage and lapsed into alcoholism. Still, the predisposition to rebellion remains hard to dismiss. Alienation and self-doubt certainly ran especially deep among these sensitive, socially conscious young people. Besides, America in the 1820s appeared to many a complex and bewildering place. Certain social realities were soon to seem disturbingly at variance with their high expectations and fixed moral codes.

These future abolitionists entered young adulthood at a time when rapid mobility, technological advance, and dizzying geographic expansion were transforming traditional institutions. Those who took up pastorates, seminary study, or positions in benevolent agencies were shocked to discover that the Protestant establishment was hardly free from the acquisitive taint and bureaucratic selfishness that they had been brought up to disdain. Expecting to lead communities of godfearing, Christian families, young ministers like Amos A. Phelps, Elizur Wright, Jr., and Charles T. Torrey confronted instead a fragmented society of entrepreneurs. Theodore Dwight Weld, for example, wrote critically to the great evangelist Charles G. Finney that "*revivals* are fast becoming with you a sort of trade, to be worked at so many hours a day." Promoters of colonization, such as James G. Birney and Joshua Leavitt, became increasingly disturbed that many of their coworkers were far less interested in Christian benevolence than in ridding the nation of inferior blacks. In politics, Lewis Tappan, William Jay, and William Lloyd Garrison searched desperately and without success for a truly Christian leader, an alternative to impious Andrew Jackson and the godless party he led.

Predictably, misgiving became ever more frequent among young evangelicals. They began to question their abilities, to rethink their choices of career, and to doubt the Christianity of the churches, seminaries, and benevolent societies. Just possibly, the nation was far more deeply mired in sin than anyone had imagined. Just possibly, parental formulas for godly reformation were fatally compromised. And, most disturbing of all, just possibly the idealist-reformer himself needed reforming—a new relationship with God, a new vision of his responsibility as a Christian American.

The powerful combination in the 1820s of Yankee conservatism, revivalist benevolence, New England upbringing, and social unrest was leading young evangelicals toward a genuinely radical vision. Given this setting, it hardly seems surprising that a militant abolitionist movement began to take shape. Opposition to slavery certainly constituted a dramatic affirmation of one's Christian identity and commitment to a life of Protestant purity. Economic exploitation, sexual license, gambling, drinking and dueling, disregard for family ties—all traits associated with slaveowning—could easily be set in bold contrast with the pure ideals of Yankee evangelicalism.

There were a few militant antislavery spokesmen in the upper south in the 1820s, but their influence on young New Englanders was negligible. The manumission societies organized largely by evangelical Quakers and Moravian Brethren in Tennessee, Kentucky, and other border areas were already collapsing at the start of New England's crusade for immediate emancipation. The southern antislavery movement's chief spokesman, editor Benjamin Lundy, had retreated northward from Tennessee. By 1829 he was living in Baltimore and had hired a zealous young editorial assistant from Newburyport, Massachusetts: William Lloyd Garrison.

The sudden emergence of immediate abolitionism in New England thus cannot be explained as a predictable offshoot of Yankee revivalism or a legacy from the upper south. Instead, one must emphasize the interaction between the rebellious feelings of these religious men and women and the events of the early 1830s. As the 1830s opened in an atmosphere of crisis, their attentions became intensely fixed on slavery. As in the early 1820s, the nation was again beset by black rebellions and threats of southern secession. Concurrently, events in England and in its sugar islands empire seemed to confirm the necessity of demanding the immediate emancipation of all slaves, everywhere. An unprecedented array of circumstances and jarring events suddenly converged on these anxious young people and launched them upon the lifetime task of abolishing slavery.

By far the most alarming was the ominous note of black militancy on which the new decade opened. In Boston in 1829, an ex-slave from North Carolina, David Walker, published the first edition of his famous *Appeal*. A landmark in black protest literature, Walker's *Appeal* condemned colonization as a white supremacist hoax, excoriated members of his own race for their passivity, and called, as a last resort, for armed resistance. "I declare," wrote Walker, "that one good black man can put to death six white men." Whites have never hesitated to kill blacks, he advised, so "if you commence . . . do not trifle, for they will not trifle with you." Other events, even more shocking, were to follow. In 1831, William Lloyd Garrison, now living in Boston, issued a call for immediate emancipation in the *Liberator*. Soon after, Southampton County, Virginia, erupted in the bloody Nat Turner insurrection, the largest slave revolt in ante-bellum America. Still another massive slave rebellion broke out in British Jamaica in 1831. Coinciding with these racial traumas was the Nullification Crisis of 1831–32, a confrontation ignited by South Carolina's opposition to national tariff policy and by the deeper fear that the federal government might someday abolish slavery. Intent on preserving state sovereignty and hence slavery, South Carolina politicians led by John C. Calhoun temporarily defied national authority, threatened secession, and risked occupation of federal troops.

As these frightening events unfolded, young evangelicals cast aside their self-doubt. Unfocused discontent gave way to soul-wrenching commitments to eradicating the sin of slavery. The combined actions of Nat Turner, the South Carolina "Nullifiers," and David Walker suggested with dramatic force that slavery was the fundamental cause of society's degraded state. As Theodore D. Weld observed, the abolitionist cause "not only *overshadows* all others, but . . . absorbs them into itself. Revivals, moral Reform etc. will remain stationary until the temple is cleansed." The step-by-step solutions advocated by their parents suddenly appeared to invite only God's retribution. Like Garrison, Arthur Tappan, and many others, James G. Birney sealed his commitment to immediate abolition by decrying colonization. The Colonization Society, Birney charged, acted as "an opiate to the consciences" of those who would otherwise "feel deeply and keenly the sin of slavery."

In one sense, these sudden espousals of immediate abolition can be understood as a strategic innovation developed because of the manifest failures of gradualism. Slaveholders had certainly shown no sympathy to moderate schemes. In England, too, where immediatism was also gaining followers, the general public had remained unmoved by gradualist proposals. Demands for "immediate, unconditional, uncompensated emancipation" thus appealed to young American idealists—at least the slogan was free of moral qualifications. Indeed, in 1831 the British government, responding to immediatist demands, enacted a massive program of gradual, compensated emancipation in the West Indies. But, even more important, by dedicating themselves to immediatism, the young reformers performed acts of self-liberation akin to the experience of conversion.

By freeing themselves from the shackles of gradualism, American abolitionists had finally triumphed over their feelings of selfishness, unworthiness, and alienation. Now they were morally fit to take God's side in the struggle against all the worldliness, license, cruelty, and selfishness that slaveowning had come to embody. Immediatists sensed themselves involved in a cosmic drama, a righteous war to redeem a fallen nation. They now felt ready to make supreme sacrifices and prove their fitness in their new religion of antislavery. "Never were men called on to die in a holier cause," wrote Amos A. Phelps in 1835 as he began his first tour as an abolitionist lecturer. It was far better, he thought, to die "as the negro's plighted friend" than to "sit in silken security, the consentor to & abettor of the manstealer's sin."

The campaign for Protestant reassertion had thus brought forth a vibrant romantic radicalism. Orthodox evangelicals quite rightly recoiled in fear. Abolitionists now put their faith entirely in the individual's ability to recognize and redeem himself from sin. No stifling traditions, no restrictive loyalties to institutions, no timorous concern for moderation or self-interest should be allowed to inhibit the free reign of Christian conscience. In its fullest sense, the phrase "immediate emancipation" described a transformed state of mind dominated by God and wholly at war with slavery. "The doctrine," wrote Elizur Wright, Jr., in 1833, "may be thus briefly stated":

> It is the duty of the holders of slaves to restore them to their liberty, and to extend to them the full protection of the law . . . to restore to them the profits of their labors, . . . to employ them as voluntary laborers on equitable wages. Also it is the duty of all men . . . to proclaim this doctrine, to urge upon slaveholders *immediate emancipation*, so long as there is a slave—to agitate the consciences of tyrants, so long as there is a tyrant on the globe.

Embedded in this statement was a vision of a new America, a daring affirmation that people of both races could re-establish their relationships on the basis of justice and Christian brotherhood. Like many other Americans who took up the burdens of reform, abolitionists envisioned their cause as leading to a society reborn in Christian brotherhood. Emancipation, like temperance, women's rights and communitarianism, became synonymous with the redemption of mankind and the opening of a purer phase of human history.

Abolitionists constantly tried to explain that they were not expecting some sudden Day of Jubilee when, with a shudder of collective remorse, the entire planter class would abruptly strike the shackles from all two million slaves and beg their forgiveness. Emancipation, they expected, would be achieved gradually; still it must be immediately begun. Immediatists were also forced to rebut the recurring charge that their demand promoted emancipation by rebellion on the plantations. "Our objects are to save life, not destroy it," Garrison exclaimed in 1831. "Make the slave free and every inducement to revolt is taken away." Few Americans believed these disclaimers. Instead, most suspected that immediate emancipation would suddenly create a large and mobile free population of inferior blacks. Most in the north were quite content to discriminate harshly against their black neighbors while the slaves remained at a safe distance on faraway plantations. According to Alexis de Tocqueville, the unusually acute foreign observer of ante-bellum society of the early 1830s: "Race prejudice seems stronger in those states that have abolished slavery than in those states where it still exists, and nowhere is it more intolerant than in those states where it has never been known." White supremacy and support for slavery were thus inextricably bound up with all phases of American political, economic, and religious life. Immediatist agitation was bound to provoke hostility from nearly every part of the social order.

As we have seen, by the 1830s the northeast and midwest enjoyed a thriving trade with the south, and the nation's economic well-being had become firmly tied to slave labor. Powerful financial considerations could thus dictate that abolitionism be harshly suppressed. Religious denominations were also deeply enmeshed in slavery, for southerners were influential among the Methodists, Presbyterians, Anglicans, and Baptists. Little wonder that most clergymen vigorously rejected demands that their churches declare slaveholders in shocking violation of God's Law.

But by far the most consistent opponents of the abolitionist crusade were found in politics. Young reformers had long ago come to abhor what they saw as the hollow demagoguery and secularism of Jacksonian mass politics. By 1830 they were fully justified in adding the politician's unstinting support of slavery to their bill of particulars. As Richard H. Brown has shown, Jackson's Democratic Party was deliberately designed to uphold the planters' interests. Jacksonian ideology soon became synonymous with racism and antiabolition. In the north, men who aspired to careers in Democratic Party politics had to solicit the approval of slaveholding party chiefs like Amos Kendall, John C. Calhoun, and Jackson himself. When anti-Jacksonian dissidents finally coalesced into the Whig Party during the 1830s, they, too, relied upon this formula for getting votes and recruiting leaders. Obviously, neither party dared to alienate proslavery interests in the south or racist supporters in the north. Moreover, as the Missouri and Nullification controversies had shown, political debates about slavery caused party allegiances to break ominously along sectional lines. For these reasons, party loyalty meant the suppression of all discussions of slavery.

The challenges that the abolitionists faced as they began their crusade were thus enormous. So was their own capability for disruption, although they were hardly aware of it at first. The ending of slavery whether peacefully or violently would require great changes in American life. Yet, if immediate emancipation provoked fear and violent hostility, it was nevertheless a doctrine appropriate to the age. The evangelical outlook with its rejection of tradition and expedience both embodied and challenged the culture that had created it. In retrospect, moderate approaches to the problem of slavery hardly seemed possible in Jacksonian America.

As a result, immediatist goals were anything but limited. Abolitionists now proposed to transform hundreds of millions of dollars worth of slaves into millions of black citizens by eradicating two centuries of American racism. Nevertheless, they sincerely felt that they promoted a conservative enterprise, and in certain respects this was an understandable (if misleading) self-assessment. Their unqualified attacks on slavery were, as they understood them, simply emulations of well-established evangelical methods. The Temperance Society's assault on liquor and the revivalist's denunciation of unbelief had hardly been characterized by restraint. Besides, immediatists were simply proposing an ideal by which all Christians were to measure themselves. They were not planning bloody revolution. They relied solely on voluntary conversion and rejected violence. As agitators, they defined their task as restoring time-honored American freedoms to an unjustly deprived people. Except for their opposition to racism, they offered no criticism of ordinary Protestant values. Was it anarchy, they wondered, to urge that pure Christian morality replace what they believed was the sexual abandon of the slave quarters? "Are we then fanatics," Garrison asked, "because we cry, *Do not rob! Do not murder!?*"

In their own eyes, then, abolitionists were hardly behaving like incendiaries as they opened their crusade. In slaveholding they discovered the ultimate source of the moral collapse that so deeply disturbed them. The race violence of Nat Turner and the secession threats of the "Nullifiers" constituted evidence that the nation had jettisoned all her moral ballasts. But immediate abolition seemed to hold forth the promise of Christian reconciliation between races, sections, and individuals. All motive for race revolt, all reason for political strife, and all inducement for moral degeneracy would be swept away. Indeed, the alternative of silence only invited the further spread of anarchy in a nation that Garrison described in 1831 as already "full of the blood of innocent men, women and babies—full of adultery and concupiscence—full of blasphemy, darkness and woeful rebellion against God—full of wounds and bruises and putrefying sores." Abolitionists were thus filled "with burning earnestness" when they insisted, as Elizur Wright did, that "the instant abolition of the whole slave system is safe." Most other Americans remained firm in their suspicions to the contrary.

Nevertheless, the abolitionists launched their crusade on a note of glowing optimism. Armed with moral certitude, they were also completely naive politically. "The whole system of slavery will fall to pieces with a rapidity which will astonish," wrote Samuel E. Sewall, one of the first adherents to immediatism. Weld predicted in 1834 that complete equality for all blacks in the upper south was but two years away, and that "scores of clergymen in the slaveholding states . . . *are really with us.*" Anxious for the millennium, abolitionists had wholly misjudged the depth of northern racism, not to mention the extent of southern tolerance.

All the same, there was wisdom in the naïveté. Without this romantic faith that God would put all things right, abolitionists would have lacked the incentive and creative stamina necessary for sustained assaults against slavery. Moreover, by stressing intuition as a sure guide to reality, abolitionists made an unprecedented attempt to establish empathy with the slave. One result, to be sure, was racist sentimentalism, a not surprising outcome considering the gulf that separated a Mississippi field hand from an independently wealthy Boston abolitionist. Yet the abolitionists were trying hard to imagine what it was like to be stripped of one's autonomy, prevented from protecting one's family, and deprived of legal safeguards and the rewards of one's own labor. This view of slavery made piecemeal reform completely unacceptable. To give slaves better food, fewer whippings, and some education was not enough. They deserved immediate justice, not charity. So convinced, and certain of ultimate victory, abolitionists set out to induce each American citizen to repent the sin of slavery.

To learn more about abolition and the movement for colonization in Liberia, visit the website for the African-American Mosaic: A Library of Congress Resource Guide for the Study of Black History and Culture *at* http://www.loc.gov/exhibits/african/afam001.html.

@ ON THE WEB

SOURCES

Commission to Theodore Dwight Weld, 1834

Abolitionists have often been pictured as rampant individualists who wanted to throw off the shackles of the existing social order. But, like other reformers of their day, most of them belonged to organizations that put a premium upon concerted action, the power of numbers, rather than individual initiative. The American Anti-Slavery Society, which was formed in 1833, wanted to build up massive followings, which through pressure-group tactics would force others in line. By 1838 the society had organized 1,350 auxiliaries in the North. Here are the society's instructions to its most famous organizer, Theodore Dwight Weld.

*American Anti-Slavery Society**

Commission to Theodore D. Weld

Dear Sir,

You are hereby appointed and commissioned, by the Executive Committee of the American Anti-Slavery Society, instituted at Philadelphia in 1833, as their Agent, for the space of one year commencing with the first day of January, 1834, in the State of Ohio and elsewhere as the Committee may direct.

The Society was formed for the purpose of awakening the attention of our whole community to the character of American Slavery, and presenting the claims and urging the rights of the colored people of the United States; so as to promote, in the most efficient manner, the immediate abolition of Slavery, and the restoration of our colored brethren to their equal rights as citizens.

For a more definite statement of the objects of your agency, and the methods of its prosecution, the Committee refer you to their printed "Particular Instructions," communicated to you herewith; a full acquaintance and compliance with which, according to your ability, you will, on accepting this commission, consider as indispensable.

The Committee welcome you as a fellow-laborer in this blessed and responsible work; the success of which will depend, in no small degree, under

This commission is a printed form, with the name of Theodore Weld, the dates, etc., written in.

From Gilbert H. Barnes and Dwight L. Dumond, eds., *Letters of Theodore Dwight Weld, Angelina Grimké Weld, and Sarah Grimké, 1822–1844,* American Historical Association, Washington, D.C., 1934, pp. 124–128. Reprinted by permission.

God, on the results of your efforts. Their ardent desires for your success will continually attend you; you will have their sympathy in trials; and nothing, they trust, will be wanting, on their part, for your encouragement and aid.

They commend you to the kindness and co-operation of all who love Zion; praying that the presence of God may be with you, cheering your heart, sustaining you in your arduous labors, and making them a means of a speedy liberation of all the oppressed.

Given at the Society's Office, No. 130 Nassau-street, New-York, the twentieth day of February in the year of our Lord eighteen hundred and thirty-four.

Arthur Tappan
Chairman of the Executive Committee

Attest,

E. Wright Jr.
Secretary of Domestic Correspondence.

❧ *Particular Instructions*

To Mr. T. D. Weld

Dear Sir—You have been appointed an Agent of the American Anti-Slavery Society; and will receive the follo wing instructions from the Executive Committee, as a brief expression of the principles they wish you to inculcate, and the course of conduct they wish you to pursue in this agency.

The general principles of the Society are set forth in the Declaration, signed by the members of the Convention which formed it at Philadelphia, Dec. 7, 1833. Our object is, the overthrow of American slavery, the most atrocious and oppressive system of bondage that has ever existed in any country. We expect to accomplish this, mainly by showing to the public its true character and legitimate fruits, its contrariety to the first principles of religion, morals, and humanity, and its special inconsistency with our pretensions, as a free, humane, and enlightened people. In this way, by the force of truth, we expect to correct the common errors that prevail respecting slavery, and to produce a just public sentiment, which shall appeal both to the conscience and love of character, of our slaveholding fellow-citizens, and convince them that both their duty and their welfare require the immediate abolition of slavery.

You will inculcate every where, the great fundamental principle of IMMEDIATE ABOLITION, as the duty of all masters, on the ground that slavery is both unjust and unprofitable. Insist principally on the SIN OF SLAVERY, because our main hope is in the consciences of men, and it requires little logic to prove that it is always safe to do right. To question this, is to impeach the superintending Providence of God.

We reprobate the idea of compensation to slave holders, because it implies the right of slavery. It is also unnecessary, because the abolition of slavery will be an advantage, as free labor is found to be more profitable than the labor of slaves. We also reprobate all plans of expatriation, by whatever specious pretenses covered, as a remedy for slavery, for they all proceed from prejudice against color; and we hold that the duty of the whites in regard to this cruel prejudice is not to indulge it, but to repent and overcome it.

The people of color ought at once to be emancipated and recognized as citizens, and their rights secured as such, equal in all respects to others, according to the cardinal principle laid down in the American Declaration of Independence. Of course we have nothing to do with any equal laws which the states may make, to prevent or punish vagrancy, idleness, and crime, either in whites or blacks.

Do not allow yourself to be drawn away from the main object, to exhibit a detailed PLAN of abolition; for men's consciences will be greatly relieved from the feeling of present duty, by any objections or difficulties which they can find or fancy in your plan. Let the *principle* be decided on, of immediate abolition, and the plans will easily present themselves. What ought to be done can be done. If the *great* question were decided, and if half the ingenuity now employed to defend slavery were employed to abolish it, it would impeach the wisdom of American statesmen to say they could not, with the Divine blessing, steer the ship through.

You will make yourself familiar with FACTS, for they chiefly influence reflecting minds. Be careful to use only facts that are well authenticated, and always state them with the precision of a witness under oath. You cannot do our cause a greater injury than by overstating facts. Clarkson's "Thoughts," and Stuart's "West India Question," are Magazines of facts respecting the safety and benefit of immediate emancipation. Mrs. Child's Book, Stroud's Slave Laws, Paxton's and Rankin's Letters, D. L. Child's Address, are good authorities respecting the character of American slavery. The African Repository and Garrison's Thoughts will show the whole subject of expatriation.

The field marked out by the Committee for your agency is the State of Ohio.

The Committee expect you to confine your labors to that field, unless some special circumstances call you elsewhere. And in such case you will confer with the Committee before changing your field, if time will allow. And if not, we wish immediate notice of the fact.

In traversing your field, you will generally find it wise to visit first several prominent places in it, particularly those where it is known our cause has friends. In going to a place, you will naturally call upon those who are friendly to our objects, and take advice from them. Also call on ministers of the gospel and other leading characters, and labor specially to enlighten them and secure their favor and influence. Ministers are the hinges of community, and ought to be moved, if possible. If they can be gained, much is gained. But if not, you will not be discouraged; and if not plainly inexpedient, attempt to obtain a house of worship; or if none can be had, some other convenient place—and hold a public meeting, where you can present our cause, its facts, arguments and appeals, to as many people as you can collect, by notices in pulpits and newspapers, and other proper means.

Form Auxiliary Societies, both male and female, in every place where it is practicable. Even if such societies are very small at the outset, they may do much good as centres of light, and means of future access to the people. Encourage them to raise funds and apply them in purchasing and circulating anti-slavery publications gratuitously; particularly the Anti-Slavery Reporter, of which you will keep specimens with you, and which can always be had of the Society at $2.00 per 100. You are at liberty, with due discretion, to recommend other publications, *so far* as they advocate our views of immediate abolition. We hold ourselves responsible only for our own.

You are not to take up collections in your public meetings, as the practice often prevents persons from attending, whom it might be desirable to reach. Let this be stated in the public notice of the meeting. If you find individuals friendly to our views, who are able to give us money, you will make special personal application, and urge upon them the duty of liberally supporting this cause. You can also give notice of some place where those disposed can give you their donations. Generally, it is best to invite them to do this *the next morning*.

We shall expect you to write frequently to the Secretary for Domestic Correspondence, and give minute accounts of your proceedings and success. If you receive money for the Society, you will transmit it *by mail*, WITHOUT DELAY, to the Treasurer.

Always keep us advised, if possible, of the place where letters may reach you.

Believing as we do, that the hearts of all men are in the hand of Almighty God, we wish particularly to engage the prayers of all good men in behalf of our enterprise. Let them pray that *we* and our agents may have Divine guidance and zeal; and slave-holders, penitence; and slaves, patience; and statesmen, wisdom; so that this grand experiment of moral influence may be crowned with glorious and speedy success. Especially stir up ministers and others to the duty of making continual mention of the oppressed slaves in all social and public prayers. And as far as you can, procure the stated observance of the LAST MONDAY EVENING in every month, as a season of special prayer in behalf of the people of color.

We will only remind you, that the Society is but the almoner of the public—that the silver and the gold are the Lord's—that the amount as yet set apart by his people for promoting this particular object is small—our work is great and our resources limited—and we therefore trust that you will not fail to use a faithful economy in regard to the expenses of traveling, and reduce them as low as you can without impairing your usefulness.

The Anti-Slavery Record, 1835–1836

In 1835, thanks to a sudden reduction in the costs of printing, the American Anti-Slavery Society was able to flood the country with propaganda. Able agitators, abolitionists were among the first to use lithographs for political ends. Images of women being whipped or separated from their children and of men being beaten were the bread-and-butter of the antislavery message. Here are some of the pictographs that appeared on the front page of the Anti-Slavery Record, *the pamphlet with by far the greatest circulation.*

Anti-Slavery Record

Anti-Slavery Record

Anti-Slavery Record

Anti-Slavery Record

Anti-Slavery Record

Anti-Slavery Record

"Fathers and Rulers" Petition

The abolitionists, like other reformers of the age, relied heavily on churchwomen. While lacking the right to vote, women were generally regarded to be inherently more moral than men, and hence their opinions on moral questions were highly respected. Capitalizing on this sentiment, women gathered thousands of signatures for massive petitions to Congress calling for the end of slavery in Washington, D.C. To shut off the flood, Congress in 1836 passed a "gag law," which was designed to keep the petitions from being read, printed, or considered by Congress. The law remained in effect until 1844. Here is one of the more famous "female petitions."

[NOVEMBER (?) 1834]

To the Hon. Senate and House of Representatives of the U. States, in Congress Assembled

Petition of Ladies resident in _____ County, State of Ohio.*
Fathers and Rulers of our Country,
    Suffer us, we pray you, with the sympathies which we are constrained to feel as wives, as mothers, and as daughters, to plead with you in behalf of a long oppressed and deeply injured class of native Americans, residing in that portion of our country which is under your exclusive control. We should poorly estimate the virtues which ought ever to distinguish your honorable body could we anticipate any other than a favorable hearing when our appeal is to men, to philanthropists, to patriots, to the legislators and guardians of a Christian people. We should be less than women, if the nameless and unnumbered wrongs of which the slaves of our sex are made the defenseless victims, did not fill us with horror and constrain us, in earnestness and agony of spirit to pray for their deliverance. By day and night, their woes and wrongs rise up before us, throwing shades of mournful contrast over the joys of domestic life, and filling our hearts with sadness at the recollection of those whose hearths are desolate.

*This is a printed form. The signatures of the petitioners were to be secured separately and pasted upon the form, and the whole petition then mailed to a congressman in Washington. This was by far the most popular form for "female petitions" until 1840. Tens of thousands are in the files of the House of Representatives (boxes 85–126) in the Library of Congress. Except for short "sentence forms" distributed by the American Anti-Slavery Society during the period 1837–1840, it was the commonest form in the campaign.

From Gilbert H. Barnes and Dwight L. Dumond, eds., *Letters of Theodore Dwight Weld, Angelina Grimké Weld, and Sarah Grimké, 1822–1844,* American Historical Association, Washington, D.C., 1934, pp. 175–176. Reprinted by permission.

Nor do we forget, in the contemplation of their other sufferings, the intellectual and moral degradation to which they are doomed; how the soul formed for companionship with angels, is despoiled and brutified, and consigned to ignorance, pollution, and ruin.

Surely then, as the representatives of a people professedly Christian, you will bear with us when we express our solemn apprehensions in the language of the patriotic Jefferson "we tremble for our country when we remember that God is just, and that his justice cannot sleep forever," and when in obedience to a divine command "we remember them who are in bonds as bound with them." Impelled by these sentiments, we solemnly purpose, the grace of God assisting, to importune high Heaven with prayer, and our national Legislature with appeals, until this Christian people abjure forever a traffic in the souls of men, and the groans of the oppressed no longer ascend to God from the dust where they now welter.

We do not ask your honorable body to transcend your constitutional powers, by legislating on the subject of slavery within the boundaries of any slaveholding State; but we do conjure you to abolish slavery in the District of Columbia where you exercise exclusive jurisdiction. In the name of humanity, justice, equal rights and impartial law, our country's weal, her honor and her cherished hopes we earnestly implore for this our humble petition, your favorable regard. If both in Christian and in heathen lands, Kings have revoked their edicts, at the intercession of woman, and tyrants have relented when she appeared a suppliant for mercy, surely we may hope that the Legislators of a free, enlightened and Christian people will lend their ear to our appeals, when the only boon we crave is the restoration of rights unjustly wrested from the innocent and defenseless.—And as in duty bound your petitioners will ever pray.

NAMES	NAMES

Slavery as It Is, 1839

The most impressive antislavery indictment was compiled by Theodore Dwight Weld, his wife, Angelina, and her sister, Sarah Grimké. The two women spent six months going through thousands upon thousands of southern newspapers, looking for items in which slaveholders effectively condemned themselves. Weld then assembled the clippings into a book, Slavery as It Is: The Testimony of a Thousand Witnesses, *which was published in 1839 and quickly sold 22,000 copies. Here is an excerpt from that book.*

The slaves are often branded with hot irons, pursued with firearms and *shot*, hunted with dogs and torn by them, shockingly maimed with knives, dirks, &c.; have their ears cut off, their eyes knocked out, their bones dislocated

From Theodore Dwight Weld, *Slavery as It Is*, American Anti-Slavery Society, New York, 1839, pp. 79–81.

and broken with bludgeons, their fingers disfigured with scars and gashes, *besides* those made with the lash.

We shall adopt, under this head, the same course as that pursued under previous ones,—first give the testimony of the slaveholders themselves, to the mutilations, &c. by copying their own graphic descriptions of them, in advertisements published under their own names, and in newspapers published in the slave states, and, generally, in their own immediate vicinity. We shall, as heretofore, insert only so much of each advertisement as will be necessary to make the point intelligible.

✍ *Testimony*

"Ranaway, a Negro woman and two children; a few days before she went off, *I burnt her with a hot iron*, on the left side of her face, *I tried to make the letter M.*"

"Ranaway a Negro man named Henry, *his left eye out*, some scars from a *dirk* on and under his left arm, and *much scarred* from the whip."

"One hundred dollars reward for a Negro fellow Pompey, 40 years old, he is *branded* on the left *jaw.*"

"Ranaway a Negro named Arthur, has a considerable *scar* across his *breast* and *each arm*, made by a knife; loves to talk much of the goodness of God."

"Ranaway a Negro named Mary, has a small scar over her eye, *a good many teeth missing*, the letter A. *is branded on her cheek and forehead.*"

"Ranaway a Negro named Hambleton, *limps* on his left foot where he was *shot* a few weeks ago, while runaway."

"Ranaway a Negro boy name Mose, he has a *wound* in the right shoulder near the backbone, which was occasioned by *a rifle shot.*"

"Was committed to jail a Negro man, says his name is Josiah, his back very much scarred by the whip, and *branded on the thigh and hips, in three or four places*, thus (J.M.) the *rim of his right ear has been bit or cut off.*"

"Ranaway from the plantation of James Surgette, the following Negroes, Randal, *has one ear cropped*; Bob, *has lost one eye*; Kentucky Tom, *has one jaw broken.*"

"Was committed, a Negro man, has a *scar* on his right side by a burn, one on his knee, and one on the calf of his leg *by the bite of a dog.*"

"Fifty dollars reward, for the Negro Jim Blake—has a *piece cut out of each ear*, and the middle finger of the left hand cut off to the second joint."

To read more about the American Anti-Slavery Society and its efforts to end slavery as well as other groups involved in the anti-slavery movement, see the abolition section of the "African American Odyssey" at http://lcweb2.loc.gov/ammem/aaohtml/exhibit/aopart3.html, *the website for the Library of Congress.*

To read Slavery as It Is *in its entirety, visit the "Documenting the American South" website of the University of North Carolina Library at* http://docsouth.unc.edu/neh/weld/menu.html.

"Ranaway, the mulatto wench Mary—has a *cut on the left arm, a scar on the shoulder, and two upper teeth missing.*"

"Ranaway, my man Fountain—has *holes in his ears, a scar* on the right side of his forehead—has been *shot in the hind parts of his legs*—is marked on the back with the whip."

THE BIG PICTURE

Antislavery was just one of the many reform movements that sprang up in Jacksonian America, but it was easily the most divisive. Why did it arise when it did? Was it a success—a limited success—or largely a failure? Were the abolitionists truly radical, or were they really conservatives?

Chapter 11

Westward Expansion

Interpretive Essay by J. S. Holliday 257

Sources 270

    Two Views of the West 270

    Poker Flat and Points West 274

    The Other Side of the Story 275

The Big Picture 279

*A*ndrew Jackson and his colleagues were anxious to silence the aboli-tionists and to keep slavery out of politics. But at the same time they were zealous expansionists. Arguing that it was God's will for the United States to expand over North America, Jackson and his followers drove the Indians off their ancestral lands in Georgia, Alabama, Mississippi, and other states in the 1830s; annexed Texas in 1845; secured by treaty much of the vast Oregon country in 1846; and took California and the Southwest from Mexico in 1848. Jacksonian expansionism doubled the size of the country, but the process left ugly scars. Force, fraud, and murder were necessary to exact choice Indian lands, and war was necessary to wrest lands from Mexico.

Jacksonian expansionism also accentuated the western march of America's pioneers. For several generations, young men had been told to "go west" and seek their fortune, and occasionally the same advice had been given to young women and family farmers. The Indian tribes or foreign governments that stood in their path had long been dismissed as temporary barriers. But there still had been much doubt about how far west pioneers could go. Somewhere beyond the Mississippi, so the mapmakers had indicated, was the Great American Desert, where white settlement would have to stop because "the land was fit for no one except Indians."

By the 1840s, however, land-hungry settlers began pushing their way across the formidable desert, through Indian country and land legally claimed by Mexico. Some headed toward Oregon, hoping to find new and fertile farmland. Others made their way to California and lived as illegal aliens on Mexican soil. By 1845 some 6,000 had settled in Oregon, with another 2,000 in California. The following year, still others headed toward Utah, where a new and rapidly growing church, known popularly as the Mormons, hoped to establish an isolated community where they could practice their religion without outside interference.

Then in 1848, thanks to the Mexican War, the United States annexed the northern third of Mexico—over 1 million square miles—including California and most of what is now the American Southwest. None of the treaty's negotiators expected the patterns of migration to change immediately. But nine days before the treaty was signed, an itinerant carpenter from New Jersey found gold on the land of a Swiss immigrant, now a Mexican citizen, who hoped to build an agricultural empire in the Sacramento Valley.

Within a year came the great California gold rush. By the thousands farmers cast aside their plows, doctors their pills, lawyers their briefs, and made their way west to dig gold. Soon, within another year or two, the human stampede to California made earlier migrations seem small and insignificant—mere specks in the course of western migration.

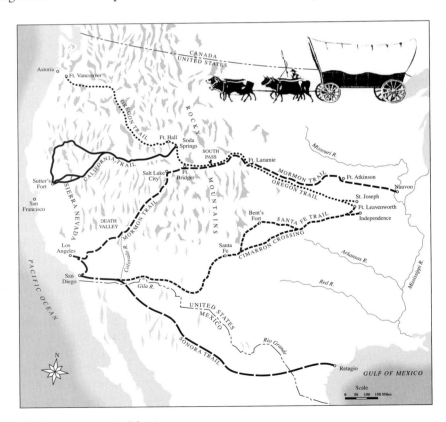

Overland routes to California.

The World Rushed In

J. S. Holliday

The author of the following selection began studying the great California migration in 1948, a century after it began, when a friend handed him two leather-bound notebooks in the Yale University library. The notebooks turned out to be the diary of a twenty-seven-year-old farmer from upstate New York who, despite his deep love for his wife and newborn daughter, took off for California to get rich. Building on this diary, the author spent the next three decades tracing the triumphs and tribulations of the diarist and his compatriots. This selection shows how California changed overnight from a sleepy backwater into the talk of the nation, how it became an enticement that disrupted the lives of hundreds of thousands of Americans. Why, in your judgment, did it have the impact that it did? Why, in particular, would a devoted young husband abandon his eastern roots upon hearing of California gold? And why would he, a New Yorker, decide to take the overland trail to California rather than travel by sea? Did his behavior make any sense at all?

After two years of war, the United States and Mexico on February 2, 1848, signed a treaty which ceded to the victor the vast expanse west from Texas and north to Oregon. With this territorial acquisition, President Polk achieved for his country its Manifest Destiny—one nation from Atlantic to Pacific.

Nine days before the treaty signing, a native of New Jersey, a carpenter named James Marshall, chanced to find several pieces of gold at a place called Coloma, in what was yet Mexican California. His discovery the morning of January 24, 1848, might have been made at some far earlier date by one of the Spanish explorer-looters who had found gold from Aztec to Inca cities and searched the continents for more. Or Mexican soldiers in pursuit of Indians might have uncovered the first nugget and thus have provided Mexico City the means and the will to resist Yankee expansion. Instead, California's gold remained hidden through seven decades of Spanish and Mexican rule, a historical irony and a testament to Yankee luck. Some Protestant preachers proclaimed the discovery to be the work of God, who had hidden the gold as long as Popery—the Catholics—held sway over California.

That gold should be found in a place so difficult to reach by land or by sea was foretold in 1510 when a romantic novel published in Seville described "an island called California very close to the Terrestrial Paradise."

From J. S. Holliday, *The World Rushed In: The California Gold Rush Experience*, Simon and Schuster, New York, 1981, pp. 25–39, 41, 45–54.

Ruled by an Amazon queen named Calafia, "the island everywhere abounds with gold and precious stones and upon it no other metal is found." The far-away land stirred Spanish imagination. Fiction seemed more like fact when Cortez, following his conquest of the Aztecs in 1521, wrote of an island northwest of Mexico which he called California. But the fable did not come true until by God's design, destiny or luck, a few gold specks caught the eye of the American carpenter—who worked for John Sutter, native of Switzerland, Mexican citizen, a man whose ambitious plans for an agricultural empire would be destroyed by the gold found on his land.

Everything about California would change. In one astonishing year the place would be transformed from obscurity to world prominence, from an agricultural frontier that attracted 400 settlers in 1848 to a mining frontier that lured 90,000 impatient men in 1849; from a society of neighbors and families to one of strangers and transients; from an ox-cart economy based on hides and tallow to a complex economy based on gold mining; from Catholic to Protestant, from Latin to Anglo-Saxon. The impact of that new California would be profound on the nation it had so recently joined.

But nothing about the old California, except the fable of Queen Calafia, vaguely hinted at its future. Reports of the first Spanish explorers told of a bleak coastline with natives so primitive as to have no knowledge of gold. After 1602, exploration ceased. California remained Spanish only by the work of royal mapmakers who often showed it as an island.

One hundred and sixty-seven years later, Spanish interest revived, not in hope of gold but from fear of Russian expansion south from Alaska. To thwart that presumed threat, the viceroy in Mexico City determined to create an outpost of empire on the California coast. In 1769–70 a sickly expedition built a mission and a presidio, frail structures, at both San Diego and Monterey. To Christianize and control the Indians, the vice-regal government in 1771 sent ten Franciscan priests and sixty soldiers; that same year three new missions were established. Thus Spain sought to colonize California—at the very time England's colonies on the Atlantic Coast were beginning their struggle to break free.

More than missionary zeal and courage, California needed colonists. But a far frontier without prospect of gold held little attraction for the citizens of Mexico. With few exceptions, only the most miserable and ignorant from city streets could be induced to emigrate. To augment the policy of shipping "idle, undesirable people," convicts from Mexican jails were exiled to California. Most of the soldiers conscripted for the protection of the expanding mission system were drunkards, assorted criminals and deserters from the regular army. Faced with such colonists to intermarry with the Christianized Indians and such soldiers to protect and control the Indians living at the missions, the head of the Franciscan padres, Junipero Serra, begged the government "not to look upon California and its missions as the China of exile. . . . Being sent to our missions should not be a form of banishment, nor should our missions be filled with worthless people who serve no purpose but to commit evil deeds."

Toward the end of the century, the feeble hold that Spain had placed on California earned the scorn of a British sea captain, George Vancouver, who sailed along the coast and visited several presidios in the 1790s. In his report he noted that "should any civilized nation" have the ambition to seize California, the Spanish military "could not make the least resistance." The weakness he observed forecast the collapse of Spain's New World empire, not from the ambition of her imperial enemies, France, England and Russia, but because of internal disruption. From 1808 into the 1820s, Spain's colonies were in revolt, with Mexico gaining independence in 1821.

California drifted through those years of turmoil so isolated that little was known of political affairs in faraway Mexico City. In 1822 the province quietly came under the rule of the new Mexican government. Relations with the capital changed little from Spanish days. For most Mexicans, "to speak of California was like mentioning the end of the world." And so the policy of exporting convicts as colonists continued. Called *cholos* (rascals or mongrels) by Californios, the thieves and political prisoners settled in the towns of Los Angeles and San Jose and in the villages attached to the presidios. Their brawling, drunkenness, gambling and abuse of Indians gave those places a rough character.

During the Mexican period, 1822–46, the policy that had the most profound effect on California was the secularization of the twenty-one Franciscan missions, a process by which millions of acres of land and herds of livestock were to be allotted to the Indian converts, with the Franciscan padres reduced to curates of the parish churches. Given the wealth to be distributed, the pitiful unpreparedness of the Indians to manage their own affairs and the political rivalries in Mexico and California which produced a succession of bickering governors, it was inevitable that the vast holding of the missions should end up not in the ownership of the Indians but sold, leased or granted to retired soldiers, government officials and anyone else with the right connections. By the mid-1840s, 8 million acres of mission lands and the authority of the Franciscans had been transferred to some 800 families who made up the new social order. They lived on ranchos, some of them encompassing more than 250,000 acres, where their cattle grazed unfenced over quiet valleys and rolling hills.

For the mission Indians who had been ruled for decades by the Franciscan padres, the breakup of the mission system was disastrous. Dispossessed of land that was supposedly theirs, unready for their homeless freedom, they were demoralized by liquor and violence, with large numbers of them exploited as servants of townspeople and rancheros. They suffered as well from white men's diseases, especially syphilis, which had spread as an epidemic for years within the missions and beyond to the unconverted Indians. By the late 1830s the missionized Indians had declined to fewer than 4,000 from an estimated 30,000 in 1820.

A new California evolved, a pastoral society of large families living on vast ranchos, far from their neighbors. Blessed with a comfortable climate, plenty of land and cheap Indian labor, the ranchero, patriarch of his realm, enjoyed a good life, celebrated in history and legend as a "pastoral Arcadia." A household might include nineteen or even twenty-nine children, plus a number of poor relatives and transient strangers enjoying unstinted hospitality, all supported by Indian servants grinding corn for tortillas, serving in the kitchen, washing clothes and sewing or spinning. One rancho had 600 Indians as servants and field hands. . . .

Far more important to California's frantic future, there came into the Sacramento Valley late in the fall of 1841 a party of overland emigrants from Missouri and other western states. Frontiersmen, farmers, they were the kind of people who had moved America westward from Virginia to the Missouri River. Setting out from Independence, Missouri, in the spring, they had found their way through the wilderness of deserts and mountains by following trails opened in the 1830s by fur trappers ("those men who made the unknown known"). Though it had taken this first overland party six months to make the journey, they had survived—the first of hundreds of land-seeking American pioneers who would follow their route along the Humboldt River to the passes through the Sierra Nevada and down to the warmth of the Sacramento Valley. After 1841 this route would be known as the California Trail. . . .

* * *

During 1847, the last year before gold finally took charge, California drowsed along at its old tempo. However, two places changed and grew rapidly, as if preparing for their central roles in the next year's drama—Yerba Buena on the shores of San Francisco bay and Sutter's ranch on the banks of the American River in the Sacramento Valley.

After years as a scruffy village of adobe huts, one store and a few tents where hide traders and whalers did some business, Yerba Buena gained a sudden population boost when a ship from New York, via Cape Horn, dropped anchor in July 1846. Two hundred and thirty-eight Mormon men, women and children came ashore under the leadership of a printer named Sam Brannan. They had sailed from the East Coast hoping to find in California a haven from American persecution, possibly a place to which Brigham Young could bring the other Saints. Faced with the unwelcome news that California was under United States rule, Brannan sent some of his men into the Sacramento Valley (where they settled near Sutter's ranch), while the others took shelter in the Mexican custom house or shivered in tents. In January 1847, the alcalde (an elected position that combined the duties of mayor, judge, lawyer and marshal) renamed the town San Francisco. He also authorized a plan with streets to be laid out American-style, intersecting at right angles. That same month Sam Brannan started printing a newspaper, the *California Star.* By the end of 1847 San Francisco had 200 buildings and 800 inhabitants—one year later it would be the great metropolis of the Pacific coast.

Out in the valley, John A. Sutter ruled over a prospering ranch. He had landed at Monterey in 1839 and within a year had applied for Mexican citizenship and received a land grant of nearly 50,000 acres in two parcels, one at the junction of the American and Sacramento rivers, another to the north along the Feather River—names soon to be familiar to thousands of gold miners. Near the south bank of the American, on a knoll high enough to stand free from floods, Sutter built an adobe-walled fort to control the surrounding land, all of which he called New Helvetia, a place to which he would bring colonists from his home country. Furthermore, the Mexican governor appointed Sutter alcalde for the entire Sacramento Valley.

In January 1848, the fort with its dozen cannons overlooked fields cultivated and ditched by Indians in Sutter's employ, a ten-acre garden, horses, cattle and sheep, and a nearby river landing where Sutter's sloop was tied up when not sailing the Sacramento River or all the way to San Francisco. It was a lively place, the center of trade and communication for all the settlers in the valley. At once a fortress, inn, granary, warehouse and retail store, Sutter's Fort and environs had a white population of about 290, most of them frontiersmen and farmers from the United States. As well, there were a number of Hawaiians—Kanakas—and 450 Indians who worked as servants and in the fields. A man of vision to match his ambition, Sutter laid out a town, Sutterville, along the banks of the Sacramento River. Some distance up the South Fork of the American River, several of Sam Brannan's Mormons worked for Sutter in building a flour mill. Most important for Sutter's plans and for California's future, about forty-five miles from the fort James Marshall served as construction superintendent of a sawmill at a bend of the South Fork, in a gentle valley called Coloma.

While work on the sawmill continued, the millrace had to be deepened to increase the flow of water and thereby provide a greater force to turn the wheel. The morning of January 24, 1848, Marshall walked along the race to inspect the flow of water. Recalling the moment, he later reported: "My eye was caught by something shining in the bottom of the ditch. . . . I reached my hand down and picked it up; it made my heart thump, for I was certain it was gold. The piece was about half the size and shape of a pea. Then I saw another. . . ."

Buried there for endless centuries, those glittering granules and flakes of gold that Marshall held in his hand had been freed from their hiding by the digging of the race and the action of water running through, loosening and separating the rocks, gravel and sand. This very process of digging and washing, so innocently accomplished by Marshall and his workers, would be the method used by tens of thousands of men working with picks and shovels and crude mining machines in their search for gold, first along the South Fork of the American River and then, as the months passed, along scores of rivers and streams and up canyons and gorges along the western slope of the Sierra Nevada.

But first Marshall had to determine what, in truth, he had found. When he ran back to the mill with his particles of gold, he shouted, "Boys, I believe I have found a gold mine." The workers were doubtful. After testing the metal, biting and hammering a piece and finding it not brittle, several men went down to the tailrace to look for more. Work continued on the mill, but each day they found more gold. On January 28, Marshall rode over to Sutter's Fort and met with Sutter, and after more careful testing, they agreed Marshall had found gold. Excitement in Marshall, uncertainty in Sutter; the one returned immediately to the mill, the other waited until the next day. On the 29th, Sutter, Marshall and several workers examined the race, found gold all along it and more along the banks of the fork.

The growing excitement aroused in Sutter a new vision, but he could not turn easily from his plans for New Helvetia. Fearful that work on the sawmill would be interrupted, possibly stopped altogether in the face of a greater cause, he asked his workers to stay on the job, and though they could continue in their spare time to dig for gold, would they say nothing to outsiders about the discovery?

Such startling news could not be contained. Sutter himself talked of it, and in a letter he boasted: "I have made a discovery of a gold mine which, according to the experiments we have made, is extremely rich." Inevitable talk by the workers also spread the news. The Mormons working on Sutter's flour mill a few miles down the South Fork of the American River came up to the sawmill on February 27. A few days of digging and they too found enough gold to make them believers, and when they returned to their work site and noted the similarity of the riverbed and gravel bars, they scratched and dug and found more. The second "gold mine" became famous as Mormon Island.

Sutter could not hold his workers. The flour mill stood unfinished, hides rotted in the warehouse. All his plans depended on a staff of assistants, field workers, carpenters, tanners. Suddenly they were gone, with plans of their own. . . .

*   *   *

The two weekly newspapers in San Francisco, the *Californian* and the *California Star*, first mentioned the Sutter mill discovery rather casually in mid-March. Another report of gold appeared on March 25, and a more informative article followed on April 1. Then on May 12 the tune and the tempo changed. On that date, Sam Brannan returned from Coloma and brought to San Francisco's streets the kind of evidence and the kind of excited announcement needed to brush aside the doubters and the collective restraint. Holding high a bottle full of gold dust, Brannan shouted: "Gold! Gold! Gold from the American River!"

The man's enthusiasm, the electrifying words, the sight of gold, the accumulated force of rumor and expectation now released, all combined to create a contagion of belief and of impatience to get to the American River. As the agriculture of the Sacramento Valley had nurtured visions in Sutter's mind, now the gold of that place spawned dreams and concepts in the minds of hundreds of San Franciscans. One of those entranced recalled: "A frenzy seized my soul. . . . Piles of gold rose up before me . . . castles of marble, thousands of slaves . . . myriads of fair virgins contending with each other for my love—were among the fancies of my fevered imagination. The Rothschilds, Girards, and Astors appeared to be but poor people; in short, I had a very violent attack of the gold fever." . . .

By the middle of June, San Francisco stood half empty, with three-quarters of the men off to the mines, most stores closed, the alcalde's office shut, the newspapers suspended, outbound ships at anchor deserted by their crews. News from San Jose, Benicia, Sonoma, all the same—empty streets, abandoned businesses, fields of grain opened to roaming cattle. . . .

* * *

In the rush and excitement, few goldseekers bothered or had reason to keep records or otherwise report what was happening as they searched ever farther from Coloma. Fortunately Thomas O. Larkin, one of the most influential Americans in California and a successful merchant in Monterey, was in the habit of writing letters to his business associates and to Colonel Richard B. Mason, the military governor of California. On May 26, 1848, Larkin, at Pueblo de San Jose, wrote to Mason at his headquarters in Monterey, "We can hear of nothing but gold, gold, gold. An ounce a day, two or three. Last night several of the most respectable American residents of this town arrived home from a visit to the gold regions. Next week they will go with their families, and I think nine-tenths of the foreign storekeepers, mechanics or day laborers of this town and perhaps of San Francisco will leave for the Sacramento. . . . Baskets, tin pans, shovels, etc. bring any price imaginable at the gold washings."

On June 1 from San Francisco, Larkin wrote to the Secretary of State, James Buchanan, in Washington: "I have to report to the State Department one of the most astonishing excitements and state of affairs now existing in this country that perhaps has ever been brought to the notice of the Government. On the American Fork of the Sacramento and Feather rivers . . . there has been within the present year discovered a placer, a vast tract of land containing gold in small particles. . . . It is now two or three weeks since the men employed in these washings have appeared in this town with gold to exchange for merchandise and provisions. I presume near $20,000 of this gold has as yet been so exchanged. . . . I have seen several pounds of this gold and consider it very pure. . . . Fourteen to sixteen dollars in merchandise is paid for it here. . . . Common spades and shovels one month ago worth one dollar will now bring ten dollars at the gold regions. I am informed that fifty dollars has been offered for one. Should the gold continue as represented, this town will be depopulated. . . ."

Writing to Buchanan again on June 28, Larkin perceived the future: "If our countrymen in California as clerks, mechanics and workmen will forsake employment at from two to six dollars per day, how many more of the same class in the Atlantic states earning much less will leave for this country under such prospects?" . . .

By the fall of 1848 the energy and ambition of the miners had expanded the known gold regions a distance of 400 miles, from the Trinity River in the north to the Tuolumne in the south, a kingdom at last for Queen Calafia.

While her fabled domain had only women, in this California women were rare—a few wives of ranchers and mothers with children. Probably they settled at Coloma and Mormon Island, where some semblance of civilization slowly developed. But beyond those shanty villages, it was a world of men, where fifty or sixty miners might camp together on a river bar or under some sheltering trees along a river flat. A few mining camps had as many as 200 men. Nearby they dug and washed each day, hearing on all sides the shaking of rockers, the rattle of stones thrown out of hoppers, and now and then a shout that told of sudden success. Slipping and slogging in the rocks, gravel and icy water of streams pouring down from snowbanks up above in the Sierra, or digging in some otherwise quiet ravine where the stifling heat bore down at 110 degrees in the shade, these bearded goldseekers labored and cursed, sweated and shivered through July, August and September, hoping to make their fortunes before the rainy season, which might set in any time after September and cause the streams to rise and ravines to flood.

Reporting once again on these men who had transformed California, Larkin wrote a letter to Buchanan on July 20. "Some of those who first made the discovery of gold, after working a month and obtaining $1,000 to $3,000, have left the place [planning] to return when the weather is cooler. . . . A few who are working thirty or forty Indians are laying up $1,000 to $2,000 a week. None of these men had any property of consequence to commence with. . . ."

*   *   *

Across the country Americans read and talked of gold and felt increasingly envious of miners who could dig their fortunes in a matter of days or weeks. For farmers in Massachusetts or Kentucky and city folk in Cincinnati or Savannah discouraged by their prospects, for others restless after returning home from the war with Mexico, or those weary of marriage or fearful of growing debts, these first reports of gold and the resulting expectations of quick fortune might have been enough to send them on their way to El Dorado. But for most potential goldseekers in the thirty states, far more tangible evidence was needed to overcome doubts and scoffing neighbors—evidence strong enough to justify to wives and creditors, parents and business partners the expense and the danger of the long journey to California.

What the American people needed was an official endorsement of the California news. It came in December, directly from the two most trusted authorities in the nation: the President and the United States Army.

Having received Colonel Mason's official report of the diggings, President James K. Polk was prepared to speak with authority and confidence about the astonishing events in California. Mason had sent dramatic evidence (230 ounces of gold) to back up his report, and he set forth his judgment of California: "I have no hesitation in saying there is more gold in the country drained by the Sacramento and San Joaquin rivers than will pay the cost of the war with Mexico a hundred times over." Thus encouraged and more than willing to find additional justification for the recent war of conquest with Mexico, President Polk on December 5, 1848, delivered his message to the second session of the 30th Congress. Of the news from California, he stated: "The accounts of the abundance of gold in that territory are of such extraordinary character as would scarcely command belief were they not corroborated by authentic reports of officers in the public service." With this endorsement of the seemingly incredible, with the gold on display at the War Department, and with the full details of Mason's report published throughout the nation, skepticism gave way to unrestrained enthusiasm.

After December 5 and through the winter and spring of 1849, there appeared in literally every newspaper in the country continuing reports of the ever-increasing emigration to California. Whether in New York or Iowa, editors wrote of the national drama in florid phrases and excited tones, as if the wonder and impact of the news might not otherwise be fully appreciated.

On January 11, 1849, the New York *Herald* trumpeted its judgment: "The spirit of emigration which is carrying off thousands to California so far from dying away increases and expands every day. All classes of our citizens seem to be under the influence of this extraordinary mania. . . . If the government were under the necessity of making a levy of volunteers to the amount of two or three hundred thousand men for any purpose in California, the ranks would be filled in less than three months. . . . What will this general and overwhelming spirit of emigration lead to? Will it be the beginning of a new empire in the West, a revolution in the commercial highways of the world, a depopulation of the old States for the new republic on the shores of the Pacific?

"Look at the advertising columns of the *Herald* or any other journal, and you will find abundant evidence of the singular prevalence of this strange movement and agitation in favor of gold digging on the Sacramento. Every day men of property and means are advertising their possessions for sale, in order to furnish them with means to reach that golden land. Every city and town is forming societies either to cross the Isthmus or to double Cape Horn. . . .

"Poets, philosophers, lawyers, brokers, bankers, merchants, farmers, clergymen—all are feeling the impulse and are preparing to go and dig for gold and swell the number of adventurers to the new El Dorado.

"The spirit which has been thus awakened in this country by the discovery of the gold mines in California and by the authentic facts published concerning them under the authority of the government in Washington exceeds everything in the history of commercial adventure that has occurred in many ages and can only be paralleled by that which sprang up in Spain and other parts of Europe by the discovery of the mineral wealth of Mexico and Peru by the expeditions of Cortez and Pizarro."

More influential than such editorial fervor, what nurtured hopes on farms and in villages and challenged the faint-hearted were personal reports direct from California—letters sent home by settlers who had become California's first gold miners. Eagerly sought by local newspapers and then reprinted again and again by dailies and weeklies in other states, these statements written in the language of neighbors told of digging for gold along rivers called the American, Feather, Yuba and Mokelumne, where in a matter of months young men using methods that sounded simple, even haphazard, gathered fortunes totaling thousands, tens of thousands of dollars.

A letter from a man named McClellan written to his family in Jackson, Missouri, concluded: "You know Bryant, the carpenter who used to work for

Ebenezer Dixon, well, he has dug more gold in the last six months than a mule can pack." In family councils at day's end, in churchyards after the Sunday sermon, in country stores and city saloons, men used Bryant's triumph or similar reports to argue in favor of going to California. Week by week the news gathered force, more men believed and their families agreed that if they could get to California success would be assured, success that required no knowledge of mining and only a few months' work.

As the frugality of generations gave way to a contagion of optimism and ambition, responsible family men found their jobs and prospects unrewarding when set against all that California could provide. They figured how much they could bring home after a year's sojourn in the gold fields and justified the cost of the journey and the length of their absence as an investment that would guarantee financial security. And it was not just ambitious men who dreamed. In January 1849 the wife of a struggling shopkeeper wrote to her parents: "Joseph has borrowed the money to go; but I am full of bright visions that never filled my mind before, because at the best of times I have never thought of much beyond a living; now I feel confident of being well off."

In East Coast ports, shipowners announced sailing dates for steamers, schooners, brigs and old whaling ships resurrected to meet the sudden demand. Newspaper advertising columns announced the sale of businesses by men "overtaken by the gold fever." Manufacturers of money belts, tents, India-rubber wading boots and clothing, medicines, and gold testing and smelting devices proclaimed their products essential to success in the land of gold. And inventors attested to the infallibility of their patented mining machinery, including a "hydro-centrifugal Chrysolyte or California Gold Finder" and an "Archimedes Gold Washing Machine." Equally imaginative entrepreneurs announced an "aerial locomotive" capable of carrying fifty to one hundred passengers from New York to California "pleasantly and safely" in three days at a cost of $200—and they assured their readers that two hundred tickets had already been sold.

Those more aware of the realities of geography and commerce knew that the journey would require many weeks—even months—of arduous, possibly dangerous travel by wilderness trails or ocean voyages. For those on the Atlantic Coast with seafaring traditions, the ocean routes seemed the only way to go. For forty years New England merchants and whalers had sent their ships around Cape Horn, an 18,000-mile voyage, to the coves and harbors of California, there to trade or obtain fresh food and water. This commercial tradition helped build confidence in the Cape route (despite the distance and four to six months on shipboard), so much so that all but twenty-two of the 124 gold-rush companies that organized in Massachusetts during 1849 sailed around the Horn, taking a total of 6,067 emigrants from that state alone.

In contrast to the time that would be spent on board a ship sailing around South America, goldseekers could reach California in a matter of weeks by taking a steamer from New York to the town of Chagres on the Atlantic side of the Isthmus of Panama. From there it took two or three days through dense jungle to reach the ancient Pacific port of Panama City, where another line of steamers tried to accommodate the ever-pressing demand for passage to San Francisco. If they sailed from New York to Panama in January, February or even March, they could be in the diggings before the first overland emigrants even set out from the western frontier. In all, about 6,500 emigrants took the Panama route in 1849; but disease, exorbitant costs, overcrowding and too few steamers on the Pacific route caused delays of weeks and sometimes months throughout that first year of the rush.

For those who lived inland and had farming as a background, the ocean voyage seemed fearful, the overland trails practical, even familiar. The well-known history of travel from the Missouri frontier to Santa Fe and to Oregon increased their confidence. During the winter and early spring of 1849 tens of thousands of men throughout the United States prepared for the overland trek that would begin with the first good weather in April or May. In cities and country villages they organized joint-stock companies, each member paying an equal amount to provide funds for the company's purchase of wagons, teams and provisions. Organized as the Pittsburgh and California Enterprise Company, the Illinois and California Mining Company, the Sagamore and Sacramento Mining and Trading Company and many more, goldseekers joined together more as ambitious businessmen than as carefree adventurers. In Ithaca, New York, a company of fifty men, with a capital of $25,000 and a credit of $25,000 more at a local bank, planned to leave the western frontier in early April and reach the gold country in June. There, as the Ithaca *Journal* reported on March 21, 1849, "they will select a suitable location, erect cabins and proceed to rake in the dust."

In addition to reporting the financial arrangements of the overland companies, the local newspapers often printed each company's membership lists and their lengthy constitutions, or "Rules of Regulation," which more often than not prohibited swearing, drinking and violation of the Sabbath. Some companies issued uniforms, elected officers with military titles and drilled their members. Some purchased ships which carried cargoes of supplies and trade goods around Cape Horn to San Francisco, there to await the members' arrival by overland trail. One company included in its equipage eleven "gold finders" and a machine for making gold coins.

To raise money to join an overland company or to purchase a wagon, team and other "California fixings," goldseekers mortgaged or sold homes and farms, took out life savings, or borrowed from friends and fathers-in-law. The financial impact of this money raising caused concern in several states, with editors lamenting the loss of capital withdrawn from the local economy to support the sudden needs of men afflicted with gold fever. On March 27 a newspaper in Ann Arbor, Michigan, estimated that $30,000 had been taken out of Washtenaw County alone, with each man spending an average of $400 to pay for his outfit and transportation to the frontier. Many had to find additional money to provide for their wives and children until their return. A man in Ann Arbor, father of six daughters, sold his home to his brother for $1,200; a farmer on February 24, 1849, sold his acreage to his father-in-law for $1,300. More often, such funds came from mortgages, but some would-be goldseekers found that a mortgage was not always enough—they had to enter into a contract to share equally with the moneylender the gold that would be found in California. Such contracts suggest the contagion of optimism that spring of 1849.

Ignorant of guns and camping life except for what they had heard or read in legend and literature, thousands of city and rural men studied John C. Frémont's famous *Report of the Exploring Expedition to the Rocky Mountains in the Year 1842 and to Oregon and North California in the Years 1843–44* and the accounts of other western travelers. In part motivated by such reading and by the traditional fear of Indians, these emigrants purchased a remarkable number of guns, an impulse encouraged by the U.S. War Department's February 1849 offer to sell pistols, rifles and ammunition at cost to California (and Oregon) emigrants.

In further preparation for their long journey, they probably bought one of the several "emigrant guides" issued that spring to tell the greenhorns how to find their way through the vastness of mountains and deserts. These publications, along with newspaper articles describing "Travel in the Far West," gave the goldseekers advice on what equipment and food they should purchase, whether oxen or mules made the best teams, where the Indians would be most dangerous. There were even tables of distances which set down the specific mileages from point to point—water sources, river crossings, major topographic features. All this information reflected the fact that the trails from the western frontier across the wilderness half of the continent had been explored and traveled for many years—by fur trappers and traders to Santa Fe since 1822, and to Oregon since 1812. Exploration or trailblazing would not be necessary for the crowds of inexperienced goldseekers or Californians as they were often called.

They had a choice of two primary routes: the Santa Fe Trail through territory newly acquired by conquest from Mexico, with various branches leading to southern California; or the far more publicized Oregon-California Trail, which since 1841 had been traveled by settlers headed for the Willamette or Sacramento valleys. Both of these well-established trails started at the major outfitting towns on the frontier, Independence and St. Joseph.

The goldseekers came to the frontier from every state in the Union, even from East Coast cities where the sea routes would have a strong appeal and from southern states where the routes through Texas and Mexico were open year-round. In all, at least 30,000 men, with possibly 1,000 women, traveled to the Missouri frontier. Never before had this country, or any other, experienced such an exodus of civilians, all heavily armed or intending to purchase rifles and pistols, mostly young men on the road for the first time, many organized into formal companies, others alone or with a few friends from their neighborhood. Impatient, curious, somewhat fearful of the uncertainties and dangers ahead, yet buoyed by their common expectations, they were not unlike a great volunteer army traveling from all parts of the nation to mobilize at the frontier.

Many who lived on farms and in villages and cities in Illinois, Wisconsin, Iowa and Missouri packed their gear in their wagons and rolled down the nearest road, headed for the Missouri river towns. Thousands from farther east began their journey on river steamers down the Ohio and Mississippi, with typical cost $9 per man (including stateroom) for seven days from Pittsburgh to St. Louis. Others traveled west on the great Erie Canal across northern New York or across Pennsylvania on the Portage and Canal System. On Great Lakes steamers they often experienced their first bout of seasickness, while from East Coast cities they rode in crowded railroad cars to connect with river and canal transportation to the West.

Along the way some of these men kept their promise to write home, and thus began a dynamic process by which the entire nation was emotionally involved in the rush to California. Scores of thousands of Americans who stayed home—wives, parents, sweethearts, relatives, friends who doubted the California stories, business partners and bankers who had helped finance the enterprise—received, shared, or read in local newspapers letters sent back by the goldseekers. The first of these letters reached homes in March and April; they continued to come from St. Louis, then from the frontier, and later from military posts in the Far West; some from the Mormons' embryo city at Salt Lake, and finally from California. For some families, the letters came for years from husbands and sons who could not give up their quest for gold. Through these letters (and after the men came home, through their diaries) America saw the great West—Indians, buffalo, deserts, the Rocky Mountains—for the first time through hometown eyes and vicariously experienced life in the Sierra mining camps and in the astonishing cities of Marysville, Sacramento, Sonora and San Francisco.

One of the thousands who set out that spring of 1849 promising to write letters and to keep a diary was a man named William Swain, aged twenty-seven, from a farm near the village of Youngstown, New York, north of Niagara Falls. He had read of California's gold in the local newspapers. By February, California had become the focus of his future. . . .

Two Views of the West

Easterners were always of two minds about the American West, one positive, the other negative. Typical of the positive view of the West is this painting by John Gast, "Manifest Destiny," which shows the goddess of Destiny moving westward bearing a schoolbook in one hand and a telegraph in the other. In front of the goddess, white Americans push the Indians and buffalo ever westward. What is the order of white settlement as envisioned by Gast? What kinds of people are the typical settlers? What do you make of the fact that there are no blacks in the picture?

"Manifest Destiny," John Gast. Library of Congress.

Easterners also liked to belittle people who went west, and especially those who went to California. Following are several examples. What is the primary message of these drawings? That the would-be settlers didn't have a clue about what they were getting into? Or that only oddballs, misfits, and wishful thinkers went to California?

1849 cartoon spoofing the wild rush to get to California. Note the imaginary dirigible and rocket ship. Chicago Historical Society.

1849 cartoon of a greenhorn setting off for the gold fields. H. R. Robinson, "A Gold Hunter on His Way to California, Via St. Louis," ca. 1849. Lithograph. California Historical Society, [FN-16057, X70-23-2-2].

Another greenhorn going west. Joseph Goldsborough Bruff, "Another Greenhorn Going West." Yale Collection of Western Americana, Beinecke Rare Book and Manuscript Library.

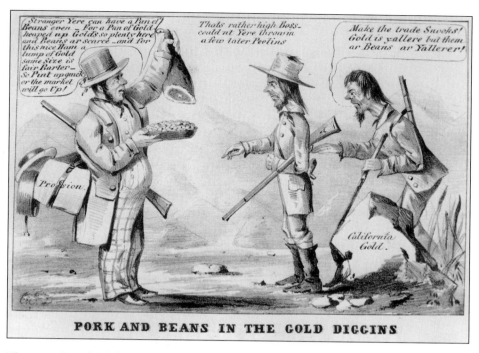

The true value of California gold. © Collection of The New-York Historical Society, [16261].

California justice.
American Heritage Picture
Collection.

Poker Flat and Points West

Also contributing to the eastern disdain for California were the names that prospectors gave to their settlements. What would you have thought had you seen this map in 1850? What do the names tell you about the first settlers? Years later, some of the names were changed. Guess which ones.

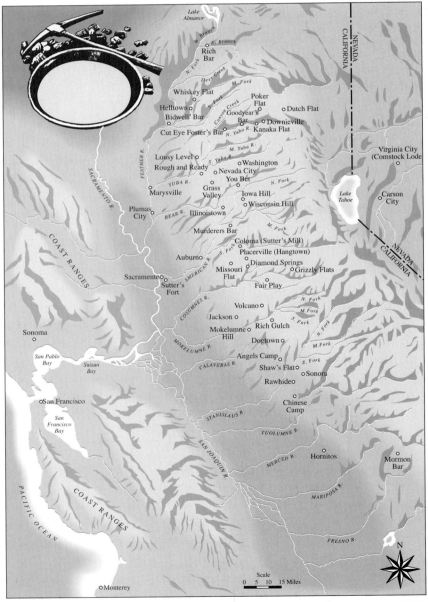

The California gold fields, showing some of the more important mining camps, c. 1850.

The Other Side of the Story

Most accounts of the great California migration were written by white men and women. Here is the other side of the story, from the perspective of a little Paiute girl, Sarah Winnemucca. About six or seven years old at the time of the great migration, she later lived briefly with a trader's family, learned English, and became a translator for the United States Army. As you read her account, try to recall the experiences of the Catawbas and other eastern tribes, as presented in Chapter 1. Do you discern any similarities? Any differences?

VOICES

I was born somewhere near 1844, but am not sure of the precise time. I was a very small child when the first white people came into our country. They came like a lion, yes, like a roaring lion, and have continued so ever since, and I have never forgotten their first coming. My people were scattered at that time over nearly all the territory now known as Nevada. My grandfather was chief of the entire Piute nation, and was camped near Humboldt Lake, with a small portion of his tribe, when a party travelling eastward from California was seen coming. When the news was brought to my grandfather, he asked what they looked like? When told that they had hair on their faces, and were white, he jumped up and clasped his hands together, and cried aloud,—

"My white brothers,—my long-looked for white brothers have come at last!"

He immediately gathered some of his leading men, and went to the place where the party had gone into camp. Arriving near them, he was commanded to halt in a manner that was readily understood without an interpreter. Grandpa at once made signs of friendship by throwing down his robe and throwing up his arms to show them he had no weapons; but in vain,— they kept him at a distance. He knew not what to do. He had expected so much pleasure in welcoming his white brothers to the best in the land, that after looking at them sorrowfully for a little while, he came away quite unhappy. But he would not give them up so easily. He took some of his most trustworthy men and followed them day after day, camping near them at night, and travelling in sight of them by day, hoping in this way to gain their confidence. But he was disappointed, poor dear old soul! . . .

The next year came a great emigration, and camped near Humboldt Lake. The name of the man in charge of the trains was Captain Johnson, and they stayed three days to rest their horses, as they had a long journey before them without water. During their stay my grandfather and some of his people called upon them, and they all shook hands, and when our white brothers were going away they gave my grandfather a white tin plate. Oh, what a

From Sarah Winnemucca Hopkins, *Life Among the Piutes: Their Wrongs and Claims*, ed. by Mrs. Horace Mann, Cupples, Upham, and Company, Boston, 1883, pp. 5–13, 20–21.

time they had over that beautiful gift,—it was so bright! They say that after they left, my grandfather called for all his people to come together, and he then showed them the beautiful gift which he had received from his white brothers. Everybody was so pleased; nothing like it was ever seen in our country before. My grandfather thought so much of it that he bored holes in it and fastened it on his head, and wore it as his hat. He held it in as much admiration as my white sisters hold their diamond rings or a sealskin jacket. . . .

The third year more emigrants came, and that summer Captain Fremont, who is now General Fremont.

My grandfather met him, and they were soon friends. They met just where the railroad crosses Truckee River, now called Wadsworth, Nevada. Captain Fremont gave my grandfather the name of Captain Truckee, and he also called the river after him. Truckee is an Indian word, it means *all right*, or *very well*. A party of twelve of my people went to California with Captain Fremont. I do not know just how long they were gone. . . .

That same fall, very late, the emigrants kept coming. It was this time that our white brothers first came amongst us. They could not get over the mountains, so they had to live with us. It was on Carson River, where the great Carson City stands now. You call my people bloodseeking. My people did not seek to kill them, nor did they steal their horses,—no, no, far from it. During the winter my people helped them. They gave them such as they had to eat. They did not hold out their hands and say:—

"You can't have anything to eat unless you pay me." No,—no such word was used by us savages at that time; and the persons I am speaking of are living yet; they could speak for us if they choose to do so.

The following spring, before my grandfather returned home, there was a great excitement among my people on account of fearful news coming from different tribes, that the people whom they called their white brothers were killing everybody that came in their way, and all the Indian tribes had gone into the mountains to save their lives. So my father told all his people to go into the mountains and hunt and lay up food for the coming winter. Then we all went into the mountains. There was a fearful story they told us children. Our mothers told us that the whites were killing everybody and eating them. So we were all afraid of them. Every dust that we could see blowing in the valleys we would say it was the white people. In the late fall my father told his people to go to the rivers and fish, and we all went to Humboldt River, and the women went to work gathering wild seed, which they grind between the rocks. The stones are round, big enough to hold in the hands. The women did this when they got back, and when they had gathered all they could they put it in one place and covered it with grass, and then over the grass mud. After it is covered it looks like an Indian wigwam.

Oh, what a fright we all got one morning to hear some white people were coming. Every one ran as best they could. My poor mother was left with my little sister and me. Oh, I never can forget it. My poor mother was carrying my little sister on her back, and trying to make me run; but I was so frightened I could not move my feet, and while my poor mother was trying to get me along my aunt overtook us, and she said to my mother: "Let

Sarah Winnemucca.
Nevada Historical Society.

us bury our girls, or we shall all be killed and eaten up." So they went to work and buried us, and told us if we heard any noise not to cry out, for if we did they would surely kill us and eat us. So our mothers buried me and my cousin, planted sage bushes over our faces to keep the sun from *burning them*, and there we were left all day.

Oh, can any one imagine my feelings *buried alive*, thinking every minute that I was to be unburied and eaten up by the people that my grandfather loved so much? With my heart throbbing, and not daring to breathe, we lay there all day. It seemed that the night would never come. Thanks be to God! the night came at last. Oh, how I cried and said: "Oh, father, have you forgotten me? Are you never coming for me?" I cried so I thought my very heartstrings would break.

At last we heard some whispering. We did not dare to whisper to each other, so we lay still. I could hear their footsteps coming nearer and nearer. I thought my heart was coming right out of my mouth. Then I heard my mother say, "'Tis right here!" Oh, can any one in this world ever imagine what were my feelings when I was dug up by my poor mother and father? . . .

Well, while we were in the mountains hiding, the people that my grandfather called our white brothers came along to where our winter supplies were. They set everything we had left on fire. It was a fearful sight. It was all we had for the winter, and it was all burnt during that night. My father took some of his men during the night to try and save some of it, but they could not; it had burnt down before they got there.

These were the last white men that came along that fall. My people talked fearfully that winter about those they called our white brothers. My people said they had something like awful thunder and lightning, and with that they killed everything that came in their way.

This whole band of white people perished in the mountains, for it was too late to cross them. We could have saved them, only my people were afraid of them. We never knew who they were, or where they came from. So, poor things, they must have suffered fearfully, for they all starved there. The snow was too deep. . . .

I tell you we children had to be very good, indeed, during the winter; for we were told that if we were not good they would come and eat us up. We remained there all winter; the next spring the emigrants came as usual, and my father and grandfather and uncles, and many more went down on the Humboldt River on fishing excursions. While they were thus fishing, their white brothers came upon them and fired on them, and killed one of my uncles, and wounded another. Nine more were wounded, and five died afterwards. My other uncle got well again, and is living yet. Oh, that was a fearful thing, indeed!

After all these things had happened, my grandfather still stood up for his white brothers. . . .

While my grandfather was talking, he wept, and men, women, and children, were all weeping. One could hardly hear him talking.

After he was through talking, came the saddest part. The widow of my uncle who was killed, and my mother and father all had long hair. They cut off their hair, and also cut long gashes in their arms and legs, and they were all bleeding as if they would die with the loss of blood. This continued for several days, for this is the way we mourn for our dead. . . .

To "experience" the Gold Rush for yourself and learn more about the people, places, and events involved, visit the website of the Oakland Museum of California at http://www.museumca.org/ goldrush/ *and the website of the Virtual Museum of the City of San Francisco.*

THE BIG PICTURE

The West was always a magnet, but in the 1840s it became a huge attraction, a lure for hundreds of thousands of people. Why were so many easterners willing to pick up stakes and take off for the promised land? Many of them literally walked across the country. What prompted them to do so?

Chapter 12

Sectional Conflict

Interpretive Essay by William L. Barney 282

Sources 294
 The Kansas-Nebraska Act, 1854 294
 Two Portraits of the West 295
 The Lincoln-Douglas Debates, 1858 297

The Big Picture 305

*I*n doubling the size of the country, the followers of Andrew Jackson brought slavery into the center of American politics. That was not the intention of most Jacksonians. The vast majority still wanted to keep slavery out of politics, silence the abolitionists, and focus on other issues. Western expansion, however, raised troublesome questions. What was to become of the new acquisitions? Were they to become slave states or free states? And in what proportion?

In 1845 Texas was admitted to the Union as a slave state, with the right to subdivide into as many as four additional states. Having lost Texas to slavery, antislavery forces in Congress were determined to keep slavery out of the territory seized from Mexico during the Mexican War. In 1846 an obscure Pennsylvania congressman named David Wilmot added to a money bill a proviso declaring that none of the territory acquired from Mexico should ever be open to slavery. Although solid opposition from the South, plus crucial votes from some northern Democrats, killed the Wilmot Proviso, it was added to bill after bill. It was never adopted, but it infuriated southern congressmen.

Even more infuriating to southern congressmen was the decision of California's leaders in 1849 to become a free state. Although proslavery men had considerable power in California, especially in the upper echelons of the California Democratic Party, they were no match for the miners. Earlier that year, miners along the Yuba River had forcibly ordered one slaveholder and his slaves out of the region, hanged a "major domo" who had refused to remove his Chilean peons, and cut off the ears of another slaveholder who had ignored their warnings. Rather than defy this sentiment, the territory's constitutional convention outlawed slavery by unanimous vote. Not only did those who disliked slavery in principle vote for the ban; so too did men from the Deep South who still had slaves back in their native states. Shortly thereafter, the leader of the latter group appeared in Washington seeking statehood for California.

The Congress that met that December quickly became raucous. With legislators screaming and shouting at one another, carrying Bowie knives and revolvers, the House took three weeks and sixty-three ballots to elect a Speaker, twenty-one ballots to elect a clerk, three ballots to elect a chaplain, and eight ballots to elect a sergeant at arms. In the Senate, the aged Henry Clay tried to rally the forces of moderation and compromise by presenting an omnibus bill covering all the disputed questions arising from the slavery issue. That hardly ended the turmoil. Northern Whigs complained bitterly about the new Fugitive Slave Act that was part of Clay's "compromise," and southern Democrats fumed that the admission of California as a free state would upset the balance of slave and free states in the Senate.

Clay's proposal finally passed in 1850 and led to what one historian has called an "armistice." But peace and tranquility were short-lived. The issue of slavery in the territories rose again and again, snapping the bonds of union, shattering the national political parties, and, by 1861, splitting the country itself into warring nations.

INTERPRETIVE ESSAY

The Quest for Room

William L. Barney

It was one thing for politicians in Washington to debate the future of the West, and another for New England and New York reformers to see the West as a fateful breeding ground for slavery. But what of the southerners themselves, the men who actually owned the slaves? Many historians have argued that the West was really irrelevant, that no white southerner in his right mind would have thought seriously of taking slaves into Nebraska, let alone California or Arizona. But another argument, represented in the following essay by William L. Barney, holds that the West was important to the slaveholders as a place where they might transport their "peculiar institution."

The history of slavery in the south was largely the story of its expansion. This expansion, from the tidewater of Virginia and the Carolinas in the late seventeenth century to the river valleys of eastern Texas by the mid-nineteenth century, enabled successive generations of southerners to carry slavery into new territories. These surges of growth not only were converted into political power in Washington through increased representation but also satisfied two basic internal needs of the south. Additional slave territory sustained the economic viability of slavery by providing fresh land to replace the exhausted soil of the older plantation regions, creating markets for the sale of surplus and agriculturally unprofitable slaves from the upper south, and enlarging opportunities for both the slaveholders and those striving to attain that status. Moreover, the diffusion of slaves through expansion permitted southerners to avoid the fundamental problem of how to maintain control over a growing number of slaves confined to a closed area. The slaves had to be kept ignorant and tied to the land, because urbanization and industrialization entailed too grave a risk of slackened discipline and eventual race warfare. But a given amount of land subjected to an exploitive agriculture could support both whites and blacks for only a limited period before losing its fertility. Meanwhile, the concentration of slaves would grow ever denser until it reached unmanageable proportions. Soon—within a generation, some southerners prophesied—the master would be fleeing his slaves. This was the southern dilemma. The continual maturation of slavery within a fixed geographical area created class and racial stresses that could be relieved only through expansion. The extension of slavery, in turn, generated powerful opposition, capped in 1860 by the triumph of the Republican party,

From William L. Barney, *The Road to Secession: A New Perspective on the Old South*, Praeger, New York, 1972, pp. 6–17. Reprinted by permission of William L. Barney.

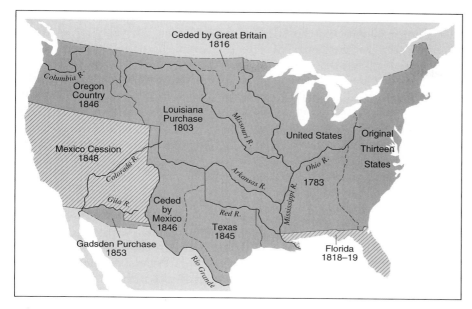

Westward expansion.

which was pledged to the strict containment of slavery within its existing limits. For the south, the dilemma had become a question of survival.

Land as the Economic Elixir

Of the many myths spawned by the plantation legend of the old south, few are as alluring, or as deceptive, as the languorous, timeless image of the white-columned plantation, the homestead of the planter—that polished aristocrat with deep ties to the land, moving with grace and ease in a milieu of wealth, stability, and refinement. In fact, most planters were grasping parvenus, and their homes were simply overgrown log cabins. But what most distorts reality in this image is the absence of a sense of time and movement. It was precisely the restlessness and dynamism of most planters that attracted the attention of contemporaries. Thomas Cobb, a leading jurist of ante-bellum Georgia, described the planters as a class that was "never settled. Such a population is almost nomadic." Cobb explained this mobility by noting that the prime determinant of a planter's wealth and status was not his land but his slaves. As a result, his surplus income was invested in more slaves rather than in improvements to the land.

> The homestead is valued only so long as the adjacent lands are profitable to cultivation. The planter himself having no local attachments, his children inherit none. On the contrary, he encourages in them a disposition to seek new lands. His valuable property (his slaves) are easily removed to fresh lands, much more easily than to bring the fertilizing materials to the old.

Mobility was characteristic of all southerners and appears to have been a function of economic class. In Jefferson County, Mississippi, an alluvial planting area on the banks of the Mississippi, about 87 percent of the nonslaveholders left the county during the 1850s. This percentage dropped among slaveholders in proportion to the number of slaves held, until it reached a low of 17 percent for those owning 100 slaves or more. The main flow of migration was from the worn-out lands of the Southern Atlantic states to the virgin soils of the southwest and across Louisiana into Texas. By 1860, South Carolina, an older state, had lost to emigration nearly half of all white natives born after 1800. (The annual and even seasonal movement was also quite heavy, but, because of gaps in the census returns, it cannot be measured.) Writing from the newly opened Alabama frontier in the mid-1830s, a planter's daughter noted that there were "a great many persons moving away from the place and going to the Choctaw [P]urchase and [a] great many coming in which keeps the number pretty much the same."

Whole counties were virtually depopulated by the Texas land fever, only to be refilled by a new wave of settlers. So prevalent was the wanderlust that many resorted to religious metaphor or cited positive secular values to explain their drive. In explaining his lifestyle, which had seen him constantly on the move, the yeoman farmer Gideon Linecum pointed to his "belief and faith in the pleasure of frequent change of country." Eli Lide, a planter's son who had moved to Alabama from South Carolina in the 1830s, rationalized his move to Texas twenty years later in terms of "something within me [that] whispers onward onward and urges me on like a prisoner who has been 58 years and idles in his Lord[']s vineyard and lived on his bounty and made no returns for the favors received."

Southern institutions were transplanted across the Appalachians with but minimal disruptions. Planters frequently sent ahead a younger son or a trusted overseer with a few field hands to stake out the new territory and clear the land. When the planter arrived with his wagons, livestock, family, and slaves, he quickly re-established the community leadership to which he was accustomed. He assumed the responsibility of meeting the frontier's rudimentary cultural needs by hiring private tutors, perhaps setting up one of the few schools, and donating land or funds for the upkeep of an imported minister. In a few years, his slaves would have carved out of the wilderness the plantation on which his economic primacy rested. Finally, as long as he catered to the democratic sensibilities of the yeoman farmers, he could be virtually assured of political influence and, even, office. No concessions of substance were required, only of style. For example, it was always politically wise to express antiaristocratic sentiments and to show an acceptably egalitarian spirit in one's personal dealings, no matter what one's natural inclinations. These were the rules of the game, and to violate them brought opprobrium—as one Virginia planter newly arrived on Mississippi discovered. A local farmer, observing that the good gentleman disdained soiling his hands, did not hesitate to tell him that, if he had "taken hold of a plough" and worked by the farmer's side, his help would have been welcomed, but "to see him sitting up on his horse with his gloves on, directing his Negroes how to work," was not to the farmer's taste. Most planters learned the rules soon enough. Generally speaking, then, there was a remarkably successful transfer of the prior structure of institutions and leadership from the old south of Jefferson to the newer one of Jefferson Davis.

A potential source of conflict in the spread of the plantation was class competition for the better lands. This was usually not a problem, however, because the emigrants, naturally enough, sought out a region similar in soil and climate to what they had left behind. Traditionally, the yeomanry had avoided the heavy, sticky prairie soils and the wet, marshy bottomlands. These areas were thought to be unhealthy and required a much greater initial investment to cultivate than the lighter soils in the uplands or the sandy loam back on the ridges. As a result, when the southwest was opened up, much of the prairie and alluvial soils, the most productive and fertile in the south, were left by default to the planters. Where competition did exist, it was usually short-lived. The average farmer was a speculator. For him, it was good business to enter a new region, put up a log cabin, clear the forest and make other improvements, and then sell out for a profit after a few years. If a wealthy planter should want the land, all the better. With plenty of land to the west, one could repeat the process several times in a lifetime.

The expansion of the south meant a continual renewal of slave society. Yet, southerners always had the nagging doubt that the process itself had not solved any problems but only perpetuated them. The doubt, akin to a fear of overdependence, can be understood by looking at the economic forces that fueled the south's search for land.

The nature of plantation agriculture and the consistently low ratio of land to labor costs explain much of the south's outward thrust. Besides initially requiring large units of land, staple-crop production on the plantations exhausted the soil at an alarming rate. Throughout most of the ante-bellum period, good land was so cheap and available in such quantity, especially relative to slave labor, that it was more profitable to ruin a plantation, pick up stakes, and start anew on virgin soil than to practice soil-conserving agriculture through crop rotation, deep plowing, and the use of fertilizers. Soil erosion and sterility became serious problems not only in scattered localities but in entire districts. By the early 1850s, the plantation belt of middle Georgia was described as a region of "red old hills stripped of their native growth and virgin soil, and washed with deep gullies, with here and there patches of Bermuda grass, and stunted pine shrubs, struggling for a scanty subsistence on what was one of the richest soils in America." Before 1860, the supposedly inexhaustible new cotton lands of the southwest had already exhibited the "painful signs of senility and decay" familiar to residents of the seaboard states. The complaint of a Georgia editor in 1858 that from the Chesapeake to the Mississippi there was "something fundamentally wrong in southern agriculture" was little more than a stock refrain.

Within a generation, the planters monopolized the agricultural wealth of any given area with the land and transportation facilities suitable for plantation agriculture. Five percent of the south's farmers owned 36 percent of the region's agricultural wealth; the poorest 50 percent of all farmers owned only 6 percent of the land. Indeed, even in the uplands and pine barrens—regions where the plantation never took root and that were supposedly the haven of the small farmer—a slaveholding elite controlled more land and more valuable land than the majority of the yeomanry. With their large labor force, extensive credit arrangements, and the capital resources to buy and utilize the best lands, the planters enjoyed competitive advantages over their small farmer neighbors and gradually were able to displace them.

This encroachment of the planter was not a matter of economic necessity only. As much as the planter needed fresh land to replace what he had destroyed or as a hedge for the future, he was also concerned about the security problems of having his slaves come into contact with nonslaveholders. The poorer whites were accused of interfering with slave discipline by setting an example of shiftlessness and by encouraging the slaves to steal plantation property to exchange for liquor and cheap trinkets. A Louisiana sugar planter told Frederick Law Olmsted, perhaps the most perceptive of all northern travelers in the south, that he wanted to buy out all the poor whites living around his plantation.

> It was better that negroes never saw anybody off their own plantation; that they had no intercourse with other white men than their owner or overseer; especially, it was best that they should not see white men who did not command their respect, and whom they did not always feel to be superior to themselves, and able to command them.

Wasteful agricultural practices, monopolistic patterns of land ownership, and displacement of the yeomanry combined to create the south's land hunger. Down to the 1850s, there had always been a new cotton frontier—whether in the Georgia-Carolina uplands before the War of 1812, the prairies of Alabama and Mississippi in the Jacksonian period, or the river valleys of Arkansas and Texas just before and after the Mexican War—to satisfy this hunger and prevent social tensions from building up. "The way we have been able to give land to the lacklanders, to extend this great country, and to supply the landless with land, has been by the extension of the empire by arms and by money," boasted Senator Robert Toombs of Georgia, as he argued in 1859 for the acquisition of Cuba. Even the moderate Jefferson Davis claimed an economic right of expansion: "We at the South are an agricultural people, and we require an extended territory. Slave labor is a wasteful labor, and it therefore requires a still more extended territory than would the same pursuits if they could be prosecuted by the more economical labor of white men."

The Failure of Expansionism

The 1850s witnessed a widening gap between the south's desire to gain more territory and her ability to do so within the Union. The decade opened with the loss of California to the free-soil north. California was the great prize in the lands recently wrested from Mexico. Already noted for its deep ocean ports and its rich valley agriculture, the area became, with the discovery of gold, a mecca for fortune-seeking Americans.

The antislavery forces, with some backing from southern Whigs, argued that the United States was honor-bound to respect the Mexican decrees that had prohibited slavery in the provinces of California and New Mexico. Southern Democrats reacted scornfully to this position. They stressed that the south had contributed more than her fair share of men and arms to the conquest of these territories and thus had a military, as well as a constitutional, right to carry slaves there. Racial stereotypes were employed. "Do they mean to assert," wondered Senator Albert Gallatin Brown of Mississippi, "that the victorious and proud-hearted American is to go, cap in hand, to the miserable, cringing Mexican peon, and ask his permission to settle on the soil won by the valor of our troops at Buena Vista, or before the walls of Mexico?"

To arguments that the climate and soil of these territories were unsuitable for slavery, that the institution was debarred by a "decree of Nature," southerners responded by citing the great profitability of slavery in mining. "Slave labor is never more profitably employed than in mining," said Brown in a letter to his constituents, "and you may judge whether slaves could be advantageously introduced into that country, when I inform you . . . that an able-bodied negro is worth in California from two to six thousand dollars per annum." The slaves were so valuable in the mines, contended a Virginia senator, that, unless the black race were excluded altogether from California, slaveholders could bring them in by the thousands under contracts calling for their manumission within a few years, work them until then, and still show a large profit. Senator Jefferson Davis of Mississippi was certain that, with irrigation, southern California could support a lucrative commercial agriculture in cotton, grapes, and olives. This agriculture, however, required slave labor. The individual pioneer could not settle upon this dry land and support his family with his own exertions as he had traditionally done in the more humid east. Associated labor was needed to establish and maintain the irrigation system. Because Mexican peonage was clearly inconsistent with American law, Davis concluded that black slavery was the only solution.

The admission of California as a free state was a bitter blow to the south. A small but strategically placed proslavery wing of the California Democracy continued to fight for the introduction of slavery and even succeeded by its control of the judiciary in allowing a limited use of slave labor in the mines until the mid-1850s. But the battle had been lost. Although they alleged improper executive interference by the administration of President Taylor with the statehood movement, southerners generally blamed their defeat on the constant antislavery agitation of northerners and the refusal of slaveholders to risk their property under such unsettling conditions. Had it not been for this agitation, insisted Representative Thomas Clingman of North Carolina, "our southern slaveholders would have carried their negroes into the mines of California in such numbers, that I have no doubt but that the majority there would have made it a slaveholding State."

Clingman, however, underestimated the extent of antislavery feelings. S. R. Thurston, the territorial representative from Oregon, explained that white Californians had excluded slavery not from any hostility to the south, nor even from opposition to slavery in the abstract, but solely out of economic self-interest: They feared that the slaveholders would monopolize the wealth of the mines. "One man might work a thousand [slaves], and consequently, on the ground that a slave will do as much work as a white man, the southerner might make a thousand dollars to the northerner['s] one." The miners would never permit such an aristocracy of wealth to arise. So, it was fortunate, Thurston continued, that slavery had never gained legal protection; for, if any man had taken large numbers of slaves into the mines, "they would have been cut down—yes, sir, cut down—cut down by white men. . . . To have maintained slave labor there, during this last year, would have required a standing army of fifty thousand men; and whenever it is desired to redden those mountain streams with human gore, take your slaves there."

Kansas, although economically less significant than California, represented an even more serious psychological defeat for the south. Badly misjudging the strength and sensitivity of the antislavery movement, many southerners had deluded themselves into believing that the Kansas-Nebraska Act, by expressly revoking the Missouri Compromise line of 36° 30′, would take the issue of territorial slavery out of politics and allow the settlers to decide the question for themselves. Even Alexander Stephens of Georgia, a very cautious and moderate politician and a leading congressional spokesman for the Whigs, interpreted the act as a moral victory for the south by its removal of the stigma of slavery exclusion. Far more perceptive was the comment of a Tennessee congressman who predicted that passage of the act would result in a "most impolitic and mad moment for the South, no practical good can come of it because there is none in it."

Infuriated by the organized efforts of some abolitionists groups to send free-soil settlers into Kansas, the south committed herself to an ideological contest that she could not win. Most slaveholders simply were not interested in the flat, windy prairies of Kansas. Hemp and tobacco could be grown profitably in the eastern river valleys of the region, as they were in neighboring Missouri, but few planters wanted to hazard their slaves for such limited economic returns. Although led by slaveholders, the Southern bands that made the long trek to Kansas were composed mainly of land-hungry adventurers. These men were outnumbered by the free-soil settlers, more mobile than slave labor, who moved rapidly into the territory, and who were determined to keep slavery out.

Southern Democrats fought desperately to gain legal recognition of slavery in Kansas. Entrenched among the territorial office-holders, the proslavery forces pushed through the Kansas Lecompton Constitution in a boycotted election. This document, which could not be amended for several years, protected the slave property already within the territory. In attempting to bring Kansas into the Union under this constitution, the southern Democrats downplayed economic motives. They insisted that the issue was whether slavery would ever again be permitted to expand. John Slidell of Louisiana told the Senate that the south was "struggling for the maintenance of a principle, barren, it is true, of present practical fruits, but indispensable for our future protection." If Kansas was refused admission because slavery "nominally and temporarily exists there, what may we expect," he asked, "when application shall be made by a State of which it will be a real and enduring institution?" Representative William Porcher Miles of South Carolina wanted Kansas as a "wall of defense" for Missouri—and for the two additional proslavery votes she would provide in the Senate. In a racist appeal, Brown of Mississippi accused the free-soilers of wanting to force a government upon the white settlers and thereby create a free Kansas that "makes the negro free by enslaving the white man; but my free Kansas makes the white man free, and leaves the negro where the Constitution left him— subject to the authority of his master." As to charges of corruption and irregularities surrounding the Lecompton Constitution, southern Democrats replied that these were no worse than similar problems that had beset California. "Are we of the South to be made to see California hurried into the Union against all law and all precedent *because she is a free state* and Kansas subjected to the rigors of the inquisition because she *has a chance* of being a slave state?" demanded a Mississippi congressman.

In March 1855, David Atchison, a Missouri senator and leader in the struggle to open up Kansas for slavery, offered an early version of the domino theory: "If we win we carry slavery to the Pacific Ocean; if we fail we lose Missouri, Arkansas, and Texas and all the territories; the game must be played boldly. I know that the Union as it exists is in the other scale, but I am willing to take the holyland." In the view of Python, a pseudonymous contributor to DeBow's Review in the late 1850s, all the dominoes would fall if the south lost Kansas; for the entire western flank of slavery would be endangered. The emboldened abolitionists, he warned, would first attack slavery in Missouri, then move south into the Oklahoma Indian territories and Texas, and finally turn west into New Mexico and Arizona. The upper south would be the next target, and soon slavery would end up confined to the gulf states.

Southern Whigs, on the other hand, while conceding that the admission of new slave states was vital to southern interests, refused to believe that Kansas represented slavery's Armageddon. For one thing, the south, they argued, was capable of standing on higher ground than the Lecompton Constitution, which one Whig denounced as the "most barefaced fraud and cheating the world ever saw." For another, few of them expected slavery to take permanent hold in Kansas. Senator John Bell of Tennessee, for example, pointed out, in the spring of 1858, that the number of slaves in Kansas had declined in the previous year from about three hundred to no more than one hundred.

In the end, the south was hoisted with her own petard. If the eventual admission of Kansas as a free state was a humiliating defeat, it was largely because too many southerners had made the issue a test of sectional strength and determination. "It will be useless to attempt explanations and excuses, we are condemned, and I think justly," wrote a Georgia judge to Alexander Stephens in June 1857. "We have made the people believe it will be a slave state and we ought to make it good or not assume to hold the reins of power."

Cuba and Mexico offered unique advantages to southern expansionists. The former was already a slave society, and the latter seemed ripe for the taking. Although the unyielding Republican opposition to the expansion of slavery was sufficient to block most designs on these areas, internal resistance within the south was itself a major deterrent.

The pro-Cuban forces were centered in the Democratic party, and they had some support from the northern wing of the party, as exemplified by James Buchanan's acquiescence in the Ostend Manifesto of 1854. In this declaration, three American foreign ministers crudely served warning on Spain that the United States meant to have Cuba. Many of their arguments would sound familiar a century later. Cuba, lying just ninety miles off Florida, was deemed the key to the commerce and defenses of the Caribbean. But, of course, slavery was the overriding issue. "I want Cuba, and I know that sooner or later we must have it. . . . I want Tamaulipas, Potosi, and one or two other Mexican States; and I want them all for the same reason—for the planting or spreading of slavery," announced Albert Gallatin Brown in a speech at Hazlehurst, Mississippi. Cuba was to be the linchpin in a tropical empire founded on outright annexation or on the creation of satellite states. This empire, by giving the south a virtual monopoly over the production of tropical goods, would ensure the perpetuation of slavery.

The annexationists charged that the British were scheming to effect emancipation in Cuba. Furthermore, they warned that the unstable Spaniards might decree emancipation in order to punish the rebellious Creole planters or to make the island unattractive to Americans. A free black government in Cuba was depicted as a threat to slave security all along the Gulf Coast. "Indeed," in the vivid phrase of John Van Evrie, a proslavery propagandist, "Cuba would be a volcano of 'free negroism,' constantly vomiting fire and blood on the neighboring coast." Annexation not only would eliminate this threat but would also prove a boon to the Cuban slaves. Stephen Mallory of Key West assured his Senate colleagues that, under the paternalism of a southern master, "the plantation negro in Cuba would be what he is in Florida, the freest from disease and care, the happiest and the most enduring of his race on the face of the earth."

The southern opposition, once again led by the Whigs, contended that if Cuban sugar were admitted duty-free, the sugar planters of Louisiana, Texas, and Florida would be ruined. These planters depended on tariff protection for their economic survival. If hurt by Cuban competition, they might shift their resources to cotton production, thus depressing the price of that staple. The Whigs stressed that Cuba, unlike Texas in the 1840s, was a settled, heavily populated country that had no room for southern emigrants. The living conditions of the slaves would improve under American rule, but this would result in an even higher population density, which could not absorb the south's own rapidly increasing slave population. "We want land without people on it, and not land and people together," said a Tennessee representative. The problems of assimilating the Cuban people were seen as insurmountable. Their language, religion, and extraction differed from ours, stressed Senator John Thompson of Kentucky, "and our people have regarded them as aliens and outlaws from the pale of humanity and civilization. . . . Saying nothing about color, I think I have been at more respectable weddings than it would be to bring her into the household." The Republicans agreed. Cuban whites were "ignorant, vicious, and priest-ridden," according to one Republican senator, and another wondered what the United States would do with the 200,000 free blacks on the island.

The Whigs could not see how Cuban annexation would strengthen slavery. The old fear of the future of slavery in the upper south was revived. If, as most people expected, the African slave trade with Cuba were prohibited under the Americans, the planters would turn to the upper south to replenish their labor supply and thereby hasten the abolitionizing of these states. One Whig congressman based his opposition on the ground that he did not want to see the area of slavery contracted. Because Spain hated and feared the United States, he reasoned, she would spitefully free the Cuban slaves if she ever became convinced that the island was about to fall into American hands. On the other hand, if Cuba, by some unexpected stroke of good fortune, were acquired with slavery intact, the Whigs foresaw an explosion of antislavery agitation. England and France, suspecting that the United States coveted, and would therefore try to seize, other West Indian islands, would be poised for war.

Despite considerable influence within the Pierce and Buchanan administrations, the Cuban annexationists got nowhere. Their most flamboyant leader, Governor John Quitman of Mississippi, was in constant difficulty with federal authorities over his open defiance of the neutrality laws through his filibustering activities. Quitman was convinced that the south would be able to expand within the Union only if she forced a drastic revision of these neutrality statutes, which barred Americans from private military enterprises against other sovereign powers. Then, southern armies, privately financed and recruited, would be free, he hoped, to carry slavery into the Caribbean and Central America. Quitman was immensely popular in Mississippi, but most southerners rejected his dramatic program. After all, even in the case of Cuba, the expansionists had not resolved certain paradoxes. On the other hand, they predicted that, as a result of the closing of the African slave trade and of American paternalism, the Cuban slave population would be better treated and would increase rapidly by natural causes. With a longer life expectancy, their value would rise, and this, in turn, would inflate the production costs of Cuban sugar, making it more competitive with American sugar. Yet, if the slave population grew after annexation, the island could hardly serve as the outlet the south demanded for her own increasing numbers of slaves.

For some, Mexico could serve as that outlet. In a speech before Congress, Representative O. R. Singleton of Mississippi reasoned that, because there was no settled government in Mexico, the United States had every right to intervene to promote order and set up a stable government. And, "when we have wound it up, there being no better heirs than ourselves, we will be compelled to hold that territory." Such altruism had its rewards. Much of Mexico, Singleton declared, was suitable for cotton, rice, and sugar cultivation. The south would have her outlet. "In my opinion we must, and we are compelled to, expand in that direction, and thus perpetuate it [slavery]—a hundred or a thousand years it may be."

In 1858, William Burwell of Virginia, in urging Senator R. M. T. Hunter of Virginia to exert pressure for a more aggressive Mexican policy, suggested that the acquisition of all Mexico could serve both as a popular issue for the next presidential election and as a means for the south to reestablish her political equality within the Union.

> . . . you have within your grasp a country accessible, abounding in all the metals and staples which civilised man most values, and a territory so extensive as that you can by only promoting the existing communities of Mexico to an equality with the present members of the Union preserve the balance in the Council of States, and so guarantee the peculiar rights of those States of which you are one of the guardians and representatives.

Burwell was confident that southern whites could easily control the racially mixed population. Movement into Mexico would be relatively easy on the railroads, and, with the telegraph, communications would be no problem. In that sense, Mexico was no farther away from Washington than Alabama or Tennessee had been twenty years earlier. If Mexico were not won for slavery, Burwell contended, it would be abolitionized by the north. "And if the worst should befall us could we not cut loose from the Union, throw an emigrant army into Mexico and make it as safe as Texas?" There was no alternative. "The North has more states and more territory than the South. It has the immigration of Europe to aid it. Your subjugation is as certain as the unrelenting operation of these great causes can render it." Out of self-protection, the South must "seize upon all the territory which produces those great staples of social necessity which the world cannot go without. Do so and you are safe."

Southern Democrats did implement a pale replica of the Singleton-Burwell program. The Buchanan administration tried to purchase the northern Mexican states or at least establish a protectorate over them, to extract commercial concessions, and to win diplomatic recognition of the right of the United States to intervene directly in Mexican affairs. These approaches, which met with some success, were held back by the same racial antipathies that had defeated the All-Mexico movement in the aftermath of the Mexican War. This racism was common to nearly all Americans. To Senator A. H. Sevier of Arkansas, the Mexicans were "a people bigoted, superstitious, cruel and ignorant; crossed, in the first place, in blood with the Moor and Spaniard, and recrossed with the negro and Indian." Representative C. Delano of Ohio believed that this intermixture produced a "slothful, indolent, ignorant race of beings." In his Barnwell, South Carolina, speech of 1858, Senator James Hammond used these racial slurs in denouncing any effort to take slavery into Mexico. Not only were Mexicans incapable of self-government, he asserted, but they could not even sustain slavery. Moreover, any attempt to incorporate them into the Union would result in a loss of racial purity.

> Sweep in Mexico at present, and it is the beginning of amalgamation. That is a people of mixed race and blood. So far from marking a line of discrimination between black and white, it is almost utterly obliterated, and

would step over, and gradually spread itself over, and instead of aiding this country, debauch it.

There was no better indication of the difficulties, if not outright futility, plaguing the expansionists than the opposition within the south to the reopening of the African slave trade. There were many factors behind the opposition: the vested interest of the upper south in high slave prices; fear of losing racial control by importing savage, heathen Africans; the wish to avoid agitating such a divisive issue; the threat of lower-class discontent if wages were severely depressed by cheap slave competition; and the conviction that the trade was morally wrong. These factors combined to hamstring the expansionists, for southerners of both parties agreed that, without a surplus of cheap slave labor to throw into the territorial competition with free labor, the south had little chance of adding any more slave states. "This great truth seems to take the people by surprise," wrote the Georgia Whig Alexander Stephens. "Some shrink from it as they would from death. Still it is as true as death." Albert Gallatin Brown realized this truth, but, ever sensitive to the land hunger of his piney-woods constituency and aware that land prices in Mississippi had more than doubled during the 1850s, he demanded more land before the trade was reopened. "If . . . labor is trenching, is close upon the lands—I mean lands worth cultivating—then we ought to get more land before we get more labor, since labor without land will be a burden rather than a profit."

The positions of Stephens and Brown were irreconcilable as long as the south remained in the Union. The south needed the slave trade in order to expand, but, even if the north consented to the reopening of the trade, the south feared that she had insufficient land on which to support the additional slaves. As an independent country, however, she would no longer face the political necessity of matching the northern expansion of free labor with her slaves and, even without reviving the African slave trade, could stake out additional slave territory to be occupied whenever economic pressures dictated. . . .

Explore the PBS site for "Africans in America," Part 4: 1831–1865, at http://www.pbs.org/wgbh/aia/part4/narrative.html *to read what other notable historians have had to say about westward expansion and slavery.*

@ ON THE WEB

The Kansas-Nebraska Act, 1854

Was there any way to quiet the slavery controversy? Senator Stephen A. Douglas, the North's leading Democrat, thought he had a way. In his eagerness to organize Kansas and Nebraska country, the Illinois senator gave in to southern demands and in 1854 sponsored a bill that specifically repealed the Missouri Compromise of 1820, which barred slavery north of 36° 30'. Douglas proposed that the fate of the territories be decided by "popular sovereignty." Under this system the actual settlers would have the opportunity to vote on slavery, either approving it or prohibiting it.

Below is a map of the country after the Kansas-Nebraska Act was passed by Congress. Do you think the 36° 30' line was a real barrier to slavery or just of

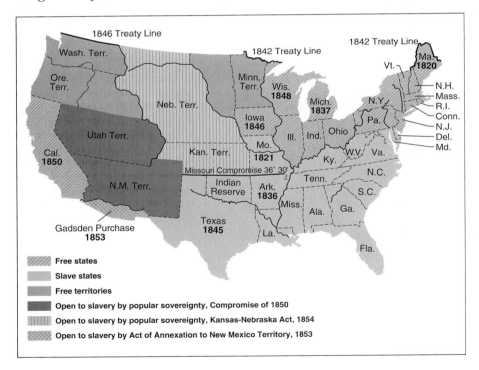

The United States, 1854.

To read the Congressional Debates on the Compromise of 1850, the Kansas-Nebraska Act, the secession crisis, and any other issues debated between 1833 and 1873, visit the Library of Congress American Memory site at http://www.memory.loc.gov/ammem/amlaw/lwcg.html, choose "Search this title through the Collection Search Page," then type in the search box the name of the debate you want to read, for example, Compromise of 1850.

ON THE WEB

symbolic importance? Do you think its repeal was really a meaningless gesture to calm southern nerves, as Douglas claimed? If you were a northerner in 1854, would you have been concerned?

Two Portraits of the West

The Kansas-Nebraska Act raised a storm of protest throughout the North, and almost overnight Anti-Nebraska groups sprang up to fight the extension of slavery. Some called themselves "Republican," which had a nice Jeffersonian ring to it, and the name stuck. Douglas expected the storm to blow itself out once northerners realized that his bill provided millions of acres for land-hungry farmers and a railroad route to the newly discovered gold fields of California. Moreover, argued Douglas, Kansas and Nebraska were obviously unsuited to slavery, and the "principle of dollars and cents" would keep slaveholders out.

But the storm did not blow itself out, and the brand-new Republican Party did incredibly well at the polls, routing northern Democrats in one congressional district after another, and carrying eleven of sixteen northern states in the presidential election of 1856. Douglas had clearly misread northern opinion. To many northerners it did not matter that slavery was never likely to take root on the prairies. To them, merely allowing the possibility was an outrage, and even more outrageous was the fact that the federal government had reversed itself and legally opened free territory to slavery.

The following two cartoons will help you understand this outrage. The first is from an English magazine, Punch, which had a strong following among antislavery men and women on both sides of the Atlantic. What do you make of the details? Why has Washington's likeness become a footrest? Who now controls the "land of liberty"?

The second illustration is a Republican cartoon showing Douglas, with the help of other leading northern Democrats, trying to force slavery down the throat of a Free-Soiler. What do you make of the Free-Soiler? Is he at all like the character in the Punch cartoon? And why is he so concerned about his wife and children? Is the message of the cartoon racist as well as antislavery? Why do you think keeping slavery out of the West had broad appeal, while abolishing slavery had very limited appeal?

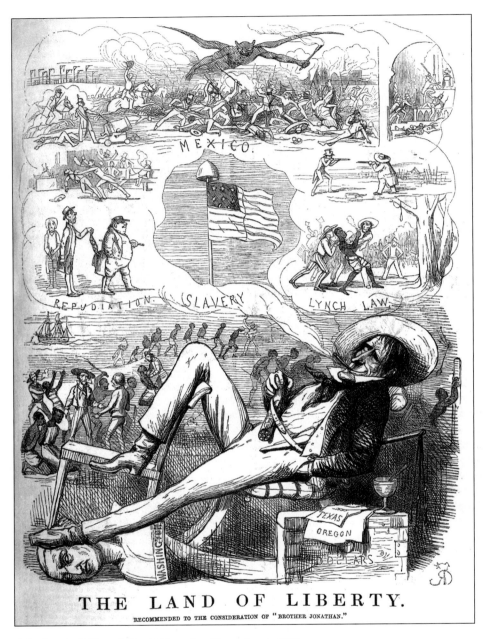

"The Land of Liberty" *Punch* Magazine, December 4, 1847.

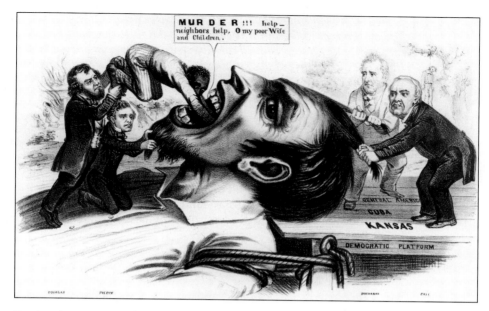

Forcing slavery down the throat of a Free-Soiler. Library of Congress.

The Lincoln-Douglas Debates, 1858

*While Republicans were blasting the Kansas-Nebraska Act in national politics,
Kansas itself became a battleground with northerners and southerners fighting for
control. Proslavery forces in Kansas put forward the Lecompton Constitution,
which the majority in Kansas clearly opposed. Nevertheless, President James
Buchanan, a Pennsylvania Democrat, backed the Lecompton Constitution and
tried to bring Kansas into the Union as a slave state. At the same time, the
Supreme Court, in the Dred Scott case, declared that Congress had no right to bar
slavery from the territories.*

*It was against this background that Senator Douglas, who broke with the
White House over the Lecompton Constitution, ran for reelection in 1858. His
opponent was a cunning Republican lawyer, Abraham Lincoln, who claimed that
Douglas's policy of "squatter sovereignty" had become an invitation to chaos.
Douglas attacked Lincoln as an abolitionist "Black Republican" whose principles
would lead not only to disunion but also to the "amalgamation" of the races and
the downfall of white America. Across Illinois the two men battled in debate.*

From *Political Debates Between Abraham Lincoln and Stephen A. Douglas in the Celebrated
Campaign of 1858 in Illinois,* The Arthur H. Clark Company, Cleveland, Ohio, 1902, pp. 1,
14, 18, 33, 101–117 *passim.*

*Read newspaper editorials addressing the Kansas-Nebraska Act, the Caning of Charles Sumner, the
Dred Scott decision, and John Brown's Raid at* http://history.furman.edu/~benson/docs/.

 ON THE WEB

Here are some highlights from these famous debates. Douglas won reelection. Do you think he also won the debates? How did the two men differ on such basic issues as slavery, race, local self-government, and the possibility of civil war? Today Lincoln is often referred to as a "racist." If Lincoln was a racist, how would you describe Douglas?

 ## DEBATES

Lincoln, at Springfield

"A house divided against itself cannot stand." I believe this government cannot endure permanently half slave and half free. . . . I do not expect the house to fall; but I do expect it will cease to be divided. It will become all one thing, or all the other.

Douglas, at Chicago

Mr. Lincoln advocates boldly and clearly a war of sections, a war of the North against the South, of the Free States against the Slave States. . . . He objects to the Dred Scot decision because it does not put the negro in the possession of citizenship on an equality with the white man. I am opposed to negro equality. . . . I am in favor of preserving, not only the purity of the blood, but the purity of the government from any mixture or amalgamation with inferior races.

Lincoln, at Chicago

I protest, now and forever, against that counterfeit logic which presumes that because I do not want a negro woman for a slave, I do necessarily want her for a wife. My understanding is that I need not have her for either, but, as God made us separate, we can leave one another alone, and do one another much good thereby. . . . The Judge regales us with the terrible enormities that take place by the mixture of races. . . . Why, Judge, if we do not let them get together in the Territories, they won't mix there.

Douglas, at Ottawa

Prior to 1854 this country was divided into two great political parties, known as the Whig and Democratic parties. Both were national and patriotic, advocating principles that were universal in their application. An Old Line Whig could proclaim his principles in Louisiana and Massachusetts alike. Whig principles had no boundary section line, they were not limited by the Ohio river, nor by the Potomac, nor by the line of the free and slave states, but applied and were proclaimed wherever the Constitution ruled or the American flag waved over the American soil. So it was, and so it is with the great Democratic party, which, from the days of Jefferson until this period, has proven itself to be the historic party of this nation. While the Whig and Democratic parties differed in regard to a bank, the tariff, distribution, the specie circular and the sub-treasury, they agreed on the great slavery question which now agitates the Union. I say that the Whig party and the Democratic party agreed on this slavery question while they differed on those matters of expediency to which I have referred. The Whig party and the Democratic party jointly adopted the compromise measures of 1850 as the basis of a proper and just solution of this slavery question in all its forms. Clay was the great leader, with Webster on his right and Cass on his left, and sustained by the patriots in the Whig and Democratic ranks, who had devised and enacted the compromise measures of 1850. . . .

Thus you see that up to 1853–'54, the Whig party and the Democratic party both stood on the same platform with regard to the slavery question. That platform was the right of the people of each state and each territory to decide their local and domestic institutions for themselves, subject only to the federal Constitution. . . .

In 1854, Mr. Abraham Lincoln and Mr. Trumbull entered into an arrangement, one with the other, and each with his respective friends, to dissolve the old Whig party on the one hand, and to dissolve the old Democratic party on the other, and to connect the members of both into an Abolition party under the name and disguise of a Republican party. . . . Lincoln went to work to abolitionize the Old Whig party all over the state, pretending that he was then as good a Whig as ever; and Trumbull went to work in his part of the state preaching abolitionism in its milder and lighter form, and trying to abolitionize the Democratic party, and bring old Democrats handcuffed and bound hand and foot into the abolition camp. . . .

Mr. Lincoln, following the example and lead of all the little Abolition orators, who go around and lecture in the basements of schools and churches, reads from the Declaration of Independence, that all men were created equal, and then asks how can you deprive a negro of that equality which God and the Declaration awards to him. . . . I do not question Mr. Lincoln's conscientious belief that the negro was made his equal, and hence is his brother, but for my own part, I do not regard the negro as my equal, and positively deny that he is my brother or any kin to me whatever. . . .

. . . He belongs to an inferior race, and must always occupy an inferior position. I do not hold that because the negro is our inferior that therefore he ought to be a slave. By no means can such a conclusion be drawn from what I have said. On the contrary, I hold that humanity and Christianity both require that the negro shall have and enjoy every right, every privilege, and even immunity consistent with the safety of the society in which he lives. On that point, I presume, there can be no diversity of opinion. You and I are bound to extend to our inferior and dependent being every right, every privilege, every facility and immunity consistent with public good. The question then arises what rights and privileges are consistent with the public good. This is a question which each state and each territory must decide for itself. . . .

Illinois Senator Stephen A. Douglas. Corbis Images.

Abraham Lincoln in 1858. The Lloyd Ostendorf Collection, Dayton, Ohio.

Lincoln, at Ottawa

Now gentlemen, I hate to waste my time on such things, but in regard to that general abolition tilt that Judge Douglas makes, when he says that I was engaged at that time in selling out and abolitionizing the old Whig party— I hope you will permit me to read a part of a printed speech that I made then at Peoria, which will show altogether a different view of the position I took in that contest of 1854.

VOICE: Put on your specs.

MR. LINCOLN: Yes, sir, I am obliged to do so; I am no longer a young man.

. . . we have before us, the chief materials enabling us to correctly judge whether the repeal of the Missouri Compromise is right or wrong.

I think, and shall try to show, that it is wrong; wrong in its direct effect, letting slavery into Kansas and Nebraska—and wrong in its prospective principle, allowing it to spread to every other part of the wide world, where men can be found inclined to take it.

This *declared* indifference, but as I must think, covert *real* zeal for the spread of slavery, I can not but hate. I hate it because of the monstrous injustice of slavery itself. I hate it because it deprives our republican example of its just influence in the world—enables the enemies of free institutions, with plausibility, to taunt us as hypocrites—causes the real friends of freedom to doubt our sincerity, and especially because it forces so many really good men amongst ourselves into an open war with the very fundamental principles of civil liberty—criticising the Declaration of Independence, and insisting that there is no right principle of action but *self-interest.*

Before proceeding, let me say I think I have no prejudice against the Southern people. They are just what we would be in their situation. If slavery did not now exist amongst them, they would not introduce it. If it did now exist amongst us, we should not instantly give it up. This I believe of the masses North and South. Doubtless there are individuals, on both sides, who would not hold slaves under any circumstances; and others who would gladly introduce slavery anew, if it were out of existence. We know that some Southern men do free their slaves, go north, and become tip-top Abolitionists; while some Northern ones go south, and become most cruel slave-masters.

When Southern people tell us they are no more responsible for the origin of slavery, than we; I acknowledge the fact. When it is said that the institution exists, and that it is very difficult to get rid of it, in any satisfactory way, I can understand and appreciate the saying. I surely will not blame them for not doing what I should not know how to do myself. If all earthly power were given me, I should not know what to do, as to the existing institution. My first impulse would be to free all the slaves, and send them to Liberia,—to their own native land. But a moment's reflection would convince me, that whatever of high hope, (as I think there is) there may be in this, in the long run, its sudden execution is impossible. If they were all landed there in a day, they would all perish in the next ten days; and there are not surplus shipping and surplus money enough in the world to carry them there in many times ten days. What then? Free them all, and keep them among us as underlings? Is it quite certain that this betters their condition? I think I would not hold one in slavery, at any rate; yet the point is not clear enough to me to denounce people upon. What next? Free them, and make them politically and socially, our equals? My own feelings will not admit this; and if mine would, we well know that those of the great mass of white people will not. Whether this feeling accords with justice and sound judgment, is not the sole question, if indeed, it is any part of it. A universal feeling, whether well or ill-founded, can not be safely disregarded. We can not, then, make them equals. It does seem to me that systems of gradual emancipation might be adopted; but for their tardiness in this, I will not undertake to judge our brethren of the South.

When they remind us of their constitutional rights, I acknowledge them not grudgingly, but fully, and fairly; and I would give them any legislation for the reclaiming of their fugitives, which should not in its stringency, be more likely to carry a free man into slavery, than our ordinary criminal laws are to hang an innocent one.

Now gentlemen, I don't want to read at any greater length, but this is the true complexion of all I have ever said in regard to the institution of slavery and the black race. This is the whole of it, and anything that argues me into his idea of perfect social and political equality with the negro, is but a specious and fantastic arrangement of words, by which a man can prove a horse chestnut to be a chestnut horse. I will say here, while upon this subject, that I have no purpose directly or indirectly to interfere with the institution of slavery in the states where it exists. I believe I have no lawful right to do so, and I have no inclination to do so. I have no purpose to introduce political and social equality between the white and the black races. There is a physical difference between the two, which in my judgment will probably forever forbid their living together upon the footing of perfect equality, and inasmuch as it becomes a necessity that there must be a difference, I, as well as Judge Douglas, am in favor of the race to which I belong, having the superior position. I have never said anything to the contrary, but I hold that notwithstanding all this, there is no reason in the world why the negro is not entitled to all the natural rights enumerated in the Declaration of Independence, the right to life, liberty and the pursuit of happiness. I hold that he is as much entitled to these as the white man. I agree with Judge Douglas he is not my equal in many respects—certainly not in color, perhaps not in moral or intellectual endowment. But in the right to eat the bread, without leave of anybody else, which his own hand earns, *he is my equal and the equal of Judge Douglas, and the equal of every living man.* . . .

When he [Douglas] undertakes to say that because I think this nation, so far as the question of slavery is concerned, will all become one thing or all the other, I am in favor of bringing about a dead uniformity in the various states, in all their institutions, he argues erroneously. The great variety of the local institutions in the states, springing from differences in the soil, differences in the face of the country, and in the climate, are bonds of union. They do not make "a house divided against itself," but they make a house united. If they produce in one section of the country what is called for by the wants of another section, and this other section can supply the wants of the first, they are not matters of discord but bonds of union, true bonds of union. But can this question of slavery be considered as among these varieties in the institutions of the country? I leave it to you so say whether, in the history of our government, this institution of slavery has not always failed to be a bond of union, and, on the contrary, been an apple of discord and an element of division in the house. . . . If so, then I have a right to say that in regard to this question, the Union is a house divided against itself, and when the Judge reminds me that I have often said to him that the institution of slavery has existed for eighty years in some states, and yet it does not exist in some others, I agree to the fact, and I account for it by looking at the position in which our fathers originally placed it—restricting it from the new territories where it had not gone, and legislating to cut off its source by the abrogation of the slave trade, thus putting the seal of legislation *against its spread.* The public mind *did* rest in the belief that it was in the course of ultimate extinction. But lately, I think—and in this I charge nothing on the Judge's motives—lately, I think, that he, and those acting with him, have placed that institution on a new basis, which looks to the *perpetuity and nationalization of slavery.* And while it is placed upon this new basis, I say, and I have said, that I believe we shall not have peace upon the question until the opponents of slavery arrest the further spread of it, and place it where the public mind shall rest in the belief that it is in the course of ultimate extinction; or, on the other hand, that its advocates will push it forward until it shall become alike lawful in all the states, old as well as new, North as well as South. Now, I believe if we would arrest the spread, and place it where Washington, and Jefferson, and Madison placed it, it *would be* in the course of ultimate extinction, and the public mind *would,* as for eighty years past, believe that it was in the course of ultimate extinction. The crisis would be past and the institution might be let alone for a hundred years, if it should live so long, in the states where it exists, yet it would be going out of existence in the way best for both the black and white races. . . .

When I made my speech at Springfield, of which the Judge complains, and from which he quotes, I really was not thinking of the things which he ascribes to me at all. I had no thought in the world that I was doing anything to bring about a war between the free and slave states. I had no thought in the world that I was doing anything to bring about a political and social equality of the black and white races. It never occurred to me that I was doing anything or favoring anything to reduce to a dead uniformity all the local institutions of the various states. But I must say, in all fairness to him, if he thinks I am doing something which leads to these bad results, it is none the better that I did not mean it. It is just as fatal to the country, if I have any influence in producing it, whether I intend it or not. But can it be true, that placing this institution upon the original basis—the basis upon which our fathers placed it—can have any tendency to set the Northern and the Southern states at war with one another, or that it can have any tendency to make the people of Vermont raise sugar cane, because they raise it in Louisiana, or that it can compel the people of Illinois to cut pine logs on the Grand Prairie, where they will not grow, because they cut pine logs in Maine, where they do grow? . . .

@ ON THE WEB

Read the full text of the Lincoln-Douglas Debates at http://www.nps.gov/liho/debates.htm.

THE BIG PICTURE

It has often been argued that the rise of the West made sectional conflict inevitable. It also has been argued that the West was unfit for slavery. What are the merits of these two arguments? And why were Lincoln and Douglas, northerners and southerners, so often at loggerheads? Why didn't they find a lasting compromise?

Chapter 13

The Civil War

Interpretive Essay by James M. McPherson 309
Sources 320
>   The Photographers' War 320
>   Sherman's March Through Georgia, 1865 327
The Big Picture 335

$\mathcal{A}$mericans have studied the Civil War with almost obsessive fascination. The main reason is that the Civil War was the nation's great trauma. It was the one instance where orderly democratic processes failed miserably. With Lincoln's election in 1860, the lower South refused to abide by the dictates of the electorate, play democratic politics, and try to regain power in the next election. During the first seventy-two years of the American republic, slaveholders had held the presidency for fifty years. Now the nation had a president who was committed to the "ultimate extinction" of slavery. Now the nation was governed by a northern party that owed nothing to the South. Indeed, the Republicans were not even on the ballot in ten southern states, and Lincoln captured only 26,000 votes in the slaveholding states as compared with 1,800,000 in the free states. With Lincoln's victory, the lower South seceded from the Union, and when the first shots were fired four states in the upper South followed suit.

The Civil War was also a brothers' war. If we wish, we can blame the American Revolution on the British, the Mexican War on the Mexicans, World War I on German submarines, World War II on the Japanese and Hitler, Korea and Vietnam on the communists; but we can blame the Civil War on nobody but Americans. Thus, even though Americans have studied this war with fascination, they have never been able to agree which brother—if either—was to blame.

The Civil War was also a bloodbath. That, in fact, is what distinguished it from earlier American wars. The War of 1812 cost the country

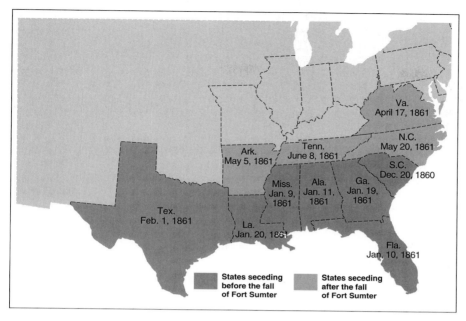

The Union disintegrates.

only 7,000 lives, with fewer than 2,000 men dying in action. The Mexican War cost the nation fewer than 2,000 lives on the battlefield and some 11,000 from diseases. Most Americans in 1861 expected the Civil War to be much the same. But it was not. By the time it was over, more than 600,000 men were dead, and many of the "lucky" survivors were missing arms and legs.

The war has fascinated Americans, too, because of its totality. Indeed, some historians have argued that it was the first modern war not only because of its scale, but also because of the unprecedented extent to which both sides were mobilized. North and South, the Civil War touched more aspects

Deaths in the Civil War and Other Wars

	Total Deaths	Deaths per 100,000 Population
Civil War	618,000	1,967
World War II	318,000	241
Revolutionary War	4,000	144
World War I	115,000	109
Mexican War	13,270	57
War of 1812	2,200	31
Vietnam War	56,000	28
Korean War	33,000	22
Spanish-American War and Philippine Insurrection	9,700	13

of more lives than any other had done. Factories and railroads became crucial objects of strategic concern. Women and children were involved as supporters—their traditional roles—but also as victims on a scale that Americans had not known before. Blacks were active participants in a war fought over the issue of slavery and its political consequences. In the end, too, the war sought not only a political statement but a social and economic one that went to the heart of the institutions by which half a nation had ordered its life.

INTERPRETIVE ESSAY

A Band of Brothers

James M. McPherson

The Civil War was so bloody that it is hard for us today to grasp how ordinary men, Yankee and Confederate, bore the brunt of it.

They were hardly well-trained professionals. The professional army in 1861 was minute, consisting of only 16,000 men; most of the several million men who fought in the war were members of volunteer regiments that had been pieced together in their home states and home communities. These men saw themselves as civilians who were just temporarily in uniform to do a necessary job and return home as quickly as possible. In most instances, they had the right to elect their own company officers, who usually had no more combat experience than they did. And in most instances, they went off to battle with just a month or two of training.

So why was it that these ordinary men were able to bear the brunt of some the bloodiest fighting the world had witnessed? This is a tough question to answer and many able historians have tried their hand at it. One of the ablest is James M. McPherson, probably the most popular Civil War historian practicing today. His answer is multifaceted. What follows is a key part of it.

Civil war soldiers wrote much about *courage, bravery, valor*—the three words meant the same thing. The quality they described was the mark of honor. But soldiers wrote even more about cowardice—the mark of dishonor. Many soldiers lacked confidence in their courage. But most of them wanted to avoid the shame of being known as a coward—and that is what gave them courage. Civil War soldiers went forward with their comrades into a hail of bullets because they were more afraid of "showing the white feather" than they were of death. The soldier who visibly skulked out of combat could never hold up his head again as a man among men. S. L. A. Marshall wrote of soldiers in World War II: "Personal honor is the one thing valued more than life itself by the majority of men." Civil War soldiers would have agreed. "Death before dishonor" is a phrase that occurs in their letters and diaries more times than one can count. And they really seem to have meant it.

A postwar novel by a Civil War veteran included an episode depicting a visit by wives and mothers to soldiers in camp. The women praised their manly courage and contrasted it with the timorous nature of womanhood. The second lieutenant replied: "We are as much afraid as you are, only we are more afraid to show it." To show fear was to court contempt. A captain in the 14th New Hampshire expressed pride at having so few skulkers in his

From James M. McPherson, *For Cause and Comrades: Why Men Fought the Civil War,* Oxford University Press, New York, 1997, pp. 77–89. Reprinted by permission of Oxford University Press.

company "and the others shame those few so much that they must of necessity come up to scratch or be in disgrace." After a soldier in the 16th Mississippi had fallen to the rear at Malvern Hill, "he is irretrievably disgraced," reported his sergeant. "Not one of the Regt. deign to notice him at all."

Few soldiers with "any pride of manhood in them" could bear the shame of such contempt. "I cannot boast of much pluck," wrote a private in the 39th Ohio after his first battle, "but I have got my full share of pride and could die before I could disgrace the name I bear." He was confident that his wife also "would sooner hear of my death than my disgrace." It is by no means clear that wives and mothers shared this sentiment. But husbands and sons liked to think they did. A New York private wrote his wife in 1863: "I would not show myself [a coward] if I was ever so big a one, *would you?*" A sergeant in the 64th Ohio informed his mother that "it is better to die the deth of a brave Soldier than to liv a cowards life." The wife of a Texas infantry captain was probably not thrilled by a letter from her husband in 1863 declaring that if he ever showed "the white feather" in battle, "I hope that some friend will immediately shoot me so that the disgrace shall not attach either to my wife or children." He was later killed not by a friend but by the enemy, at the battle of Pleasant Hill.

Before their first battle many soldiers were apprehensive that they would not pass this test of manhood. Those who did pass uttered a sigh of relief after it was over. "I am so afraid I shall prove a coward," an officer in the 8th Connecticut told his family. "I can hardly think of anything else." But after the battle of Newbern he wrote elatedly that he was "a little shaky at first but soon got used to the music. I know no one will say that I behaved cowardly in the least." While waiting to go into action for the first time, a private in the 36th Pennsylvania feared that he might "find myself acting the coward," but in fact "the opposite was the case; I was never more cool and self possessed than while in the hottest of the fight." Before attacking Confederate trenches at Fort Donelson, an Iowa corporal "did not know whether I had pluck enough to go through," but afterward, "I have no fear but I can do my duty. . . . I would rather be in a soldier's grave than to have acted as some of our boys did," especially the "fist-cuff rowdies" from the waterfront slums of Davenport, who were last seen "running away into the timber" while "all the Wolf Creek boys did their duty bravely."

In Civil War argot, one of the favorite devices of men who wanted to skulk out of combat was to "play off"—to feign sickness—when their real ailment was "cannon fever." Letters from fighting soldiers are full of contempt for men in their companies who were "taken very suddenly ill" when action portended. A captain in the 63rd Ohio wrote in his diary after a fight that "the usual number of cowards got sick and asked to be excused." A private in a Kentucky Confederate regiment damned the "infurnel cowards" in his company who "reported Sick when the fight was expected." But he was proud that all of his messmates "walk out like men" to meet the enemy. A soldier in the 38th Tennessee told his wife after Shiloh that "some of our Company disgraced themselves by falling back, pretending to be very lame. I would have gone in if I had to have gone in on one leg."

To avoid the taint of cowardice, many genuinely sick soldiers did go into battle on one leg, so to speak. A corporal in the 24th Michigan wrote in his diary during the battle of Fredericksburg: "Feel quite sick. If it were not for being called a Sneak and a coward I would not be in the ranks today." A sergeant in the 155th Pennsylvania disobeyed the surgeon's order sending him to the hospital during the Bristoe campaign because "there are so many get off by pretending to be sick that a man is always looked upon with suspicion if he goes to a hospital, especially if there is a fight expected soon." A lieutenant in the renowned 15th Alabama was "quite sick" at the battle of Gaines Mill, he admitted to his wife afterward, "but I was determined to not have it said that our Comp. was in a fight and I not with them."

Soldiers who went into action despite a real illness sometimes paid a steep price. A private in the 62nd Pennsylvania remained with his regiment despite the surgeon's orders to the contrary, for "if I had of Staid behind I would have been called a coward." He later regretted this decision, for he became seriously ill and did not recover for weeks just because "my foolish Pride kept me in the ranks." A corporal in the 1st Minnesota fought at First Bull Run despite sickness and afterward lost sixty pounds and almost died during three months in an army hospital. The 2nd Massachusetts was one of the war's elite regiments, with many of its officers from Boston's Brahmin class. One of them, Robert Gould Shaw, reported that four of his fellow officers refused to stay out of the battle of Cedar Mountain even though they were "quite ill." "It was splendid," Shaw wrote his mother, "to see those sick fellows walk straight up into the shower of bullets, as if it were so much rain." For that splendor three of the four paid with their lives.

Most of the men in a volunteer company had enlisted from the same community or county. Many of them had known each other from childhood. They retained close ties to that community through letters home, articles in local newspapers, and occasional visits by family members to the regiment's camp. Because of this close relationship between community and company, the pressure of the peer group against cowardice was reinforced by the community. The absence of censorship meant that reports of cowardice would quickly find their way back to the community. The soldier who proved a sneak in battle could not hold up his head again in his company *or* at home.

Fighting soldiers did not hesitate to name skulkers in their letters home. "I am sorry to say that Norman Hart is a D———n coward," wrote a private in the 10th Wisconsin after Stones River. "He run away from the company just as we were going under fire the first day. . . . I tell you I do hate a coward. I am a big enough coward my self but never will desert in a trying time like Hart so help me God." A private in the 20th Indiana wrote home after a skirmish at Mine Run that "we did have A lot of skedadlers." He named nine of them, adding that "they should be published to the world." Likewise a private in the 18th Mississippi wrote an amusing letter describing the antics of men in his company who found excuses to disappear when the drums beat the long roll for action. One of these men was harried out of the regiment by the ridicule of his fellows. He could never go home again because "the boys have written so much about him."

Officers did not escape this kind of censure; indeed, they were held to a higher standard. "Capt. Lucy of our company has resigned and gone home," wrote a lieutenant in the 17th Connecticut after Chancellorsville. "The company called him a coward and we told him that we hoped the folks at home would treat him as such." A captain in the 47th Ohio reported to his wife a rumor that another captain from their community "ran away and left his men" during a skirmish. "I hope not for the honor of our town." When the same officer "proved himself a coward" in another battle, it polluted forever "his family alter—what a stigma for men to transmit to their posterity—your father a coward!"

That was why so many soldiers echoed the words of a private in the 20th Georgia: "I had rather dye on the battle field than to disgrace my self & the hole family." Or like a lieutenant in the 26th Tennessee they proudly wrote home after a battle that "I did not disgrace our name. . . . The Boys all know it & can tell of it." Two brothers in the 10th Connecticut who fought at Newbern informed their father after the battle that "shame need not settle on your face in behalf of your two sons."

In some cases, soldiers who had been assigned to safe duty behind the lines pulled strings to return to their regiments at the front because folks back home might think they were playing off. As a private in the 21st Mississippi explained it, "I prefer the ranks" because his detachment as brigade clerk "is what is technically known as a 'Bomb proof' & that is something that I never want." Similarly a private in the 36th Massachusetts who had been detailed for two months as a teamster was "glad of the chanch to com back to the company" because "I should not lik to go home with the name of a couhard."

Some studies of combat motivation have found that the felt need of a soldier to prove himself in the eyes of his comrades is strongest in his first battle or two. After that the veteran believes he has done enough to demonstrate his courage, and subsequently his fear of death or a crippling wound sometimes overmasters his fear of showing fear. One study finds the same to be true for the Civil War, in which the seemingly endless carnage by 1863 supposedly eroded the Victorian notions of manhood, courage, and honor that soldiers had carried into the army.

Soldiers' letters offer some evidence for this interpretation. Reluctance to fight often characterized "short-timers" during their final weeks of enlistment—especially those Union soldiers whose three-year terms expired in 1864 and who had not reenlisted. "The 2nd RI has got but 4 days more and if they get into a fight I don't think they will last a minute," wrote a lieutenant in the 10th Massachusetts, another regiment in the same brigade, in June 1864. "It makes all the difference in the world with the mens courage. They do dread awfully to get hit just as thier time is out." A private in the 3rd New York Cavalry with a good combat record confessed when he had only three weeks left of his enlistment that "I am what the Boys call 'playing off'" by pretending not to have recovered from an illness. "I have been sent for half a dozen times but So far have got out of going. . . . I am in hopes that it may last until my time is out." This psychology did not exist in the

Confederate army because there was no such thing as a Confederate short-timer. The Richmond Congress required men whose enlistments expired to reenlist or be drafted.

A majority of Union soldiers served through the end of the war unless killed or badly wounded, however, because half of the three-year volunteers of 1861 reenlisted and the terms of the 1862 three-year volunteers did not expire before Appomattox. Among these men, and among most Confederate soldiers, little change in the values of honor and courage they brought into the war is reflected in their letters and diaries. "I do most earnestly hope that I may be enabled to meet my duties like a man when the breath of battles blows around me," wrote a corporal in the 64th Ohio in language that sounds like 1861 but was actually written in 1864 as he returned from his reenlistment furlough. Although he had fought in such bloody battles as Shiloh, Perryville, Stones River, Chickamauga, and Missionary Ridge, he expressed the same sentiments that had animated him three years earlier: "I do hope I may be brave and true for of all names most terrible and to be dreaded *is coward.*" Another reenlisted veteran of many battles, a private in the 2nd Vermont of the Vermont brigade, which suffered more combat deaths than any other brigade in the Union army, wrote after his regiment lost 80 men killed and 254 wounded in the Wilderness that "I am sure if I had acted just as I felt I should have gone in the opposite direction [i.e. to the rear] but I wouldn't act the coward. . . . I clenched my musket and pushed ahead determined to die if I must, in my place and like a man."

These were far from isolated examples. If anything, the motivating power of soldiers' ideals of manhood and honor seemed to increase rather than decrease during the last terrible year of the war. A veteran in the 122nd Ohio wrote in 1864 that "I would rather go into fifty battles and run the risk of getting killed than as to be . . . a coward in time of battle." The lieutenant colonel commanding the 70th Indiana in Sherman's Atlanta campaign broke down from stress in June 1864 after a month of almost continuous fighting. Although he was still sick and exhausted, he returned to his regiment after a week in the hospital because "those who keep up are full of ugly feelings toward those who fall [behind], intimating in every way possible that it is cowardice that is the cause. . . . By being with the rest [I] can prevent anyone feeling that I lack the pluck to face what others do." And on the eve of marching through South Carolina with Sherman in 1865, a veteran corporal in the 102nd Illinois wrote simply, in language he might have used three years earlier, of "the soldier's person—more valuable to him than all else in the army, save his honor."

The pride and honor of an individual soldier were bound up with the pride and honor of his regiment, his state, and the nation for which he fought, symbolized by the regimental and national flags. "None but soldiers can know how sensitive the men of a good Regiment are of its reputation," wrote a lieutenant in the 2nd Michigan. Unit pride created a sense of rivalry with other regiments that sometimes took the form of denigrating their courage. A soldier in the elite 5th Wisconsin wrote with contempt of the

26th New Jersey, which "ran like sheep" at Chancellorsville, leaving the 5th to fight the enemy front and flank. While the 26th "turned their backs to the Rebels . . . not a man in our Regiment was shot in the back and all our dead lay with their heads toward the enemy."

This disparagement of a regiment from another state was typical. Regimental honor was associated with state pride. When several hundred men from New York regiments broke and ran at the battle of Kinston in December 1862, soldiers in the 23rd Massachusetts threatened to shoot them, according to a member of that regiment. "Our boys called them cowards, and told them to go back to their regiments but they did not know where their regiments were—though the bullitts were whistling around us we had to laugh at the excuses of these cowards."

In the Confederacy, North Carolina regiments endured a great deal of disdain from those of other states, especially Virginia. Union victories over small armies composed mainly of North Carolina troops at Hatteras Inlet, Roanoke Island, and Newbern early in the war rubbed salt in the psychological wounds of North Carolinians. One general from the Tarheel State made the soldiers in his brigade pledge "not to visit wife, children, or business till we have done our full share in retrieving the reputation of our troops and our state." When North Carolinians fought courageously in later battles with the Army of Northern Virginia, particularly at Fredericksburg, a major in the 46th North Carolina was elated. The conceited Virginians had been put in their place. "It was the proudest day of my life," wrote the major after Fredericksburg. "It was a proud day for the old state."

Individual soldiers whose courage nobody questioned nevertheless shared the humiliation of units with which they were identified—company, regiment, state. A lieutenant in the 75th New York, a veteran of many battles in which his regiment had performed well, was deeply ashamed when the regiment broke at Third Winchester. "This was the first time the 75th had ever run and I felt the disgrace," he wrote in his diary. "I never felt so bad in my life . . . and I cared little whether I was shot." Such a feeling of dishonor could become a powerful spur to courage in the next battle. When the 22nd Wisconsin fell apart in its first two battles and was subsequently assigned to rear-area guard duty in Tennessee, a private wrote with bitter shame that "the regiment is disgraced in the eyes of this army and its Commander." He hoped they would be sent to the front and get a chance to salvage their reputation, "for pride is what makes a soldier. It seems to me as if I could not bear the thought of the 22nd going back [home] as they are now." The regiment did redeem itself as part of one of the best brigades in the 20th Corps during Sherman's Georgia campaign of 1864.

Unit pride and loyalty prompted many three-year veterans in Union regiments to reenlist in 1864. "I have studied on your advice," wrote a sergeant in the 12th Iowa to his parents, who had urged him not to reenlist. But he did, because more than three-quarters of the veterans in the 12th had reenlisted and the regiment would therefore retain its designation. The 12th had a proud history, and if this sergeant did not reenlist he feared he would be "put in another Regt to serve the remainder of my term, perhaps that

Regt has disgraced itself in some previous engage[ment]." Anyway, what would he do after leaving the army if the war still raged? "Do you have the least idea that I could remain quiately at home and see those boys who have been with me constantly for over two years, who have endured the same hardships have been through the same dangers, and now leave them to bear my burden? *Not much.*"

The most meaningful symbols of regimental pride were the colors—the regimental and national flags, which bonded the men's loyalty to unit, state, and nation. The flags acquired a special mystique for Civil War soldiers. Color bearers enjoyed a special pride of place—and also a special risk, since the enemy directed its heaviest fire against the colors. But "the post of danger is the post of honor," to quote a Civil War phrase used so often that it became a cliché. There was rarely any shortage of volunteers to carry the flags if the color bearers were shot down. One of the most honorable feats a regiment could accomplish was to capture enemy colors; the worst shame imaginable was to lose its own colors to the enemy.

Perhaps the best description of the powerful mystique associated with the colors comes from a noncombatant. In December 1862 Walt Whitman visited his brother George, a lieutenant in the 51st New York, after he had been wounded at Fredericksburg. Finding his war-time vocation, Walt Whitman stayed in Washington as a volunteer nurse, learning as much about soldiers as anyone outside that fraternity could learn. In April 1864 he described to his mother a regimental flag he had received from a wounded soldier he tended. "It was taken by the secesh in a cavalry fight, and rescued by our men in a bloody little skirmish. It cost three men's lives, just to get one little flag, four by three. Our men rescued it, and tore it from the breast of a dead Rebel—all that just for the name of getting their little banner back again. . . . There isn't a reg't . . . that wouldn't do the same."

Perhaps the only achievement that could eclipse the honor of taking enemy colors or retaking one's own was to plant the national flag on a captured enemy position. Regimental rivalries to be the first to do so help explain the reckless courage of many Civil War assaults. In 1864 an officer in the 12th New York described a successful attack on Confederate lines defending the Weldon Railroad near Petersburg. When the American flag appeared above the battle smoke on the enemy works, "it is impossible to describe the feelings one experiences at such a moment. God, Country, Love, Home, pride, conscious strength & power, all crowd your swelling breast . . . proud, proud as a man can feel over this victory to our arms—if it were a man's privilege to die when he wished, he should die at such a moment."

This identification with regiment, state, country, and flag is related to but not precisely the same as the "primary group cohesion" that has been the focus of most writings about combat motivation since World War II. The soldier's primary group consists of the men closest to him with whom he interacts every day in camp, on the march, in combat. For the Civil War soldier this group may have been as large as his company but was likely to be smaller: his messmates, the men from his town or township with whom he enlisted, the squad commanded by his sergeant. All other groups were "secondary": regiment, brigade army, country, even community and family so long as he remained in the army.

Bonded by the common danger they face in battle, this primary group becomes a true band of brothers whose mutual dependence and mutual support create the cohesion necessary to function as a fighting unit. The survival of each member of the group depends on the others doing their jobs; the survival of the group depends on the steadiness of each individual. It is the primary group that enforces peer pressure against cowardice. If any member of the group "plays off" or succumbs to "cannon fever" during combat, he not only dangers his own and the others' survival but he also courts their contempt and ostracism; he loses self-respect as a man and may be exiled by the group. For many soldiers this could be quite literally a fate worse than death; it was a powerful incentive for fight rather than flight.

Primary group cohesion has presumably existed among combat soldiers from time immemorial and has been implicitly understood by those who experienced it. But it was the studies of German, American, and British soldiers in World War II by social scientists that gave the concept a hard analytical edge and a language to describe it. These studies have multiplied since the 1940s; most armies have incorporated the theory of primary group cohesion into their training and doctrine.

"For the key to what makes men fight," wrote one modern student of combat motivation, "we must look hard at military groups and the bonds that link the men within them." The answer, according to another analysis, lies in "the intense loyalty stimulated by close identification with the group. The men are now fighting for each other and develop guilty feelings if they let each other down. . . . This spirit of self sacrifice, so characteristic of the combat personality, is at the heart of good morale." In World War II the soldier "became increasingly bound up with his tiny fraternity of comrades. . . . In the last analysis, the soldier fought for them and them alone." Or as William Manchester put it in his memoirs of service in the American Marine Corps during World War II: "Those men on the line were my family, my home. They were closer to me than . . . my friends had ever been or ever would be. They had never let me down, and I couldn't do it to them. . . . Men, I now knew, do not fight for flag or country, for the Marine Corps or glory or any other abstraction. They fight for one another."

Civil War armies presented no exception to the importance of primary groups. Indeed, the territorial basis of company recruitment reinforced this cohesion by bringing friends and relatives together in the same unit, thus linking primary groups at home with those in the army. In many cases, especially in Confederate regiments, two or more biological brothers enlisted in the same company. Soldiers' letters contain many references to the "band of brothers" theme—literal as well as metaphorical. "We feel like the kindest of brothers together" (10th Virginia Cavalry). "You would not believe that men could be so attached to each other we are all like brothers" (1st Ohio Heavy Artillery). "We love each other like a band of brothers" (11th Georgia). We all "seem almost like brothers. We have suffered hardships and dangers together and are bound together by more than ordinary ties" (8th

Texas Cavalry). A corporal in the 9th Alabama returned to his regiment in October 1862 after convalescence at home from a wound in the battle of Glendale. "A soldier is always nearly crazy to get away from the army on furloughs," he observed, "but as a general thing they are more anxious to get back. There is a feeling of love—a strong attachment for those with whom one has shared common dangers, that is never felt for any one else, or under any other circumstances.

The significance of this bonding became clear in combat. A veteran in the 122nd New York tried to explain how it worked. His sister had asked what kept him going through the carnage of the Wilderness, Spotsylvania, Cold Harbor, and Petersburg. "You ask me if the thought of death does not alarm me," he replied. "I will say I do not wish to die. . . . I myself am as big a coward as eny could be," he admitted in July 1864, "but give me the ball [bullet] before the coward when all my friends and companions are going forward. Once and once only was I behind when the regt was under fire, and I cant discribe my feelings at that time none can tell them only a soldier. I was not able to walk . . . but as soon as the rattle of musketry was heard and I knew my Regt was engaged I hobbled on the field and went to them. . . . The untrained and old soldier are different in many respects. As to life the new one looks out for himself in or out of Battle, the old one when away from his companions thinks of them and goes in and the danger to himself is forgotten."

The experience of combat did more than strengthen existing bonds; it also dissolved the petty rivalries and factions that existed in some regiments and forged new bonds among men who saw the elephant together. "Those who had stood shoulder to shoulder during the two terrible days of that bloody battle," wrote an officer in the 54th Ohio after Shiloh, "were hooped with steel, with bands stronger than steel." After the 6th Missouri (Union) fought its first battle at Chickasaw Bluffs, a captain who had previously lamented the bickering and backbiting among its officers wrote that "we all feel proud of our men and there is a better feeling among the officers." After the 83rd Pennsylvania suffered 75 percent casualties in the Seven Days battles, a private commented that "it seems strange how much the rest of our company has become united since the battles. They are almost like brothers in one family now. We used to have the 'aristocratic tent' and 'tent of the upper ten,' and so on, but there is nothing of that kind now. We have all lost dear friends and common sorrow makes us all equal."

The fire of battle could even fuse the breach that existed in many companies between the pious and the profane. Not only did some of the profane suddenly get religion, but also some of the pious found surprisingly admirable qualities in their blasphemous brethren. "I have now spent a whole year with my comrads in battle," wrote a teetotaling private in the 23rd Massachusetts. "Every one of them is as a brother to me. . . . The members of Company F have won from me a lasting love. It is true many of them are very profane and the demon whiskey is not refused by many of them but with all their faults I love them because they are brave, generous, intelligent, and noble-hearted."

The ties of comradeship caused many a soldier to resist a soft assignment away from his company or even to refuse promotion if it meant transfer to another unit. An aristocratic South Carolinian turned down a chance to transfer from the infantry to an elite cavalry outfit because "I am very proud of this company . . . & I am too much attached to my intimate friends to seek an opportunity of parting with them." A lieutenant in the 20th Massachusetts refused promotion to captain in another company. "It is a pretty hard thing to throw away a chance of rising," he explained to his father, but "I can't make up my mind to leave my own company. I have got really attached to the fellows." A Quaker captain in the 5th New Jersey faced a different kind of decision. His wife and mother pressed him to resign; his Quaker brethren threatened to read him out of Meeting if he did not do so. "Yet I should leave with much regret the men who stood manfuly by me in the hours of dainger through which I have passed," he told his wife. In the end he could not bring himself to leave them, and was killed at Second Manassas.

This officer's death separated him from his company more decisively than resignation would have done. As the war went on, casualties rent the cohesion of some veteran regiments almost to the vanishing point. Cohesion is a renewable resource, with new men bonding to old and veterans bonding more closely. In time, however, attrition became a deadly foe to cohesion— and therefore to the qualitative as well as quantitative combat effectiveness of a unit. By August 1862 the South Carolina infantryman who had refused to leave his company to join the cavalry the preceding May left it to join the artillery because his company had "been stripped of some of my best friends" by casualties in the Peninsula campaign. A sergeant in the 55th Illinois found it "very lonely here" after Shiloh. "Most of the boys from the village are either in their long home or have been sent down the river on account of wounds." After the Shenandoah Valley campaign of 1864 had decimated Jubal Early's army, a Confederate officer lamented that "my best friends have fallen so fast, that in the army I feel as if I were left alone."

One of the most influential studies of primary group cohesion attributed the persistent fighting power of the Wehrmacht even as the Third Reich collapsed around them to the bonds of camaraderie among squads and platoons in the German army. The principal critique of this interpretation, however, points out that the enormous casualties and consequent turnover of personnel in the Wehrmacht by 1942 left no core primary group around which to cohere. "*Real* 'primary groups' do not fully explain combat motivation due to their unfortunate tendency to disintegrate when they are most needed," wrote Omar Bartov in his study of *Hitler's Army*, but "the *idea* of attachment to an *ideal* 'primary group' . . . clearly does have a powerful integrating potential." By ideal primary group Bartov meant the Nazi ideology of Aryan racial brotherhood. "The Wehrmacht began to manifest its most remarkable 'fighting power' precisely at a time when the network of 'primary groups' which had ensured its cohesion during previous Blitzkrieg campaigns began to disintegrate." Nazi ideology portrayed the Soviet Union as a mortal threat to German civilization. These "ideological arguments . . . [and the] ideological cohesion of the troops" enabled the Wehrmacht to continue fighting after 1942 "with far greater determination and against far greater odds than at any other time."

Bartov's thesis, while perhaps overstated, offers a suggestive way to analyze the ideological attachments of Civil War soldiers to something beyond their comrades in squad or company: to nationalism, liberty, democracy, self-government, and so on. When primary groups disintegrated from disease, casualties, transfers, and promotions, these larger ideals remained as the glue that held the armies together. Whether or not these commitments constituted "combat motivation," they certainly provided "sustaining motivation" for armies composed mainly of volunteers. Sustaining motivation is not unrelated to combat motivation, for armies cannot fight if they do not exist. And with respect to Civil War armies, a strong case can be made that the most patriotic and ideologically committed volunteers were the best combat soldiers, because they believed in what they were fighting for. It is time to examine what Civil War soldiers called "the Cause."

Read for yourself about the experience of soldiering through one of the largest online collections of American Civil War Soldiers' diaries and letters at the website of the American Civil War Collection at the Electronic Text Center at http://etext.virginia.edu/civilwar/#Letters.

@ ON THE WEB

The Photographers' War

The Civil War was the first war in history to be photographed on a large scale. Matthew Brady, Alexander Gardner, T. H. O'Sullivan, and others used large box cameras on tripods and collodion-coated glass plates that had to be sensitized in one chemical bath before exposure and developed immediately after in another chemical bath. The process was incredibly awkward, and it was impossible to take action shots. But the photographers produced a magnificent record of the war.

Abraham Lincoln, Springfield, Illinois, June 3, 1860. Photographer, Alexander Hesler. Chicago Historical Society, ICHi-20265.

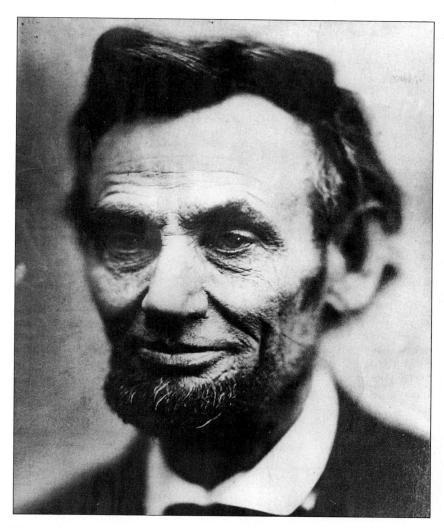

Library of Congress.

Here are two memorable photographs that demonstrate the strain of war. The one on page 320 shows Abraham Lincoln in Springfield, Illinois, on June 3, 1860. Compare this with the above photograph of Lincoln, taken in Washington on April 10, 1865, after four years of war.

The photograph on top of page 322 gives some idea why Lincoln aged so quickly. It shows the dead of both sides lying together after the battle of Gettysburg, where 150,000 men fired their muskets for several days, hour after hour, and left the ground littered with over 7,000 corpses.

Following is a series of pictures that more or less speak for themselves. Most are the work of Matthew Brady, who followed the Union Army, and especially the wagons that collected the dead after battle.

Library of Congress.

Private Edwin Francis
Jennison, Georgia
infantry. Killed at
Malvern Hill. Library of
Congress.

The 107th U.S.
Colored Infantry.
Library of Congress.

Powder monkey, USS
New Hampshire. Off
Charleston, South
Carolina, 1865. The
Brady Collection/Library of
Congress.

Ruins of Charleston,
South Carolina, 1865.
The National Archives.

Union dead. Trapped in the sunken road, Battle of Chancellorsville, May 3–5, 1863. The Brady Collection/Library of Congress.

Union wounded. Battle of Chancellorsville, May 3–5, 1863. Library of Congress.

The Richmond and Petersburg railroad depot, 1865. Library of Congress.

Richmond, Virginia, at war's end. Library of Congress.

Freedmen in Richmond, Virginia. Library of Congress.

John Wilkes Booth's accomplices (Mary Surratt, David Herold, Lewis Paine, George Atserodt) in a Washington jailyard, July 7, 1865, three months after Lincoln's assassination. Booth himself had been shot and killed earlier, two weeks after he killed Lincoln. Library of Congress.

 ON THE WEB   *To view more photographs from the Civil War, visit the "American Memory" website of the Library of Congress at* http://memory.loc.gov/ammem/cwphtml/cwphome.html.

Sherman's March Through Georgia, 1865

David P. Conyngham

The South had lost the war by 1865, and southerners knew it. One reason was General William Tecumseh Sherman's army, which in 1864 marched through Georgia and destroyed a civilization. Along with Sherman's army went a young newspaperman, David P. Conyngham, who was hired by the New York Herald to write on-the-spot reports. Here are some of his observations. What effect do you think they had on the people back home?

✍ The Red Badge of Courage

Night had set in. The ground was strewn with the dead and wounded. Our men slept beside their arms, for the rebel lines were quite close to them. The living, the dying, and the dead slept beside one another. Rebel and Union officers and men lay piled together; some transfixed with bayonet wounds, their faces wearing that fierce, contorted look that marks those who have suffered agony. Others, who were shot dead, lay with their calm faces and glassy eyes turned to heaven. One might think they were but sleeping.

Others had their skulls crashed in by the end of a musket, while the owner of the musket lay stiff beside them, with the death grip tightened on the piece.

Clinging to one of the guns, with his hand on the spoke, and his body bent as if drawing it, lay a youth with the top of his head shot off. Another near him, with his body cut in two, still clung to the ropes.

Men writhing in pain, men stark and cold; broken caissons, rifles, and bayonets; bloody clothes and torn haversacks with all the other debris of war's havoc, were the price we paid for two old cannon.

A battle-field, when the carnage of the day is over, when the angry passions of men have subsided; when the death silence follows the din and roar of battle; when the victors have returned triumphant to their camps to celebrate their victory, regardless of the many comrades they have left behind; when the conquered sullenly fall back to a new position, awaiting to renew the struggle,—is a sad sight. It is hard to listen to the hushed groans and cries of the dying, and to witness the lacerated bodies of your fellow-soldiers strewn around, some with broken limbs, torn and mangled bodies, writhing in agony. How often has some poor fellow besought me to shoot him, and put him out of pain! It would be a mercy to do so, yet I dared not.

Piled up together in a ditch, near a battery which they supported with their lines, I found several rebel dead and wounded. I dragged some of the wounded out under the shelter of the trees.

From David P. Conyngham, *Sherman's March Through Georgia*, Sheldon and Company, New York, 1865, passim.

The ghouls of the army were there before me; they had rifled the pockets of the dead and wounded indiscriminately.

I gave many a poor fellow a reviving drink, amidst silent prayers.

In one place I found a mere boy of about fifteen. His leg was shattered with a piece of shell. I placed his knapsack under his head. Poor child! what stories he told me about his mother, away down in Carolina; and his little sisters, how glad they would be, now that he was wounded, to see him home.

They never saw him home, for he went to the home where the weary are at rest.

I came up to the corpse of a rebel soldier, over whom a huge Kentuckian federal soldier was weeping.

"My man," I exclaimed, "why do you weep over him? Look at your comrades around you."

"True, sir," he replied, wiping his eyes; and pointing to a federal soldier near, he said, "There is my brother; this man shot him: I killed him in return. He was my bosom friend. I loved him as a father loves his child."

Next morning, as we were removing our wounded to hospital, I saw a group collected. I rode up, and found that they were some raw troops jeering and insulting rebel wounded. Veteran troops will never do this, but share their last drink and bite with them. I rated them pretty roundly, and ordered the cowardly sneaks to their regiments. After another battle or two, these very boys would feel indignant at such conduct.

It is an affecting sight to witness the removal of the dead and wounded from a battle-field, and the manner in which the former are interred. In some case, deep pits are sunk, and, perhaps, a hundred or more bodies are flung promiscuously into it, as if no one owned them, or cared for them.

In other cases, where the bodies had been recognized, they were buried with some semblance of decency. I was once riding with a column over a battle-field, in which the skeletons of the hastily buried were partly exposed. . . .

Women and children were dreadfully frightened at the approach of our army. It was almost painful to witness the horror and fear depicted on their features. They were schooled up to this by lying statements of what atrocious murders we were committing.

The country people trembled at our approach, and hid themselves away in woods and caves. I rode out one evening alone to pay a visit to another camp which lay some six miles beyond us. In trying to make a short way through the woods, I lost the road, and rambled on through the forest, trying to recover it. This is no easy matter, as I soon discovered; for I only got deeper and deeper into the forest. I then turned my horse's head down a valley that I knew would lead me out on a camp somewhere.

In riding along this, I thought I saw a woman among the trees. I rode in the direction, and saw her darting like a frightened deer towards a thick copse of tangled briers, wild vines, and underbrush.

Fearing some snare, I followed, with pistol in hand; and heavens, what a sight met my view! In the midst of the thicket, sheltered by a bold bluff, were about a dozen women, as many children, and three old men, almost crazy with fear and excitement.

Some of them screamed when they saw me, and all huddled closer, as if resolved to die together. I tied my horse, and assured them that they had no cause for fear; that I was not going to harm them, but would protect them, if needed. Thus assured, they became somewhat communicative.

They told me that they thought the soldiers would kill them, and that they hid here on our approach. Thinking that we were only passing through, they had brought nothing to eat or to cover them. They were here now near three days, and had nothing but the berries they picked up in the woods. They looked wretched, their features wan and thin, their eyes wild and haggard; and their lips stained from the unripe wild fruit. Some of them were lying down, huddled together to keep themselves warm; their clothes were all saturated from the dew and a heavy shower of rain which fell during the day.

I do not think one could realize so much wretchedness and suffering as that group presented. Some of the women were evidently planters' wives and daughters; their appearance and worn dresses betokened it; others were their servants, or the wives of the farm-laborers.

There were two black women, and some three picaninnies. Under the shelter of a tree, I saw a woman sitting down, rocking her baby to and fro, as she wept bitterly.

I went over to her. Beside her was a girl of some fourteen years, lying at full length. As I approached, she looked so pale and statuelike, I exclaimed,—

"What's the matter. Is she in a faint?"

"Yes; in one that she won't waken from," said an old crone near.

"Dead!" I exclaimed.

"Well, stranger, I reckon so; better for her to go, poor darling, than have the Yankees cotch her."

It was so. She was dead. I understood she was delicate; and the hunger and cold had killed her. So much were they afraid of being discovered that they had not even a fire lighted.

I inquired my way to the camp, and soon returned with some provisions. The dead body was removed, and the sorrowing group returned to their homes; but some of them had no homes, for the soldiers, on the principle that all abandoned houses belong to rebels, had laid them in ashes. . . .

On one occasion General Johnston sent a flag of truce to Sherman, in order to give time to carry off the wounded and bury the dead, who were festering in front of their lines.

A truce followed, and Rebels and Federals freely participated in the work of charity. It was a strange sight to see friends, to see old acquaintances, and in some instances brothers, who had been separated for years, and now pitted in deadly hostility, meet and have a good talk over old times, and home scenes, and connections. They drank together, smoked together, appeared on the best possible terms, though the next day they were sure to meet in deadly conflict again.

Even some of the generals freely mixed with the men, and seemed to view the painful sight with melancholy interest.

An officer, speaking of this sad burial, said, "I witnessed a strange scene yesterday in front of Davis's division. During the burial of the dead, grouped together in seemingly fraternal unity, were officers and men of both contending armies, who, but five minutes before, were engaged in the work of slaughter and death."

Under the shelter of a pine, I noticed a huge gray Kentuckian rebel, with his arm affectionately placed around the neck of a Federal soldier, a mere boy. The bronzed warrior cried and laughed by turns, and then kissed the young Federal.

Attracted by such a strange proceeding, I went over to them, and said to the veteran, "Why, you seem very much taken by that boy; I suppose he is some old friend of yours."

"Old friend, sir! Why, he is my son!"

I have often seen a rebel and a Federal soldier making right for the same rifle-pit, their friends on both sides loudly cheering them on. As they would not have time to fight, they reserved their fire until they got into the pit, then woe betide the laggard, for the other was sure to pop him as soon as he got into cover. Sometimes they got in together, and then came the tug of war; for they fought for possession with their bayonets and closed fists. In some cases however, they made a truce, and took joint possession of it.

It was no unusual thing to see our pickets and skirmishers enjoying themselves very comfortably with the rebels, drinking bad whiskey, smoking and chewing worse tobacco, and trading coffee and other little articles. The rebels had no coffee, and our men plenty, while the rebels had plenty of whiskey; so they very soon came to an understanding. It was strange to see these men, who had been just pitted in deadly conflict, trading, and bantering, and chatting, as if they were the best friends in the world. They discussed a battle with the same gusto they would a cock-fight, or horse-race, and made inquiries about their friends, as to who was killed, and who not, in the respective armies. Friends that have been separated for years have met in this way. Brothers who parted to try their fortune have often met on the picket line, or on the battlefield. I once met a German soldier with the head of a dying rebel on his lap. The stern veteran was weeping, whilst the boy on his knee looked pityingly into his face. They were speaking in German, and from my poor knowledge of the language, all I could make out was, they were brothers; that the elder had come out here several years before; the younger followed him, and being informed that he was in Macon, he went in search of him, and got conscripted; while the elder brother, who was in the north all the time, joined our army. The young boy was scarcely twenty, with light hair, and a soft, fair complexion. The pallor of death on his brow, and the blood was flowing from his breast, and gurgled in his throat and mouth, which the other wiped away with his handkerchief. When he could speak, the dying youth's conversation was of the old home in Germany, of his brothers and sisters, and dear father and mother, who were never to see him again.

In those improvised truces, the best possible faith was observed by the men. These truces were brought about chiefly in the following manner. A rebel, who was heartily tired of his crippled position in his pit, would call out, "I say, Yank!"

"Well, Johnny Reb," would echo from another hole or tree.

"I'm going to put out my head; don't shoot."

"Well, I won't."

The reb would pop up his head; the Yank would do the same.

"Hain't you got any coffee, Johnny?"

"Na'r a bit, but plenty of rot-gut."

"All right; we'll have a trade."

They would meet, while several others would follow the example, until there would be a regular bartering mart established. In some cases the men would come to know each other so well, that they would often call out,—"Look out, reb; we're going to shoot," or "Look out, Yank, we're going to shoot," as the case may be. . . .

❧ *The Siege of Atlanta*

From several points along the lines we could plainly see the doomed city, with the smoke of burning houses and bursting shells enveloping it in one black canopy, hanging over it like a funeral pall.

The scene at night was sublimely grand and terrific! The din of artillery rang on the night air. In front of General Geary's headquarters was a prominent hill, from which we had a splendid view of the tragedy enacting before us. One night I sat there with the general and staff, and several other officers, while a group of men sat near us enjoying the scene, and speculating on the effects of the shells. It was a lovely, still night, with the stars twinkling in the sky. The lights from the campfires along the hills and valleys, and from amidst the trees, glimmered like the gas-lights of a city in the distance. We could see the dark forms reclining around them, and mark the solemn tread of the sentinel on his beat. A rattle of musketry rang from some point along the line. It was a false alarm. The men for a moment listened, and then renewed their song and revelry, which was for a while interrupted. The song, and music, and laughter floated to our ears from the city of camps, that dotted the country all round.

Sherman had lately ordered from Chattanooga a battery of four and a half inch rifles, and these were trying their metal on the city.

Several batteries, forts, and bastions joined in the fierce chorus. Shells flew from the batteries, up through the air, whizzing and shrieking, until they reached a point over the devoted city, when down they went, hurling the fragments, and leaving in their train a balloon-shaped cloud of smoke. From right, and left, and centre flew these dread missiles, all converging towards the city. From our commanding position we could see the flash from the guns, then the shells, with their burning fuses, hurtling through the air like flying meteors.

"War is a cruelty," said the general beside me; "we know not how many innocents are now suffering in this miserable city."

"I'm dog gone if I like it," said a soldier, slapping his brawny hand upon his thigh; "I can fight my weight of rattlesnakes; but this thing of smoking out women and children, darn me if it's fair."

On the night of September 1, Hood blew up all the magazines and ammunition, destroyed all the supplies he could not move, comprising eight locomotives, and near one hundred cars laden with ammunition, small arms, and stores, and then retreated. Our troops, advancing near the city, met with no resistance. Observing that it was evacuated, they entered it about 11 o'clock on the morning of September 2, 1864.

Atlanta was now in our hands, the crowning point of Sherman's great campaign. Hood had been outgeneraled, outmanoeuvred, and outflanked, and was now trying to concentrate his scattered army. On the night of the 1st, when the rebel army was vacating, the stampede was frightful to those engaged, but grandly ludicrous to casual spectators. . . .

The city had suffered much from our projectiles. Several houses had been burned, and several fallen down. In some places the streets were blocked up with the rubbish. The suburbs were in ruins, and few houses escaped without being perforated. Many of the citizens were killed, and many more had hair-breadth escapes. Some shells had passed through the Trout House Hotel, kicking up a regular muss among beds and tables.

One woman pointed out to me where a shell dashed through her house as she was sitting down to dinner. It upset the table and things, passed through the house, and killed her neighbor in the next house.

Several had been killed; some in their houses, others in the streets.

When the rebels were evacuating, in the confusion several of our sick and wounded escaped from the hospitals, and were sheltered by the citizens.

Almost every garden and yard around the city had its cave. These were sunk down with a winding entrance to them, so that pieces of shells could not go in. When dug deep enough, boards were placed on the top, and the earth piled upon them in a conical shape, and deep enough to withstand even a shell. Some of these caves, or bomb-proofs, were fifteen feet deep, and well covered. All along the railroad, around the intrenchments and the bluff near the city, were gopher holes, where soldiers and citizens concealed themselves.

In some cases it happened that our shells burst so as to close up the mouths of the caves, thus burying the inmates in a living tomb.

. . . The first fire burst out on the night of Friday, the 11th of November, in a block of wooden tenements on Decatur Street, where eight buildings were destroyed.

Soon after, fires burst out in other parts of the city. These certainly were the works of some of the soldiers, who expected to get some booty under cover of the fires. . . .

It was hard to restrain the soldiers from burning it down. With that licentiousness that characterizes an army they wanted a bonfire.

On Sunday night a kind of long streak of light, like an aurora, marked the line of march, and the burning stores, depots, and bridges, in the train of the army.

The Michigan engineers had been detailed to destroy the depots and public buildings in Atlanta. Everything in the way of destruction was now considered legalized. The workmen tore up the rails and piled them on the smoking fires. Winship's iron foundery and machine shops were early set on fire. This valuable property was calculated to be worth about half a million dollars.

An oil refinery near by next got on fire, and was soon in a fierce blaze. Next followed a freight warehouse, in which were stored several bales of cotton. The depot, turning-tables, freight sheds, and stores around, were soon a fiery mass. The heart was burning out of beautiful Atlanta. . . .

ᴥ *Atlanta to the Sea*

It was pretty well known that Sherman was going to cut loose from all communications, and to destroy all the factories, founderies, railroads, mills, and all government property, thus preventing the rebels from using them in his rear. After the troops destroyed Rome, Kingston, and Marietta, tore up the track, and set fire to sleepers, railroad depots, and stores, Sherman issued a special field order:

"The army will forage liberally on the country during the march. To this end each brigade commander will organize a good and efficient foraging party, under command of one or more discreet officers. To regular foraging parties must be instructed the gathering of provisions and forage at any distance from the roads travelled.

"As for horses, mules, wagons, &c., the cavalry and artillery may appropriate freely and without limit. Foraging parties may also take mules or horses to replace the jaded animals of their trains, or to serve as pack-mules for the regiments or brigades."

These orders were all right, if literally carried out; but they were soon converted into licenses for indiscriminate plunder. The followers of an army, in the shape of servants, hangers-on, and bummers, are generally as numerous as the effective force. Every brigade and regiment had its organized, foraging party, which were joined by every officer's servant and idler about the camps. . . .

"Living off the country" was fast becoming the order. The men knew that Sherman had started with some sixteen days' supplies, and they wished to preserve them if possible; besides, they thought that a change of diet would be good for their health. There was nothing to be got the first two days' march, as the country all around Atlanta had been foraged by Slocum's corps while hemmed in there. Now we were opening on a country where pits of sweet potatoes, yards of poultry and hogs, and cellars of bacon and flour, were making their appearance. A new spirit began to animate the men; they were as busy as so many bees about a honey-pot, and commenced important voyages of discovery, and returned well laden with spoils. Foragers, bummers, and camp followers scattered over the country for miles, and black clouds of smoke showed where they had been. Small lots of cotton were found near most of the plantation houses. These, with the gins and presses, were burned, oftentimes firing the houses and offices. Near Madison we passed some wealthy plantations; one, the property of a Mr. Lane, who was courteous enough to wait to receive us, was full of decrepit, dilapidated negroes, presided over by a few brimstone-looking white ladies. They were viciously rabid, and only wished they could eat us with the same facility that the troops consumed all the edibles on the place, and eloped with plump grunters and indignant roosters, and their families. . . .

@ ON THE WEB   *To learn more about the Civil War's impact on the Southern homefront, visit the website of "Documenting the American South: The Southern Homefront, 1861–1865" at* http://docsouth.unc.edu/imls/.

THE BIG PICTURE

The Civil War became the central event in the lives of nineteenth-century Americans. Yet why that happened is open to dispute. Was it the bloodshed? The end of slavery? The defeat of the Confederacy? The emergence of northern dominance? The heroics of Robert E. Lee? Lincoln? Just what was it?

Chapter 14

Reconstruction

Interpretive Essay by Elizabeth Rauh Bethel 338

Sources 351
>   The Meaning of Freedom 351
>   The Cartoonist's View of Reconstruction 353
>   The South Redeemed 363

The Big Picture 364

When it was first coined in the crisis months between the election of Lincoln and the beginnings of the Civil War, the term "Reconstruction" meant simply the reunification of the nation. By the time the war ended in 1865, the idea of Reconstruction was more complicated: it now meant more than simple political reestablishment of the Union; it meant reconstructing the South, refashioning its social and economic life to some degree or other. For the freedmen—many only days removed from slavery—Reconstruction would soon come to represent freedom itself. Even in 1865, most southern blacks realized that without thoroughgoing Reconstruction, in which freedmen obtained land as well as the right to vote, freedom would mean only a new kind of economic oppression.

Twelve years later, in 1877, many people, north and south, realized that Reconstruction had ended. But by then the term had taken on intense moral meanings. To most white southerners, it was a term of resentment, the name of a bleak period during which vindictive Yankee politicians had tried to force "black rule" on a "prostrate South." The North tried and finally failed, for the South had, in the end, been "redeemed" by its own leaders. Slavery had ended, but white supremacy had been firmly reestablished. To perhaps a majority of whites in the North, Reconstruction had over the years become a nuisance, and they were glad to let go of it, to reaffirm the value of the Union, and to let the bitter past die. There were other northerners, however, who looked back from 1877 to twelve years of moral failure, of lost opportunities to force freedom and equality on an unrepentant South.

There were hundreds of thousands of freedmen who experienced this "moral failure" in very real ways. Instead of farming their own land, they farmed the lands of whites as tenants and sharecroppers. Far from benefiting from meaningful voting rights, most blacks were denied the franchise, and those who continued to exercise it did so in a climate of hostility hardly conducive to political freedom. Nonetheless, it was possible for blacks to look back positively at the Reconstruction experience. The 1866 Civil Rights Act granted blacks both citizenship and all the civil rights possessed by whites. When the constitutionality of that statute seemed in doubt, Congress made ratification of the Fourteenth Amendment (accomplished in 1868) a precondition for southern restoration to the Union. In theory, that amendment made the federal government the protector of rights that might be invaded by the states. Under "Radical" Reconstruction, carried out by Congress after 1867, hundreds of thousands of southern blacks voted, and many held high elective office. And in 1875, when whites had reestablished their authority throughout most of the region, a new civil rights act "guaranteed" blacks equal rights in theaters, inns, and other public places. If in the end it proved impossible to maintain these gains, Reconstruction still remained the bright spot in the lives of many former slaves.

INTERPRETIVE ESSAY

Promised Land

Elizabeth Rauh Bethel

Most accounts of the Reconstruction period have been written largely from the perspective of powerful white men such as presidents, northern congressmen, or southern "Redeemers." As a result, students often get the impression that all decisions were made by whites, and blacks were idly sitting on their hands, just the beneficiaries or victims of white actions. That was not the case. Throughout the South black men and women, just months after the end of slavery, actively shaped their own futures and challenged the power and prejudices of their white neighbors. Most wanted to own land and become family farmers. The odds against them were immense, and many struggled valiantly only to see their hopes dashed by their lack of money, or by political decisions made in distant Washington, or by white terrorists such as the Ku Klux Klan. But some, as Elizabeth Rauh Bethel documents in the following selection, overcame great obstacles and established tightly knit communities. What do you think accounts for the courage and determination of the families Bethel describes? Do you think the course of American history would have been changed if most black families during Reconstruction had obtained a forty-acre farm? In what respect?

The opportunity to acquire land was a potent attraction for a people just emerging from bondage, and one commonly pursued by freedmen throughout the south. Cooperative agrarian communities, instigated in some cases by the invading Union Army and in other cases by the freedmen themselves, were scattered across the plantation lands of the south as early as 1863. Collective land purchases and cooperative farming ventures developed in the Tidewater area of Virginia, the Sea Islands of South Carolina and Georgia, and along the Mississippi River as refugees at the earliest contraband camps struggled to establish economic and social stability.

These initial land tenure arrangements, always temporary, stimulated high levels of industrious labor among both those fortunate enough to obtain land and those whose expectations were raised by their neighbors' good fortunes. Although for most freedmen the initial promise of landownership was never realized, heightened expectations resulted in "entire families laboring together, improving their material conditions, laying aside money that might hopefully be used to purchase a farm or a few acres for a homestead of their own" during the final years of the war.

From Elizabeth Rauh Bethel, *Promiseland: A Century of Life in a Negro Community*, Temple University Press, Philadelphia, 1981, pp. 5–8, 17–21, 23, 25–33, 39–40. © 1981 by Temple University. Reprinted by permission of Temple University Press.

The desire for a plot of land dominated public expressions among the freedmen as well as their day-to-day activities and behaviors. In 1864 Secretary of War Stanton met with Negro leaders in Savannah to discuss the problems of resettlement. During that meeting sixty-seven-year-old freedman Garrison Frazier responded to an inquiry regarding living arrangements by telling Stanton that "we would prefer to 'live by ourselves' rather than 'scattered among the whites.'" These arrangements, he added, should include self-sufficiency established on Negro-owned lands. The sentiments Frazier expressed were not unusual. They were repeated by other freedmen across the south. Tunis Campbell, also recently emancipated, testified before the congressional committee investigating the Ku Klux Klan that "the great cry of our people is to have land." A delegate to the Tennessee Colored Citizens' Convention of 1866 stated that "what is needed for the colored people is land which they own." A recently emancipated Negro representative to the 1868 South Carolina Constitutional Convention, speaking in support of that state's land redistribution program, which eventually gave birth to the Promised Land community, said of the relationship between landownership and the state's Negro population: "Night and day they dream" of owning their own land. "It is their all in all."

At Davis Bend, Mississippi, and Port Royal, South Carolina, as well as similar settlements in Louisiana, North Carolina, and Virginia, this dream was in fact realized for a time. Freedmen worked "with commendable zeal . . . out in the morning before it is light and at work 'til darkness drives them to their homes" whenever they farmed land that was their own. John Eaton, who supervised the Davis Bend project, observed that the most successful land experiments among the freedmen were those in which plantations were subdivided into individually owned and farmed tracts. These small farms, rather than the larger cooperative ventures, "appeared to hold the greatest chance for success." The contraband camps and federally directed farm projects afforded newly emancipated freedmen an opportunity to "rediscover and redefine themselves, and to establish communities." Within the various settlements a stability and social order developed that combined economic self-sufficiency with locally directed and controlled schools, churches, and mutual aid societies. In the years before the Freedmen's Bureau or the northern missionary societies penetrated the interior of the south, the freedmen, through their own resourcefulness, erected and supported such community institutions at every opportunity. In obscure settlements with names like Slabtown and Acreville, Hampton, Alexandria, Saxtonville, and Mitchelville, "status, experience, history, and ideology were potent forces operating toward cohesiveness and community." . . .

. . . In South Carolina, perhaps more intensely than any of the other southern states, the thirst for land was acute. It was a possibility sparked first by General William T. Sherman's military actions along the Sea Islands, then dashed as quickly as it was born in the distant arena of Washington politics. Still, the desire for land remained a goal not readily abandoned by the state's freedpeople, and they implemented a plan to achieve that goal at the first opportunity. Their chance came at the 1868 South Carolina Constitutional Convention.

South Carolina was among the southern states that refused to ratify the Fourteenth Amendment to the Constitution, the amendment that established the citizenship of the freedmen. Like her recalcitrant neighbors, the state was then placed under military government, as outlined by the Military Reconstruction Act of 1867. Among the mandates of that federal legislation was a requirement that each of the states in question draft a new state constitution incorporating the principles of the Fourteenth Amendment. Only after such new constitutions were completed and implemented were the separate states of the defeated Confederacy eligible for readmission to the Union.

The representatives to these constitutional conventions were selected by a revolutionary electorate, one that included all adult male Negroes. Registration for the elections was handled by the army with some informal assistance by "that God-forsaken institution, the Freedman's Bureau." Only South Carolina among the ten states of the former Confederacy elected a Negro majority to its convention. The instrument those representatives drafted called for four major social and political reforms in state government: a statewide system of free common schools; universal manhood suffrage; a jury law that included the Negro electorate in county pools of qualified jurors; and a land redistribution system designed to benefit the state's landless population, primarily the freedmen.

White response to the new constitution and the social reforms that it outlined was predictably vitriolic. It was condemned by one white newspaper as "the work of sixty-odd Negroes, many of them ignorant and depraved." The authors were publicly ridiculed as representing "the maddest, most unscrupulous, and infamous revolution in history." Despite this and similar vilification, the constitution was ratified in the 1868 referendum, an election boycotted by many white voters and dominated by South Carolina's 81,000 newly enfranchised Negroes, who cast their votes overwhelmingly with the Republicans and for the new constitution.

That same election selected representatives to the state legislature charged with implementing the constitutional reforms. That body, like the constitutional convention, was constituted with a Negro majority; and it moved immediately to establish a common school system and land redistribution program. The freedmen were already registered, and the new jury pools remained the prerogative of the individual counties. The 1868 election also was notable for the numerous attacks and "outrages" that occurred against the more politically active freedmen. Among those Negroes assaulted, beaten, shot, and lynched during the pre-election campaign months were four men who subsequently bought small farms from the Land Commission and settled at Promised Land. Like other freedmen in South Carolina, their open involvement in the state's Republican political machinery led to personal violence.

Wilson Nash was the first of the future Promised Land residents to encounter white brutality and retaliation for his political activities. Nash was nominated by the Republicans as their candidate for Abbeville County's seat in the state legislature at the August 1868 county convention. In October of that year, less than two weeks before the general election, Nash was attacked and shot in the leg by two unidentified white assailants. The "outrage" took place in the barn on his rented farm, not far from Dr. Marshall's farm on Curltail Creek. Wilson Nash was thirty-three years old in 1868, married, and the father of three small children. He had moved from "up around Cokesbury" within Abbeville County, shortly after emancipation to the rented land further west. Within months after the Nash family was settled on their farm, Wilson Nash joined the many Negroes who affiliated with the Republicans, an alliance probably instigated and encouraged by Republican promises of land to the freedmen. The extent of Nash's involvement with local politics was apparent in his nomination for public office; and this same nomination brought him to the forefront of county Negro leadership and to the attention of local whites.

After the attack Nash sent his wife and young children to a neighbor's home, where he probably believed they would be safe. He then mounted his mule and fled his farm, leaving behind thirty bushels of recently harvested corn. Whether Nash also left behind a cotton crop is unknown. It was the unprotected corn crop that worried him as much as his concern for his own safety. He rode his mule into Abbeville and there sought refuge at the local Freedman's Bureau office where he reported the attack to the local bureau agent and requested military protection for his family and his corn crop. Captain W. F. DeKnight was sympathetic to Nash's plight but was powerless to assist or protect him. DeKnight had no authority in civil matters such as this, and the men who held that power generally ignored such assaults on Negroes. The Nash incident was typical and followed a familiar pattern. The assailants remained unidentified, unapprehended, and unpunished. The attack achieved the desired end, however, for Nash withdrew his name from the slate of legislative candidates. For him there were other considerations that took priority over politics.

Violence against the freedmen of Abbeville County, as elsewhere in the state, continued that fall and escalated as the 1868 election day neared. The victims had in common an involvement with the Republicans, and there was little distinction made between direct and indirect partisan activity. Politically visible Negroes were open targets. Shortly after the Nash shooting young Willis Smith was assaulted, yet another victim of Reconstruction violence. Smith was still a teenager and too young to vote in the elections, but his age afforded him no immunity. He was a known member of the Union League, the most radical and secret of the political organizations that attracted freedmen. While attending a dance one evening, Smith and four other League members were dragged outside the dance hall and brutally beaten by four white men whose identities were hidden by hoods. This attack, too, was an act of political vengeance. Like other crimes committed against politically active Negroes, this one remained unsolved.

On election day freedmen Washington Green and Allen Goode were precinct managers at the White Hall polling place, near the southern edge of the Marshall land. Their position was a political appointment of some prestige, their reward for affiliation with and loyalty to the Republican cause. The appointment brought them, like Wilson Nash and Willis Smith, to the attention of local whites. On election day the voting proceeded without incident until midday, when two white men attempted to block Negroes from entering the polling site. A scuffle ensued as Green and Goode, acting in their capacity as voting officials, tried to bring the matter to a halt and were shot by the white men. One freedman was killed, two others injured, in the incident that also went unsolved. In none of the attacks were the assailants ever apprehended. Within twenty-four months all four men—Wilson Nash, Willis Smith, Washington Green, and Allen Goode—bought farms at Promised Land.

Despite the violence surrounding the 1868 elections, the Republicans carried the whole of the state. White Democrats refused to support an election they deemed illegal, and they intimidated the newly enfranchised Negro electorate at every opportunity. The freedmen, nevertheless, flocked to the polls in an unprecedented exercise of their new franchise and sent a body of legislative representatives to the state capitol of Columbia who were wholly committed to the mandates and reforms of the new constitution. Among the first legislative acts was one that formalized the land redistribution program through the creation of the South Carolina Land Commission.

The Land Commission program, as designed by the legislature, was financed through the public sale of state bonds. The capital generated from the bond sales was used to purchase privately owned plantation tracts that were then subdivided and resold to freedmen through long-term (ten years), low-interest (7 percent per annum) loans. The bulk of the commission's transactions occurred along the coastal areas of the state where land was readily available. The labor and financial problems of the rice planters of the low-country were generally more acute than those of the up-country cotton planters. As a result, they were more eager to dispose of a portion of the landholdings at a reasonable price, and their motives for their dealings with the Land Commission were primarily pecuniary.

Piedmont planters were not so motivated. Many were able to salvage their production by negotiating sharecropping and tenant arrangements. Most operated on a smaller scale than the low-country planters and were less dependent on gang labor arrangements. As a consequence, few were as financially pressed as their low-country counterparts, and land was less available for purchase by the Land Commission in the Piedmont region. With only 9 percent of the commission purchases lying in the up-country, the Marshall lands were the exception rather than the rule.

The Marshall sons first advertised the land for sale in 1865. These lands, like others at the eastern edge of the Cotton Belt, were exhausted from generations of cultivation and attendant soil erosion; and for such worn-out land the price was greatly inflated. Additionally, two successive years of crop failures, low cotton prices, and a general lack of capital discouraged serious planters from purchasing the lands. The sons then advertised the tract for rent, but the land stood idle. The family wanted to dispose of the land in a single transaction rather than subdivide it, and Dr. Marshall's farm was no competition for the less expensive and more fertile land to the west that was opened for settlement after the war. In 1869 the two sons once again advertised the land for sale, but conditions in Abbeville County were not improved for farmers, and no private buyer came forth.

Having exhausted the possibilities for negotiating a private sale, the family considered alternative prospects for the disposition of a farm that was of little use to them. James L. Orr, a moderate Democrat, former governor (1865 to 1868), and family son-in-law, served as negotiator when the tract was offered to the Land Commission at the grossly inflated price of ten dollars an acre. Equivalent land in Abbeville County was selling for as little as two dollars an acre, and the commission rejected the offer. Political promises took precedence over financial considerations when the commission's regional agent wrote the Land Commission's Advisory Board that "if the land is not bought the (Republican) party is lost in this district." Upon receipt of his advice the commission immediately met the Marshall family's ten dollar an acre price. By January 1870 the land had been subdivided into fifty small farms, averaging slightly less than fifty acres each, which were publicly offered for sale to Negro as well as white buyers.

The Marshall Tract was located in the central sector of old Abbeville County and was easily accessible to most of the freedmen who were to make the lands their home. . . .

The farms on the Marshall Tract were no bargain for the Negroes who bought them. The land was only partially cleared and ready for cultivation, and that which was free of pine trees and underbrush was badly eroded. There was little to recommend the land to cotton farming. Crop failures in 1868 and 1869 severely limited the local economy, which further reduced the possibilities for small farmers working on badly depleted soil. There was little credit available to Abbeville farmers, white or black; and farming lacked not only an unqualified promise of financial gain but even the possibility of breaking even at harvest. Still, it was not the fertility of the soil or the possibility of economic profit that attracted the freedmen to those farms. The single opportunity for landownership, a status that for most Negroes in 1870 symbolized the essence of their freedom, was the prime attraction for the freedmen who bought farms from the subdivided Marshall Tract.

Most of the Negroes who settled the farms knew the area and local conditions well. Many were native to Abbeville County. In addition to Wilson Nash, the Moragne family and their in-laws, the Turners, the Pinckneys, the Letmans, and the Williamses were also natives of Abbeville, from "down over by Bordeaux" in the southwestern rim of the county that borders Georgia. Others came to their new farms from "Dark Corner, over by McCormick," and another nearby Negro settlement, Pettigrew Station— both in Abbeville County. The Redd family lived in Newberry, South Carolina before they bought their farm; and James and Hannah Fields came to Promised Land from the state capital, Columbia, eighty miles to the east.

Many of the settlers from Abbeville County shared their names with prominent white families—Moragne, Burt, Marshall, Pressley, Frazier, and

Pinckney. Their claims to heritage were diverse. One recalled "my grandaddy was a white man from England," and others remembered slavery times to their children in terms of white fathers who "didn't allow nobody to mess with the colored boys of his." Others dismissed the past and told their grandchildren that "some things is best forget." A few were so fair skinned that "they could have passed for white if they wanted to," while others who bought farms from the Land Commission "was so black there wasn't no doubt about who their daddy was."

After emancipation many of these former bondsmen stayed in their old neighborhoods, farming in much the same way as they had during slavery times. Some "worked for the marsters at daytime and for theyselves at night" in an early Piedmont version of sharecropping. Old Samuel Marshall was one former slaveowner who retained many of his bondsmen as laborers by assuring them that they would receive some land of their own—promising them that "if you clean two acres you get two acres; if you clean ten acres you get ten acres" of farmland. It was this promise that kept some freedmen on the Marshall land until it was sold to the Land Commission. They cut and cleared part of the tract of the native pines and readied it for planting in anticipation of ownership. But the promise proved empty, and Marshall's death and the subsequent sale of his lands to the state deprived many of those who labored day and night on the land of the free farms they hoped would be theirs. "After they had cleaned it up they still had to pay for it." Other freedmen in the county "moved off after slavery ended but couldn't get no place" of their own to farm. Unable to negotiate labor or lease arrangements, they faced a time of homelessness with few resources and limited options until the farms became available to them. A few entered into labor contracts supervised by the Freedman's Bureau or settled on rented farms in the county for a time.

The details of the various postemancipation economic arrangements made by the freedmen who settled on the small tracts at Dr. Marshall's farm, whatever the form they assumed, were dominated by three conscious choices all had in common. The first was their decision to stay in Abbeville County following emancipation. For most of the people who eventually settled in Promised Land, Abbeville was their home as well as the site of their enslavement. There they were surrounded by friends, family, and a familiar environment. The second choice this group of freedmen shared was occupational. They had been Piedmont farmers throughout their enslavement, and they chose to remain farmers in their freedom.

Local Negroes made a third conscious decision that for many had long-range importance in their lives and those of their descendants. Through the influence of the Union League, the Freedman's Bureau, the African Methodist Church, and each other, many of the Negroes in Abbeville aligned politically with the Republicans between 1865 and 1870. In Abbeville as elsewhere in the state, the alliance was established enthusiastically. The Republicans promised land as well as suffrage to those who supported them. If their political activities became public knowledge, the freedmen "were safe nowhere"; and men like Wilson Nash, Willis Smith, Washington

Green, and Allen Goode who were highly visible Negro politicians took great risks in this exercise of freedom. Those risks were not without justification. It was probably not a coincidence that loyalty to the Republican cause was followed by a chance to own land.

. . . The Land Commission first advertised the farms on the Marshall Tract in January and February 1870. Eleven freedmen and their families established conditional ownership of their farms before spring planting that year. They were among a vanguard of some 14,000 Negro families who acquired small farms in South Carolina through the Land Commission program between 1868 and 1879. With a ten-dollar down payment they acquired the right to settle on and till the thin soil. They were also obliged to place at least half their land under cultivation within three years and to pay all taxes due annually in order to retain their ownership rights.

Among the earliest settlers to the newly created farms was Allen Goode, the precinct manager at White Hall, who bought land in January 1870, almost immediately after it was put on the market. Two brothers-in-law, J. H. Turner and Primus Letman, also bought farms in the early spring that year. Turner was married to LeAnna Moragne and Letman to LeAnna's sister Francis. Elias Harris, a widower with six young children to raise, also came to his lands that spring, as did George Hearst, his son Robert, and their families. Another father-son partnership, Carson and Will Donnelly, settled on adjacent tracts. Willis Smith's father, Daniel, also bought a farm in 1870.

Allen Goode was the wealthiest of these early settlers. He owned a horse, two oxen, four milk cows, and six hogs. For the other families, both material resources and farm production were modest. Few of the homesteaders produced more than a single bale of cotton on their new farms that first year; but all, like Wilson Nash two years earlier, had respectable corn harvests, a crop essential to "both us and the animals." Most households also had sizable pea, bean, and sweet potato crops and produced their own butter. All but the cotton crops were destined for household consumption, as these earliest settlers established a pattern of subsistence farming that would prevail as a community economic strategy in the coming decades.

This decision by the Promised Land farmers to intensify food production and minimize cotton cultivation, whether intentional or the result of other conditions, was an important initial step toward their attainment of economic self-sufficiency. Small-scale cotton farmers in the Black Belt were rarely free agents. Most were quickly trapped in a web of chronic indebtedness and marketing restrictions. Diversification of cash crops was inhibited during the 1870s and 1880s not only by custom and these economic entanglements but also by an absence of local markets, adequate roads, and methods of transportation to move crops other than cotton to larger markets. The Promised Land farmers, generally unwilling to incur debts with the local lien men if they could avoid it, turned to a modified form of subsistence farming as their only realistic land-use option. Through this strategy many of them avoided the "economic nightmare" that fixed the status of other small-scale cotton growers at a level of permanent peonage well into the twentieth century.

The following year, 1871, twenty-five more families scratched up their ten-dollar down payment; and upon presenting it to Hollinshead obtained conditional titles to farms on the Marshall Tract. The Williams family, Amanda and her four adult sons—William, Henry, James, and Moses—purchased farms together that year, probably withdrawing their money from their accounts at the Freedmen's Savings and Trust Company Augusta Branch for their separate down payments. Three of the Moragne brothers—Eli, Calvin, and Moses—joined the Turners and the Letmans, their sisters and brothers-in-law, making five households in that corner of the tract soon designated "Moragne Town." John Valentine, whose family was involved in A.M.E. organizational work in Abbeville County, also obtained a conditional title to a farm, although he did not settle there permanently. Henry Redd, like the Williamses, withdrew his savings from the Freedman's Bank and moved to his farm from Newberry, a small town about thirty miles to the east. Moses Wideman, Wells Gray, Frank Hutchison, Samuel Bulow, and Samuel Burt also settled on their farms before spring planting.

As the cluster of Negro-owned farms grew more densely populated, it gradually assumed a unique identity; and this identity, in turn, gave rise to a name, Promised Land. Some remember their grandparents telling them that "the Governor in Columbia [South Carolina] named this place when he sold it to the Negroes." Others contend that the governor had no part in the naming. They argue that these earliest settlers derived the name Promised Land from the conditions of their purchase. "They only promised to pay for it, but they never did!" Indeed, there is some truth in that statement. For although the initial buyers agreed to pay between nine and ten dollars per acre for their land in the original promissory notes, few fulfilled the conditions of those contracts. Final purchase prices were greatly reduced, from ten dollars to $3.25 per acre, a price more in line with prevailing land prices in the Piedmont.

By the end of 1873 forty-four of the fifty farms on the Marshall Tract had been sold. The remaining land, less than seven hundred acres, was the poorest in the tract, badly eroded and at the perimeter of the community. Some of those farms remained unsold until the early 1880s, but even so the land did not go unused. Families too poor to consider buying the farms lived on the state-owned property throughout the 1870s. They were squatters, living there illegally and rent-free, perhaps working a small cotton patch, always a garden. Their condition contrasted sharply with that of the landowners who, like other Negroes who purchased farmland during the 1870s, were considered the most prosperous of the rural freedmen. The freeholders in the community were among the pioneers in a movement to acquire land, a movement that stretched across geographical and temporal limits. Even in the absence of state or federal assistance in other regions, and despite the difficulties Negroes faced in negotiating land purchases directly from white landowners during Reconstruction, by 1875 Negroes across the south owned five million acres of farmland. The promises of emancipation were fulfilled for a few, among them the families at Promised Land.

Settlement of the community coincided with the establishment of a public school, another of the revolutionary social reforms mandated by the 1868 constitution. It was the first of several public facilities to serve community residents and was built on land still described officially as "Dr. Marshall's farm." J. H. Turner, Larkin Reynolds, Iverson Reynolds, and Hutson Lomax, all Negroes, were the first school trustees. The families established on their new farms sent more than ninety children to the one-room school. Everyone who could be spared from the fields was in the classroom for the short 1870 school term. Although few of the children in the landless families attended school regularly, the landowning families early established a tradition of school attendance for their children consonant with their new status. With limited resources the school began the task of educating local children.

The violence and terror experienced by some of the men of Promised Land during 1868 recurred three years later when Eli and Wade Moragne were attacked and viciously beaten with a wagon whip by a band of Klansmen. Wade was twenty-three that year, Eli two years older. Both were married and had small children. It was rumored that the Moragne brothers were among the most prominent and influential of the Negro Republicans in Abbeville County. Their political activity, compounded by an unusual degree of self-assurance, pride, and dignity, infuriated local whites. Like Wilson Nash, Willis Smith, Washington Green, and Allen Goode, the Moragne brothers were victims of insidious political reprisals. Involvement in Reconstruction politics for Negroes was a dangerous enterprise and one that addressed the past as well as the future. It was an activity suited to young men and those who faced the future bravely. It was not for the timid.

The Republican influence on the freedmen at Promised Land was unmistakable, and there was no evidence that the "outrages" and terrorizations against them slowed their participation in local partisan activities. In addition to the risks, there were benefits to be accrued from their alliance with the Republicans. They enjoyed appointments as precinct managers and school trustees. As candidates for various public offices, they experienced a degree of prestige and public recognition that offset the element of danger they faced. These men, born slaves, rose to positions of prominence as landowners, as political figures, and as makers of a community. Few probably had dared to dream of such possibilities a decade earlier.

During the violent years of Reconstruction there was at least one official attempt to end the anarchy in Abbeville County. The representative to the state legislature, J. Hollinshead—the former regional agent for the Land Commission—stated publicly what many local Negroes already knew privately, that "numerous outrages occur in the county and the laws cannot be enforced by civil authorities." From the floor of the General Assembly of South Carolina Hollinshead called for martial law in Abbeville, a request that did not pass unnoticed locally. The editor of the *Press* commented on Hollinshead's request for martial law by declaring that such outrages against the freedmen "exist only in the imagination of the legislator." His response was probably typical of the cavalier attitude of southern whites toward the problems of their former bondsmen. Indeed, there were no further reports of violence and attacks against freedmen carried by the *Press*, which failed to note the murder of County Commissioner Henry Nash in February 1871. Like other victims of white terrorists, Nash was a Negro.

While settlement of Dr. Marshall's farm by the freedmen proceeded, three community residents were arrested for the theft of "some oxen from Dr. H. Drennan who lives near the 'Promiseland.'" Authorities found the heads, tails, and feet of the slaughtered animals near the homes of Ezekiel and Moses Williams and Colbert Jordan. The circumstantial evidence against them seemed convincing; and the three were arrested and then released without bond, pending trial. Colonel Cothran, a former Confederate officer and respected barrister in Abbeville, represented the trio at their trial. Although freedmen in Abbeville courts were generally convicted of whatever crime they were charged with, the Williamses and Jordan were acquitted. Justice for Negroes was always a tenuous affair; but it was especially so before black, as well as white, qualified electors were included in the jury pool. The trial of the Williams brothers and Jordan signaled a temporary truce in the racial war, a truce that at least applied to those Negroes settling the farms at Promised Land.

In 1872, the third year of settlement, Promised Land gained nine more households as families moved to land that they "bought for a dollar an acre." There they "plow old oxen, build log cabin houses" as they settled the land they bought "from the Governor in Columbia." Colbert Jordan and Ezekiel Williams, cleared of the oxen stealing charges, both purchased farms that year. Family and kinship ties drew some of the new migrants to the community. Joshuway Wilson, married to Moses Wideman's sister Delphia, bought a farm near his brother-in-law. Two more Moragne brothers, William and Wade, settled near the other family members in "Moragne Town." Whitfield Hutchison, a jack-leg preacher, bought the farm adjacent to his brother Frank. "Old Whit Hutchison could sing about let's go down to the water and be baptized. He didn't have no education, and he didn't know exactly how to put his words, but when he got to singing he could make your hair rise up. He was a number one preacher." Hutchison was not the only preacher among those first settlers. Isaac Y. Moragne, who moved to Promised Land the following year, and several men in the Turner family all combined preaching and farming.

Not all the settlers came to their new farms as members of such extensive kinship networks as the Moragnes, who counted nine brothers, four sisters, and an assortment of spouses and children among the first Promised Land residents. Even those who joined the community in relative isolation, however, were seldom long in establishing kinship alliances with their neighbors. One such couple was James and Hannah Fields, who lived in Columbia before emancipation. While still a slave, James Fields owned property in the state capital, which was held in trust for him by his master. After emancipation Fields worked for a time as a porter on the Columbia and Greenville Railroad and heard about the up-country land for sale to Negroes as he carried carpet bags and listened to political gossip on the train. Fields went to

Abbeville County to inspect the land before he purchased a farm there. While he was visiting, he "run up on Mr. Nathan Redd," old Henry Redd's son. The Fields's granddaughter Emily and Nathan were about the same age, and Fields proposed a match to young Redd. "You marry my granddaughter, and I'll will all this land to you and her." The marriage was arranged before the farm was purchased, and eventually the land was transferred to the young couple.

By the conclusion of 1872 forty-eight families were settled on farms in Promised Land. Most of the land was under cultivation, as required by law; but the farmers were also busy with other activities. In addition to the houses and barns that had to be raised as each new family arrived with their few possessions, the men continued their political activities. Iverson Reynolds, J. H. Turner, John and Elias Tolbert, Judson Reynolds, Oscar Pressley, and Washington Green, all community residents, were delegates to the county Republican convention in August 1872. Three of the group were landowners. Their political activities were still not received with much enthusiasm by local whites, but reaction to Negro involvement in politics was lessening in hostility. The *Press* mildly observed that the fall cotton crop was being gathered with good speed and "the farmers have generally been making good use of their time." Cotton picking and politics were both seasonal, and the newspaper chided local Negroes for their priorities. "The blacks have been indulging a little too much in politics but are getting right again." Iverson Reynolds and Washington Green, always among the community's Republican leadership during the 1870s, served as local election managers again for the 1872 fall elections. The men from Promised Land voted without incident that year.

Civic participation among the Promised Land residents extended beyond partisan politics when the county implemented the new jury law in 1872. There had been no Negro jurors for the trial of the Williams brothers and Colbert Jordan the previous year. Although the inclusion of Negroes in the jury pools was a reform mandated in 1868, four years passed before Abbeville authorities drew up new jury lists from the revised voter registration rolls. The jury law was as repugnant to the whites as Negro suffrage, termed "a wretched attempt at legislation, which surpasses anything which has yet been achieved by the Salons in Columbia." When the new lists were finally completed in 1872 the Press, ever the reflection of local white public opinion, predicted that "many of [the freedmen] probably have moved away; and the chances are that not many of them will be forthcoming" in the call to jury duty. Neither the initial condemnation of the law nor the optimistic undertones of the *Press* prediction stopped Pope Moragne and Iverson Reynolds from responding to their notices from the Abbeville Courthouse. Both landowners rode their mules up Five Notch Road from Promised Land to Abbeville and served on the county's first integrated jury in the fall of 1872. Moragne and Reynolds were soon followed by others from the community—Allen Goode, Robert Wideman, William Moragne, James Richie, and Luther (Shack) Moragne. By 1874, less than five years after settlement of Dr. Marshall's farm by the new Negro landowners began, the residents of

Promised Land remained actively involved in Abbeville County politics. They were undaunted by the *Press* warning that "just so soon as the colored people lose the confidence and support of the North their doom is fixed. The fate of the red man will be theirs." They were voters, jurors, taxpayers, and trustees of the school their children attended. Their collective identity as an exclusively Negro community was well established. . . .

The representatives to the 1868 South Carolina Constitutional Convention who formulated the state's land redistribution hoped to establish an economically independent Negro yeomanry in South Carolina. The Land Commission intended the purchase and resale of Dr. Marshall's farm to solidify the interests of radical Republicanism in Abbeville County, at least for a time. Both of these designs were realized. A third and unintended consequence also resulted. The land fostered a socially autonomous, identifiable community. Drawing on resources and social structures well established within an extant Negro culture, the men and women who settled Promised Land established churches and schools and a viable economic system based on landownership. They maintained that economic autonomy by subsistence farming and supported many of their routine needs by patronizing the locally owned and operated grist mills and general store. The men were actively involved in Reconstruction politics as well as other aspects of civil life, serving regularly on county juries and paying their taxes. Attracted by the security and prestige Promised Land afforded and the possible hope of eventual landownership, fifty additional landless households moved into the community during the 1870s, expanding the 1880 population to almost twice its original size. Together the eighty-nine households laid claim to slightly more than four square miles of land, and within that small territory they "carved out their own little piece of the world."

@ ON THE WEB   *To further explore the experience of Reconstruction, visit the "Civil War and Reconstruction, 1861–1877" page of the Library of Congress website and access the links entitled "The Freedmen," "Reconstruction and Rights," and "The Travails of Reconstruction" at* http://lcweb2.loc.gov/ammem/ndlpedu/features/timeline/civilwar/civilwar.html.

The Meaning of Freedom

What did it mean to be free? As Bethel's account of the settlers of Promised Land indicates, there were many obstacles in the path of every freedman and only a few succeeded in becoming independent small farmers. Some twentieth-century writers have argued that the gains for most blacks were miniscule, that being a poor tenant farmer or sharecropper was often even worse than being a slave. But these writers, of course, never experienced the change from slavery to freedom. Here is a man who did.

VOICES

Dayton, Ohio, August 7, 1865

To My Old Master, Colonel P. H. Anderson, Big Spring, Tennessee

Sir: I got your letter and was glad to find you had not forgotten Jourdon, and that you wanted me to come back and live with you again, promising to do better for me than anybody else can. I have often felt uneasy about you. I thought the Yankees would have hung you long before this for harboring Rebs they found at your house. I suppose they never heard about your going to Col. Martin's to kill the Union soldier that was left by his company in their stable. Although you shot at me twice before I left you, I did not want to hear of your being hurt, and am glad you are still living. It would do me good to go back to the dear old home and see Miss Mary and Miss Martha and Allen, Esther, Green, and Lee. Give my love to them all, and tell them I hope we will meet in the better world, if not in this. I would have gone back to see you all when I was working in the Nashville hospital, but one of the neighbors told me Henry intended to shoot me if he ever got a chance.

I want to know particularly what the good chance is you propose to give me. I am doing tolerably well here; I get $25 a month, with victuals and clothing; have a comfortable home for Mandy (the folks here call her Mrs. Anderson), and the children, Milly, Jane and Grundy, go to school and are learning well; the teacher says Grundy has a head for a preacher. They go to Sunday-School, and Mandy and me attend church regularly. We are kindly treated; sometimes we overhear others saying, "Them colored people were slaves" down in Tennessee. The children feel hurt when they hear such remarks, but I tell them it was no disgrace in Tennessee to belong to Col.

From Lydia Maria Child, ed., *The Freedmen's Book*, Ticknor and Fields, Boston, 1865, pp. 265–267.

Anderson. Many darkies would have been proud, as I used to was, to call you master. Now, if you will write and say what wages you will give me, I will be better able to decide whether it would be to my advantage to move back again.

As to my freedom, which you say I can have, there is nothing to be gained on that score, as I got my free-papers in 1864 from the Provist-Marshal-General of the Department at Nashville. Mandy says she would be afraid to go back without some proof that you are sincerely disposed to treat us justly and kindly—and we have concluded to test your sincerity by asking you to send us our wages for the time we served you. This will make us forget and forgive old scores, and rely on your justice and friendship in the future. I served you faithfully for thirty-two years and Mandy twenty years. At $25 a month for me, and $2 a week for Mandy, our earnings would amount to $11,680. Add to this the interest for the time our wages has been kept back and deduct what you paid for our clothing and three doctor's visits to me, and pulling a tooth for Mandy, and the balance will show what we are in justice entitled to. Please send the money by Adams Express, in care of V. Winters, esq., Dayton, Ohio. If you fail to pay us for faithful labors in the past we can have little faith in your promises in the future. We trust the good Maker has opened your eyes to the wrongs which you and your fathers have done to me and my fathers, in making us toil for you for generations without recompense. Here I draw my wages every Saturday night, but in Tennessee there was never any pay day for the negroes any more than for the horses and cows. Surely there will be a day of reckoning for those who defraud the laborer of his hire.

In answering this letter please state if there would be any safety for my Milly and Jane, who are now grown up and both good-looking girls. You know how it was with poor Matilda and Catherine. I would rather stay here and starve and die if it comes to that than have my girls brought to shame by the violence and wickedness of their young masters. You will also please state if there has been any schools opened for the colored children in your neighborhood, the great desire of my life now is to give my children an education, and have them form virtuous habits.

P.S.—Say howdy to George Carter, and thank him for taking the pistol from you when you were shooting at me.

From your old servant,
Jourdon Anderson

The Cartoonist's View of Reconstruction

Thomas Nast was America's foremost political cartoonist. He also was a Radical Republican who had no love for the white South or the Democratic Party. The touchstone cause of Radical Republicans was black civil rights—particularly the right to vote—and conflict with the Democrats and the white South often focused on this issue. Nast's drawings in Harper's Weekly, *as you will notice, illustrated vividly this ongoing battle. The high point for Nast came when Hiram Revels, a black, occupied the Senate seat from Mississippi once held by Jefferson Davis. The low point came shortly afterward. What effect do you think each cartoon had on the electorate? Were any more compelling than the others?*

Columbia—"Shall I trust these men, . . .

and not this man?" Thomas Nast, *Harper's Weekly,* August 5, 1865.

"This Is a White Man's Government."
"We regard the Reconstruction Acts (so called) of Congress as usurpations, and unconstitutional, revolutionary, and void."—Democratic platform. Thomas Nast, *Harper's Weekly*, September 5, 1868, Courtesy of The Research Libraries, The New York Public Library, Astor, Lenox and Tilden Foundations.

"Time Works Wonders Government." Thomas Nast, *Harper's Weekly*, April 9, 1870.

The commandments in South Carolina.
"We've pretty well smashed that; but I suppose, Massa Moses, you can get another
one." Thomas Nast, *Harper's Weekly*, September 26, 1874.

"To Thine Own Self Be True." Thomas Nast, *Harper's Weekly*, October 24, 1874.

The target.
". . . They (Messrs. Phleps & Potter) seem to regard the White League as innocent as a Target Company."—Special dispatch to the N.Y. *Times*, from Washington, Jan. 17, 1875. Thomas Nast, *Harper's Weekly*, February 6, 1875.

"These Few Precepts in Thy Memory."
Beware of entrance to a quarrel; but, being in,
Bear it that the opposer may beware of thee.
Give every man thine ear, but few thy voice:
Take each man's censure, but reserve thy judgment.
Costly thy habit as thy purse can buy,
But not express'd in fancy; rich, not gaudy:
For the apparel oft proclaims the man.

This above all,—To thine own self be true;
And it must follow, as the night the day,
Thou canst not then be false to any man.
                                        —Shakespeare

Thomas Nast, *Harper's Weekly*, April 24, 1875.

The "Civil Rights" scare is nearly over.
The game of (Colored) fox and (White) goose. Thomas Nast, *Harper's Weekly*, May 22, 1875.

"Is *This* a Republican Form of Government? Is *This* Protecting Life, Liberty, or Property? Is *This* the Equal Protection of the Laws?"
Mr. Lamar (Democrat, Mississippi): "In the words of the inspired poet, 'Thy gentleness has made thee great.'" [Did Mr. Lamar mean the colored race?] Thomas Nast, *Harper's Weekly*, September 2, 1876. The Newberry Library.

@ ON THE WEB   *To learn more about Thomas Nast and view more of his political cartoons relative to Reconstruction, visit* http://cartoons.osu.edu/nast/index.htm.

The South Redeemed

As Nast's cartoons indicate, the crusade for black voting rights and other civil rights ran into stiff opposition and eventually failed. By 1877, white supremacy was firmly reestablished throughout the South, and black political voices were almost completely stilled. The South, according to many white southerners, had been "redeemed" by its white leaders. But the white South did not get back everything it wanted. Black men had refused to work as gang laborers, and black families had refused to let women and children work long hours in the field. Grudgingly, white landowners had let blacks work the land in family plots, usually as either tenant farmers or sharecroppers. Thus, despite "redemption," the southern landscape would look startlingly different from Reconstruction. Here are maps of the same Georgia plantation in 1860 and in 1880. What, in your judgment, were the important features in the new and the old landscape? Do the changes match up with the kinds of attitudes discussed in Bethel's essay? How many of the 1880 families, would you guess, once lived in the old slave quarters?

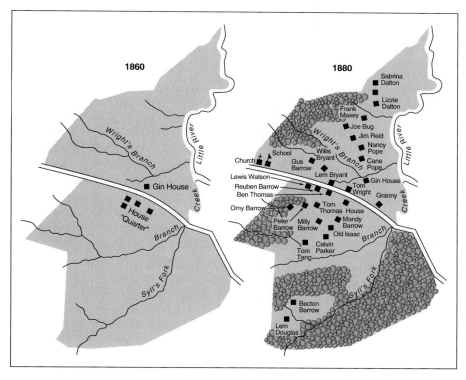

The Barrow plantation, 1860 and 1880. Adapted from *Scribner's Monthly*, vol. 21, April 1881, pp. 832–833.

To read Frederick Douglass's perception of Reconstruction, visit http://classiclit.about.com/library/bl-etexts/fdouglass/bl-fdoug-reconstruction.htm.

THE BIG PICTURE

The problem of Reconstruction was to bring eleven states back into the Union, rebuild the war-torn nation, and achieve racial justice. The latter did not happen. Why didn't it happen? What, in your opinion, would have been an appropriate and effective method for achieving racial justice in 1865?